Secondary Education

DAVID G. ARMSTRONG
TEXAS A&M UNIVERSITY

TOM V. SAVAGE
CALIFORNIA STATE UNIVERSITY, LONG BEACH

Secondary Education

An Introduction

SECOND EDITION

MACMILLAN PUBLISHING COMPANY
NEW YORK

Editor: Robert Miller

Production Supervision: Publication Services, Inc.

Text Design: Robert Freese

Cover Design and Art: Armen Kojoyian

This book was set in Baskerville by Publication Services, Inc. and printed and bound by R. R. Donnelley & Sons Co. The cover was printed by Phoenix Color Corp.

Macmillan Publishing Company
866 Third Avenue, New York, 10022

Collier Macmillan Canada, Inc.

LIBRARY OF CONGRESS CATALOGING-IN-PUBLICATION DATA

Armstrong, David G.
    Secondary education : an introduction / David G. Armstrong, Tom
V. Savage.
        p.   cm.
    Includes bibliographies and indexes.
    ISBN 0-02-304091-2
    1. Education, Secondary.   I. Savage, Tom V.   II. Title.
LB1607.A75   1990   89-33798
373—dc20   CIP

Printing: 1 2 3 4 5 6 7   Year: 0 1 2 3 4 5 6

Preface

Debates about the quality of the nation's secondary schools have become commonplace since the middle 1980s. The vast majority of national reform reports, which first began to appear in 1983, have focused on concerns about programming in secondary schools. Mediocre student performances on standardized tests, poor showings in terms of academic achievement as compared with students from other lands (particularly with those from Japan), high dropout rates (particularly among Hispanic and black student populations), and other problems have attracted the attention of many would-be reformers. Politicians have recognized the growing national interest in secondary schools, and many of them have publicly endorsed one or more of prescriptions that have been suggested for "improving our schools."

Some of the ideas for making secondary education "better" are mutually contradictory. On the one hand, there have been proposals to toughen the curriculum by reducing numbers of electives and by making required courses more difficult. On the other hand, there have been concerns about the very high dropout rates among Hispanic and black students. Impartial observers have noted that implementing proposals to make secondary course work more difficult may result in even higher numbers of students dropping out of school before they graduate.

An important issue in the debate about secondary education that has been rarely referenced directly in discussions about school quality is the fate of the comprehensive high school. For most of this century, there has been an assumption that the high school, as a single comprehensive institution, should provide educational experiences *both* for students planning to go on to college and universities and for students planning to enter the work force after completing the high school program.

Some of the reform recommendations put forward in recent years, if implemented, might so narrow the scope of the high school that it could no longer meet the needs of all students it presently serves. Part of the continuing debate over secondary education's quality may well center on whether the nation's traditional commitment to the comprehensive high school should be abandoned. Would it be better to establish one kind of senior secondary school for college-bound and another for vocationally-oriented students? This question, whether made explicit or not, seems certain to be a feature of continuing debates about the quality of secondary education.

This new edition of *Secondary Education: An Introduction* seeks to provide those who are considering a career in secondary education with an understanding of major issues that are being argued today. Increasingly, professional educators are making research-based policy and instructional decisions. The text draws together salient research findings with implications for effective school organization and administration and for effective teaching. Beginning secondary school teachers need sound information about instruction. This edition provides broad coverage of instructional procedures that have been validated in the classroom. Additional attention is devoted to issues related to unit and lesson planning, the diverse nature of the secondary-school population (with especial attention to handicapped students and gifted-and-talented students), legal issues affecting teachers and students, emerging technologies and the schools, and on-going professional development of career teachers.

Part I, "Contexts for Secondary Education," including Chapters 1, 2, and 3 of the text, introduces (a) a number of recent reform proposals and their implications for secondary schools, (b) research focusing on effective schools and effective teaching, and (c) information about student characteristics. Material in these chapters describes today's secondary-education milieu.

Part II, "Selecting, Delivering, Evaluating," places a heavy emphasis on issues associated with organizing, delivering, and assessing instruction. Chapters 4 through 13 focus on issues related to instructional effectiveness, content selection, motivation and management, alternative teaching techniques, and evaluation of learning. Among techniques included are those associated with direct instruction (for example, lecture, demonstration, and discussion), group learning, inquiry, individualized instruction, and affective learning.

Part III, "Formal Planning," features two chapters on basic approaches to program organization. Chapter 14 outlines procedures for planning instructional units. This focus of Chapter 15 is on content sequencing and lesson planning.

Part IV, "Special Instructional Concerns," includes Chapters 16, 17, and 18. Chapter 16 suggests some appropriate teacher responses to needs of handicapped students and gifted-and-talented students. Many secondary school students are not proficient readers. Chapter 17 suggests some ways teachers can work with students to maximize their learning from prose materials. Chapter 18 introduces prospective teachers to problems and prospects associated with newer instructional technologies.

Part V, "Professional Concerns," features three chapters that focus on some issues that are of career-long interest to teachers. Chapter 19 introduces information about the legal environment within which secondary school teachers and students operate. Chapter 20 introduces the idea that teacher preparation is an ongoing process that continues throughout a teacher's entire professional life.

Any book of this nature requires the assistance of many people. We particularly wish to acknowledge the help of several who are very special. Ford Button, who for many years served as a high-school art teacher in Rochester, New York and who is a well-known professional cartoonist, provided the cartoons that are featured in the book. We appreciate his encouragement, and, of course, his good humor.

Marsha Savage, an expert in English/language arts instruction, who taught high school for many years in College Station, Texas, provided invaluable assistance to us in the preparation of the material relating to reading problems of secondary school students. Her help is much appreciated.

Thanks, too, are due to Wendy Jordan and Radhika Viruru. They patiently proofread final copies of the manuscript and caught many errors we had overlooked.

We also wish to thank professors Bob L. Taylor, University of Colorado at Denver; Walter E. McPhie, University of Utah; James Dick, University of Nebraska at Omaha; Anne J. Russ, Wells College; Charles E. Jackson, Tarleton State University; and Larry Johnson, Creighton University. The final version of the book benefited from their sound suggestions.

Finally, our families provided an environment that allowed us to complete this project. We thank them for their tolerance and for their patience.

D. G. A.
T. V. S.

Contents

CHAPTER 5
Selecting Content and Establishing Objectives   95

CHAPTER 6
Motivating Students   126

CHAPTER 7
Classroom Management and Control   149

CHAPTER 20
The Career Secondary Teacher   527

Author Index   549

Subject Index   553

PART I

Contexts for
Secondary Education

CHAPTER 1

Secondary Education in an Age of Reform

AIMS

This chapter provides information to help the reader to:

1. Identify differences in the historical development of the nation's high schools, junior high schools, and middle schools.

2. Point out some issues raised by people who have noted important differences in academic achievement levels of American students and foreign students.

3. Describe some concerns about the secondary school curriculum that, in the view of some critics, have contributed to an erosion of school quality.

4. Discuss issues addressed in the educational reform reports that began to appear in the early and middle 1980s.

5. Cite examples of specific reform reports and describe several of their recommendations to improve the secondary schools.

PRETEST

DIRECTIONS: Using your own paper, answer these true/false questions. For each correct statement, write the word "true." For each incorrect statement, write the word "false."

_____ 1. High schools in the United States developed at about the same time as elementary schools.

_____ 2. Junior high schools developed in this country before middle schools.

_____ 3. A higher percentage of American students than Japanese students complete high school.

_____ 4. Dropout rates in urban high schools, particularly those in the inner cities, are much higher than in other settings.

_____ 5. Many recent school reform reports place an extremely heavy emphasis on the need to provide more vocational programs in high schools.

Introduction

Not too many years ago, fans gathered around the radio for the Fight of the Week. As the boxers went about their business, announcers sent vivid word pictures to eager listeners throughout the country. Their excited voices described left jabs, thunderous uppercuts, and courageous counterpunches. Between rounds, these dedicated sportscasters commented on cuts and bruises, speculated on the condition of the fighters, and urged the audience at home to stock up on quality razor blades and good Wisconsin beer. The Fight of the Week drew people in many communities together for compelling moments of shared excitement.

Today, appreciation of conflict often extends beyond the vicarious pleasures of listening to blow-by-blow accounts from distant rings. When a great national issue captures the public imagination, a kind of verbal pugilism often ensues. One such issue is public education, particularly as it is being delivered in the nation's secondary schools.

In a country that prides itself on diversity, it is natural that people have vastly different views regarding the characteristics of a "good" school. Some of these positions are mutually compatible. Others are not. The latter often provide the bases for heated debates in legislatures, in the press, at school board meetings, and in other settings. These debates are healthy, reflecting a pattern of citizen concern for education. Secondary schools, in particular, have been the focus of this concern.

The nation's secondary schools–middle schools, junior high schools, and senior high schools–have evolved from diverse beginnings into the kinds of institutions they are today. In part, criticisms made of sec-

"The vote is three in favor, five opposed, and Mr. Kay's 'you've gotta be kidding'."

ondary schools today result from changing public perceptions of what they should do. To understand calls for secondary school reform, some basic grasp of the historical evolution of these schools is desirable.

Development of the Secondary Schools

Secondary schools are institutions that include one or more of the grades from 6 or 7 through 12. They are known by various names. The three most common secondary-school types are (1) the senior high school, (2) the junior high school, and (3) the middle school. These institutions share some common features, but each has important characteristics of its own.

The Senior High School

The first public high school in the United States, established in 1821, was the Boston English Classical school. The program of study emphasized the useful and practical subjects and attended less to subjects that seemed to have no clear connections to the demands of daily living.

Interest in the high school as an institution developed slowly. Even as late as 1860, there were only about 40 public high schools in the entire country (Barry 1961). One important barrier to the rapid spread of the high school concerned finances. The principle of public support for elementary schools went back to early colonial times. However, for many years, there was doubt about the legality of using tax money to support secondary schools. A key decision in this area was the famous *Kalamazoo* case of 1874 [*Stuart v. School District No. 1 of the Village of Kalamazoo*, 30 Mich. 69 (1874)], which supported the right to state legislatures to pass laws permitting local communities to levy taxes to support secondary as well as elementary schools.

Once the legality of public financing of high schools was ensured, the number of high schools in the country increased rapidly. By 1900, there were over 6,000 high schools serving over half a million students. Today, there are over 11 million students in the nation's high schools (Stern and Chandler 1987, p. 60).

The latter years of the nineteenth century and the first decades of the twentieth were a time of great debate about the nature of the high school program. In its simplest terms, the argument concerned whether the high school's primary role should be to prepare students for the world of work or for the academic world of the university.

In the 1890s the National Education Association's Committee of Ten issued a report suggesting that the high school should be almost exclusively devoted to preparing students for college-level work. The Committee recommended that all high school students take (1) Latin; (2) Greek; (3) English; (4) a modern foreign language; (5) mathematics; (6) sciences; including physics, astronomy, and chemistry; (7) natural history; (8) history, civil government, and political economy; and (9) geography (Tanner and Tanner 1980; National Education Association 1893). Box 1.1 shows the Committee's recommendations for sophomores.

This view quickly came under attack by those who observed the tremendous enrollment growth of high schools. These critics suggested that high schools were taking in many students who would be entering the work force immediately after they graduated. A purely academic program, they argued, would not adequately prepare students for the survival skills they would need in the world of work. Positions of these critics were reflected in the final report of the National Education Association's Committee of Nine issued in 1911. The Committee of Nine suggested that high schools had a responsibility to produce "socially efficient" individuals, by which it meant persons who were committed to fundamental American values and were capable of making real contributions to the technical and social development of the country (National Education Association 1911).

Box 1.1

The Sophomore Year in High School as Envisioned by the 1893 Committee of Ten

In 1893, the Committee of Ten proposed that the following subjects be taken by all high school sophomores (National Education Association 1893, p. 4).

Latin

Greek

English Literature

English Composition

German (continued from the freshman year)

Algebra (could be replaced by bookkeeping or commercial arithmetic)

Geometry

Botany

English History to 1688

What Do You Think?

1. How do you think people today would react to a proposal to install the above program in the nation's high schools?

2. If such a program were required, how do you think most students would fare?

3. Would homework expectations be changed if such a program were required? If so, in what ways?

4. How would you personally have reacted if you had faced such a program of study during your sophomore year?

In 1918, a grand compromise was finally struck that bridged the gap between those favoring a college-preparatory high school and those favoring a practical, world-of-work-oriented high school. The report of the National Education Association's Commission on the Reorganization of Secondary Education of 1918 is widely regarded as a seminal document in the development of the American high school. It promulgated the view that the public high school should be "comprehensive."

In its inspired use of the word "comprehensive," the commission suggested that the high school should serve multiple purposes. This broad view of the high school's purpose was expressed in the commission's (1918) description of the "cardinal principles" of secondary education. These cardinal principles, promoted as goals to be developed by a high school education, were

1. Health
2. Command of fundamental processes
3. Worthy home membership

4. Vocational preparation
5. Citizenship
6. Worthy use of leisure time
7. Ethical character

The comprehensive high school and its associated cardinal principles have been the guiding assumptions of high school education for over 70 years. The promise to provide something for every kind of student usually has allowed school leaders to maintain working majorities in support of this general approach.

At the same time, this solution has bred resentment on the part of some community members. Certain individuals have felt that the comprehensive high school has emphasized breadth of services at the expense of quality. Many of the reform reports of the 1980s have indirectly challenged the need for a comprehensive high school. There have been proposals for a high school with a much more limited range of purposes. A subsequent section of this chapter reviews many of these reform reports.

The Junior High School

Junior high schools were not established until the early years of the twentieth century. The movement to establish them began late in the nineteenth century, when large numbers of public high schools were being built. Academic programs offered in the high schools generally were quite demanding compared to those in the elementary schools. Some people viewed the junior high school as a school that would help learners prepare for the academic rigors of high school.

Others were attracted to the idea that a special school could respond to the special physical and emotional needs of preadolescents and early adolescents. The views of those who saw the junior high school as primarily a training ground for the academic challenges of high school and those who saw it as an institution to serve the unique developmental needs of the learners often resulted in heated debates about the curriculum (see Box 1.2). These debates have continued unabated since the nation's first junior high school was established in Berkeley, California in 1909.

The school organizational pattern developed in Berkeley was copied by large numbers of school districts throughout the country. This 6-3-3 scheme features a six-year elementary school, a three-year junior high school, and a three-year senior high school (Popper 1967). The predominant pattern was for the junior high school to serve students in grades 7, 8, and 9. However, some schools called junior high schools featured other grade-level groupings.

Box 1.2

How Should a School System Be Organized?

Throughout the twentieth century, there have been recurring debates about how grades K through 12 should be divided among different school types. These arguments continue even today.

What Do You Think?

1. Do you like the idea of having a system featuring either a junior high school or a middle school to serve students between their elementary and senior high school years? If so, what features of this scheme do you find attractive? If not, what alternative might you propose?

2. Some taxpayers believe it would be more economical to adopt a system featuring only two kinds of schools: a grades K to 8 elementary school and a grades 9 to 12 high school. What strengths and weaknesses do you see in this proposal?

3. What kind of a school or schools did you attend between your elementary and senior high school years? What features of this school arrangement did you like and dislike?

4. What do you predict the dominant pattern of grade distributions in different school types such as elementary schools, middle schools, junior high schools, and senior high schools will be in the year 2000? Why do you think so?

By the end of World War I, the debate between those who saw the junior high school as an academic preparatory experience for high school and those who saw it as a school to respond to learners' special developmental needs had largely been won by the partisans of the academic preparation position. Although some lip service continued to be paid to serving the special needs of preadolescents and early adolescents, mastery of subject matter had become the order of the day.

Junior high schools drew teachers from college and university preparation programs that were heavily oriented toward the senior high school. With few exceptions, junior high school teachers were expected to have secondary rather than elementary certificates. Large numbers of junior high school teachers saw teachers in high school as their professional role models. Many of them hoped to teach at the senior high school level. Ever sensitive to negative comments that might come their way from teachers in the senior high school, many junior high school teachers worked hard to demonstrate to potential skeptics that there was nothing "academically soft" about junior high school programs.

One consequence of all this was to divert attention from specialized needs of junior high school students. This situation had always prompted criticism from people concerned about growth and development issues, and these critics become more numerous in the years following World War II. Drawing on the work of developmental psychologists and physiologists as an intellectual rationale, critics of the junior high school in the early 1960s were proposing the establishment of a new kind of school to serve preadolescents and early adolescents. They proposed that the new school be called a *middle school*, a term borrowed from European education.

The Middle School

The middle school concept began to catch on during the 1960s. In general, middle schools were organized so as to include at least three but not more than five grades that must include grades 6 and 7 (Lounsbury and Vars 1978). Supporters of the middle school were concerned not so much with grade levels as with age levels of students—from about 11 to about 14 years (Egnatuck et al. 1975).

Many middle school educators were committed to the idea that high school preparation should not be the primary focus of the school program. They argued that certain psychological and physiological characteristics of students in the 11- to 14-year-old group require a special set of educational conditions.

Since they first began to appear in the 1960s, middle schools' popularity has continued to increase. Middle schools are rapidly displacing junior high schools as the dominant intermediate school type.

The specific arrangement of schools between the elementary school and the senior high school varies considerably from place to place. Some communities have only middle schools; others have only junior high schools, and still others have both middle schools and junior high schools. This inconsistent pattern sometimes becomes even more confusing when programs offered by these schools are considered.

As originally conceived, middle schools were supposed to be schools heavily oriented toward serving students' special developmental needs. Many institutions called middle schools do reflect this pattern of concern. On the other hand, many other middle schools are organized very much along the lines of senior high schools. They reflect an orientation toward academic content that differs little from that of the junior high school programs that initially prompted the establishment of middle schools.

Similarly, some junior high schools continue to see their roles as academic preparation institutions for the senior high schools. However, other schools called junior high schools have student-oriented curricula that are every bit as responsive to learners' developmental needs as those in similarly oriented middle schools. It is simply not accurate today to suggest that "middle schools care about students," whereas "junior high schools care about subjects." There are too many place-to-place variations. Conclusions about these schools must be based on an examination of their individual programs, not on whether they are called middle schools or junior high schools.

How People View Senior High Schools, Junior High Schools, and Middle Schools

Junior high schools and middle schools have not enjoyed the same prestige as senior high schools. A variety of explanations have been suggested for these status differences. Some observers have noted that many people mistakenly believe that little can be done with learners between their elementary and senior high school years. The view that the senior high school needs a new building but that the old one is perfectly all right for the junior high school students has been often expressed.

School district administrative officers sometimes perpetuate the idea that middle school and junior high school education is not terribly important. One school district personnel officer, known to the authors, frequently commented that he liked to place new secondary students in a middle school or a junior high school for "seasoning." Presumably, after a few years of working at this level, the individuals would be "sent up" to the senior high school where quality teaching might make a difference. This personnel director assumed that middle school and junior high school teachers would learn from their mistakes. Further, these mistakes would come at no real cost in that even an inept teacher could not do much harm to preadolescents and early adolescent students, who were presumed to be in an intellectual "holding pattern."

The National Middle School Association, groups of interested teachers, and others concerned about education in the years between the elementary and senior high schools have been working hard to promote a wider appreciation of the importance of middle school and junior high school experiences. There are teachers, strongly committed working in these schools, who would resist a suggestion that they transfer either to an elementary school or a senior high school.

Public interest in these schools is increasing. For example, a recent report by the Carnegie Council on Adolescent Education called for a reorganization plan that would divide large schools into several small administrative units. Teachers in each unit would establish close personal relationships with students, build a "community of learning," and take action to assist each student to succeed (Jackson, 1989).

Secondary schools number in the thousands. They come in many shapes and sizes. This is one example.

Reform of Secondary Education: Some Issues

Since the early 1980s, there has been great public interest in the quality of American schools. This interest has prompted many studies and the preparation of dozens of reports on the general subject of improving the schools. Reports have been issued by many groups reflecting a variety of perspectives. For all of their diversity, however, some themes do recur in these reports. This section highlights several key issues that have been addressed in many of the reform proposals.

Survival Skills for a Technological Economy

The kinds of jobs growing most rapidly in urban areas where most Americans live are service and information jobs (Coughlin 1988). These positions require employees who have good technical and analytical skills. Economic disadvantage and unemployment are prevalent among groups of individuals who are not proficient in these areas.

To serve the employment needs of the nation and to reduce poverty levels, some critics of current school practice argue that educational programs must be more finely tuned to the needs of a technological economy. If adjustments to school curricula are not made, there may be a serious erosion of our nation's "intellectual capital." It is argued that this deterioration could reduce our standard of living and threaten our national security. This threat is particularly serious because some other nations of the world seem to be doing a better job of developing high levels of technical proficiency among their students. These nations may develop powerful economies that could threaten our own in the years ahead.

Disappointment with Scholastic Aptitude Test Scores

Many colleges and universities require applicants to furnish their scores on the Scholastic Aptitude Test (S.A.T.) as part of their application for admission. Students typically take this examination during their senior year in high school. Results are believed to provide a rough measure of a student's aptitude for college and university work.

State and national S.A.T. averages are widely reported. Though the S.A.T. test is not designed to measure the relative worth of individual high school programs, many people have come to regard the scores as a source of information about the relative quality of secondary education programs. The educational reform movement that began in the early 1980s was in part a public response to years of generally declining S.A.T. scores. For example, from 1963 to 1977, there was a 49 point drop in verbal S.A.T. scores and a 32 point drop quantitative S.A.T. scores (*On Further Examination* 1977).

In the 1980s, the trend of S.A.T. score decline witnessed during the 1960s and 1970s shifted and scores began to rise slightly or to remain about the same (Stern and Chandler 1987, p. 20). Nevertheless, scores continued to lag behind those of the 1960s and early 1970s. Concern with S.A.T. scores is reflected in many of the 1980s era reform proposals.

International Comparisons

The reform proposals of the 1980s also reflect a concern that American students' academic performance is inferior to that of students in other countries. American students have not compared well with students from many western European countries and Japan on standardized tests. It has been established that these differences cannot be explained by differences in native intelligence (Gordon 1987). Hence, some critics have charged that American secondary schools are teaching a program that is inferior to that offered to students in many other countries.

One response to this criticism has been the argument that many European high schools enroll a smaller percentage of their young people in secondary schools than their American counterparts. In Sweden, for example, only about 45 to 55 percent of students complete high school. In this country, the figure is about 75 percent (Felt 1985).

This argument may make sense when comparisons are made between students in Western European and American high schools. It breaks down, though, when high schools in Japan and the United States are considered. The Japanese graduate fully 95 percent of their students from high school (Felt 1985). This suggests that an even higher percentage of intellectually less-able students are in Japanese high schools during the senior year than are in American high schools.

Japanese high school students have consistently outperformed American students on international achievement test comparisons (Felt 1985). This level of academic performance in a country that keeps a high percentage of its students in school through the 12th grade has led to increasing interest in Japanese educational practices.

Comparative studies of Japanese and American practices have revealed some interesting differences. One such difference is the general attitude toward young people and learning. The Japanese tend to assume that all students are capable of learning the material that is presented. They believe failure in school results more from a failure to study hard than from any innate deficiency in learning ability. The Japanese "believe the key to learning is hard work. Americans, by contrast, express delight and pride in their children's native ability and do not push them diligently." (Gordon 1987, p. 5).

The general Japanese view makes for a much more restricted curriculum than that characterizing American high schools. For example, there are no separate courses for high ability, intermediate ability, and low ability students. Because the curriculum includes fewer subjects, the Japanese have succeeded in reaching much more consensus regarding the specific content to be covered in each course.

This means that courses fit together more precisely than they often do in American high schools. A student finishing one course has learned exactly what he or she needs to begin the material introduced in the subsequent course. Because of this careful content arrangement, Japanese teachers spend much less time than American teachers at the beginning of the course making sure that students have basic information they will need before they can begin working with new content.

Academic pressures on Japanese students are enormous compared to those experienced by most secondary students in the United States. Japanese students spend 240 days a year in school, including a half-day of instruction on Saturdays. (Thorp 1987). This compares with about 180 days for Americans. Access to a good university is very important for Japanese students, as graduates of the best universities are selected for high-paying, prestigious jobs. University admission depends on getting a high score on college entrance examinations taken during the senior year of high school. To prepare for these examinations, large numbers of Japan's seniors spend three or more hours a day after school in special *juki*, or cram schools. Once they get home, these students spend additional hours studying. Many students sleep only four or five hours a night during their senior year (Thorp 1987).

Some critics of Japanese education have expressed concern abut these pressures. While many Japanese students do not enjoy their secondary school years, stories about excessively high suicide rates are exaggerated; the suicide rate among American teen-agers is in fact higher than that among Japanese (Gordon 1987). One might suspect that the pressure to do well on college entrance examinations would stultify interests in artistic and creative endeavors. Apparently, it does not. All Japanese students, by the time they graduate from high school, will have participated in the production of one dramatic production each year and have learned to play two musical instruments (Gordon 1987).

Are Japanese educational successes bound up in cultural variables unique to Japan? Can American educators import some features of Japanese education? These questions are being widely debated today. Many educational reform reports suggest that American secondary schools might well study some Japanese practices as they consider ways to improve their programs.

Narrowing the Scope of the Secondary Curriculum

The typical American comprehensive high school offers a tremendous variety of courses. Supporters of this approach to secondary education have argued that this variety is healthy. It is designed to serve young people with very different personal needs and aspirations. Some recent critics, however, have taken a contrary view (see Box 1.3).

One argument is that there has been too much fragmentation of the curriculum. Because educational resources are limited, attempting to do something for everyone results in mediocrity. It would be better to concentrate resources and to provide students with more depth in a limited number or areas.

Some critics are suggesting that more emphasis be placed on traditional academic subjects. With some exceptions, they have tended to be less interested in programs designed to promote students' personal development and in programs with a vocational orientation. Part of the impetus for the movement to emphasize academic subjects more

Box 1.3

The Question of High School Electives

In recent years, there have been concerns about the large numbers of electives available to students. Some critics have argued that this situation has produced a generation of students who lack a solid grounding in important core subjects such as history and English. They suggest the present system encourages students to choose easy courses. This might be pleasant for students in the short run. However, it has serious long-term implications for students' development and for the nation as a whole.

What Do You Think?

1. How many electives did you have when you were in high school? Was your situation typical or not typical? Do you think you and your friends made wise choices of electives?

2. How to you react to the general argument that the high school program has been cluttered with too many electives? On what do you base your opinion?

3. The suggestion that numbers of electives should be reduced often has been accompanied by a recommendation that all students should take a certain basic academic program. This is not to suggest that there should be *no* electives. Rather, the idea is to reduce their number and to insist that all students be required to take certain courses. How do you react to this idea? If you were to decide on courses every student should take, what would you require?

heavily has come from a focus on S.A.T. scores and on comparisons between academic performance levels of American students and students in countries such as Japan.

Another concern of those who have suggested a narrowing of the secondary curriculum is that the high school experience should provide a sort of "intellectual glue" that holds the nation together. They argue that part of our national identity should come from a set of rich, shared intellectual experiences. A more standardized high school curriculum featuring a narrower range of required subjects would provide a common intellectual experience for all citizens. This would facilitate communication among people from all parts of the nation and build a sense of national community.

Such books as E. D. Hirsch, Jr.'s *Cultural Literacy: What Every American Needs to Know* and Chester E. Finn, Jr. and Diane Ravitch's *What Do Our 17-Year-Olds Know?: A Report on the First National Assessment of History and Literature* reflect this perspective. It is also present in many of the 1980s reform proposals.

Box 1.4

Changing Times Schools Are Open to Meet Student Needs

Problems faced by inner city schools have been addressed in several school reform proposals. One issue these reports mention concerns family obligations of high school students. Large numbers of these students have jobs. Their families are heavily dependent on the income these students bring in. Teenagers' earnings often contribute significantly to a family's total income. This is particularly true in the many families headed by just one parent.

School instructional programs typically take place during the very same hours as most jobs are available. This situation often forces young people to make a difficult choice between staying in school or staying on a job. Economic pressures often force students to drop out of a school to maintain the income flow to their family.

What Do You Think?

1. What is your general reaction to the argument that traditional school hours contribute to a heightened dropout rate in many urban areas?

2. What do you think about offering classes in high schools continuously from 6 a.m. to midnight? (The assumption would be that teachers would work in different shifts.) Would this arrangement reduce the dropout rate?

3. What problems might be associated with a plan to greatly extend the numbers of hours high schools offer instruction? How would different community groups react?

Special Problems of Urban Schools

Another theme present in some of the reform reports is that secondary schools are failing to serve the needs of students in urban schools, particularly in inner city schools. Recent data suggest that dropout rates are at extremely high levels in many of these schools. In some New York City high schools they may be as high as 90 percent (Perlez 1987).

Some critics suggest that traditional school practices are inappropriate for the students they serve. For example, many students in high schools come from impoverished single-parent families. These students are encouraged to work to supplement family income. Most jobs are available during the same hours the school is open. It may be that much larger numbers of urban high schools should consider shifting to night hours to allow students to work and to complete their high school educations in the evening (Perlez 1987). Box 1.4 presents this view.

The kinds of jobs that are growing most rapidly today are those requiring people with good technological skills. As a group, people in the inner cities are very poorly prepared for these kinds of positions. It is argued that secondary schools in the urban areas have a special obligation to prepare students for the kinds of employment skills in demand today.

The number of poor people in the inner cities is growing rapidly (Coughlin 1988), and the nation could face a heavy social cost if something is not done to provide the poor with more marketable employment skills. In recognition of this problem, there is an emerging interest in improving the quality of inner city secondary education.

A Summary of Selected Reform Reports

As noted in the preceding section, certain common themes run through a number of the reform reports of the 1980s. However, these themes are by no means represented in all of the reports.

Some of the earlier reports were particularly critical of classroom teachers and their practices. The concern led to criticism of how teachers were being prepared. Somewhat later, reports began to focus on the conditions under which teachers work in the school and to suggest changes. Many recent recommendations have recognized the vast differences among schools and the need to decentralize decision-making to allow officials at the local school level to exercise more control over their programs (Michaels 1988). Recent reports have also begun to take a look at the total undergraduate academic preparation of teachers, rather than their teacher education courses alone. There has also been a trend toward considering how secondary schools are meeting the needs of specific segments of the population such as the urban poor.

Summaries of a selection of reform reports with recommendations for the nation's secondary schools are provided in this section. These reports represent a cross-section of thinking represented in the much larger number of reports that have been issued since 1983.

The Paideia Proposal

In *The Paideia Proposal: An Educational Manifesto (1982)*, Mortimer Adler, a long-time proponent of education for intellectual development, suggested that schools are in trouble because they are stretching limited funds too far. Too many "nonessential" courses are offered. For example, programs designed to prepare students for the world of work take resources away from more important efforts to provide students with a solid academic foundation.

A common curriculum is proposed as the remedy to many of the school's problems. In particular, *The Paideia Proposal* recommended that all students should be exposed to experiences to (1) promote their acquisition of organized knowledge, (2) develop their intellectual skills, and (3) improve their grasp of important ideas and values.

The high school program to implement these ideas would be rigorous. All students would study mathematics through at least one year of calculus. There would be a heavy use of seminars in such courses as history, and basic documents such as *The Federalist Papers*, the Constitution, and the Declaration of Independence would be studied. Development of students' ability to engage in sophisticated thinking is an important objective.

The Paideia Proposal was a direct attack on the principle of the comprehensive high school. It took an unequivocal stand in support of the view that academic education should virtually be the exclusive goal of secondary education. Proponents hint that students who emerge with the kinds of understanding and thinking skills they will have at the end of this program will easily adapt to the challenges of the work place and of productive citizenship.

A Nation at Risk

A Nation at Risk: The Imperative for Education Reform was a widely read report of the U. S. Department of Education's Commission on Excellence in Education released in 1983. It led to a tremendous renewal of national interest in the quality of the schools. *A Nation at Risk* is probably the best known of all the 1980s reform reports.

A Nation at Risk made many recommendations for improving the schools. Some of these focused on teachers, on administrative arrangements, and on the curriculum. With regard to teachers, the report suggested that the best performers be identified and rewarded. A "career ladder" was proposed featuring "rungs" to which teachers would be assigned depending on their levels of competence and their range of responsibilities. Teachers on higher rungs would receive higher salaries and have more responsibilities than teachers on lower rungs.

The report took schools to task for placing too many administrative responsibilities on teachers. It recommended that ways be found to remove some of these burdens to allow them more time to work directly with students. The concern that teachers and students were not spending enough time on productive learning activities was reflected in other recommendations for increasing the amount of learning time each day and for increasing the number of days students attend schools each year.

A theme that recurs throughout the report is that the range of school offerings should be limited. Curriculum proposals called for an emphasis on five "basics," including (1) English, (2) mathematics, (3) science, (4) social science, and (5) computers. High schools' programs should be rigorous and challenging. In the emphasis on academics, and the relatively sparse attention to vocational subjects and personal development of students, *A Nation at Risk* poses a direct challenge to the traditional concept of the comprehensive high school.

High School

High School: A Report on Secondary Education In America, a book written by Ernest L. Boyer, appeared in 1983. It was based on a study conducted under the auspices of the Carnegie Foundation for the Advancement of Teaching.

High School's suggestions included recommendations for improving the quality of secondary-school teachers, reorganizing the curriculum, and modifying administrative arrangements. Recruitment and retention of talented people to teaching were established as important priorities. Talented individuals should be identified as early as the high school years and systematically recruited to the teaching profession. Special scholarships should be provided to the top five percent of students seeking admission to teacher preparation programs.

Attention should also be given to improving teachers' working conditions. Individual high schools were urged to establish a "teacher excellence fund" to provide resources for teachers who devise and implement promising new approaches. The school year should be modified to include a two-week professional development term. During this time teachers would work together to improve their instructional skills.

The report, similar to several others, suggested that many high school curricula today are fragmented. *High School* proposed that all students be exposed to a common core of learnng experiences. This core should include courses designed to improve facility in English, promote the development of analytical thinking, develop an appreciation for our connections to other peoples and other times, and stimulate interests related to the world of work.

High School's core is somewhat broader in scope than that recommended by some of the other reform reports (e.g., *The Paideia Proposal* and *A Nation at Risk*). In particular, there is a heavier emphasis on preparing students for the world they will face after graduation. During their junior and senior years, students should be exposed as directly as

Box 1.5

Can Increasing High Schools' Autonomy Lead to Excellence?

Several of the educational reform reports suggest that our high schools are over-regulated. They point out that guidelines from federal, state, and local authority often fail to respond to the special characteristics of students in individual schools. To remedy this situation, there have been suggestions that more decision-making authority be given to administrators and teachers in individual buildings. It has been argued that, if empowered to do so, educators in each school would be able to design instructional programs well suited to their own needs.

Others argue that high schools have gotten themselves into trouble by a failure of local, state, and federal authorities to pay attention to what they are doing. Too much authority has been placed in the hands of principals and teachers in individual buildings. A result has been a highly fragmented and academically "soft" high school program.

What Do You Think?

1. What problems do you see with the suggestion to place more authority in the hands of local building principals and teachers?

2. What strengths do you see in this idea?

3. If you could make the decisions, what specific kinds of decisions would you leave in the hands of principals and teachers in individual buildings? Which ones would you want made by local, state, or federal authorities?

possible to work, service and academic environments, and other settings they might encounter once they leave school.

High School strongly supported the idea that school reform is best accomplished at the individual school level. The report suggested that principals be given more freedom to control programs at their schools and that they be provided with the financial resources funds to support special projects in their buildings. The issue of control is discussed in Box 1.5.

Horace's Compromise

Theodore R. Sizer wrote *Horace's Compromise: The Dilemma of the American High School* in 1984. The book was based on information initially reported in "A Study of High Schools," a five-year study supported by the National Association of High School Principals and the National Association of Independent Schools. The "Horace" in the title is an extremely talented teacher who finds that he has to deviate from what he knows is best for his students. He must compromise because of the many demands the school puts on his time.

Sizer's book took schools to task for the constraints they place on teachers' behavior. Teachers should be provided working conditions that allow them to help each learner progress. This is possible only when there is time for teachers to design learning tasks for individuals that are of appropriate levels of difficulty. Every effort should be made to make it possible for learners to succeed.

Sizer argued that students' success is partly derived from their ability to think analytically. There should be direct instruction in seminar-like settings to develop students' thinking skills. To succeed, these give-and-take discussions should take place under conditions where teachers work with fewer than 20 students.

Educators should worry more about depth rather than breadth of content coverage. A recurring theme in *Horace's Compromise* is that "less is more." To promote depth, it is desirable that the dozens of fragmented courses in the high school curriculum be replaced. The new curriculum would feature a program focusing on four key areas: (1) inquiry and expression; (2) mathematics and science; (3) literature and the arts; and, (4) philosophy and history. Both required courses and electives should be accommodated within these themes. Vocational courses should not be allowed to rob time from courses associated with these major areas of study.

To implement a high school featuring teachers who would work intensively with each student, Sizer proposed organizing schools into small administrative units. He suggested that no teacher should be responsible for working with more than 80 students. To keep themselves fresh and armed with a variety of perspectives, teachers ought to play different roles throughout the course of a career. For example, in addition to working with students, at some times during their careers teachers might serve as counselors or as curriculum developers.

Personalization of instruction to assure student learning is a paramount objective of the school reorganization plan reflected in *Horace's Compromise*. The proposals share with a number of other reports a view that many current high school curricula are crowded with too many courses. Sizer's book, however, places primary emphasis on the need to provide instruction that leads to learning. Reorganizing courses into a limited number of major themes is proposed as one means to this end.

Time for Results

The National Governors' Association released its report on American education, *Time For Results*, in 1986. It focused heavily on state-level policy changes that might be undertaken to improve the overall quality of the nation's schools.

Several earlier reports, including *High School* and *Horace's Compromise*, argued that the focus for educational improvement should be the individual school. The governors, as they studied problems facing the school, generally agreed with this view. *Time for Results* makes a strong case in support of the argument that state authorities should reduce the number and complexity of regulations affecting individual schools. This recommendation responded to concerns that bureaucratic red tape was diverting educators in the schools away from their primary mission – instructing students.

The report also pointed out that many existing regulatory practices promote mediocrity. Instances were cited of policies that allowed extra funds to go to troubled schools, but only under conditions calling for them to be withdrawn once there was evidence of improvement. *Time for Results* suggested such regulations reinforce poor performance and fail to reward teachers and school leaders who do well. The report recommended that extra state money provided to problem schools should continue to be paid once positive results were observed.

Time for Results' discussion of when and how to spend public money to improve education reflects one of education's classic "chicken-and-egg" questions. Individuals interested in education have long pondered whether it is better to spend "seed" money in schools with poor programs to make them better or whether it is better to find evidence that some schools are doing well and to provide them with extra money in recognition of their excellence. This issue seems certain to remain an ongoing feature of improvement-of-the-schools discussions.

American Memory and What Do Our 17-Year-Olds Know?

American Memory, written by Lynne V. Cheney, was published by the National Endowment for the Humanities in 1987. Later that year, Chester E. Finn's and Diane Ravitch's book, *What Do Our 17-Year-Olds Know?: A Report on the First National Assessment of History and Literature*, appeared. Both reports drew heavily on data gathered by the National Assessment of Education Progress.

In *American Memory*, Cheney pointed out that tests of teenagers' understanding of pivotal past events reveal startling knowledge gaps. Many cannot identify when the Civil War occurred, when Columbus arrived in the Americas, or when the Constitution was signed. Cheney suggested that this lamentable lack of information has resulted from an inappropriate school curriculum.

In particular, Cheney decried an overemphasis on "process" teaching that has come at the expense of "product" teaching. She suggested that too much time has been spent in literature courses teaching basic reading skills rather than in teaching the actual content conveyed by the reading material. As a result, students have failed to concentrate on critical information.

Cheney noted, too, that part of the problem results from fragmentation of the curriculum. For various reasons, extraneous topics have been introduced that have displaced more important ones. She pointed out, for example, that in some places even drivers' education has been included in the social studies curriculum. As a result of such practices, students in many places receive only about four years of solid history instruction in the entire grades K to 12 program.

To remedy this situation, Cheney recommended a curriculum featuring more attention to solid subject matter. In particular, she favored a program with more traditional content from the humanities.

Many concerns raised by Cheney were also addressed in Finn's and Ravitch's *What Do Our 17-Year-Olds Know?* They, too, pointed to distressing statistics regarding these students' levels of understanding of basic historical events. They pointed out, for example, that one-third of the 17-year-olds tested by the National Assessment of Educational Progress did not know that the Declaration of Independence marked the formal separation of the American colonies from Britain.

Finn and Ravitch suggested that these results provide a strong rationale for critically examining existing school curricula. They specifically recommended a core curriculum of history and literature courses for all students.

The reports of Cheney and of Finn and Ravitch are among those that see "curriculum failure" as one of the most pressing problems facing education. They favor reducing the number of elective courses. Further, the courses they would retain have a heavily academic flavor. Their contention is that school curricula have accommodated too many meaningless courses over the years. Improvement will require trimming the curriculum back to emphasize more traditional academic content.

William J. Bennett's "Madison High School"

In late 1987, United States Secretary of Education William J. Bennett put forward a plan for a rigorous high school program of studies. In Bennett's fictitious "Madison High School," a student would take a program consisting of a prescribed amount of course work in these seven core areas (Voreacas 1987):

4 years of English

3 years of science

3 years of mathematics

3 years of social studies

2 years of foreign languages

2 years of physical education-health

1 semester of art

1 semester of music-fine arts

Bennett described this as a program to be worked toward by the nation's high schools, not something that should be legislated and necessarily required of every school. Course work would be difficult. At the ninth grade level, the English program would require students to read classics of western literature including Homer's *Odyssey*, several of Shakespeare's plays, and the Bible. Students would take three years of mathematics to be selected from geometry, algebra 1, algebra 2, statistics, and calculus.

Bennett's 'Madison High School" proposal focused heavily on academics. So heavily, in fact, that even some people generally sympathetic to more emphasis on traditional subject matter publicly argued against it. Mortimer Adler argued that "Bennett's program, aimed at the survival of the fittest who go on to college, is ill-conceived" (Adler 1988, p. 6).

The view promoted in the "Madison High School" proposal is generally consistent with other suggestions that have been made to restrict the range of subjects available to high school students. A number of reports have made the same point. While these reports differ regarding what students should take, they agree that the availability of too many course options has weakened the intellectual quality of the high school experience.

An Imperiled Generation: Saving Urban Schools

The Carnegie Foundation for the Advancement of Teaching released its report, *An Imperiled Generation: Saving Urban Schools*, in 1988. The report was based on data gathered during visits to a number of urban schools. These visits revealed problems associated with high dropout rates, low levels of teacher morale, and poor facilities. There was also evidence that many of these schools were faced with so many rules and regulations that they found it very difficult to implement needed changes.

Consistent with several other reform reports, *An Imperiled Generation: Saving Urban Schools* recommended that teachers and administrators be given more freedom to operate their own schools and school programs. Since each school would have broad latitude in planning its own program, the individual school could be held more directly accountable for its students' learning.

The report recommended establishment of special after-school and summer-school programs for urban children from poor families. Governments were urged to set up funds to provide low interest loans to urban school districts seeking to upgrade their physical facilities. Funds should also be provided for the development and implementation of curricula relevant to the urban setting. Similarly, financial incentives should be provided to colleges and universities to encourage them to take a more active role in upgrading programs in urban schools.

An Imperiled Generation: Urban Schools noted that many students in urban schools have obligations that conflict with schooling. Large numbers of high school students work. Others are parents themselves or have other family obligations. High schools should develop more flexible programs that would allow students to attend at different times of the day and to take more than four years to complete graduation requirements.

The report highlighted the idea that schools in different settings have different needs. This theme is one that increasingly has been emphasized in reform reports released since the middle 1980s. Like *Horace's Compromise, An Imperiled Generation: Saving Urban Schools* expressed a concern that students' learning problems may be associated with the large size of many urban schools. The report recommended that schools be divided so that no unit would have a total of more than 450 students. The effort here would be to help students develop a more personal identity with their school.

Key Ideas in Summary

1. The quality of American education has become an important public concern. Varying perceptions of what constitutes a "good" school have resulted in much debate. A large number of reform recommendations with implications for secondary schools have resulted from these discussions.

2. There are three basic secondary school types. These are the senior high school, the junior high school, and the middle school. The oldest of these types is the senior high school, which began developing in the nineteenth century. Senior high schools expanded rapidly once the legal principle of tax support for senior high schools was firmly established.

3. The first junior high schools appeared in the early 1900s. This school type developed because of a need to provide a "bridge" between the elementary school and the academically rigorous high school. From its inception, there were debates regarding whether junior high schools should focus more on teaching academics or on personal development of students. A feeling that junior high schools were becoming too much oriented to the academic program of the high school led to the development of the middle school in the 1960s. Middle schools were initially supported by people who wanted a school heavily oriented to developmental needs of preadolescents and early adolescents. Middle schools are growing in popularity.

4. A number of major themes have been featured in criticisms of American secondary schools. Sliding Scholastic Aptitude Test Scores in the 1960s and 1970s led many people to believe schools' standards had slipped. International comparisons of student performance often have not reflected well on American students. There has been a concern that secondary students have too many elective choices. Lagging performance levels of students in the nation's cities have led to concerns about the quality of urban schools.

5. During the 1980s, an unprecedented number of reports containing recommendations to reform the schools were issued. Recommendations in these reports addressed many issues critics have seen as threats to educational quality. Among the most widely read of these reports were: *The Paideia Proposal: An Educational Manifesto; A Nation at Risk: The Imperative for Educational Reform; High School: A Report on Secondary Education in America; Horace's Compromise: The Dilemma of the American High School; Time for Results; American Memory; What Do Our 17-Year-Olds Know?;* and *An Imperiled Generation: Saving Urban Schools.*

POSTTEST

DIRECTIONS: Using your own paper, answer these true/false questions. For each correct statement, write the word "true." For each incorrect statement, write the word "false."

_____ 1. In the 1890s, the National Association's Committee of Ten suggested that the major objective of the high school should be to provide vocational courses to prepare students for the world of work.

_____ 2. In recent years, some critics have pushed for improvement in secondary education by arguing that present programs are failing to give students the kind of technical skills they need for many of today's jobs.

_____ 3. A common theme running through proposals to reform the nation's high schools is that high schools today offer too many elective courses.

_____ 4. A number of reform reports suggest that high schools are too large and that teachers should work with smaller numbers of students.

_____ 5. One proposal for reforming schools serving younger secondary students recommends dividing large schools into several smaller administrative units.

Bibliography

ADLER, MORTIMER. "Learning Disputes." *Los Angeles Times*. January 10, 1988. Section 5, pp. 1, 6.

ADLER, MORTIMER J. *The Paideia Proposal: An Educational Manifesto.* New York: Macmillan Publishing Co., Inc., 1982.

BARRY, THOMAS NEWMAN. *Origin and Development of the American Public High School in the Nineteenth Century.* Unpublished doctoral dissertation. Stanford University, 1961.

BOYER, ERNEST L. *High School: A Report on Secondary Education in America.* New York: Harper & Row, 1983.

CARNEGIE FOUNDATION FOR THE ADVANCEMENT OF TEACHING. *An Imperiled Generation: Saving Urban Schools.* Lawrenceville, N.J.: Princeton University Press, 1988.

CHENEY, LYNNE V. *American Memory.* Washington, DC: National Endowment for the Humanities, 1987.

COMMISSION ON THE REORGANIZATION OF SECONDARY EDUCATION. *Cardinal Principles of Secondary Education.* Washington, DC: U.S. Government Printing Office, 1918.

COUGHLIN, ELLEN K. "Worsening Plight of the 'Underclass' Catches Attention of Researchers." *The Chronicle of Higher Education.* March 30, 1988, pp. A5; A7–A8.

EGNATUCK, TONY; GEORGIADY, NICOLAS P; MUTH, C. ROBERT; AND ROMANO, LOUIS G. *The Middle School.* East Lansing: Michigan Association of Middle School Educators, 1975.

FELT, MARILYN CLAYTON. *Improving Our Schools: Thirty-Three Studies that Inform Local Action.* Newton, MA: Education Development Center, Inc., 1985.

FINN, CHESTER E. JR. AND RAVITCH, DIANE. *What Do Our 17-Year-Olds Know?: A Report on the First National Assessment of History and Literature.* New York: Harper & Row, 1987.

FISKE, EDWARD B. "Schools Criticized on the Humanities." *New York Times.* September 8, 1987, pp. A1, B8.

GORDON, BONNIE. "Cultural Comparisons of Schooling. " *Educational Researcher*. August-September, 1987, pp. 4–7.

HECHINGER, FRED M. *"Governors Learn Lesson on Schools." New York Times,* August 26, 1986, Section 3, 9.

HIRSCH, E. D., JR. *Cultural Literacy: What Every American Needs to Know.* New York: Houghton-Mifflin, 1987.

JACKSON, TONY. (ED.) *Turning Point in Preparing American Youth for the 21st Century.* Washington, D.C. : Carnegie Council on Adolescent Education, 1989.

LOUNSBURY, JOHN H., AND VARS, GORDEN E. *Curriculum for the Middle Years.* New York: Harper & Row, 1978.

MICHAELS, KEN. "Caution: Second-Wave Reform Taking Place." Educational Leadership. February, 1988, p. 3.

A NATION AT RISK: THE IMPERATIVE FOR EDUCATIONAL REFORM. Washington, DC: National Commission on Excellence in Education, U.S. Department of Education, 1983.

NATIONAL EDUCATION ASSOCIATION. *Report of the Committee of Ten on Secondary School Studies.* Washington, DC: NEA, 1893.

NATIONAL EDUCATION ASSOCIATION. *Addresses and Proceeedings.* Washington, DC: NEA, July 11, 1911.

ON FURTHER EXAMINATION: REPORT OF THE ADVISORY PANEL ON THE SCHOLASTIC APTITUDE TEST DECLINE. New York: College Entrance Examination Board, 1977.

PERLEZ, JANE. "Dropouts: Data Maze." *New York Times.* March 4, 1987, B24.

POPPER, SAMUEL H. *The American Middle School: an Organizational Analysis.* Waltham, MA: Blaisdell Publishing Company, 1967.

SIZER, THEODORE R. *Horace's Compromise: The Dilemma of the American High School.* Boston: Houghton-Mifflin, 1984.

STERN, JOYCE D. (ED.) AND CHANDLER, MARJORIE O. (ASSOC. ED.). *The Condition of Education.* Washington, DC: U.S. Department of Education, Office of Educational Research and Improvement, Center for Education Statistics, 1987.

TANNER, DANIEL, AND TANNER, LAUREL N. *Curriculum Development: Theory Into Practice.* 2nd ed. New York: Macmillan, 1980.

THORP, MIKE. "High Schoolers in U.S. Lack Drive of Japan's But Show Spontaneity." *The Wall Street Journal.* March 10, 1987, pp. 1, 20.

TIME FOR RESULTS. Washington, DC: National Governors' Association, Center for Policy Research, August, 1986.

VOREACAS, DAVID. "Tougher High School Studies Urged. " *Los Angeles Times.* December 30, 1987. Part I, p. 4.

CHAPTER 2

Effective Schools

AIMS

This chapter provides information to help the reader to:

1. Identify some basic problems that have faced researchers who have tried to identify "effective" schools.
2. Suggest ways in which the "culture" of a given school might influence behavior patterns of teachers.
3. Describe characteristics of "effective" schools initially suggested by Ronald Edmonds.
4. Explain several criticisms that have been made of Edmonds' conceptions of "effective" schools.
5. Describe several characteristics of "effective" schools suggested by the work of Lawrence Stedman.

PRETEST

DIRECTIONS: Using your own paper, answer these true/false questions. For each correct statement, write the word "true." For each incorrect statement, write the world "false."

_____ 1. Most schools have been found to share one or two common problems.

_____ 2. Recent research has shown a consistent relationship between the characteristics of "effective" schools identified by Ronald Edmonds and increased levels of student achievement.

_____ 3. Lawrence Stedman's work has revealed a relationship between parent participation in a school and its "effectiveness."

_____ 4. There is some evidence that when students are given some important responsibilities within the school their attitude toward the school improves.

_____ 5. Recent research suggests that many effective schools are characterized by collaborative leadership involving principals, teachers, and parents.

Introduction

During the past decade, many solutions to problems facing the nation's secondary schools have been proposed. Some researchers have tried to identify examples of schools thought to be serving students well. Their purpose has been to describe features of these "effective schools" carefully so that they could be understood and adopted by other schools. The idea has been to promote the adoption of effective school practices as a means of upgrading the general quality of all the nation's secondary schools.

The diversity among schools has been a vexing problem for effective-schools researchers. Ralph Tyler, one of the leading educational researchers and thinkers of this century, has commented that "because of wide variations among schools, they rarely share in common any single, serious problem" (Tyler 1987, p. 278). Since problems facing individual schools are so different, practices that might be "effective" in one setting may have little application in another.

Despite these differences, researchers interested in improving school quality have argued that there are still some important commonalities among schools. Throughout much of the 1980s and on into the 1990s there has been a continued interest in identifying these general characteristics of "effective" schools.

What Makes a School Effective?

In part, differences among schools are explained by variations in patterns of interpersonal relationships. Each school develops its own "culture." This culture includes expected patterns established regarding relationships among teachers, students, administrators, and parents (Feiman-Nemser and Floden 1986).

Variations in school cultures may affect teachers' behaviors in important ways. For example, in one school, there may be a tradition of viewing teachers as autonomous professionals. In such a setting, there may be little inclination for teachers to consult with one another about their instructional practices. Indeed, a request for help might even be regarded by some staff members as an embarrassing confession of intellectual weakness.

Another building might have a long tradition of cooperative, collegial planning. Teachers might routinely visit one another's classrooms. Parents, teachers, administrators, and students might regularly confer about various aspects of the instructional program. Forces conditioning a teacher's behavior in a setting of this kind are quite different from those in a school where teachers are expected to be independent, stand-alone professionals.

Part of the effort to identify effective schools has required research into variables that go together to shape the specific culture of a school. A number of lists of these characteristics have been developed. Much of the discussion about the attempt to identify features of effective schools centers on the adequacy of the variables that individual researchers have identified.

One of the most influential effective-schools researchers was the late Ronald Edmonds. Edmonds' research led him to identify the following characteristics of effective schools (Edmonds 1982, p. 4):

1. Strong instructional leadership by the principal
2. High academic expectations of students by teachers
3. Strong emphasis on basic skills instruction
4. An orderly environment
5. Frequent, systematic evaluation of students

Edmonds' list of characteristics attracted an enormous following in the early and middle 1980s. His list of effective-schools characteristics, sometimes supplemented by a sixth characteristic (increased instructional time), was adopted by many school systems throughout the country as a model for their school improvement projects. Among them were Chicago, Milwaukee, Minneapolis, San Diego, St. Louis, and Washington, DC (Stedman 1987, p. 215).

Recent research has begun to raise doubts about the adequacy of these five or six characteristics of school effectiveness (Stedman 1987; Zirkel and Greenwood 1987). Some follow-up studies have not demonstrated a consistent association between the presence of these school-effectiveness characteristics and improved learner achievement. In evaluating the worth of improvement programs based on the Edmonds characteristics, one of the difficulties has been achieving agreement on the question of "what constitutes improvement?"

Some schools that have followed Edmonds' recommendations have claimed success because achievement scores have shown modest increases. Critics charge, however, that often these scores have remained well below national grade-level averages and represent little cause for celebration. It has also been noted that there has been a lack of consistency in achievement levels in many of these schools. In one year, scores may have been up, but in another they had fallen back to previous levels (Stedman 1987).

The appropriateness of focusing on academic achievement to identify effective schools has been challenged. If there is too much emphasis on improvement of students' scores on standardized tests, there is a danger that the school program may become excessively narrow. Students may improve their test scores, but the schools may develop into places lacking the kind of warm and caring atmosphere that many parents and other community members have long associated with good schools.

A number of the specific components of the Edmonds' list of characteristics have been challenged. The suggestion that effective schools focus heavily on basic skills instruction has led some schools to emphasize lower-level thinking skills (Stedman 1987). It has narrowed the curriculum to focus on basic content for which standardized tests are readily available. Since there has been great concern about "improving" schools in inner-city areas where student achievement levels have not been high, there has been an especially notable tendency in these schools to avoid content focusing on higher-level thinking and to restrict student options. One unintended side effect may be "a widening of the social class achievement gap, as many suburban schools move rapidly into high-tech, problem-solving curricula, while urban schools remain focused on lower-order test items" (Stedman 1987, p. 217).

The idea that the school principal, in his or her role as an instructional leader, can have an important influence on the overall effectiveness of the school program has been widely endorsed. The assumption that the principal is a key figure in any effort to improve school quality makes so much intuitive sense that, for many years, the proposition was rarely challenged. In recent years, investigators have begun to look more closely at the relationship between the principals' instructional leadership and its impact on school effectiveness. In general, results are beginning to suggest that this may not be as important a factor as Edmonds and others have implied (Stedman 1987; Zirkel and Greenwood 1987) (See Box 2.1).

Box 2.1

Is It Realistic to Expect Every Principal to Be an Instructional Leader?

It is unrealistic to expect all principals to be instructional leaders. Take the example of a principal in a large high school. This person has responsibility for managing a very complex curriculum. There are incredibly complex decisions to be made to assure that all classes that need to be taught are covered by qualified teachers. Budgetary responsibilities are enormous.

In short, a busy principal in a crowded secondary school has too many difficult managerial responsibilities for him or her also to be the school's instructional leader. This role can much more effectively be played by widely-respected competent teacher who has few administrative responsibilities.

What Do You Think?

Read the statement above and answer these questions:

1. What advantages and disadvantages do you see in an educational system that regards the principal as the school's undisputed "instructional leader"?

2. This article suggests that, in some schools, it is not realistic to expect the principal to be the instructional leader. Do you agree?

3. Who do you think should provide instructional leadership in the school? What barriers stand in the way of implementing your proposal?

Unthinking adherence to the idea that the principal is a key figure in any effort to improve school quality, particularly as measured by academic achievement gains, may place the principal in an impossible situation. The research base simply is not there to support the idea that the principal's behavior is a key factor in students' achievement (Zirkel and Greenwood 1987). More recent reviews of the research seem to suggest that instructional leadership must be a concern of a broader constituency. Evidence mounts that reform is more often accomplished when there is shared instructional leadership. When principals, teachers, parents, and other community members jointly commit to support school change, the impact on students' achievement has been observed to be positive (Stedman 1987).

The work of Lawrence Stedman (1987) is representative of that of researchers who are trying to establish criteria for effective schools that have a solid research base. Stedman suggests that school programs should be regarded as effective when there is a record of improved achievement on the part of students from low-income families that has been sustained over several years. Though much additional research needs to be done, Stedman has suggested the following categories for inclusion in a list of characteristics of effective schools (Stedman 1987; p. 218):

1. Ethnic and racial pluralism
2. Parent participation
3. Shared governance with teachers and parents
4. Academically rich programs
5. Skilled use and training of teachers
6. Personal attention to students
7. Student responsibility for school affairs
8. An accepting and supportive environment; and
9. Teaching aimed at preventing academic problems

Ethnic and Racial Pluralism

Many effective-school projects that have been modeled after characteristics suggested by Edmonds (1982) have placed heavy emphasis on teaching basic skills and on classroom management and discipline procedures. In a sense, these recommendations propose a restricted, tightly controlled curriculum that has little claim to meet the wide-ranging needs of students in today's secondary schools. Some critics have charged that these programs have never served students from minority groups well (Stedman 1987). There are fears that a reemphasis on basic skills instruction and on heavy-handed classroom management might lead to even greater disparities between achievement levels of white, middle-class students and those from minority groups and from lower-income families.

Schools that have been found to be doing a good job of meeting the needs of economically deprived students, minority students, and inner city students adjust their programs to reflect special perspectives of these learners. Such schools have programs specifically designed to improve the self-images and self-worth of all students in the school. The curriculum takes into account special contributions of people from different ethnic groups. There may be school recognition of holidays important to students from some of the cultural groups represented in the school. There are sometimes efforts to communicate to parents and other school patrons in languages other than English. For example, school notices might be sent to parents of some students in both English and Spanish (Stedman 1987).

The thrust of programs directed toward ethnic and racial minorities is to enhance the sense of "ownership" in the school and the school program on the part of these students and their parents. Secondary schools with large numbers of ethnic and racial minorities are generally more effective when the culture of the school encourages broad toleration and acceptance of differences among students. Such schools scrupulously avoid sending an unintended message to students that "it would really be better if you were white and middle class."

Parent Participation

One measure of the effectiveness of a secondary school is the level of parental involvement. When parents have a strong interest in school, their children do better on academic tests and they also feel better about the school in general (Henderson 1981).

When there is little parental involvement, there is a good chance parents will sense themselves to be "outsiders." If they lack information about what is really going on in the school, they may be more willing to listen to and pass on unfounded rumors. Such parents know very little about what their children are really experiencing in school. Hence, they have little sound information to assess the accuracy of something they have heard about their children's school. If parents know little about their children's middle, junior high, or senior high school, they will find it difficult to assist their children to prepare themselves to succeed in the school program.

Parental participation in effective schools takes place on two basic levels. First, there needs to be a system that results in frequent two-way communication between parents and teachers. Second, parents need to be directly involved in activities that bring them into the school building and the classroom.

Communication with parents needs to provide more than simply a means for school officials and teachers to tell parents what the school is doing. Effective communication demands that parents also have open avenues of communication with the school. There must be a way for parental views to be openly and easily transmitted to the educators who work with their children.

Some schools have adopted such procedures as scheduling small group meetings of parents, teachers, and administrators in order to share their views. Others mail questionnaires to parents soliciting their reactions to contemplated policy changes. Still others provide workshops for parents to show them how they might do things at home to reinforce what students are learning in their school classes. One such program taught grandparents, parents, and older brothers and sisters how

Box 2.2

Involving Parents: Some Problems

Researchers who have studied practices that tend to make schools more effective have noted that successful schools often involve parents directly in instructional programs. Suggesting that it makes sense to involve parents is one thing. Developing practical procedures to do so is quite another.

This is particularly difficult in schools that enroll large numbers of economically deprived minority students. Such students are among those that have been found to be especially responsive to parental improvement. However, large numbers of parents of such students work and it is not possible for them to come to school during the day. This places some limits on the scope of parent-involvement programs in these schools.

What Do You Think?

Read the comments above and respond to these questions.

1. Do you agree with the idea that some schools find it more difficult than others to involve parents?

2. Does the difficulty many parents of economically deprived and minority students have in visiting schools during the day mean that most parent-involvement programs will take place in middle and upper class schools?

3. How might parents be directly involved in instruction even though it may not be possible for them to come to school during the day?

---

to work with students at home to improve their verbal skills (Stedman 1987).

Because many parents work, it is not always easy to make arrangements to get them into the school during the working day. Even when they cannot visit during the day, programs to get parents into the school building can help develop positive attitudes toward the school. The more parents know about the school and the more they are listened to, the more likely they are to develop a sense of pride and "ownership" in the school program. A parent who is convinced that the school program is sound can reinforce what teachers are saying to students about the importance of study and learning.

Parental understanding takes a giant step forward when parents are directly involved in school classes. Some effective high schools have large parent-aide programs. The most successful of these involve parents in activities that allow them to work with individual students. For example, they may tutor students who are having difficulty with mathematics assignments or with writing tasks. Successful parent-aide programs avoid asking parents to do unpleasant clerical tasks such as running copying machines. The question of parent involvement is discussed in Box 2.2.

Effective schools take care to communicate with parents when their students have done something good. Historically, outside of report card time, many schools initiated direct contacts with parents only when their children became ill, misbehaved, or had gotten themselves into difficulty of some other kind. Many parents have come to view any letter or call from the school as a harbinger of bad news. A communication from a school administrator or a teacher about some especially good student work does wonders for a parent's self esteem. Parents who receive such calls often become very strong supporters of the school and its programs.

Shared Governance with Teachers and Parents

Some of the early research on effective schools suggested that the instructional leadership role of the principal was a critically important factor. More recent work has suggested that although leadership is important, effective schools tend to have collaborative leadership patterns. Particularly, decision making reflects cooperative work among principals, teachers, and parents (Stedman 1987).

Researchers have suggested that in good schools a majority of teachers express satisfaction with their positions, and turnover rates among them are low (Purkey and Smith 1983). An important aspect of teacher satisfaction is the degree to which they sense themselves to have control over decisions regarding how they do their jobs. There are high levels of dissatisfaction among teachers who sense themselves to be working in impersonal bureaucracies (Feiman-Nemser and Floden 1986). This is a particular problem when teachers feel administrators are forcing instructional practices on them that are inconsistent with their own views. In effective schools, teachers feel that general school policies are responsive to their own needs (Good and Brophy 1986). To assure a congruence between policies and teachers' priorities, effective secondary schools often involve teachers directly in the policy-making process.

Parents, too, are often involved in policy making in these schools. They may serve on committees that are formed to consider changes in school curricula, in rules for students, and in other areas. Parental participation has several important benefits. First, it gives the parents who are involved a sense that their views count when policy alternatives are being considered. Involved parents often serve as effective "ambassadors" to the wider community. Their actions can increase levels of general public interest in these changes.

Second, parental involvement in the decision-making process subtly changes the assumptions of the school's administrators and teachers. Once it is known that parents will play a direct part in making decisions, there is a tendency for all school professionals to attend more closely to the views of the larger community that are reflected in the perspectives of the participating parents. This can lead to more closely aligned school policies and community priorities. Over time, this often results in a broadened base of support for the schools.

Academically Rich Programs

A theme running through a number of the educational reform reports of the 1980s is that there should be a reduction in the number of course options available to students in secondary schools. One argument in support of this proposal is that too many electives tend to divert students' attention away from critically important content. It has been suggested that a narrower secondary curriculum with fewer choices for students will focus their academic energies on "important" content.

"Look, Tommy, there's something you should know about summer school!"

Both the student and the society will benefit. This logic was reflected in Edmonds' (1982) dictum that one defining characteristic of effective schools was an emphasis on basic skills.

More recent reviews of effective-schools research have revealed that these schools tend *not* to have restricted students' course options. On the contrary, schools where economically deprived students were consistently found to do well had a very rich array of course offerings. Further, learning experiences within individual courses tended to be very diverse. There was a distinct absence of focus on basic skills learning to the exclusion of other kinds of content. Instruction was found to be "neither narrow, standardized, or drill-based" (Stedman 1987, p. 220).

Teachers in these effective schools recognize that their students have very different backgrounds, abilities, and interests. They motivate students by drawing on many kinds of materials and providing a variety of learning experiences. The breadth and richness of these schools' programs apparently prompt students to work harder and learn more. Severely delimiting course offerings by focusing on basic skills may have unintended consequences. Students may become bored with the school program. If they do, achievement scores are unlikely to improve. Uninspired students rarely do well on tests.

Skilled Use and Training of Teachers

Effective schools have been found to place their strongest teachers in what leaders have identified as high-need areas. For example, some school districts have used outstanding teachers to work in their remedial programs (Stedman 1987). The logic here is that these learners need the best instruction available if they are to master content and stay in school. Only the services of excellent teachers are likely to have a positive impact on such students.

Other effective schools have established small groups of outstanding teachers to serve as roving teacher-consultants and trouble-shooters. They work with other teachers in the schools. They model successful teaching procedures and help other teachers respond to specific instructional problems. Effective schools tend to provide relevant inservice experiences for their teachers. These inservice sessions generally focus on practical needs identified by teachers themselves (Stedman 1987). Principals in these schools tend to be highly supportive of teachers' individual development needs (Good and Brophy 1986). Specific inservice programs are designed with heavy participation of the teachers involved.

Box 2.3

The Induction Year: What Is it?

The idea of an "induction year" immediately following undergraduate teacher preparation courses and student teaching has been widely discussed in recent years. The idea is to provide a smooth transition from the preparation program to the world of the school. Various induction-year schemes have been suggested. Many of them share certain features.

Commonly, teachers in the induction year are fully responsible for the classrooms they teach and are paid a regular salary. There usually are provisions for continuing assistance. In some places, there continue to be occasional visits from college or university professors of education. Often an experienced teacher is assigned to the induction-year teacher as a mentor who provides both professional assistance and emotional support. Some induction-year programs reduce the teaching load of beginning teachers to allow for more preparation time.

In some places, there has been a requirement for a formal evaluation of the teacher to take place at the end of the induction year. A passing induction-year evaluation is a requirement for a regular teaching certificate. This scheme has drawn some criticism. The argument is that the induction year should be a positive nurturing experience. Induction-year teachers, some suggest, should not be placed under the kind of stress that results when they know their performances are being assessed for certification purposes.

Effective secondary schools pay particular attention to the needs of first-year teachers. In schools where special characteristics of beginning teachers have not been considered, there is a chance they will be assigned to classes where their likelihood of having a successful experience is low. When this happens to a beginning teacher, his or her confidence may vanish. Many people who have had an unfortunate first-year placement never return for a second year of teaching.

In effective schools, administrators try to arrange teaching assignments in such a way that beginning teachers will achieve success, develop their confidence, and, ultimately, commit to a career in the teaching profession. Some schools provide extra preparation periods for these teachers (Urbanski 1988), giving them more time to prepare their lessons. They also allow time for beginners to observe classes of outstanding teachers with years of experience in the building.

Many effective schools are beginning to formalize programs for beginning teachers into what is sometimes called an "induction year." Induction programs attempt to provide a series of experiences for newcomers to ease their entry into the profession. Sometimes a new teacher will be assigned to a formal mentor—a highly qualified experienced teacher. The mentor works with the newcomer, reacts to his or her ideas, and generally serves as a source of encouragement and support. Sometimes professors from teacher-preparation programs continue to work with beginning teachers as part of an induction-year team.

Personal Attention to Students

Researchers have noted that effective schools tend to have high academic expectations of their students (Purkey and Smith 1983). This observation raises as many questions as it answers. For example, do the high academic expectations themselves bring about high levels of student achievement? Or are there other factors in effective schools that go along with high academic expectations to produce improved achievement levels? Increasingly, researchers are beginning to suggest that high expectations alone are not a sufficient expectation. What seems to be needed is a school atmosphere characterized by very careful attention to individual student needs.

Stedman (1987) points out that many effective schools have "designed their programs so that they could provide close, personal attention to students" (p. 221). This personal attention has been provided in a number of ways. A general theme running through these approaches has been to increase the number of contacts between an individual student and someone else who can assist him or her with assigned learning tasks. For example, some effective schools have large programs that bring adult volunteers into the classroom to help students. In other schools, older and brighter students are enlisted to work with students.

When the teacher has parents or other aides available, he or she can spend more time with those students who are in particular need of help. Under these conditions, personalized explanations tailored to the needs of individual students become a real possibility. These explanations greatly enhance the probability that learners who are having difficulty will master assigned content.

Use of teaching assistants also allows more continuous and systematic monitoring of students' progress. There is a growing body of research to support the proposition that consistent monitoring of students is associated with improved academic performance (Good and Brophy 1986). Monitoring provides feedback to students, allows them to correct mistakes, and increases the likelihood that they will master assigned content. Academic success is a very strong motivator. Students who do well tend to think more positively about themselves and about their school. These positive attitudes, in turn, increase their likelihood of success on subsequent learning tasks.

Effective schools are characterized by comfortable, respectful relationships between teachers and students.

Student Responsibility for School Affairs

Effective schools have policies that provide students with important responsibilities. These often are of both an academic and nonacademic nature. In some schools, more able students are systematically organized into teams of tutors. These student-tutors work with other students who need help to master assigned content (Stedman 1987). In some schools, student representatives participate with teachers, parents, administrators, and community representatives on curriculum councils that consider ways to improve the academic program.

Nonacademic duties of students in effective schools are varied. In some schools, organized student groups assume responsibility for removing litter from the grounds and for keeping halls and restrooms in good order. Student councils may play important roles. Student groups may assist teachers and administrators in monitoring student groups in such areas as the cafeteria and at athletic events.

Providing students with some important responsibilities can help them develop a sense of pride in the school and its programs. Effective secondary schools have been found to offer many opportunities of this type. The better programs give students opportunities to make some important decisions. Researchers have found two important benefits to be associated with an increase in students' authority and responsibility at school. When this occurs, achievement levels tend to go up, and episodes of undesirable classroom behavior tend to decrease in number (Rutter 1983, Good and Brophy 1986). These effects become more pronounced as the number of learners given responsibilities increases (Rutter 1983).

An Accepting and Supporting Environment

Emotional climates of effective secondary schools are warm and accepting. These schools are happy places where administrators do not rigidly impose rules on teachers and students (Stedman 1987). Such schools are concerned about discipline. However, special provisions are often made to minimize discipline problems. In one school, for example, a special place is provided for students who are feeling pressured. They use this place to cool down, get temporarily out of a frustrating situation, and settle down before they return to the classroom (Stedman 1987).

Teachers in an accepting and supporting school environment have what sometimes has been described as a "sense of efficacy" (Ashton and Webb 1986). This means that these teachers have great confidence in their abilities to transmit content to students. They sense their work to be important, and they take pride in what they do.

Teachers' attitudes are important in shaping the atmosphere of a given school (Lightfoot 1983). In schools characterized by warm and caring atmospheres, most teachers are pleased with their jobs and rates of teacher turnover are low (Purkey and Smith 1983).

In schools with caring and supporting environments, teachers feel that they personally exercise a great deal of personal control over the nature of their work. They sense that school policies in the district and in the building are responsive to their needs (Feiman-Nemser and Floden 1986). Teachers feel that they have the authority to modify instructional programs as they see fit to meet their students' needs.

Box 2.4

Improving the Environment of the School

Researchers have found that students tend to feel schools are "warmer" and more caring places when the physical surroundings of the school are pleasant. This research establishes a sound rationale for a good school maintenance program. It also suggests that teachers have an obligation to do what they can to assure the physical environment of the school is pleasant.

What Do You Think?

1. What do you recall about the physical condition of your own high school? Were conditions uniformly good or bad throughout? Or, were some areas better than others? What might have accounted for place-to-place differences within the school?

2. If you have an opportunity to do so, walk through a local secondary school. Take some notes on the physical environment. What impressed you? What things might be improved?

3. Think about the courses you will be teaching. What kinds of things might you do to create a pleasant atmosphere in your room?

Schools with positive school climates often make efforts to recognize student achievement of all kinds. This kind of recognition goes well beyond more familiar practices of displaying athletic trophies and otherwise acknowledging athletic prowess. For example, such schools often prominently display names of high academic achievers, academic scholarship winners, instrumental music champions, one-act play competition winners, and other students who have achieved something special. The idea is to develop school-wide support for students who do well in all areas.

Schools that have been found to have warm, supportive, positive atmospheres often feature pleasant physical surroundings (Rutter 1983). The word "pleasant" by no means implies "new," "well-landscaped," or "spacious." In fact, many of these effective secondary schools are very old buildings in inner cities. What makes the atmosphere pleasant is the attention given to repair and maintenance of the facility. In effective schools, repairs are done quickly. Disfigurations of all kinds are removed. The buildings are neatly decorated, and there is an absence of clutter. The effort to maintain the physical appearance of the school reinforces the idea that schooling is important and that all who use the school take pride in the building (see Box 2.4).

Teaching Aimed at Preventing Academic Problems

Effective schools try to deal with potential academic problems before they become serious. A number of approaches have been developed in response to this need. Some schools have developed a parental "early warning" scheme. Teachers call or write to parents as soon as they have a preliminary indication that a student is not doing well in a course (Stedman 1987).

For example, a foreign language teacher might call a parent if a student fails to learn the appropriate way to conjugate the present tense. If the parents and teacher can work with such a student early to overcome this difficulty, the student has an excellent chance of profiting from subsequent instruction. Without early intervention of this kind, the probability is high that the student will become hopelessly lost when the class moves on to more complex verb forms that presume an understanding of the present tense.

Attending to early warning signals of academic problems requires teachers to work very closely with individual students. Teachers in effective schools know their learners well, and they are able to spot difficulties and to provide appropriate instructional responses. Instructional activities are varied to meet special needs of individual students. This kind of responsive instruction is a goal espoused by many teachers. In effective secondary schools, teachers manage to deliver this kind of personalized instruction more consistently than often is the case in less effective schools.

Key Ideas in Summary

1. The search for criteria to use in identifying "effective schools" has drawn much attention from researchers in recent years. Wide variations among schools have contributed to the difficulty of this task.

2. Qualitative differences among schools are explained, in part, by differences in variables that collectively comprise a school's "culture." Setting variables tend to result in different patterns of behaviors among administrators, teachers, learners, and parents.

3. The late Ron Edmonds was a very influential effective-schools researcher. In 1982, Edmonds suggested that effective schools were characterized by (a) strong instructional leadership by the principal; (b) high academic expectations of students by teachers; (c) strong emphasis on basic skills instruction; (d) an orderly environment; and (e) frequent, systematic evaluation of students.

4. A number of school districts adopted the Edmonds' framework to establish programs that they hoped would make their schools better. Results of these efforts, generally, have not been as promising as had been hoped. Part of the difficulty seems to have been a failure to adequately define what would be considered evidence that "improvement" had occurred. There has been a failure to ascertain that the categories identified by Edmonds really represent the most critically important characteristics of "effective" schools.

5. More recent researchers have been expanding the list of characteristics of "effective" schools. Stedman (1987), for example, has suggested a list of nine characteristics. Further, he advocates using academic progress of at-risk students from low-income families as the major measure of improvement. Stedman's review of the relevant research has led him to identify these characteristics of effective schools: (a) ethnic and racial pluralism; (b) parent participation; (c) shared governance with teachers and parents; (d) academically rich programs; (e) skilled use and training of teachers; (f) personal attention to students; (g) student responsibility for school affairs; (h) an accepting and supportive environment; and (i) teaching aimed at preventing academic problems.

POSTTEST

DIRECTIONS: Using your own paper, answer these true/false questions. For each correct statement, write the word "true." For each incorrect statement, write the word "false."

_____ 1. Ronald Edmonds suggested that one characteristic of an "effective" school was its strong emphasis on basic skills instruction.

_____ 2. One problem researchers have had in assessing the success of programs designed to improve schools' effectiveness has been deciding exactly what should be taken as evidence of "improvement."

_____ 3. Contrary to effective-schools research of the early 1980s, more recent research has suggested that effective schools have an academically rich program, not a program focusing heavily on basic skills introduction.

_____ 4. Parent-aide programs have been found to be most effective when parents have been asked to perform clerical tasks rather than to assist directly in the instructional process.

_____ 5. "Effective" schools have been found to treat new teachers no differently that "non-effective" schools.

Bibliography

ASHTON, P. T. AND WEBB, R. B. *Making a Difference: Teachers' Sense of Efficacy and Student Achievement*. New York: Longman, 1986.

BRANDT, RON. "On Leadership and Student Achievement: A Conversation with Richard Andrews." *Educational Leadership* (November, 1987), pp. 9–16.

CAWELTI, GORDON. "Why Instructional Leaders are So Scarce." *Educational Leadership* (September, 1987), p. 3.

EDMONDS, RONALD R. "Programs of School Improvement: An Overview." *Educational Leadership* (December, 1982), pp. 4–11.

FEIMAN-NEMSER, S. AND FLODEN, R. E. "The Cultures of Teaching." In Wittrock, M.C. *Handbook of Research on Teaching*, 3rd ed., New York: Macmillan Publishing Company, 1986, pp. 505–526.

GOOD, T. L. AND BROPHY, J. E. "School Effects." In Wittrock, M.C. *Handbook of Research on Teaching*, 3rd ed., New York: Macmillan Publishing Company, 1986, pp. 570–602.

HENDERSON, ANNE (ED.). *Parent Participation—Student Achievement: The Evidence Grows*. Columbia, Maryland: National Committee for Citizens in Education, 1981.

LIGHTFOOT, S. L. *The Good High School: Portraits of Character and Culture*. New York: Basic Books, 1983.

PURKEY, S. C. AND SMITH, M. S. "Effective Schools: A Review." *Elementary School Journal* (March, 1983), pp. 427–452.

RUTTER, M. "School Effects on Student Progress: Research Findings and Policy Implications." in Shulman, L.S. and Sykes, G., (eds.) *Handbook of Teaching and Policy*. New York: Longman, 1983.

STEDMAN, LAWRENCE C. "It's Time We Changed the Effective Schools Formula." *Phi Delta Kappan* (November, 1987), pp. 215–224.

TYLER, RALPH W. "Education Reforms." *Educational Leadership* (December, 1987), pp. 227–280.

URBANSKI, ADAM. "Rochester Plan: A Collaborative Model." Address given at the Second Annual Holmes Group Spring Faculty Conference. Houston, Texas: South Central Holmes Group Region, April 23, 1988.

ZIRKEL, PERRY A. AND GREENWOOD, SCOTT C. "Effective Schools and Effective Principals: Effective Research?" *Teachers College Record* (Winter, 1987), pp. 255–267.

CHAPTER 3

Profiles of Secondary Students

AIMS

This chapter provides information to help the reader to:

1. Recognize the tremendous diversity that exists within the total population of secondary students.
2. Note trends that have implications for numbers of students expected in the nation's secondary schools in the years ahead.
3. Point out high school completion rates for students from different backgrounds.
4. Recognize general patterns of physical development of secondary school students.
5. Suggest patterns of intellectual development expected in students of secondary school age.

PRETEST

DIRECTIONS: Using your own paper, answer these true/false questions. For each correct statement, write the word "true." For each incorrect statement, write the word "false."

_____ 1. The diversity in secondary schools tends to reflect the diversity in American society as a whole.

_____ 2. There is expected to be a substantial increase in the numbers of students enrolled in secondary schools in the late 1990s as compared to the late 1980s and early 1990s.

_____ 3. Tests of the nation's 17-year-olds revealed that a majority of them are "adept" readers who can read and understand relatively complicated material.

_____ 4. Use of illegal drugs among the nation's secondary school students seems to be declining.

_____ 5. A lower percentage of secondary school girls have jobs today than was the case in the mid-1950s.

Introduction

If one word could be used to describe the nature of the population of the nation's secondary schools, that word might well be "diversity." Students in middle schools, junior high schools, and senior high schools represent a range of characteristics that is almost a mirror image of the population as a whole. Students differ in their physical characteristics, aspirations, intellectual capacities, interests, and values.

Today's secondary teachers must be prepared to work with many kinds of students. For beginners, this often requires some adjustments in their assumptions about what young people are like. Some students in the school are likely to be quite different from the kinds of young people beginning teachers know as personal friends. Large numbers of secondary students come from social and cultural backgrounds having little in common with those of their teachers.

The variety of students in school today is greater than it has ever been. Nearly 95 percent of American young people between the ages of 14 and 17 are in school (U.S. Department of Education 1988). This is a remarkable figure considering that the total population includes young people with severe handicaps, with unsupportive home backgrounds, with native tongues other that English, and with a host of other characteristics that have potential for interfering with their success in school.

Not surprisingly, the diverse secondary school student population brings with it certain problems. No matter how responsive teachers and schools attempt to be in establishing programs to meet the needs of specialized groups, many individual students still find little satisfaction in their school programs.

Student dissatisfaction can lead to behavior problems. The diversity of the student population has been found to correlate with the number of student behavior problems reported by teachers. In urban areas, where the student population is likely to be quite varied, 24 percent of teachers in one survey reported that student misbehavior interfered with their teaching to "a great extent." The same survey found only 8 percent

Secondary students reflect the diversity found in the general population.

of teachers in rural areas, where student populations are less diverse, reporting a similar concern (Stern and Chandler 1988, p. 111).

There is no intent here to use these figures to give a negative impression of secondary students. The point is simply that the population of students in the nation's middle schools, junior high schools, and senior high schools is varied. This diversity can and does pose challenges for teachers in these schools. Many teachers welcome these challenges and take real pride in their abilities to cope with them professionally.

This chapter introduces a number of patterns that characterize today's secondary school students. The patterns selected for review

"You are editor of the school newspaper, president of the school chorus, yearbook editor, captain of the varsity soccer team, played the lead role in the senior class play, secretary of the photography club, president of student council—exactly *when* do you attend classes, Mr. Roth?"

here represent just a sample of those that might have been discussed. Collectively, however, those that have been included provide a good overview of secondary students.

Changes in Numbers of Secondary School Students

Widespread availability of birth control technology has resulted in important changes in the age make-up of the American population. This technology came to be almost universally available during the mid

Box 3.1

As America "Grays," How Will Attitudes Toward Young People Change?

On average, the American population is getting older. By the year 2000, it is estimated that 35.6 percent of the population will be 45 years old or older (Hoffman, 1988). This represents an increase over the 1990 figure of 31.3 percent. Some people speculate that this aging population may have varying views concerning young people. Here are two possibilities.

A

As more and more people get closer to retirement, they will increase their interest in and support for education. They will do so out of self interest. Educated workers will be better paid. Their high salaries will generate sufficient tax revenues to fund programs that benefit senior citizens. Senior citizens, then, will tend to be more supportive of education as they come to see how it will benefit them personally.

B

The higher percentage of older people will use its new political muscle to direct tax dollars to programs that benefit them personally. This will result in a diversion of money away from education. Money will be spent, instead, on improved medical care for the aged, special parks and recreational facilities for older citizens, and on construction of community centers for retired people. Educational facilities for the young will be a low priority.

What Do You Think?

Read the two positions above. Then answer these questions.

1. What are your reactions to argument "A"?

2. What are your reactions to argument "B"?

3. What counterarguments might you make to each?

4. Can you think of an outcome different from both argument "A" and argument "B" that will result from the trend toward an aging American population?

to late 1950s. Its dissemination resulted in a dramatic decline in the birthrate. This marked a dramatic change from the very high birthrates in the 15 years following the end of World War II. On average, the American population is growing older. This may, as Box 3.1 suggests, affect attitudes toward young people.

The impact of the change in American birthrates on school enrollments is complex. In general, from the 1960s until about 1988, it resulted in a reduction in the total number of students enrolled in schools. In the last two years of the 1980s and into the early 1990s, this pattern seemed to be reversing as enrollments were observed to rise (Stern and Chandler 1988, p. 107). The rise in enrollments occurred because large numbers of people born after World War II had children of their own who were beginning to enter school. While fertility rates have remained low, the extremely large number of females of child-bearing age has resulted in a very large number of children. Stated in another way, the increase in the number of children results not because individual mothers are having lots of children but, rather, because there are so many mothers.

The increase in overall enrollment that began in the late 1980s was observed first in the nation's elementary schools. This will ultimately lead to enrollment growth at the secondary level. This growth, however, will not be observed until the middle 1990s. When it comes, growth in numbers of secondary students will be significant. For example, it is estimated that nearly a million more students will attend the nation's middle schools, junior high schools, and senior high schools in 1997 than attended in 1987 (Stern and Chandler 1988, p. 107).

The expected growth in numbers of secondary school students will result in a demand for much larger numbers of secondary school teachers throughout much of the 1990s. In 1988 there was an estimated total demand for 48,000 new secondary teachers. By the year 1997, it is anticipated that 83,000 new secondary teachers will be needed (Stern and Chandler 1988, p. 104). School districts may be hard pressed to find numbers of qualified teachers to fill all vacant positions.

Major Minorities Within the Secondary School Population

Many minorities are represented within the total secondary school population. The specific mix of minorities varies greatly from place to place. The two largest minority groups in schools are blacks and Hispanics.

Fertility rates among blacks and Hispanics are somewhat higher that among whites (non-Hispanics). One result is that both groups are growing as a percentage of the total school population. For example, in 1960 blacks constituted about 13.4 percent of the total school population. By 1985, blacks accounted for 15.8 percent of those enrolled. In 1960,

Box 3.2

Average Reading Scores by Race for Students in Grades 3, 7, and 11: 1986

Scores by Race (points above or below grade-level average)

Grade	Average score	Whites (non-hispanics)	Blacks	Hispanics
3	38.1	40 (+1.9)	33 (−5.1)	33 (−5.1)
7	48.9	50 (+1.1)	45 (−3.9)	44 (−4.9)
11	56.1	57 (+0.9)	52 (−4.1)	51 (−5.1)

SOURCE: Stern and Chandler 1988, p. 17.

Hispanics accounted for 6.5 percent of students in school. By 1985, Hispanics represented 9.7 percent of the total school enrollment (U.S. Department of Education 1988, p. 50).

Both the black population and the Hispanic population are overwhelmingly urban. Blacks in rural areas tend to be concentrated in the states of the Old South. Rural Hispanics tend to live in areas that are relatively close to the Mexican border. Though many Hispanics have ancestral roots in Mexico, large numbers, too, have ancestors who have come to this country from Cuba, Puerto Rico, and other areas in the Caribbean, Central America, and South America. Many Hispanics of Cuban descent live in Florida. Many with ancestral ties to Puerto Rico live in New York.

Both black and Hispanic students experience more academic difficulty in schools than do white (non-Hispanic) students. A variety of explanations has been suggested. Certainly economic circumstances of black and Hispanic families and language problems seem to be among factors contributing to this situation. Additionally, there may be unintended cultural biases in some tests used to measure achievement. For whatever reasons, the evidence seems clear that the measured achievement levels of black and Hispanic students are generally lower than those of white (non-Hispanic) students. Scores in the area of reading reflect this general pattern (see Box 3.2).

Because proficiency in reading is so critical to school success in many other subjects, researchers in recent years have been developing more refined tests to assess students' abilities in this area. Tests developed by the National Assessment of Educational Progress focus not only on very basic reading skills but also on students' abilities to derive sophisticated understandings from written material. Results of these tests revealed that "while the Nation's students had the skills to derive a surface understanding of what they had read, they had difficulty when asked to elaborate upon this surface understanding" (Stern and Chandler 1988, p. 16).

Black and Hispanic students' scores on tests of their ability to derive sophisticated understanding from reading have been well below those of white (non-Hispanic) students. The National Assessment of Educational Progress uses the label "adept" to identify a reading proficiency level characterized by the ability "to find, understand, summarize, and explain relatively complicated literary and informational material" (U.S. Department of Education 1988, p. 58). Tests of 17-year-olds conducted during school year 1983–1984 revealed that 45 percent of white (non-Hispanic) students, 15.5 percent of black students, and 19.9 percent of Hispanic students were "adept" readers (U.S. Department of Education 1988, p. 58).

A number of explanations have been suggested for the failure of black and Hispanic students to perform well on tests of more sophisticated reading abilities. One factor appears to be the kind of a community a student lives in. In general, students in disadvantaged urban communities did not do as well as students living elsewhere. Since a high percentage of black and Hispanic students live in these circumstances, this environmental variable may contribute to their lower test scores.

Researchers also have noted that students who are engaged in academic, college-bound curricula (which, presumably, include a great deal of reading) tend to score higher on tests of more sophisticated reading skills. Much smaller percentages of black and Hispanic students are enrolled in these programs than are white (non-Hispanic) students (Stern and Chandler 1988, p. 16.). This raises a troubling issue about advisement of students. Do school counselors, knowingly or unknowingly, tend to recommend "general" or "vocational" courses more frequently to black and Hispanic students than to white (non-Hispanic) students?

Percentages of black and Hispanic students who drop out of school are higher than percentages for white (non-Hispanic) students. A recent survey of the population of the nation's 16- to 24-year-olds found that 12.2 percent of the white (non-Hispanic) students, 15.1 percent of the black students, and 27.6 percent of the Hispanic students had dropped out of high school. These students represent a sad waste of the nation's intellectual capital. Few of these individuals are able to qualify for any but entry-level, low-paying jobs. Their vocational horizons are very limited. The extremely high dropout rate for Hispanic students is particularly troublesome. There is evidence that Hispanics are the nation's fastest growing minority. Unless something can be done to increase the school retention rate for Hispanics, in the future the nation will have millions of citizens who lack important economic survival skills.

There is abundant evidence that schools in the years ahead will be intensifying their efforts to meets the needs of black and Hispanic students. A number of trends that have already begun are likely to continue. One ongoing effort to enhance the school performance of blacks and Hispanics has to do with the issue of language. In a few places, black English programs have been established. The idea is to establish initial communication with black youngsters in a language they know and understand and to build a systematic language bridge to standard American English. This response has been enormously controversial both within and without the black community. Some argue that black English programs will be the salvation of black students in the school. Others contend that such programs delay black students' acquisition of patterns of standard English. This debate is certain to continue.

The language issue is also very important with respect to the schools' Hispanic population. The federal government has taken interest in problems of students who come to school speaking languages other than English. Federal bilingual education legislation requires schools to provide initial school instruction to students in their home language. This instruction is to continue until such time as students' proficiency in English is approximately equivalent to their proficiency in their home languages. Bilingual programs have been controversial. Some feel that bilingual programs facilitate the adjustment of non-native speakers of English to the school program. Others contend that they delay students' acquisition of English.

Language concerns by no means are limited to black and Hispanic students. Though there are large numbers of blacks and Hispanics in the schools, there are students from many other cultural and language backgrounds as well. In recent years, for example, millions of students of Asian heritage have entered the public school system. More than 35 percent of all immigrants to the United States in the years 1971 to 1980 came from Asia (Hoffman 1988). In the 1980s, Asians have represented an even higher percentage of total immigration to this country. In the years 1982 through 1986, about 47 percent of all immigrants came from Asia (Hoffman 1988). Especially large numbers have come from the Philippines, Korea, Vietnam, and India.

Many children of Asian immigrants speak little or no English when they come to school. It has been extremely difficult for school districts to find people to teach who are qualified for professional teacher certification and who are also fluent in one or more Asian languages. Given the continuing high rate of immigration from Asia, this problem seems likely to persist for some time.

Changing Patterns in Secondary Students' Families

The traditional American family pattern featuring a working father and a non-working mother who stays at home to care for the children is rapidly disappearing. Today, fewer than one third of students in schools come from this kind of family. Various economic pressures, accelerating divorce rates, and increases in the numbers of unmarried women bearing children have contributed to this situation.

Dramatic price increases of certain basic items have forced many married women into the work force. In particular, housing costs have skyrocketed over the past decade. Many families find it necessary for both parents to work to accumulate sufficient funds for a down payment and to handle monthly mortgage obligations. The desire to own one's own house continues to be a strongly-held value. Pursuit of the dream of home ownership is one of the most important reasons behind the trend for wives, as well as husbands, to hold regular, paying jobs. Today, in 55 percent of two-parent families both parents work (U.S. Department of Education 1988, p. 38). Box 3.3 discusses the issue of children being left home alone after school.

Divorce rates have increased tremendously over the past 40 years. In 1950, there were about 385,000 divorces in the entire country. By the middle 1980s, this number had risen to an annual rate of about 1,200,000 divorces (U.S. Department of Education 1988, p. 10). There has been an accompanying increase in the number of children involved when divorces have taken place. In 1950, 299,000 children were involved in divorces; by the middle 1980s that figure had soared to about 1,100,000 (U.S. Department of Education 1988, p. 10). There is widespread agreement that divorces are very traumatic for children. Many secondary school students bear some scars from having gone through this wrenching emotional experience.

Because of divorces and because many children have been born to unmarried mothers in recent years, large numbers of students in the schools live in one-parent homes. In 1950, only 7.1 percent of all young people under age 18 lived in a family headed by a single parent. By the middle 1980s this figure had jumped to 21 percent. More than 52 percent of black students were living with just one parent (U.S. Department of Education 1988, p. 20).

Box 3.3

Working Parents and Leaving Children Home Alone After School

In recent years, much has been written about "latch-key" children. These young people return after school to homes where parents are absent. About 47 percent of junior high school students and about 59 percent of senior high school students are home alone after school for one or more days during the school week (Stern and Chandler 1988, p. 119).

The pattern of young people's being or not being at home alone after school is closely related to whether parents are working and whether more than one parent is in the home.

	Percentage of Parents Responding	
	Child Never at Home Alone	*Child at Home One or More Days a Week*
One-parent families		
Not working	68	32
Work part-time	48	52
Work full-time	45	55
Two-parent families		
One not working	74	26
Both work, one part-time	60	40
Both work full-time	49	51

SOURCE: Stern and Chandler 1988, p. 119.

Drug Abuse

Use of illegal drugs by secondary students is greater in the United States than in any other developed country in the world (Hamburg 1986). This problem has attracted a tremendous amount of national concern. For example, the 1988 election campaign featured promises by both major candidates to take aggressive action to curb the flow of illegal drugs into the United States.

Efforts of governmental and school officials to do something about student drug abuse may be beginning to pay off. Though percentages of students who have used illegal drugs remain distressingly high, these percentages have begun a downward trend. In 1981, 65.6 percent of high school seniors had tried an illegal drug. By 1987, this figure had dropped to 56.6 percent (Stern and Chandler 1988, p. 112).

There has been particular concern about student use of cocaine. Cocaine use, too, seems to be declining. In 1985, 17.3 percent of high school seniors reported that they had tried the drug. Two years later, this figure had dropped to 15.2 percent (Stern and Chandler 1988, p. 112). Though officials are heartened by this trend, there is still much concern about student use of this very dangerous substance.

Students from Impoverished Families

Educators have long been concerned about students who come to schools from impoverished family backgrounds. Dietary deficiencies, health standards deficiencies, and other problems frequently associated with poverty can negatively affect students' school performance. Children from economically deprived homes are in disproportionate numbers ethnic minorities or children from families headed by a single female parent (Hoffman 1988, p. 542).

In general, poverty rates are higher in central cities than in the suburban fringes surrounding these cities. This configuration has important implications for public education. To sketch the case in very general terms, it is fair to say that central cities have been losing populations and tax bases to suburban areas. What this has meant is that central city school districts have not been able to raise as much tax money as they have in the past. It has become difficult for inner-city schools to provide well-funded educational programs for students coming from economically deprived home backgrounds.

In recent years, a number of legal challenges have been mounted that have sought adequate funding for schools regardless of where they are located. The logic has been that a student should not be penalized for living in an inner city or in some other place with a meager tax base. The ultimate outcome of these challenges is not yet clear. There does, however, appear to be some move toward equalizing funding levels among schools in different parts of a state.

High schools in the United States sometimes are referred to as "comprehensive" high schools. This means that they are designed to serve the entire population. Programs are supposed to be broad enough to meet students' needs regardless of their family backgrounds, their talents, and their individual aspirations. Deeply embedded in the American view of secondary education is the idea that there is a benefit in a system that brings all students together in a common school setting where they rub elbows with "everybody." The comprehensive high school has been defended as a social melting pot where all kinds of young people meet, share their differing perspectives, and grow to maturity together.

Today, some people are challenging the proposition that the comprehensive high school really serves the interests of all students. In particular, there are concerns about whether the needs of students from impoverished home backgrounds, many of them minorities, are being served. Questions have been raised about whether too many of these students have been counseled to enroll in nonacademic, vocational tracks.

Some critics are suggesting reducing the number of course options available to students to assure that higher percentages will enroll in college-preparatory work. These ideas are stimulating a good deal of discussion at the present time. (For a more extensive discussion of some of these proposals, see Chapter 1, "The Secondary School in an Age of Reform.")

A Selection of Other Issues

Teenage Pregnancy

There has been a general increase in the pregnancy rate among girls aged 15 to 17. In the early 1970s, approximately 6.4 percent of girls in this age group became pregnant each year. By the middle 1980s, this rate had increased to 7.2 percent (U.S. Department of Education 1988, p. 96). Increases in numbers of pregnant teenagers have come at a time when birth control information is widely available. Some critics have charged, however, that schools have failed to adequately disseminate such information to students. Proposals to provide this kind of information are very controversial. Some groups oppose school-based birth control information on religious grounds. Others suggest that disseminating such information might be viewed as an endorsement of undesirable early sexual activity. The issue is certain to be a subject of continued debate in the years ahead.

Part-Time Jobs

There have been some interesting changes in students' tendencies to hold part-time jobs over the past thirty to thirty-five years. These changes pertain more to female than to male students. In 1955, 37.3

percent of all 16- and 17-year-olds enrolled in school also held jobs. By 1985, there was only a slight increase to 38.0 percent. By way of contrast, only 21.4 percent of female students in this age group worked in 1955. By 1985, 38.8 percent of girls in this age group worked— a slightly higher percentage than male students (U.S. Department of Education 1988, p. 76). For teachers, these figures suggest that large numbers of their high school students have employment obligations that may divert their attention and energy away from school-related tasks.

Television

Teachers and many parents have long been concerned about the relationship between television and homework. Research has generally supported their supposition that increased television watching is accompanied by decreased time spent on homework. Of students who reported watching television six or more hours a day, only 4 percent reported spending as much as one or two hours a day on homework. On the other hand, 62 percent of students who reported they watched from zero to two hours of television a day reported they spent one to two hours daily on homework assignments (U.S. Department of Education 1988, p. 70). Because only so much discretionary time is available to students outside of school hours, it is clear that spending a high percentage of this time watching television subtracts from time available for homework.

Patterns of Physical Development in Secondary Students

Physical differences among secondary students of the same age often come as a surprise to beginning teachers. For example, 15-year-old boys may vary as much as eight inches in height (sometimes even more). There may be weight differences in excess of 30 pounds. Differences in rates of students' physical maturation result in a tremendous disparity in their coordination, physical strength, and general appearance.

To some extent, these differences are accompanied by differences in interests. A group of 14-year-olds in a ninth-grade class may have interests ranging from those of typical middle-grades elementary school students to the enthusiasms of adults. Some interest differences have obvious connections to physical differences. For example, large early-maturing boys who do well in sports are likely to be more committed to athletics than are late-maturing students who are unable to compete successfully in athletics.

Early-maturing girls, who at age 13 or 14 may have the appearance of 17-, 18- or 19-year-olds, tend to be treated differently by adults than their later-maturing age-mates. Interests of these early-maturing girls often more closely parallel those of girls who are three or four years older.

Delayed physical maturation can have important psychological effects on students. For example, late-maturing boys may not be able to compete at a time when there is considerable social payoff for students who are larger, stronger, and better coordinated. This may mean that adolescents' identification of their leaders may be set rather early in the school years and that these leaders will tend to be drawn from early-maturing students. Given this possibility, secondary school teachers need to be particularly sensitive in dealing with late-maturing students.

Differences in rates of physiological development vary by sex. Girls, in general, tend to develop at an earlier age than do boys. For example, on average, girls in the 11- to 14-year-old age ranges tend to be taller than boys. Between the ages of about nine or 10 through about age 14 and $14^{1}/_{2}$, the average girl tends to be heavier than the average boy. What in casual conversation is sometimes referred to as the adolescent "growth spurt" typically begins for girls somewhere in the nine and one half to $14^{1}/_{2}$ age range. For boys, this occurs somewhat later, typically falling somewhere in the $10^{1}/_{2}$ to 16 age span.

Within single classes, teachers may find physiological differences among learners to be even greater than what might be expected by students of a given age. For example, although the typical ninth-grader is about 14 years old, most ninth grades will include a much broader age range. For example, there may be learners as young as twelve in the classroom, and it is not unusual to find ninth-grade classes with several 16- or 17-year-olds enrolled.

Because of recent trends to expand the number of course offerings in secondary schools, teachers today probably find a greater age range in their classes than historically has been true. The expansion of curricular offerings has tended to break down traditional practices of reserving specific courses as "freshman-," "sophomore-," "junior-," or "senior-level" offerings. Although many courses tied to grade level remain in the secondary school program, today many courses may be taken by students of different grade levels. This has caused many secondary school classrooms to be filled with students who are widely scattered in terms of their progress through the entire secondary school program (see Box 3.4). Teachers in these courses find an extraordinary range of physiological development among the learners in their classrooms.

Box 3.4

Working with Late-Maturing Students

Suppose that you were teaching a class of eighth-graders. In your class you had two boys who still had yet to reach a height of five feet. Each weighed less than 90 pounds. These two youngsters were the butt of a continuous series of pranks dreamed up by a group of very physically mature students. Among other things, these youngsters have been put in student wall lockers. They have been tossed as "human footballs" outside the school building at noon and after school. And they have generally been told by other students that they are "losers" who should be back in the fifth grade.

What Do You Think?

Think about your reactions to this situation. Then respond to these questions.

1. Do you recall any similar situations from your own school years? What impact did the behavior of others have on the physically immature youngsters?

2. What specifically would you do to help these late-developing students to develop a sense of personal confidence?

3. Is there anything you would do to prevent the early-maturing youngsters from taking advantage of their much smaller age mates? If so, what?

4. Have you personally ever been either on the giving end or the receiving end of a situation where there was a confrontation between early maturing and late maturing youngsters? What happened? How did you feel about this situation?

Patterns of Intellectual Development in School Learners

There is evidence that students' intellectual development does not follow a random pattern. Rather, the kinds of thinking in which they can engage seem to follow a predictable, age-related sequence. This implies that learners of certain ages have thought processes that are describably different from those learners who are either older or younger. For the teacher this sequence suggests, for example, that a student's failure to learn may not necessarily result from his or her failure to "apply" himself or herself but rather from a confrontation with an intellectual task that demands thinking more sophisticated than he or she is capable of performing, given his or her current level of intellectual development. Clearly, instruction must be designed with some attention to the intellectual development of the students to be served.

Perhaps the best known figure in the area of sequential development of intellectual abilities has been the late Swiss psychologist Jean Piaget. Piaget suggested that young people pass through a series of four stages as they mature toward adult thinking patterns. Let us examine briefly each of these stages.

Sensorimotor Stage: Ages Zero to Two

Intellectual activity during this first intellectual stage involves almost exculusively phenomena that can be perceived directly through the senses. As the young child matures and begins acquisition of language skills, there is some preliminary application of language labels to concrete objects. The child begins to understand the connection between the name of an object and the object that is referenced by the name.

Preoperational Thought Stage: Ages Two to Seven

Language development occurs at a dramatic rate during this stage. Increasingly verbal symbols are used to reference concrete objects. Decisions tend to be made on the basis of intuition, not rational analysis. Youngsters at this age frequently amuse adults by examining unfamiliar situations and arriving at some bizarre conclusions. In part, this behavior results from their tendency to focus excessively only on selected parts of a total situation and to generalize excessively from very limited information. For example, a youngster at this age may conclude that airplanes are small objects about 12 inches in length because that is how they appear to him or her when he or she looks up and sees them flying in the sky.

Concrete Operations Stage: Ages Seven to 11

Rational logic begins to make its appearance during these years. At this stage youngsters increasingly are able to use systematic reasoning to arrive at solutions to certain kinds of problems. The kinds of problems for which they develop this facility are what we call concrete problems. That is, they are problems involving phenomena that can be perceived directly through the physical senses. They are much less adept, at this stage, in using logical reasoning to analyze abstract problems.

Learners at this stage have great difficulty in "going beyond the givens" to make sense of a school task that tends to demand more than a simple explanation of immediately available evidence. For example, they frequently become very frustrated when asked to search for "hidden meanings" in literary selections. They tend to be extremely literal-minded. In general, school instructional programs that demand a great deal of sensory contact with tangible objects tend to be successful with learners at this age. They like problems that have answers. They are not at all happy when confronted with ambiguity.

Formal Operations Stage: Ages 11 to 16

As they move into the formal operations stage, the stage characterizing adult thought, young people are able to apply rational logic to all categories of problems, abstract as well as concrete. They are able to deal with content asking them to go beyond the givens. They tend to be much less willing to take anything except formal logical explanations as evidence that something is either "true" or "false." Sometimes, particularly during the early phases of experience at this stage, young people so enamored of the power of logic that they become very upset by what they perceive to be contradictions between the nature of the world and what logic suggests to them the world really ought to be like. Many become very idealistic at this time of life. The differences between their idealistic view of what a logical world should be like and what the real world seems to be frequently make these young people very suspicious of the motives of adults whom they see to be defending an "unjust" or "unfair" society on illogical grounds.

To recapitulate, Piaget's stages suggest to us that human beings' intellectual development follows a predictable sequence. Each ascending stage is in all cases preceded by the stages that come before. The order of stages a person goes through en route to the formal operations stage is constant from individual to individual. The age ranges given are general guidelines. Some individuals enter and exit stages at ages somewhat younger than the suggested age points mentioned. Others enter and exit at somewhat older ages. The specific ages a given individual may enter or leave a stage will vary. But the passage of each individual through all four stages in the order noted is thought to be unvarying.

Implications of Piaget's Stages for Teachers

Some evidence suggests that teachers at the junior high school level are less happy than those at any other level of education. (This same pattern may be true of middle school teachers, as well. To date, insufficient descriptive data have been gathered about this group focusing on their general levels of satisfaction.) Social status of teaching at this level, sparse funding levels for buildings and materials, and many other factors doubtless contribute to junior high school teachers' dissatisfactions.

Certainly among the issues to be considered is the issue of intellectual stages of junior high school students.

Particularly in the early junior high school years (or middle or late-middle school years), many learners may well still be functioning at the concrete operations stage (remember this stage runs roughly from age seven through age 11). Highly dependent on concrete learning experiences, these learners may well tax the teacher's ingenuity to provide for large numbers of "hands-on" experiences. In the very same classrooms, there may be individuals who have passed into the early stages of the formal operations stage. Recall that many of these learners tend to become extremely idealistic and potentially suspicious of adults whom they may see as defending a real world that is not logical. Given the potential for this kind of a classroom mix of learners at the concrete operations and formal operations stages, some junior high school teachers sense themselves to be pressed on the one hand by the needs of some learners for "touch, feel, and grasp" kinds of learning experiences and on the other hand by learners who are suspicious, if not hostile, toward the teacher's judgments.

Those who seek to work with younger secondary school students need to be aware of the kinds of student needs and attitudes that are to be expected given the age levels of these learners. Old hands have had time to observe the miraculous transformation that time works on the intellectual capacities and attitudes of junior high school students. Most can speak of several students who appeared beyond salvation as eighth-graders but who today are pillars of their local communities. New teachers can benefit greatly from conversations with some of these old hands. Further, by taking time to become familiar with the work of Piaget and others who have focused on patterns of intellectual development in learners, they can develop the kind of knowledge base that is essential for understanding and appreciation of early secondary school students. Certainly time spent in acquiring such an understanding has the potential for helping teachers develop more realistic expectations of student behavior patterns during this interesting time of life.

Key Ideas in Summary

1. American schools include an incredibly diverse student population. Indeed, there is evidence that the variety of students in the nation's middle schools, junior high schools, and senior high schools is greater than it has ever been.

2. Because large numbers of children were born in the years after World War II, many women are now in their child-bearing years.

This has led to a great growth in elementary school enrollments. This growth is expected to reach the secondary schools in the middle 1990s. One result is likely to be an increased demand for teachers as secondary school enrollments increase.

3. The largest minority groups in the schools are blacks and Hispanics. Both groups are increasing as a percentage of the total school population. Highest concentrations of black students and Hispanic students are found in urban areas. Performance levels of both black students and Hispanic students lag behind those of white (non-Hispanic) students. Cultural biases of tests, poverty, and irresponsible assignment to nonacademic courses may contribute to this situation. Black students and Hispanic students also drop out of school in greater numbers than white (non-Hispanic) students. The extremely high drop-out rates for Hispanics have attracted particular attention in recent years.

4. Problems secondary students have with the English language have become a major concern of educators. Federal legislation has established bilingual programs to assist students whose home language is not English. These programs seek to provide some instruction in students' native languages until such time as they develop proficiency in English.

5. Students of Asian heritage are increasing in numbers in the nation's schools. In the middle and late 1980s, nearly half of all immigrants to the United States came from Asia. Especially large numbers have come from the Philippines, Korea, Vietnam, and India.

6. The family structure from which many secondary students come has been changing. Today, a large majority of students come from families where both parents work or from households headed by a single working parent. Many more students have been involved in divorce situations than was true twenty and thirty years ago.

7. Drug abuse is a major problem. Illegal use of drugs by secondary students in the United States is higher than in any other developed country. Though the problem remains serious, there are hopeful signs. The rate of use of illegal drugs seems to be in a pattern of gradual decline.

8. Many students from impoverished family backgrounds are enrolled in secondary schools. Especially large numbers are in urban schools. These schools, in many cases, have not been able to pay for exemplary programs. This has been true because tax bases in many urban areas have been declining, and funds available to schools have gone down. In many places, efforts are being mounted to provide more money for hard-pressed school districts.

9. Researchers have found that students pass through a number of developmental stages en route to maturity. Jean Piaget has identified (a) the sensorimotor stage, (b) the preoperational thought stage, (c) the concrete operations stage, and (d) the formal operations stage. Capabilities of students vary, depending on their developmental stage. Secondary school teachers may find large numbers of students functioning at the concrete operations stage. This suggests the need to provide "hands on" experiences, which are thought to facilitate learning for individuals at this developmental stage.

POSTTEST

DIRECTIONS: Using your own paper, answer these true/false questions. For each correct statement, write the word "true." For each incorrect statement, write the word "false."

_____ 1. Only about 50 percent of American young people aged 14 to 17 are enrolled in schools.

_____ 2. Blacks and Hispanics are the largest minority groups represented in secondary schools.

_____ 3. A majority of students in secondary schools come from homes with two parents where the father works and the mother does not.

_____ 4. In general, as time spent watching television increases, time spent doing homework decreases.

_____ 5. Increasing evidence suggests that students' intellectual development follows a predictable, age-related sequence.

Bibliography

ELKIND, DAVID AND FLAVELL, JOHN H. (EDS.). *Studies in Cognitive Development.* New York: Oxford University Press, 1969.

The Forgotten Half: Non-College Youth in America. Washington, DC: The William T. Grant Foundation Commission on Work, Family and Citizenship, January, 1988.

GINSBERG, HERBERT P. AND OPPER, SYLVIA. *Piaget's Theory of Intellectual Development.* Englewood Cliffs, NJ: Prentice-Hall, 1988.

HAMBURG, DAVID A. *Preparing for Life: The Critical Transition of Adolescence.* New York: Carnegie Corporation of New York, 1986.

HOFFMAN, MARK S. (ED.). *The World Almanac and Book of Facts, 1988.* New York: World Almanac, 1988.

SPRINTHALL, RICHARD C. AND SPRINTHALL, NORMAN A. *Educational Psychology: A Developmental Approach.* 4th ed. New York: Random House, 1987.

STERN, JOYCE D. AND CHANDLER, MARJORIE O. (EDS.). *The Condition of Education: Elementary and Secondary Education, 1988.* Volume 1. Washington, DC: United States Department of Education, National Center for Education Statistics, 1988.

UNITED STATES DEPARTMENT OF EDUCATION. *Youth Indicators 1988: Trends in the Well-Being of American Youth.* Washington, DC: U.S. Department of Education, Office of Educational Research and Improvement, August, 1988.

PART II

Selecting, Delivering, Evaluating

CHAPTER 4

Effective Teaching

This chapter provides information to help the reader to:

1. Identify the role of research in teaching.
2. Define the basic components of active teaching.
3. Explain the importance of teacher clarity.
4. Define different time decisions made by teachers and state how each is related to student achievement.
5. Provide examples of how teacher expectations might influence student achievement.
6. Identify elements of a sound teacher-questioning procedure.

PRETEST

DIRECTIONS: Using your own paper, answer these true/false questions. For each correct statement, write the word "true." For each incorrect statement, write the word "false."

_____ 1. In active teaching, the teacher acts as a guide who leads students to learning resources but who, personally, does little direct teaching.

_____ 2. Nonverbal behavior is generally used very deliberately by the teacher to enhance the clarity of the instructional message.

_____ 3. Advance organizers help provide a structure for students to follow when they are learning new material.

_____ 4. Academic learning time is that time that students are working on tasks related to instructional objectives and are experiencing high levels of success.

_____ 5. Teachers should always include a high percentage of thought questions in their lessons.

Introduction

How should people be prepared to teach in secondary schools? This question has been much debated over the years. Some people have argued that sound preparation in the subjects to be taught is the only essential ingredient in the preparation of a professional teacher. Supporters of this view sometimes question the value of professional education courses. Some of them believe that teaching is an art that basically cannot be taught. One is either born a "good" teacher or one is not.

On the other hand, some individuals are convinced that mastery of academic subject matter, alone, does not ensure a person will be effective in the classroom . They believe that there are important teaching behaviors that characterize effective and ineffective teachers. Further, they are convinced that effective behaviors can be taught to people who have interests in becoming classroom teachers.

Today, a growing body of research literature supports the view that some kinds of teacher behaviors are more effective than others. Further, these behaviors can be effectively transmitted to prospective teachers. However, researchers in education recognize that their work has some important limitations. Because educators work in many different environments and with people of all kinds, principles of teaching probably will never be discovered that are as precise and universally applicable as those in such disciplines as the physical sciences. For example, it is unlikely that any single instructional method will be found to be "best" for all teaching situations.

Research in education has pinpointed some promising general patterns of teacher behavior. For example, teaching has been identified as a decision-making process. Kinds of decisions teachers make, regardless of the specific instructional method they are using, can affect how students learn. Sections that follow identify some general patterns of teacher decisions and behaviors that have been found to facilitate student performance.

Box 4.1

Can a Person Be Taught to Become a Teacher?

A critic of teacher education made these comments:

> Teacher education is a waste of time. Individuals spend time learning how to run a film projector and put up bulletin boards. This kind of frivolous activity takes students away from courses in the subjects they will be teaching in the schools. They should take more courses in these academic subjects.
>
> Teaching, itself, is basically intuitive. It is something a person either can do or cannot do. People cannot be taught to teach. They either have the ability, or they don't. Courses in education simply don't make sense. Natural teachers don't need them. Others, who have no aptitude for teaching, cannot change their basic characteristics by taking education courses.

What Do You Think?

Read the statement above and answer these questions:

1. How would you respond to this statement?
2. Is there a body of knowledge that one needs to know about teaching that is not taught anywhere else?
3. What does a person need to know to be a good teacher?
4. How do you respond to the idea that good teachers have an inborn ability to teach well and that this characteristic cannot be taught to people lacking this trait?

Proactive Teaching

Research has indicated that many teachers who experience success in the classroom are "proactive." The proactive teacher is a person who is an active information processor and decision maker. Proactive teachers willingly accept responsibility for content selection, for planning and presenting instruction, and for their students' learning. Proactive teachers enjoy their work. They believe in both their own abilities to teach and their students' abilities to learn (Rohrkemper and Good 1987).

Proactive teachers are strongly committed to the idea that delivery of academic content is one of their primary responsibilities. They tend to be task-oriented people who approach their classrooms in a business-like manner. They understand the demands of the content to be taught, characteristics of their students, and limitations imposed by the context within which they work. They make a number of important decisions. Are these things intuitive, or can they be learned? See Box 4.1.

Making Content Decisions

Teachers' content decisions are important. Sometimes this dimension of teachers' responsibility has been overlooked. Some people, for example, have assumed that content is selected by state officials and local school boards and that teachers simply act to implement their decisions. This is true up to a point. However, often state and local curriculum guidelines address only broad, general issues. Teachers have considerable latitude as they plan specific lessons within the context of the provided guidelines. This means that two secondary school teachers who are assigned to teach the same course may make quite different decisions regarding the specific content to be covered.

Researchers have found that teachers use a number of criteria to select what they will emphasize. Schwille (1981) found that many teachers base their selections on (a) the general difficulty of the topic, (b) their estimates of the number of problems students will encounter in learning the material, and (c) their personal interest in various aspects of the subject. Teachers tend to spend more time teaching aspects of a subject they believe easier to teach and from which they derive the most personal enjoyment.

There is a clear relationship between the content that is covered and what students learn. The opportunity to learn a subject is one of the most powerful variables explaining student achievement. Not surprisingly, when little class time is spent on a given topic, students tend not to do well on tests designed to assess their mastery of the topic. (See Box 4.2.)

Because of the important relationship between time and achievement, effective teachers think very carefully about content to be taught and time allocated to each topic. Priorities are assigned to topics that are important for the overall development of learners in the classroom. It is particularly important that sufficient class time be allocated to teaching basic skills and knowledge that are prerequisites for more sophisticated kinds of learning.

In addition to identifying important content elements and providing for adequate instructional time to do them justice, teachers make other decisions about how content is presented to their students. In making these decisions, they begin by considering the difficulty level of the material as it compares to the sophistication levels of their students. Material that is too difficult may result in failure and frustration and undermine students' motivation. Effective teachers present material in ways that result in high levels of student success. Students who experience success tend to increase their levels of interest and enthusiasm for the content being introduced.

Teachers also make decisions about matching material to students' interests. It cannot be assumed that students will immediately see the

Box 4.2

Was Your Development Hindered Because of an Insufficient Opportunity to Learn?

Some teachers emphasize only those areas of the curriculum in which they are personally interested. For example, a history teacher who is a Civil War buff may spend weeks on this topic and only a day or two on the Great Depression. An English teacher who enjoys literature may devote more time to novels, short stories, and poetry than to writing skills. As a result, students may find in later years that they wish they knew more about certain subjects.

What Do You Think?

1. As you think back on your experiences in school, can you think of times when some of your teachers spent more instructional time on subjects in which they were interested at the expense of time devoted to other topics?

2. If you responded "yes," do you believe your educational development was in any way hurt by teachers' failure to treat some topics and issues at more length?

3. Should teachers be monitored carefully to assure that all important topics are being adequately covered? Or, would such an approach irresponsibly interfere with teachers' spontaneity and enthusiasm?

4. What do you see as the proper roles of (a) the state, (b) the local school district, and (c) the individual teacher in deciding how much time to spend on specific topics?

importance of new content. Effective teachers seek to create in students a "need to know." Students who see material as relevant to their own needs are more receptive learners than are students who fail to see the personal importance of school content.

Teachers make decisions about how student learning will be evaluated. There is sometimes a tendency for teachers to delay decisions about testing until quite late in an instructional sequence. As Berliner (1987) has pointed out, this practice sometimes results in a mismatch between what has been taught and what is tested. It is better to plan evaluation procedures at the same time instruction is being planned. This practice increases the likelihood that content testing will match content taught.

Program implementation follows content-planning decisions. Active and effective teachers have been observed to play an active role in presenting material to students. Several variables have been found to correlate with student achievement. Among these are actions teachers take to maintain high levels of student interest throughout the lesson.

Stimulating and Maintaining Student Interest and Involvement

Motivated students create fewer problems for teachers, and they achieve more. Motivation is not something that concerns teachers only at the beginning of an instructional sequence. There are three important phases of motivation. The first phase involves attempts to capture student interest at the beginning of a learning sequence. The second focuses on maintaining this interest during the lesson. The third centers on activities to reinforce learning at the end of the instructional sequence. The purpose of this final motivational activity is to promote student interest in pursuing the lesson topic the next time it is introduced.

Motivation at the beginning of a learning sequence sometimes is facilitated when teachers appeal to students' basic curiosity. Many students find materials or ideas that are unique or novel to be interesting. At other times, teachers take time to point out the specific relevance of new material for students and take other actions designed to stimulate a "need to know."

When appropriate, novelty can also be used to maintain interest as a lesson is being taught. Other teacher actions at this time include helping students grasp new material and to appreciate their own potential for success in learning tasks that require them to use new information. Motivation is also facilitated when teachers maintain a positive classroom atmosphere. Students feel better about themselves and their academic work when they sense the teacher and other class members are supportive. Fearful students tend not to be motivated and not to do well on academically-related tasks.

At the conclusion of a learning sequence, teachers can promote additional interest by pointing out to students what they have accomplished. A sense of personal competence builds self-confidence and motivation. Learners who feel they have been successful are likely to be receptive to later lessons building on the topic that has been introduced.

Additional, more specific information about motivation is introduced in Chapter 6.

Systematic Presentation

Active teachers take a direct role in presenting information to be learned. They work hard to keep maintain an academic focus in their classes. Their classrooms are warm, but business-like. There are few nonacademic digressions.

These teachers tend to present new material in small, logical steps. They take time to assure that students have mastered each step before they introduce the next. Active teachers monitor students' performance constantly to determine individual levels of understanding. Pacing of instruction is very much tied to an ongoing diagnosis of learner progress.

Modeling

Modeling has been found to be a highly effective instructional approach. It is one that is widely used by successful teachers. A variety of things are modeled. For example, as a means of building students' interest in a topic, teachers often share their own enthusiasm with students. Teacher enthusiasm is sometimes "catching. " So, too, are other teacher attitudes. Secondary school students are sophisticated. They are quick to sense a teacher's lack of interest in a subject.

Modeling of thinking processes is another important type of teacher modeling. If the intent is for students to engage in critical thinking, teachers sometimes "think out loud" as they demonstrate thinking processes to be used in solving a problem. This verbalization serves as valuable illustration for the class. It demonstrates the process to students and it gives it some credibility. The exercise points out that the teacher has some specific kinds of thinking processes in mind when asking students to "think critically" about problems.

Another important area of modeling has to do with the kinds of assignments students are to produce. Often students are unclear as to what a teacher's expectations are when they are given a task to complete. For example, individuals in the class may have very different ideas about what the teacher expects when they are asked to "prepare a short essay." A teacher who follows this assignment by providing students with an example of an appropriate essay and who discusses its elements with students can clarify many misunderstandings. As a result, student essays are likely to be of higher quality.

Lesson Pacing

Active teachers' instruction moves at a brisk pace. It is a brisk pace that is accompanied by high levels of learner success. These teachers do not race to "cover" the material. But they do move along as quickly as they can consistent with learners' abilities to profit from their instruction.

Successful teachers have learned how to avoid getting off the subject for long periods of time. They have developed a feel for allocating instructional time appropriately so that individual points are well developed, but that excessive time is not spent on a few issues at the expense of time that could not be spent on others. Effective teachers consistently cover more material than less effective teachers.

Academic Feedback

Providing feedback to students improves their levels of achievement. Feedback communicates to students the extent to which their responses are correct or appropriate. It can help them adjust their behavior to meet expected standards. There is some confusion about what kinds of feedback are "best."

Some teachers, out of a desire to create a supportive classroom climate, have concluded that providing generous praise to all students is effective. Researchers have found that for praise to be effective it should be specific, genuine, and moderately used. The "specificity" issue relates to the behavior being praised. When praise is given to students with little indication of what they have done to merit the praise, it has little impact on students' performance. They do not understand what they have done (and should continue to do) to merit positive statements from the teacher.

This teacher is checking on a student's work. Provision of feedback is a characteristic of effective teaching.

Box 4.3

How Can Better Feedback Be Provided to Students?

Letter grades are a traditional part of American education. A major purpose of grades is to provide feedback to students and their parents regarding students' progress. Some people feel that grades are an inadequate mechanism for conveying information about students' work in school.

What Do You Think?

1. Do you believe letter grades provide useful information to parents and students?

2. What do you see as some potential weaknesses of grades as a feedback tool?

3. What are some alternative ways information about students' progress might be provided both to students and their parents?

4. Some people have suggested that grades are a form of criticism and that criticism always undermines students' confidence? How do you react to this view?

Students are quick to detect a teacher's insincerity. Forced and formulaic praise can lead to negative student attitudes. Unless students believe the teacher's praise is sincere, it will not facilitate productive learning.

When teachers provide too much praise, praise loses its focus. It fails to cue students as to what they should be doing. Further, the words lose their emotive power. Indiscriminant use of such stock phrases as "fine," "very good," and so forth lead students to "tune out." In time, these words simply become part of the general background noise of the classroom, not necessarily harmful, but certainly nothing that will influence patterns of behavior.

There is evidence that praise may affect some students differently than it affects others. Students who are having academic difficulties and students from lower socioeconomic groups seem to need and respond well to frequent praise. On the other hand, an abundance of praise in some circumstances has been found to reduce levels of performance of higher achieving students from upper-level socioeconomic groups.

Another from of feedback is criticism. Criticism need not be harsh. Constructive criticism can be an important aid to learning. Constructive criticism is directed at a specific difficulty a learner is experiencing. It is designed to focus a student's attention on a specific problem area and to suggest ways of remedying the difficulty. Box 4.3 discusses providing feedback to students.

Teacher Clarity

Teacher clarity is concerned with the nature of the teacher's presentation of material to the class. It includes several important parts. Among them are the presentation style of the teacher, the degree to which the teacher uses clear and precise language, and the structure of the presentation.

Presentation Style

"Paralanguage" is an important dimension of a given teacher's presentation style. Paralanguage includes those features of spoken language which influence the character of the spoken message but that are not a formal part of the message itself. Paralanguage includes such variables as patterns of articulation, tone of voice, and rate of speech. Paralanguage problems sometimes occur when a teacher with speech patterns characteristic of one region of the country moves to another section where prevailing patterns are somewhat different.

Nonverbal behavior is another dimension of paralanguage. Communication in the classroom is improved when teachers' nonverbal behaviors are consistent with their verbal behaviors. When there is an inconsistency, confusion and anxiety may result. This situation might arise, for example, if a teacher frowned while, at the same time, lavishing warm verbal praise on a learner. Teachers sometimes are unaware of nonverbal messages they may be sending to students. Videotaping is sometimes used to help teachers examine their nonverbal behaviors to assure they are consistent with their verbal patterns.

Teachers' Use of Language

Teacher presentation styles that lack clarity are often characterized by false starts, digressions, and verbal mazes. All of these verbal behaviors cause breaks in the smooth flow of a lesson. Teachers whose instruction is characterized by false starts tend to begin a lesson only to stop and start again. This behavior is confusing to students. Over time, they may fail to pay attention, realizing that the teacher will stop and repeat what has already been said.

Digressions are sometimes prompted by students' questions. On other occasions, the teacher needs no such prompts and simply begins making comments bearing little connection to the main subject of the lesson. Digressions divert students' attention from lesson content. Too many digressions can result in lowered levels of student achievement.

Verbal mazes are teacher behaviors that fail to communicate information clearly and concisely. Meandering teacher discourses often result in students' failure to see connections among important ideas. Verbal mazes often result when teachers have not planned adequately. Because of a lack of planning, they begin instruction with no clear idea as to what content should be covered and how individual points should be sequentially developed.

Teachers sometimes fail the "clarity test" when they have mistaken impressions about what students already know. Inexperienced teachers frequently make too many assumptions about students' prior learning. A colleague of one of the authors once presented an inspired lecture on the topic "Emerging Political Trends." At the end of the presentation, a student cautiously raised a hand. "What is a trend?" the student asked. Because of a failure to understand the meaning of the term "trend," the student had found much of the presentation to be confusing. Had the teacher spend a few moments at the beginning of the presentation reviewing this term, the student would have taken a great deal more away from the experience.

In addition to defining important terms, teachers need to avoid using vague terms that fail to communicate clearly. There are several important classifications of vague terms. These include (a) approximation (kind of, sort, about), (b) probability statements (frequently,

"This is merit pay?"

generally, often), (c) possibility statements (chances are, could be, maybe), and bluffing (everybody knows, it's a long story, we'll get to that later). Effective teachers use these terms very sparingly. When they are overused, learner understanding is impaired.

Structure of the Presentation

The structure of a presentation is its general organizational pattern. It is a content outline the teacher follows in presenting material to students. When lessons are well planned, this structure helps students to recognize key points of content.

One way to structure a presentation is to provide students with "advance organizers." Teachers who use advance organizers provide students with a brief overview of the important concepts to be taught. This is done at the beginning of the lesson. For example, an English teacher, before introducing students to a given short story, might spend time reviewing the basic characteristics of the short-story form. This advance organizer would provide a general set of guidelines students might use in completing an assignment requiring them to read a particular short story and comment on how the story contained the general characteristics of the short-story genre.

Sometimes teachers use lesson objectives as advance organizers. The objective lets students know what the teacher expects them to be able to do as a result of their exposure to the content of the lesson. For example, a teacher might say, "When you've completed this lesson, you should be able to identify the major parts of this short story."

In addition to good advance organizers, well-structured lessons also feature "connected discourse." This means that what the teacher says flows smoothly. Points that are made are clearly connected. The lesson has an easily discernible sense of direction.

"Internal summaries" are another important feature of a well-structured lesson. These are essentially pauses the teacher makes during the lesson to recapitulate what has been presented. They serve as simple reviews that allow teachers to summarize what has been introduced, to solicit questions from students, and to clear up misconceptions.

Lesson clarity is improved when teachers use "marker expressions." These are verbal indicators the teacher uses to highlight important content. Among marker expressions are such statements as "this is important," "write this down," and "listen carefully to this point."

Some repetition or redundancy of content facilitates learning. Well-structured lessons feature some repetition of major points. The most effective repetition features some alteration in the language used or in the context within which the information is presented. A word-by-word repetition of what has been said previously is not as effective.

A final characteristic of a well-structured lesson is a well-organized conclusion. This summary includes a review of major concepts that were introduced in the lesson. The summary reinforces student learning. A good summary helps to retain the new content. Regrettably, the summary is a part of a lesson that sometimes gets less attention than it deserves. This is particularly likely to be the case when the development of the lesson takes longer than the teacher has anticipated. Under these circumstances, the teacher may not have time to do justice to the end-of-lesson summary.

Productive Use of Class Time

Effective teachers (see Box 4.4) realize that time available for instruction is scarce. They make the most of the time that is available to them. Observers have found that in some classes as much as 50 percent of the time is spent on nonacademic tasks. Time is often lost when too much time is spent on tasks such as taking role, settling students down at the beginning of a new period, distributing and collecting student work, and handling discipline problems. The more time spent on these nonacademic tasks, the less time students have to work with content. As academic learning time is reduced, students' levels of mastery are also reduced. Teachers who analyze their patterns and increase the time students spend on academic tasks only a few minutes each day may gain the equivalent of several additional instructional days when this added time is summed over an entire academic year.

Time that is allocated to instructional tasks may be divided into three distinct categories. These are (a) allocated time, (b) engaged time, and (c) academic learning time. "Allocated time" refers to the amount of time the teacher schedules for teaching something to a group of learners. Researchers have found that different teachers allocate very different amounts of time to teaching similar content. In deciding how much time to allocate, teachers need to consider questions such as these:

- Is the time allocated sufficient given the difficulty of the content?
- Is there a danger that students will become bored because too much time has been allocated?

Just because a given amount of time has been allocated to a learning activity does not necessarily mean students will spend all of this time working with content to be mastered. For example, a teacher might allocate 50 minutes for the purpose of teaching a new concept. However, when time required to start the class, distribute materials, and take care of other duties is subtracted from this figure, there may be only 30

Box 4.4

Identifying "Effective" Teachers

Think back on the secondary teachers who taught you. Who were some of the best ones you had? Try to identify some of the things they did that made them effective.

teachers tend to stay on task and avoid unnecessary digressions? When students strayed off the topic, how did these teachers respond?

What Do You Think?

1. How did these teachers provide information to students about how they were doing?

2. What were these teachers' lessons like? Were they well organized? Did these

3. Did these teachers show students what they expected them to do on assignments. Did they model appropriate behaviors for students?

4. How did the effective teachers you had exemplify some of the characteristics of effective teachers introduced in this chapter?

minutes left for work related to academic tasks. The time students actually spend on academic work is sometimes referred to as "engaged time". The amount of engaged time varies greatly from class to class. In general, teachers strive to increase the amount of engaged time.

Maintaining high levels of engaged time is especially important for students who typically have not done well in school. In order to make up learning deficits, they need to be in classes organized to provide high percentages of engaged time. Engaged time refers to academic work that bears a clear and direct relationship to lesson objectives. Time spent by students on busy-work tasks bearing little relationship to important academic content does not count as engaged time.

A third category of time is "academic learning time." This is a narrower term than "engaged time." It includes the time a student is (a) working on an academic task and (b) experiencing success. The combination of work on academic tasks and success is strongly associated with enhanced levels of learning. Effective teachers work hard to increase the percentage of academic learning time in their classrooms.

Teacher Expectations

The expectations teachers have of individual students strongly influence these students' achievement levels. Teacher expectations include inferences teachers make about the academic potential of students. They may be formed on the basis of variables such as student appearance, past school records, IQ scores, standardized achievement test scores, classroom conduct, or even on the basis of the performance of a student's older brothers and sisters (Braun 1987).

Often, teachers treat students in classrooms in a manner consistent with their prior expectations of students' abilities. This is not always in the students' best long-term interests.

For example, a teacher may ask the class a question. A student for whom the teacher has low academic expectations volunteers to answer but has some difficulty in responding. In this case, the teacher may conclude that the student's basic problem is a lack of content understanding. In an attempt to be sensitive, the teacher might praise the student for the attempt to answer. In the same spirit, the teacher may fail to provide specific feedback about any deficiencies in the answer. While the teacher may believe this kind of response is a sensitive one, it may send an undesirable message. The student could conclude that the teacher does not believe he or she is capable of answering correctly. Over time, the student may be less inclined to participate out of a feeling that he or she has been labeled as an academic "failure" by the teacher.

Teachers' expectations about students develop rather predictably. Braun (1987, p. 559) described this basic cycle.

1. The teacher develops expectations for different students. These result because of the teacher's personal beliefs, previous experiences, and personal observations of individual students.

2. The teacher interprets students' behavior in terms of their expectations. The teacher's actions toward individual students are conditioned by his or her expectations of their behavior.

3. Students interpret the teacher's actions toward them. Individual students begin to develop self-concepts that are consistent with teacher expectations. These self-concepts affect their future learning and behavior patterns.

4. Students' patterns of behavior tend to reflect the teacher's expectations. This confirms to the teacher the accuracy of his or her initial expectations.

5. Over time, students for whom the teacher has higher levels of expectation perform at higher levels and students for whom the teacher has lower levels of expectations perform at lower levels.

Researchers have identified patterns of teacher behavior toward learners that result from their expectations about individual student characteristics. The following are some behaviors that may result from teacher expectations (adapted from Good and Brophy 1987 pp. 128–129):

1. Teachers are less responsive and direct fewer nonverbal behaviors toward learners for whom they hold low expectations. Teachers tend to smile less and have less direct eye contact with these students. They provide these students with fewer signals that indicate they have been doing well.
2. Teachers call on learners for whom they hold low expectations less frequently than they call on learners for whom they have higher expectations.
3. Teachers provide less corrective feedback to learners for whom they hold low expectations than to learners for whom they hold high expectations.
4. Teachers wait a shorter amount of time for low-expectation students to respond to questions than they wait for high-expectation students.
5. Teachers tend to criticize students for whom they hold low expectations more than students for whom they hold high expectations.
6. Low-expectation students receive less praise for their successes than do high-expectation students.
7. Lessons taught to low-expectation students tend to be more drill-and-practice oriented than those provided to high-expectation students.
8. When they grade assignments and tests, teachers tend to give the benefit of the doubt more frequently to high-expectation students than to low-expectation students.

What can be done about teacher expectations? Some people have suggested that teachers should avoid developing any preconceptions about the abilities of individual students. Generally, this has been regarded as an unrealistic suggestion because human nature leads people to make inferences about other people. Probably a more realistic approach is for teachers to be aware that they are making prejudgments about students and that these opinions may be shaping their patterns of teaching. Sometimes videotaping or audio taping of lessons can provide evidence of ways teacher expectations are operating in the classroom. An awareness of the effects of teacher expectation can help teachers to monitor their behavior to assure that expectations are not leading them to act irresponsibly toward individual students.

Further, it makes sense for teachers to systematically analyze their expectations from time to time. This practice allows them to consider new information, recent patterns of classroom behavior, and other evidence that might lead to a modified set of expectations for individual students. (See Box 4.5.)

Box 4.5

Have You Ever Been Influenced by a Teacher's Expectations?

Expectations teachers have for individual students are sometimes more obvious to the students than to the teachers. Without realizing they are doing so, teachers sometimes communicate to students that they have little confidence in these students' abilities to perform well on academic tasks. By the same token, teachers sometimes unconsciously encourage students to do well by simply conveying an impression that students have the abilities to succeed.

What Do You Think?

Think about some of your own experiences as a secondary school student as you respond to these questions.

1. Can you think of examples when a teacher's behavior influenced a student to do more? To do less?

2. In general, do you think teachers' attitudes toward individual students had a great deal, a moderate amount, or rather little to do with these students' levels of performance?

3. What are some of the things that influenced teachers' expectations of individual students?

4. Can students and other people do anything to keep from being influenced too much by other people's impressions of their ability levels?

Teacher Questioning Behavior

Many researchers have investigated teachers' questioning patterns. Good questioning has long been associated with good teaching. As long ago as 1903, DeGarmo suggested that to question well is to teach well (DeGarmo 1903). Teachers use many questions every day. Ashner (1961) went so far as to describe teachers as "professional question askers."

Researchers have established a connection between the number of questions a teacher asks and student achievement. In one study, it was found that more effective junior high school mathematics teachers asked an average of 24 questions during a 50-minute class period. Less effective teachers were found to ask an average of only 8.6 questions (Rosenshine and Stevens 1986, p. 383).

Over the years, there have been many attempts to identify characteristics of "good" questions. One approach has been to classify questions in terms of their difficulty. Schemes have been developed to categorize questions in terms of the mental sophistication required to answer them. Questions that require only recall of previously learned information have been termed "lower-level" questions. Those that are more thought provoking or intellectually demanding have been labeled "higher-level" questions. Generally, teachers have been urged to develop students' thinking skills by increasing the numbers of higher-level questions they ask.

Today, it is recognized that good classroom questioning demands more than simply asking many higher-level questions. An effective teacher questioning strategy considers (a) the purpose of questioning, (b) question clarity, (c) the nature of student responses, and (d) wait time.

The Purpose of Questioning

A question that might be effective under one set of conditions may be ineffective under another. Researchers have found that if the teacher's purpose is to check students' understanding of basic information, then most questions should be lower-level, recall kinds of questions. There should be a simple pattern involving (a) a lower-level teacher question, (b) a student response, and (c) immediate teacher feedback to the student. This pattern should be fast paced.

There are several reasons for the recommendation of a brisk questioning pace under these conditions. First of all, lower-level recall questions tend to be short. Answers, too, tend to be brief. Such questions do not require a great deal of student thinking time. Additionally, the brisk pace allows teachers to ask questions of larger numbers of learners than when a slower pace is adopted. The rapid pace tends to keep students alert and provides the teacher with an opportunity to assess levels of understanding among class members.

Recommended questioning procedures may be quite different when the teacher has a different purpose in mind. For example, when the purpose is to stimulate students' creativity and promote the development of sophisticated thought processes, higher-level questions are recommended. Research has demonstrated that under these conditions higher-level questions tend to result in improved levels of student achievement (Redfield and Rousseau 1981). A successful questioning lesson of this kind, however, must take into consideration students' levels of development. There may be a need for the teacher to ask some lower-level questions to develop an adequate knowledge base among students. If this knowledge base is lacking, students will have great difficulty in responding to higher-level questions. Creative and analytical student responses do not occur in an informational vacuum. Students must have some prerequisite information before they can be expected to respond well to higher-level questions.

Question Clarity

If questions are not stated clearly, students will have difficulty in responding appropriately. Questions that lack clarity often have a number of logical answers. Suppose a teacher asked, "Who was the first President of the United States?" This question might prompt several possible student answers, including "a man," "a Virginian," "a general," or "George Washington."

The question resulting in these answers was poorly phrased. It required students to guess at what the teacher wanted. The question failed to provide students with a feel for the context the teacher had in mind. Students would have been much more adequately cued to the kind of information the teacher was seeking had the question been asked something like this: "What was the first and last name of the first President of the United States?" This rephrasing greatly reduces the number of possible "correct" responses and indicates clearly to students the kind of information the teacher is seeking.

In using questions with students, Cazden (1986) has recommended that the teacher set the stage by taking time to let students know the general focus or context of the discussion. Sometimes this is done by following a sequence whereby the teacher first asks a general question to set the stage and follows this with more specific questions. For example, a teacher might begin by asking "Where is this city located on the map on the wall?" This could be followed by a more thought-provoking question such as "How do you account for the development of a large city at this geographical location?"

In addition to failing to adequately describe the context, some teachers confuse students by asking multiple questions at the same time. When this is done, students have difficulty deciding exactly which question the teacher wants them to answer. In general, students' answers improve when single questions are asked that are clear and to the point.

Nature of the Student Response

Successful questioning sequences feature high levels of student participation and high percentages of correct answers. When the teacher's intent is to question students over basic material, the student success rate should be at least 80 percent. If the success rate is much lower, teachers need to ask themselves whether students have the knowledge base necessary to answer the questions. In summary, good questions tend to elicit good (correct) answers from students.

Wait Time

"Wait time" refers to the time between a teacher's asking a question and (a) a student's response, or (b) a teacher's decision to call on another student, or (c) a teacher's decision to rephrase the question, or (d) a teacher's decision to respond to the question himself or herself. Rowe (1986) reported that, on average, teachers tend to wait less than one second for a student to respond to a question.

Positive results have been observed when teachers increase the duration of their wait time. Increasing wait time increases the length of student responses, increases the likelihood that student answers will feature speculative thinking, improves students' self-confidence, and involves more students in a discussion (Rowe 1986). Students of teachers who wait longer after they ask questions tend to improve their scores on tests of higher-level thinking abilities. It is possible that the increase in wait time allows more time for students to think.

Increasing wait time has also been found to have interesting effects on teachers. Teachers who increased the average length of their wait times tended to ask more higher-level, thought-provoking questions. It also influenced their attitudes toward some students in their classes. Some individuals for whom teachers had had low expectations performed better than teachers had expected. Since they were provided more time to think about answers, many of these students began to respond more frequently and more accurately to questions. This, in turn, tended to prompt teachers to revise upward their expectations of these learners.

Key Ideas in Summary

1. Though there is a great deal of "artistry" in teaching, an emerging body of research is beginning to suggest some general principles that are applicable in a wide variety of instructional settings.

2. Many teachers whose students achieve well have been found to have these characteristics: (a) they play an active role in planning the curriculum; (b) they provide their students with sufficient opportunities to learn; (c) they match learning materials to individual students' ability and interest levels; (d) they plan motivational activities throughout their lessons; (e) they present content systematically; (f) they move along at a fairly brisk pace; and, (g) they provide clear and specific feedback to students about the quality of their work.

3. Clarity of presentation is an important characteristic of effective teaching. Clarity is characterized by appropriate paralanguage, a

well-defined lesson structure, connected and logical teacher discourse, provision of good marker expressions, repetition of key ideas, and avoidance of verbal mazes and digressions.

4. Three sets of decisions are important regarding amounts of instructional time. First, teachers must allocate a block of time to the teaching of a given body of content. Second, teachers work to assure that as high a percentage as possible of this allocated time actually involves students working on the assigned task. Finally, teachers seek to assure that students are achieving high levels of success as they do assigned work.

5. Teachers' expectations of individual students influence how they interpret students' performance in class and how they respond to students. There is evidence that teacher expectations strongly influence levels of student achievement.

6. Improving the quality of teacher questions involves more than simply increasing the percentage of higher-level questions teachers ask. Good questioning techniques take into consideration the purpose of the lesson, the clarity of language used in the questions themselves, the nature of student responses to the questions, and the length of time teachers wait for responses after they have asked questions.

POSTTEST

DIRECTIONS: Using your own paper, answer these true/false questions. For each correct statement, write the word "true." For each incorrect statement, write the word "false."

_____ 1. Content decisions made during the planning phase of instruction are among the most important a teacher makes.

_____ 2. When a teacher frequently uses such terms as "kind of" and "sort of" in a presentation, students may experience difficulty interpreting the specific information the teacher wishes to convey.

_____ 3. Repetition of major points by the teacher unnecessarily slows down the pace of instruction and is detrimental to the learning process.

_____ 4. What teachers expect of students has little bearing on students' levels of achievement.

_____ 5. In a classroom discussion, teachers should always provide an immediate response to a student answer.

Bibliography

ALEXANDER, L.; FRANKIEWICZ, R.; AND WILLIAMS, R. "Facilitation of Learning and Retention of Oral Instruction Using Advance and Post Organizers." *Journal of Educational Psychology* (October 1979): 701–707.

ASHNER, M. J.; GALLAGHER, J. J.; PERRY, J. M.; AND ASFAR, S. S. *A System for Classifying Thought Processes in the Conduct of Classroom Verbal Interaction.* Urbana, Illinois: The University of Illinois, 1961.

BERLINER, D. C. AND ROSENSHINE, B. V. (EDS.). *Talks to Teachers.* New York: Random House, 1987.

BRAUN, C. "Teachers' Expectations." In Dunkin, M. (ed.). *The International Encyclopedia of Teaching and Teacher Education.* New York: Pergamon Press, 1987. pp. 598–605.

BROPHY, J. E. AND GOOD, T. L. "Teacher Behavior and Student Achievement." In Wittrock, M. (ed.). *Handbook of Research on Teaching.* 3rd edition. New York: Macmillan Publishing Company, 1986. pp. 328–375.

CAZDEN, C. "Classroom Discourse." In Wittrock, M. (ed.). *Handbook of Research on Teaching.* 3rd edition. New York: Macmillan Publishing Company, 1986. pp. 432–463.

DEGARMO, CHARLES. *Interest in Education: The Doctrine of Interest and Its Concrete Application.* New York: Macmillan Publishing Company, 1903.

GOOD, T. L. AND BROPHY, J. E. *Looking in Classrooms.* 4th edition. New York: Harper and Row, 1987.

MADDOX, H. AND HOOLE, E. "Performance Decrement in the Lecture." *Educational Review* (November 1975): 17–30.

PINNEY, R. *Presentation Behavior Related to Success in Teaching.* Doctoral dissertation, Stanford University, 1969.

REDFIELD, D. AND ROUSSEAU, E. "A Meta-Analysis of Experimental Research on Teacher Questioning Behavior." *Review of Educational Research* (Summer 1981): 237–245.

ROHRKEMPER, M. AND GOOD, T. L. "Proactive Teaching." In Dunkin, M. (ed.). *The International Encyclopedia of Teaching and Teacher Education.* New York: Pergamon Press, 1987. pp. 457–460.

ROSENSHINE, B. AND STEVENS, R. "Teaching Functions." In Wittrock, M. *Handbook of Research on Teaching.* 3rd edition. New York: Macmillan Publishing Company, 1986. pp. 376–391.

ROWE, M. B. "Wait Time: Slowing Down May be a Way of Speeding Up." *Journal of Teacher Education* (January–February, 1986): 43–50.

SCHWILLE, J.; PORTER, A.; FLODEN, R.; FREEMAN, D.; KNAPPEN, L.; KUHS, T.; AND SCHMIDT, W. *Teachers as Policy Brokers in the Content of Elementary School Mathematics.* East Lansing, Michigan: National Institute of Education Contract No. P–80–0127, Institute for Research on Teaching, Michigan State University, 1981.

SHULMAN, L. S. AND SYKES, G. (EDS.). *Handbook of Teaching and Policy.* New York; Longman, Inc., 1983.

SMITH, L. AND LAND, M. "Low-inference Verbal Behaviors Related to Teacher Clarity." *Journal of Classroom Interaction* (Winter 1981): 37–42.

CHAPTER 5

Selecting Content and Establishing Objectives

This chapter provides information to help the reader to:

1. Identify content to be taught.
2. Distinguish among goals, generalizations, and concepts.
3. Recognize differences among cognitive learning, psychomotor learning, and affective learning.
4. Describe the function of instructional objectives.
5. Plan instructional objectives that vary in type and sophistication.
6. Write objectives using the ABCD format.

PRETEST

DIRECTIONS: Using your own paper, answer these true/false questions. For each correct statement, write the word "true." For each incorrect statement, write the word "false."

_____ 1. In organizing content for a course, it is always better for beginning teachers to follow the sequence of content in the course textbook.

_____ 2. Educational goals provide learners with specific information about what they are supposed to learn from a given instructional sequence.

_____ 3. Generally, more time is required for instruction developed in support of an analysis-level instructional objective than a knowledge-level instructional objective.

_____ 4. Though taxonomies have been developed for cognitive and affective learning, none exists for psychomotor learning.

_____ 5. Planning tables can help teachers identify the relative amount of instructional time needed to teach content associated with each objective.

Introduction

Normal Dalby, a new world history teacher at Carpenter High School, expressed these feelings at the end of September.

Three weeks of school behind me. A few battle scars to show for the effort, but nothing major. My enthusiasm remains high. I know I can control my classes. I am finding now that I can begin to think a bit more about "what" I am teaching. It's nice to have moved beyond an elemental concern for physical survival.

My classes and I are tromping our way through Ancient Greece. Six notebooks crammed with university lecture notes on the topic are on my desk at home. I've also gathered together some good reference books. The subject is just so deep . . .

The text we're using is one of those gems that compacts 3,000 years of historical truth into 600 pages. It purports to do Ancient Greece in 10 pages. It seems so irresponsible. We flit by something and then dash madly on to something new. I just don't feel that this quick "once-over-lightly" approach is producing much learning.

To make matters worse, the text is just too difficult for many of my students. Beyond problems with the book, many of them don't have much *context* for a lot of the material. I mean, some of them don't know where Greece is. One of them asked me the other day if Greece is in South America!

I know I should be providing more, but I just don't know exactly what. I'm not sure what I should expect these students to be able to do. I'd like to be doing better by my students, but I just don't know where to begin.

Mr. Dalby's concerns about "what to teach" and "what to expect of students" are widely shared. One way prospective teachers can reduce the intensity of these anxieties is to become familiar with general procedures related to (1) content selection and (2) development of instructional objectives.

Selecting Content

Content is selected in many ways. A few teachers turn the entire process over to the author of the textbook they are using. They begin with the first chapter and simply follow the sequence of chapters. If all goes well, their students finish the final chapter on the final day of the term. If all does not go well, instruction stops at some earlier point. (This situation has been observed frequently in high school American history courses

Teachers are encouraged to fit textbook content to the unique needs of their students. This may mean varying the sequence of content presentation from the order followed by the text.

where many instructors have found it difficult to get past World War II.)

Relying on the textbook to organize course content is an indefensible practice. There is nothing sacred about a textbook's content and sequence. Authors make subjective decisions about topics that are included, depth of coverage, and sequence. A review of a selection of textbooks for a given school subject will reveal great differences in content organization.

Textbook authors cannot know the unique characteristics of students in a given teacher's classroom. The teacher is much better informed about these characteristics. Additionally, teachers' academic preparation may have introduced them to perspectives that differ from those of the author of a given course text. Because of their understandings of their own students, of their subject areas, and of their local communities, teachers should play an active role in selecting and organizing content.

This by no means suggests that teachers are able to make these decisions without some restraints. For example, some states have quite rigid

"Fenway doesn't *select* content. He teaches it *all*."

Box 5.1

Identifying Content to Be Taught

Suppose that you accepted a teaching position in a district that had no curriculum guides for your subject. Suppose, too, that a late-summer fire had destroyed all textbooks and that no replacements would be available until the second semester.

What Do You Think?

If this happened, the principal might ask you to design your own course. How would you respond to these questions?

1. What major topics would you cover? How would you justify this selection?

2. In what sequence would you teach these topics? Why?

3. How much emphasis should each topic receive? In an 18-week course, how much time would you give to each?

4. For each major topic, what are the main concepts you would want students to understand? Are any of these ideas more important than others? Why do you think so?

guidelines regarding content to be covered. Some local districts have similar requirements. Where this is true, these guidelines limit teachers decisions' about content selection and organization. However, even where these guidelines are quite explicit, teachers still enjoy considerable planning latitude.

In addition to state and local requirements, many school districts have curriculum committees and district-level curriculum specialists. They work to identify content to be taught and to suggest appropriate instructional sequences. Results of their work often are printed and distributed to teachers. These documents, called curriculum guides can be of great help to a new teacher.

Frequently, curriculum guides identify intended learning outcomes, suggest possible content sequences, indicate alternative instructional techniques, recommend evaluation procedures, and list information sources. The information sources often provide titles and descriptions of materials that can be used to supplement content in the text. Curriculum guides need to be updated periodically. Some districts provide opportunities for teachers to react to and revise adopted guides. This prevents them from becoming rigid, static documents. Box 5.1 looks at ways to identify course content.

Not all districts have curriculum guides. When they are not available, teachers are obliged to undertake program planning on their own. Some procedures for accomplishing this task are introduced in the next section.

The Breakdown of Academic Content

Textbook writers, developers of curriculum guides, and all others who attempt to identify contents to be covered in school courses use a system to break down academic subject matter in a systematic way. Procedures for accomplishing this task can be sophisticated. Certainly only rarely would a new teacher be expected to identify the scope and sequence of the content to be taught in his or her courses without help. Although the chances that a new teacher will be asked to accomplish this task on his or her own are remote, there is still some utility in understanding how a systematic breakdown of content might proceed.

In general, in breaking down academic content, there is an effort to start with broad topic areas and follow a set of procedures that results in the identification of specific major ideas or concepts to be taught. The following four-step process is typical of many of the schemes used to accomplish this task.

Step 1. Identify topic area.

Step 2. Identify major goals of instruction related to the topic area.

Step 3. Identify generalizations summarizing knowledge related to major goals.

Step 4. Identify major concepts needed for students to grasp the identified generalizations.

Schematically, this set of steps is depicted in Box 5.2.

Identifying Topic Areas

Topic areas are broad segments of content within a given subject area. For example, topic areas in U.S. history might include "the Revolutionary War period," "the War of 1812," "the Age of Jackson," and so forth. There is no absolutely uniform pattern for selection of major topics in any subject area. There is an important force at work, however, that tends to make for rather similar sets of topics appearing time after time in breakdowns of individual subject areas.

This highly significant force is *tradition*. For example, consider that for years it has been common for history teachers to use important chronological events as major topic areas, introducing first the events most remote in time. Subsequent instruction moves through topics that become progressively more recent. But other patterns also exist. For

Box 5.2

Relationship of Steps in a Plan for Breaking Down an Academic Subject that Is to Be Taught in School

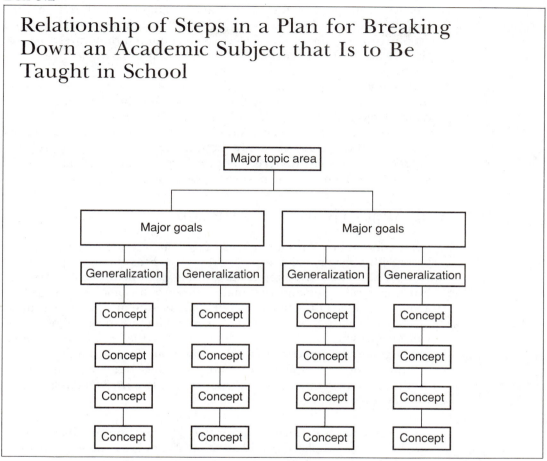

example, sometimes history courses are taught not according to chronological events but according to recurring historical themes such as revolution, war, technological innovations, and so forth. But deviations from the chronological approach are rare. The force of tradition is powerful, and it tends to make for a good deal of uniformity among topics ordinarily treated by large numbers of teachers in a given subject area.

Not surprisingly, specialized school subjects of fairly recent origin tend to be characterized by more topical diversity than are those subjects that have long been in the secondary school curriculum. One would expect to find much more diversity of topical treatment in high school courses in interpersonal communications taught by different teachers than in high school courses in chemistry. The interpersonal communications course, a high school elective encountered only rarely, has too short a history in the curriculum for tradition to have identified those topics that are almost always taught.

In summary, topic selection ordinarily does not prove to be much of a problem for a teacher charged with preparing a breakdown of an academic subject. Because of the influence of tradition, other teachers, district coordinators, and even textbooks are likely sources of information regarding this matter. Certainly the question of what topics are to be taught generates less disagreement than the question of what students should learn from their exposure to these topics.

Identifying Major Goals of Instruction

Some content breakdown schemes suggest identifying major goals even before identifying major topics. Others, such as this one, propose to identify the goals after topics have been identified. Goals are simply broad general statements that make reference to some general feelings about what kinds of benefits should come to students as a consequence of their exposure to a given topic (or, sometimes, a given set of topics). Goals represent an attempt to describe what the community at large might generally expect of students exposed to this (or these) topic(s).

Suppose, for example, that one of the topics treated in the seventh grade mathematics program was "Solving Equations. " One related goal for this topic might read

Goal: Students will learn to appreciate the relationship that exists between multiplication and addition as they are exposed to methods for applying this relationship to solving equations.

Consider another example from economics. Suppose that "inflation" had been selected as a major topic to be treated in the course. One related goal that might be selected for this topic might be

Goal: Students will come to appreciate the forces that are at work to produce the phenomenon we know as inflation.

In summary, then, goals provide very general statements about the level of competence that students are expected to have as a consequence of their exposure to a given topic (or set of topics). They tend to be rather abstract, and they do not reference specific sorts of learning that students will be expected to master.

Identifying Generalizations

Generalizations are much more specific than goal statements. Sometimes referred to as principles, generalizations are succinct expressions of relationships among important ideas or concepts. Generalizations might be thought of as propositions that have been tested over and over again and that are generally thought to be true. (It is possible in light of some future information, however, that they might have to be revised.) Generalizations represent a kind of idea-dense shorthand for summarizing a large store of knowledge. Generalizations begin to point toward the more specific kinds of learning outcomes toward which students studying a given topic will be directed.

Let us consider again the seventh grade mathematics course that includes the major topic area "Solving Equations" and see how the breakdown might look through the step of identifying generalizations. (In this example, only one goal and one generalization are included. In reality, there may be more than one of each component related to the major topic.)

MAJOR TOPIC: SOLVING EQUATIONS

Goal: Students will learn to appreciate the relationship that exists between multiplication and addition as they are exposed to methods for applying this relationship to solving equations.

Generalization: The distributive principle states that the product resulting from the multiplication of a given number and the sum of two others equals the product of this given number multiplied by the first of these two numbers *plus* the product of the given number multiplied by the second of these two numbers. Algebraically, the distributive principle is depicted as

$$a \times (b + c) = (a \times b) + (a \times c)$$

Note the great jump in specificity from the goal statement to the generalization. The generalization begins to provide specific guidance to the teacher in terms of what should be taught. In this example, it is clear that there will be a focus on developing students' ability to apply the distributive principle. But to determine just what students must understand to perform this manipulation, another step is needed.

Identifying Major Concepts

The fourth step in the breakdown of content is identifying major concepts. A concept is a major idea. Concepts sometimes are thought of as definitions. A concept means what it means because it is defined in a given way. Concepts are the building blocks of generalizations. This means that students must understand the concepts included in a generalization before they can be expected to grasp the generalization. Therefore, instruction directed toward helping students to master a generalization begins with a focus on concepts relevant to the generalization. The relevant concepts are those mentioned specifically in the generalization itself and others that the language of the generalization seems to assume students know.

Given the need to focus on concepts, let us look now at a breakdown of the topic "Solving Equations" to the concept level:

MAJOR TOPIC: SOLVING EQUATIONS

Goal: Students will learn to appreciate the relationship that exists between multiplication and addition as they are exposed to methods for applying this relationship to solving equations.

Generalization: The distributive principle states that the product resulting from the multiplication of a given number and the sum of two others equals the product of this given number multiplied by the second of these two numbers. Algebraically, the distributive principle is depicted as

$$a \times (b + c) = (a \times b) + (a \times c)$$

CONCEPTS:

Equation.

Addition process.

Subtraction process.

Multiplication process.

Division process.

Simplification.

Certainly some of these concepts may be known to students before instruction on this topic begins. A review of diagnostic information would provide some answers regarding entry-level understandings of individual students. Actual instruction would begin with a focus on those concepts with which students were not familiar. It would be with a view to helping students grasp unfamiliar concepts that instruction in this area would go forward.

In summary, then, concepts represent rather specific ideas that result from a systematic breakdown of content that begins with the identification of a major topic. Concepts provide a basis for teachers to begin

Box 5.3

Making Distinctions Among Goals, Generalizations, and Concepts

What Do You Think?

Look at items in the following list. Which ones are goals? Which ones are generalizations? Which ones are concepts? You may wish to discuss your responses with your instructor.

1. Monsoon wind.
2. Students should come to appreciate the contributions of American poets to the quality of our national life.
3. Onomatopoeia.
4. Students should come to know the properties of real numbers.
5. In technologically advanced societies, innovations tend to be adopted in the largest cities before they are adopted

in smaller cities, towns, and rural areas.

6. Successful revolutions result in a shift of political and economic power into the hands of social groups who supported the aims of the revolutionaries.
7. When temperatures go up, objects expand; when temperatures go down, objects contract.
8. Heat of fusion.
9. Moment of illumination.
10. Students should understand how temperature and heat can be measured and how changes in temperature and heat influence the environment.
11. Factoring.

---

planning the kinds of learning experiences that will provide for students within a given topic. Box 5.3 is an exercise in making distinctions among goals, generalizations, and concepts.

Preparing Instructional Objectives

In districts with well-developed curriculum guides, new teachers sometimes find that major course topics, generalizations, and concepts have been identified for them. Only rarely, though, are teachers provided with pre-established lists of instructional objectives. Typically, teachers write these themselves.

Instructional objectives describe what students should be able to do as a result of their exposure to instruction. They are written in language that references much more explicit student behaviors than do goal statements. To see the distinction between a goal and an objective, note the following:

Goal: Students will learn to appreciate the relationship that exists between multiplication and addition as they are exposed to methods for applying this relationship to solving equations.

Sample Instructional Objective: Each student will solve correctly at least 11 of 14 problem equations that require the use of combinations of addition, subtraction, multiplication, and division processes.

The objective requires students to engage in an observable behavior. This behavior is one that has been selected to serve as an indicator of the more general behavior alluded to in the goal. Other objectives might be developed that would be equally consistent with the general behavior introduced in the goal statement. No specific number of instructional objectives is right or correct for a given goal statement. Teachers must exercise their own judgment in this matter.

Instructional objectives help teachers in two ways. First, they serve as guideposts for instructional planning. Once a set of instructional objectives for a given unit of work has been prepared, subsequent instructional planning ties to these objectives. For example, selection of instructional materials is influenced by the expectations of student learning stated in the objectives. If a film has potential to help students grasp understandings associated with an objective, a good case can be made for including it in the instructional sequence. If the film has little relationship to the objectives, then teachers have a basis for eliminating it from further consideration.

A second advantage that instructional objectives provide to teachers has to do with student learning. Programs planned through the use of instructional objectives tend to be organized and purposeful. Students sense less confusion about teacher expectations. Students' academic performances improve under these conditions (Ferre 1972; Morse and Tillman 1973; Olsen 1973). This is particularly true when teachers share instructional objectives with students and make sure they understand what it is they are supposed to be learning (Good and Brophy 1987).

Development of instructional objectives is a key step in the planning process. It is preceded by identification of topics, goals, generalizations, and concepts. After instructional objectives have been prepared, teachers use them as reference points as they make decisions about instructional techniques, learning materials, evaluation, and other elements. These planning "parts" often are gathered together into systematic instructional units. Details regarding unit preparation are introduced in Chapter 13, "Planning Instructional Units."

An illustration of the relationship of instructional objectives to major concepts, a generalization, a goal, and a topic is presented in Box 5.4. Note the effort to ensure that identified major concepts have been referenced in at least one instructional objective.

Box 5.4

Relationship of Learning Objectives to Major Concepts, a Generalization, a Goal, and a Topic

Topic

Solving Equations.

Goal

Students will learn to appreciate the relationship that exists between multiplication and addition as they are exposed to methods for applying this relationship to solving equations.

Generalization

The distributive principle states that the product resulting from the multiplication of a given number and the sum of two others equals the product of this given number multiplied by the first of these two numbers plus the product of this given number multiplied by the second of these two number. Algebraically, the equality suggested by the distributive principle is depicted as follows:

$$a \times (b + c) = (a \times b) + (a \times c)$$

Major Concepts

1. Simplification.
2. Equation.
3. Addition process.
4. Subtraction process.
5. Multiplication process.
6. Division process.
7. Distributive principle.

Instructional Objectives:

1. Each student will respond correctly to 8 of 10 true/false questions related to the nature of the distributive principle.
2. Each student will solve correctly at least 7 of 10 equations requiring them to use a combination of the addition and multiplication processes.
3. Each student will solve correctly at least 11 of 14 problem equations requiring the use of combinations of the addition, subtraction, multiplication, and division processes.

   And so forth.

RELATIONSHIP OF MAJOR CONCEPTS (BY NUMBER) AND INDIVIDUAL

	Concepts						
	1	2	3	4	5	6	7
Objectives	2,3	2,3	2,3	3	2,3	3	1,2

A Format for Preparing Instructional Objectives

Of the many formats available for preparing instructional objectives, one we have used for some time is the ABCD format. This scheme presumes that a complete instructional objective includes four elements. Reference must be made in the objective to the *audience* (A) to be served, to the *behavior* (B) to be taken as an indicator of appropriate learning, to the *condition* (C) under which this behavior is measured (e.g., kind of assessment procedure to be used), and to the *degree* (D) of competency to be demonstrated before mastery of the objective is assumed. In the next sections we will look at these components of a complete instructional objective one at a time.

Selecting Content and Establishing Instructional Objectives

A = AUDIENCE. The A component of an instructional objective identifies the person or persons to whom the instructional objective is directed. This may be an entire class of students, a group even larger than a class, a small group of students, or even a single student. The purpose of the audience component of an instructional objective is to provide specific information to a given individual regarding whether or not he or she is to be held accountable for mastering the content referenced in a given objective. Typically, the A, or audience, component of an instructional objective will appear as indicated in the following examples:

"Each student will . . ."

"Louisa's group will . . ."

"All students in all sections of U.S. history will . . ."

"All fifth-period physics students will . . ."

"Joanne Smith will . . ."

B = BEHAVIOR. The B, or behavior, component of an instructional objective describes the observable performance that will be taken as an indicator that learning has taken place. The behavior in an instructional objective must be described in observable terms. This suggests a need to select verbs that describe performance in precise and specific ways and a need to avoid verbs that describe less readily observable kinds of phenomena. To illustrate this distinction, consider the following choices:

"Each student will appreciate foreign policy differences of the Republican and Democratic presidential candidates by . . ."
"Each student will describe foreign policy differences of the Republican and Democratic presidential candidates by . . ."

In the first example, it is unclear both to the teacher and the student what kind of behavior will be taken as evidence that mastery has occurred. It is not clear what kind of performance signals "appreciation." A student, given an instructional objective with a behavior statement of this kind, might well be confused as to how he or she should study the material. The use of the verb "describe" in the second option is much more precise. "Describe" suggests a behavior that is much more observable and specific than does "appreciate." A student presented with an instructional objective calling upon him or her to describe foreign policy differences can expect to be assessed on his or her ability to provide some clear indication of a familiarity with key policy points of each candidate. The use of the verb "describe" in the instructional objective suggests to students a need to study carefully specific positions of each candidiate. It is true that the verb "appreciate" *might* suggest a similar activity to some students. But the meaning of "appreciate" is much less precise than "describe." For example, some students might take the "each student will appreciate" directive to mean that they are to do nothing beyond developing a personal aesthetic satisfaction from the knowledge that, indeed, both candidates have differing foreign policy views. For a student who had this impression, there would be no deeply felt need to become thoroughly familiar with foreign policy positions of each candidate. In summary, then, a good deal of ambiguity is removed when verbs used in the behavior component of an instructional objective reference a relatively specific and an observable kind of student performance (see Box 5.5).

The following fragments of complete instructional objectives indicate how the behavior component might look:

. . . cite specific examples of . . .
. . . describe characteristics of . . .
. . . distinguish between . . .
. . . name . . .
. . . point out . . .
. . . compare and contrast . . .

Box 5.5

Kinds of Verbs Suitable for Behavior Component of an Instructional Objective

What Do You Think?

Below is a list of verbs that might be used in writing instructional objectives. Look at the list. Then identify those verbs that (1) you think would be suitable for use in an instructional objective and that (2) you do not think would be suitable for use in an instructional objective. Be prepared to defend your decisions.

compute	note
apply	evaluate
understand	critique
comprehend	select
describe	judge
compare	identify
appreciate	conjecture

C = CONDITION.   The C, or condition, component of an instructional objective describes the condition of assessment. That is, the condition details the kinds of procedures to be followed to determine whether or not the student can perform in the way described by the behavior component of the objective. In many instances, the condition is a formal test of some kind. In other instances, a less formal procedure may be described. The condition component conveys to the student information regarding how his or her learning will be assessed at the conclusion of the instructional sequence. Typically the C component of an instructional objective will appear as indicated in the following examples:

. . . on a multiple-choice test . . .

. . . during a five-minute informal conversation with the teacher . . .

. . . on an essay examination with use of notes permitted . . .

. . . on a formal paper, six to ten pages in length, footnoted
       properly . . .

. . . on a student-prepared, three-color, 3-foot by 4-foot poster . . .

D = DEGREE.   The D, or degree, component of an instructional objective details the minimum level of performance that will be acceptable as evidence that the objective has been mastered. Where such formal assessment procedures as matching tests, true/false tests, and multiple-choice tests are used, the degree frequently is described in terms of either total numbers of items that must be responded to correctly or a percentage of the total number of items that must be responded to correctly. Clearly such a procedure makes no sense for essay items. On essay items, the degree frequently refers to specific categories of content that must be included in responses that will be viewed as indicative of content mastery.

There is a good deal of teacher artistry involved in deciding what degree of competence to describe as minimal evidence a given objective has been achieved. A study by Block (1972) revealed that, when a minimum standard of about 80 percent was assigned to objectives where tests such as true/false, matching, and multiple choice were used, students generally developed a more favorable attitude toward learning than when a minimum standard of 90 percent correct was applied. We would caution, however, that research in this area is in its infancy and that teachers must rely heavily on personal intuition in identifying criterion levels they believe important. The use of criterion levels and instructional objectives' mastery for grading purposes is discussed in some detail in Chapter 11, "Measuring, Evaluating, and Reporting Student Progress."

Typically, the D component of an instructional objective will appear as indicated in the following examples:

. . . respond correctly to at least 8 of 10 . . .

. . . in an essay in which specific references are made to (a) motivations for immigration, (b) domestic resistance to immigration, and (c) psychic rewards of immigration . . .

. . . answer correctly 85 percent of the items on a . . .

. . . with no mistakes . . .

Putting It All Together: The ABCD Format

Recall that all complete instructional objectives include references to A, the audience, B, the behavior, C, the condition, and D, the degree. A number of properly prepared objectives are listed below. Individual components of each objective have been underlined and labeled.

      A   B   D   C

1. Each student will solve 8 of 10 problems on a weekly quiz featuring questions about right triangles.

      A   C   B   D

2. Laura's group, in an essay, will cite at least five reasons supporting and five reasons opposing nineteenth-century Swedish migration to the American South.

                          A   B
3. <u>The fifth-period</u> <u>class will identify examples of alliteration</u> by respon-

                          C   D
ding correctly on a <u>multiple-choice test</u> to <u>at least 8 of 10 items.</u>

Note that the audience, behavior, condition, and degree components may appear in a variety of orders. The order is not critical. What *is* important is that all four be included in every instructional objective.

In summary, the ABCD format is an easily learned procedure. Instructional objectives containing all four components (audience, behavior, condition, and degree) are capable of conveying a good deal of information to students about a teacher's expectations. For the teacher, they provide a reminder to keep instruction on track in such a way that learning experiences provided will clearly be consistent with the kinds of expectations reflected in the assessment procedures followed at the conclusion of a given instructional sequence.

Kinds of Instructional Objectives

For some years now, it has been a convention to think of learning as divided into three basic categories or "domains." These are (1) the cognitive domain, (2) the affective domain, and (3) the psychomotor domain. In very general terms, the cognitive domain includes what we might call academic or intellectual kinds of learning (see Box 5.6). The affective domain includes learning related to values, beliefs, and attitudes. The psychomotor domain includes learning related to the sensorimotor system and fine and large muscle control.

Because the general area of concern of each domain has certain unique features, it is not surprising that instructional objectives in each domain tend to be organized in slightly different ways and to be directed toward different purposes. In the sections that follow, some of these differences are introduced.

Instructional Objectives in the Cognitive Domain

The cognitive domain is concerned with rational, systematic, or intellectual thinking. When we think about subject matter content and our expectation that students will learn it, we have in mind the cognitive domain. Much of what we know about thinking in the cognitive domain stems from the work of Benjamin Bloom and others who, in the mid-

Box 5.6

Distinguishing Among Different Cognitive Levels

What Do You Think?

On the right-hand side of the page are the six levels in the cognitive Taxonomy (Bloom 1956). On the left-hand side are some tasks students might be asked to do. Look at these tasks. Decide what level of cognitive thinking might be required for students to accomplish each task. Share your responses with the rest of the class and with the instructor.

STUDENT TASKS

A. Describe the likely results of a successful effort to dig a 50-foot wide canal connecting the Mediterranean Sea with the Bay of Biscay in the Atlantic.

B. Identify the individuals who have run for president in this century whom you believe to have been "most qualified" and cite reasons for making your determinations.

C. State from memory the Preamble to the U.S. Constitution.

D. Write a sentence in which you illustrate the use of alliteration.

E. Suggest the relative importance of (1) social forces, (2) political forces, and (3) economic forces as causes of the outbreak of World War I.

F. Describe the characteristics of the halogen family.

G. Suggest procedures that must be followed to obtain a valid driver's license.

H. Name four tragedies by William Shakespeare.

I. Follow directions and build a model airplane.

LEVELS OF THE COGNITIVE DOMAIN

1. Knowledge

2. Comprehension

3. Application

4. Analysis

5. Synthesis

6. Evaluation

1950s, set about the task of developing a system for identifying categories of learning in the cognitive domain. Out of their deliberations came a ground-breaking educational document, *Taxonomy of Educational Objectives: Handbook I: Cognitive Domain* (Bloom 1956). Commonly referred to as *Bloom's taxonomy*, this document suggested that there exists a six-step hierarchy of thinking ranging from the most elemental thinking processes to the most sophisticated. Ordered in terms from simplest to most complex, the elements of Bloom's taxonomy are as follows:

Knowledge

Comprehension

Application

Analysis

Synthesis

Evaluation

For teachers, proposed learning experiences can be evaluated in terms of their intellectual complexity by referencing the intellectual demands against Bloom's taxonomy. In general, a task demanding "knowledge-level" performance will challenge students less than a task demanding "synthesis-level" performance. In thinking about instructional planning, teachers find it useful to know something about the kinds of thinking implied by each level of taxonomy. When they have made a decision regarding the kinds of intellectual demands they wish to include in their program, they then need to prepare instructional objectives that are clearly directed toward encouraging student performance at the targeted taxonomical level (knowledge, comprehension, application, analysis, synthesis, and evaluation). Let us look briefly at characteristics of each taxonomical level and at instructional objectives consistent with each.

Knowledge. Knowledge is the simple recall of a piece of previously learned information. At the knowledge level, the student is not required to do anything beyond reproducing something specific to which he or she has been exposed. No manipulation or interpretation of learned material is required. The following are examples of instructional objectives written at the knowledge level:

1. On a multiple-choice test, each student will identify the capitals of countries in NATO by responding correctly to at least 80 percent of the items.
2. Each student, on a matching test, will identify parts of a cell by responding accurately to at least 12 of 15 items.

Comprehension. Comprehension is a slightly more complex mental operation than knowledge. Comprehension requires the student to focus on more than a single piece of previously learned information with a view to understanding certain important relationships. At the comprehension level, a student may be required to change the form of previously learned material or to make a simple interpretation. Note the following examples.

1. Each student will provide literal translations from Russian to English for ten sentences making no errors in at least eight of the sentences translated.

2. Students in Laura's group will select on a matching test the correct connotative meanings of vocabulary words appearing in the first chapter of *The Red Badge of Courage* with a minimal acceptable accuracy of 80 percent correct.

Application.   Application involves the use in an unfamiliar context of information that has been learned previously. In short, application requires students to do something with what they have learned. Note the following examples of application-level instructional objectives:

1. Each student in the ninth grade geography class will compute correct air distances between ten pairs of world cities using a tape measure and a 22-inch globe so that errors of no more than 50 air miles short or long of actual distances are made on any more than two pairs of cities.

2. Each student in the eleventh grade science class will compute progeny ratios correctly on at least eight of eleven provided problems.

Analysis.   Analysis requires students to develop conclusions through a study of the constituent parts of a phenomenon. Through the process of analysis, the students attempt to understand some existing reality by looking carefully at the pieces that go together to make the reality. Some examples of analysis-level instructional objectives follow:

1. Each student will correctly identify the chemical composition of at least 15 of 18 provided unknown compounds.

2. In an essay examination, each student will describe patterns of voting in the recent presidential election on the part of voters of (a) very low incomes, (b) moderately low incomes, (c) average incomes, (d) moderately high incomes, and (e) very high incomes.

Synthesis.   Synthesis requires students to take a number of separate pieces of information and combine them to create knowledge that is new (or, more accurately, knowledge that is new to the student). Some examples of synthesis-level instructional objectives follow:

1. Making specific references to possible changes in (a) religious preferences, (b) nature of social hierarchies, (c) typical family structure, and (d) avocational interests, each student, in an essay, will suggest

what the culture of Boston might be like today if the preponderance of early settlers had come from (a) Saudi Arabia, (b) Nigeria, (c) Japan, and (d) Spain.

2. In an essay, each student will describe the likely impact on (a) climates, (b) transportation networks, (c) recreational patterns, and (d) dialects of American English were a huge mountain range, with peaks averaging in the 8,000- to 10,000-foot range, to appear along a line running roughly from Omaha to Cincinnati.

Evaluation. At the level of evaluation, students are called upon to make judgments in light of clearly identified criteria. To be at the evaluation level, it is essential for both the element of judgment and the element of established criteria to be present. Evaluation never calls upon students to engage in simplistic sharings of nonsupported personal opinion. The following instructional objectives are written at the level of evaluation.

1. Each student will compare, contrast, and critique the plays of Racine and Corneille in terms of their adherence to the "rules" of classical drama.

2. Each student will critique a selected painting by Gauguin and a selected painting by Van Gogh and determine which is the superior piece of work by completing an essay in which specific references are made to (a) the degree of coherence observed in each painting, (b) the degree to which each painting is "true" to the medium used, and (c) the degree of emotive pleasure or pain inspired by an observation of each painting.

COGNITIVE LEVEL OF INSTRUCTIONAL OBJECTIVES AND TEACHING TIME. Not surprisingly there is a relationship between the level of sophistication of thinking a teacher hopes to promote in students and the time required to get them to this level. Generally, there is an increase in instructional time needed as there is an increase in the cognitive level of the instructional objective. For example, it requires less instructional time to teach students to master a knowledge-level than it does to prepare them to master an objective at the level of comprehension (or at any higher cognitive level).

Bloom's taxonomy tells us that every higher level contains within it every lower level. This means that a student cannot be expected to think at the level of analysis unless he or she is able to think at the subordinate levels of application, comprehension, and knowledge. This relationship suggests important implications for us in planning for instruction. First, it suggests that, because of time limitations, students will not be expected to operate at higher thinking levels with respect to *all* the content of a course. This simply is unrealistic given time limitations. Consequently, there is a need to select with care those critically important areas where we feel students need to proceed toward mastery at the levels of analysis, synthesis, or even evaluation. When these areas are identified, it is necessary to build systematically the important lower-cognitive-level understandings that are prerequisite to higher-level thinking. This effort requires careful attention to sequencing and to the whole area of lesson and unit planning. Some examples of how a decision to lead students to a higher-level understanding of a given topic area might be reflected in a systematic plan for instruction are provided in Chapter 9, "Formalizing Unit and Lesson Plans."

Instructional Objectives in the Affective Domain

The affective domain, as noted previously, concerns people's values, feelings, and attitudes. Clearly in schools we are concerned about the total development of our students, not just with their mastery of academic content. We need, therefore, to consider the issue of students' values, feelings, and attitudes as the instructional planning process goes forward.

Success in the affective area often associates with success in the cognitive area; in other words, students who like and feel good about what they are doing in school tend to do better in their academic courses than do those who are unhappy in school. This does not mean that instructional planning should be directed exclusively toward the goal of "amusing the students" or "keeping them all happy all the time." What concern for students' values, feelings, and attitudes means is that every effort should be directed toward ensuring that no youngster's sense of self-worth is consciously diminished by something we do as classroom teachers.

The goal of supporting each student's growth toward self-confident and mature adulthood is not inconsistent with an instructional program that makes heavy cognitive demands on students. The critical variable is not the difficulty of the work but, rather, whether the instructional system has been designed in such a way that each youngster has a realistic chance for success. So long as students feel that they are succeeding, attitudes toward school and the teacher generally will remain positive. Success in academic work can itself be an important contributor to students' developing sense of self-worth.

The affective domain involves all areas in which the general emphasis is on values, attitudes, and feelings. But, with regard to planning instructional objectives, our focus will be limited to a small range of concerns within this broader and more general domain. The necessity for limiting our focus here results from the nature of instructional objectives.

Recall that instructional objectives suggest expected, or at least hoped for, outcomes. This purpose becomes something of a problem when we are dealing with the affective area. There is a heavy-handed, possibly authoritarian, ring to the suggestion that a given instructional program is dedicated to shaping students' values in a given way. Certainly in a society that values open discussion and democratic decision making, we have no business establishing instructional objectives that seem to say to students that certain values, attitudes, and feelings are right whereas others are wrong. A teacher who tries to do this is asking for trouble.

In thinking about the possibility of developing instructional objectives in the affective domain, we must ask ourselves this question: "In what area(s) do teachers have a legitimate need to know about students' values, attitudes, and feelings?" Perhaps there are several answers to this question. But the one that has always made the most sense to us is that teachers have a need to know how students are feeling about the instruction to which they are being exposed. For example, do they like the topics selected? How do they feel about the various school subjects? And so forth. If we accept the premise that students who feel disposed toward what is going on in their classes will do better in those classes and, hence, may grow in terms of their own feelings of competence and self-worth, then we have every reason to make some deliberate efforts to gather information that will tell us something about these kinds of student feelings.

A cautionary note is needed here. It is imperative that measures of students' values, feelings, and attitudes never be used as a basis for awarding grades. Information derived from instructional objectives in the affective area helps the teacher to take a look at how his or her program is being viewed in an attitudinal sense by his or her students. Such information may suggest a need to make changes. It may suggest a need to do nothing at all. But in every case it will provide some indication to the teacher about attitudes of youngsters toward what has been going on in the classroom. It is obvious that any attempt to use such information for grading purposes would soon undermine the reliability of the information. In addition to the ethical problem of grading students' attitudes, any such grading scheme would soon break down as clever students began to report attitudes (whether they truly held them or not) that they believed the teacher wished to hear.

In preparing instructional objectives that relate to the affective domain, it is a common practice to measure a change of attitudes that may have occurred over a period of time. Sometimes a measure of an attitude is taken at the beginning of an instructional unit and then again at the end of the same unit. Let us suppose that we were teaching a high school biology class, that we were about to begin an instructional unit on infectious diseases, and that we expected to spend a good deal of time on the subject of venereal diseases. An affective instructional objective we might prepare could look like this:

At the conclusion of the unit on infectious diseases, each student in the biology class will demonstrate greater interest in learning about venereal diseases than at the beginning of the unit as measured by a positive shift in scores from a preunit attitude inventory and a postunit attitude inventory.

Note that the same ABCD format is used for affective as for cognitive instructional objectives. The reference to an attitude inventory as the condition or means of assessing student attitudes both before the unit and after the unit refers to a procedure according to which students are asked to rank their feelings about a number of provided alternatives. An example of an attitude inventory that we might have used in connection with our sample objective follows:

Attitude Inventory

Topic: Infectious Diseases.

Directions: Listed below are a number of areas studied during a unit on infectious diseases. Look at each area. Then, place a number "1" in the blank before the area in which you have the greatest interest, a "2" in the blank before the area in which you have the second greatest interest, and so forth. Continue this pattern until you conclude with the largest number in the blank before the area in which you have the least personal interest.

_____ the body's general immunological systems
_____ veneral diseases
_____ types of immunity to disease
_____ the germ theory of disease
_____ direct versus indirect contact of disease

_____ _____
(fill in an area of your choice if you would like to do so)

_____ _____
(fill in an area of your choice if you would like to do so)

In this attitude inventory, the positive shift would be from a relatively high number on the attitude inventory when it was given before the unit (recall that the higher the number, the lower the interest in the area) to a relatively low number on the attitude inventory given at the conclusion of the unit (recall that the lower the number, the higher the interest in the area).

Clearly we would not hope for a shift on the part of all students. For example, some might already have a high interest in the study of venereal diseases even before we begin studying the unit. Obviously if a student ranked his or her interest in this area "1" on the attitude inventory given before the unit was taught, there could be no positive shift (indicating a change toward a lower number) on the attitude inventory given at the conclusion of the unit. If we had decided that we had a personal interest in prompting students' interest in the study of venereal diseases, our real concern would be to have in hand some evidence that, by the conclusion of the unit, a good many youngsters had developed a greater relative interest in the area than they had had before.

But clearly we would not expect all youngsters to express a high preference for learning about venereal diseases. Nothing would be wrong with students who prized more highly some of the other areas mentioned. Students do, after all, have varied interests. Regardless of how individual students responded, the general profile of students' attitudes regarding the area or areas (in this case, venereal diseases) that we consider important is useful to us as we think through what we did during those sections of the unit that we personally considered to be priority material. If we are displeased with the general way in which students seem to be feeling about this priority material, we may well wish to consider some revisions in our methodologies for introducing this material when teaching the unit again.

In summary, instructional objectives in the affective domain focus properly on students' reactions to the instructional program. Information about students' values, feelings, and attitudes that is derived through the use of affective instructional objectives should never be used for grading. The information is for the use of the teacher as he or she considers the impact of his or her program (or of selected parts of this program) on students' attitudes. This information can provide a basis for productive revision of instructional practices. (For further discussion, see Box 5.7.)

Instructional Objectives in the Psychomotor Domain

The psychomotor domain includes behaviors that require coordination of the body's muscular system. Specific behaviors in this area can range from activities such as running that require intensive use of large muscles to precision-drawing activities that require good control of the body's fine muscle systems. The degree to which an individual teacher

Box 5.7

Teaching Values, Attitudes, and Feelings in Schools

Recently, a school board heard testimony from citizens regarding whether or not the school program should include instruction directed at teaching certain values, attitudes, and feelings to students. Among the speakers were Ms. Johnson and Mr. Kirby. An abbreviated version of their remarks appears below.

Ms. Johnson: The schools have no business getting into the area of values, attitudes, and feelings. This whole area smacks of indoctrination. Even though we may be told that the objective is to help students understand their own feelings, what is certain to happen is that certain values, attitudes, and feelings will be identified as "right" or "correct." While I have no quarrel with the motives of teachers and administrators, I don't feel they should ever be allowed to "play God" and make clearly judgmental comments regarding very personal values, feelings, and attitudes of individual students. This whole area is something the schools should simply stay out of. It simply is not the business of the schools to poke away at students' individual differences by prying into their personal values and, by implication, weighing those values on some scale of relative merit devised by a teacher, a principal, or some other bureaucrat employed by the school system.

Mr. Kirby: Of course we should be concerned about teaching students certain values, attitudes, and feelings. The idea that we are all so individualistic, so different from one another is simple poppycock. There are certain key values that keep us from acting like barbarians. For example, is there anyone in this room who does not believe that murder is a bad thing? Shouldn't we pass this value on to our young people? Can we depend on parents to do the whole job for us without some reinforcement from the schools? I think not. We need to put a stop to this nonsense that the principle of individualism knows no boundaries. Carried to its logical extreme, this position can be used to justify the most outrageous kinds of behaviors. Do we really want a generation who, in reading about the Holocaust, can shrug their shoulders and say, "Oh, well, Hitler was just doing his thing." In my view, we can't allow such unsupportable logic to go unchallenged. We must teach values, attitudes, and feelings in the schools.

What Do You Think?

Read the comments above. Then, respond to these questions.

1. What strengths do you find in Ms. Johnson's comments? What weaknesses?

2. What strengths do you find in Mr. Kirby's comments? What weaknesses?

3. Suppose that you had been asked to state your position before the school board. What would you have said?

may have a need for instructional objectives in the psychomotor domain depends on the extent to which intended learning outcomes require students to demonstrate motor control (control of the body's muscular systems).

In preparing instructional objectives in the psychomotor domain, we can use the same ABCD format introduced earlier. Objectives in this area can be sequenced in terms of increasing difficulty by reference to four stages or levels of psychomotor activity. The simplest of these stages is level 1, the level of awareness. Somewhat akin to the cognitive level of knowledge, awareness demands only that a student be able to describe correctly the movements that need to be made to properly complete a muscular activity.

At level 2, the individual components level, the student is able to correctly demonstrate individual parts of a complex muscular activity. At level 3, the level of integration, the student can perform the entire muscular activity, including all necessary components, with some teacher guidance. Finally, at level 4, the free practice level, the student can perform the muscular activity correctly, in numerous settings, and without any prompting from the teacher. In general, students who achieve level 4 psychomotor objectives can be thought of as having complete mastery of the targeted muscular behavior. Some examples of performance objectives for each of these psychomotor levels follow.

Level 1: Awareness Each student will describe to the teacher, with no errors, the specific hand motions necessary to tie knots needed in preparing a completed Royal Coachman dry fly.
Each student will describe to the teacher, with no errors, the specific foot position changes that occur from beginning to end in a sequence of discus throwing.

Level 2: Individual components Each student, on request, will tie whatever knot called for, with no errors, that represents one knot needed in the preparation of a Royal Coachman dry fly.
Each student will demonstrate, upon the teacher's request and without error, the feet positioning that is correct for a given point in the discus-throwing sequence.

Level 3: Integration Each student will prepare, with some teacher guidance permitted, a complete Royal Coachman dry fly that includes all defining criteria for a dry fly of this type.
Each student will complete a discus throw that includes appropriate feet positioning at each phase of the activity with some teacher guidance permitted.

Level 4: Free practice Each student will prepare, with no supervision from or guidance by the teacher and on several occasions, at least five Royal Coachman dry flies that include all defining criteria for a dry fly of this type.

Each student will complete, with no teacher supervision or guidance and on several occasions, at least six discus throws characterized by appropriate feet positioning at each phase of the activity.

Teachers who wish to prepare objectives in this area need good diagnostic information about students' levels of psychomotor development. If students are asked to perform at levels that are far in excess of their ability levels, many will refuse to try out of a belief they are "beaten before they start."

Key Ideas in Summary

1. Selection of content is a problem many teachers face. It is not recommended that teachers blindly follow the content selection and organization of the course textbook. Such an approach fails to take advantage of the special knowledge teachers have about their own students and settings.

2. One procedure for breaking down academic content requires identification of four major content levels. These are (a) topics, (b) goals, (c) generalizations, and (d) concepts.

3. Instructional objectives state what students are expected to be able to do as a result of instruction. They provide a basis for teacher planning of the instructional program. There are three general categories of learning for which instructional objectives ordinarily are prepared. These are (a) cognitive-domain learning, (b) affective-domain learning, and (c) psychomotor-domain learning.

4. Cognitive-domain learning includes academic or subject-matter content learning. A framework for distinguishing various levels of cognitive learning difficulty has been identified. Known informally as Bloom's Cognitive Taxonomy (Bloom 1966), this system provides teachers with a means of scaling the difficulty of their cognitive-domain objectives. In general, less instructional time is required to prepare students for mastery of lower-level cognitive-domain objectives than for higher-level cognitive-domain objectives.

5. Affective-domain learning focuses on values, attitudes, and feelings. Care must be exercised in this area to assure that students are not subjected to irresponsible indoctrination. Our pluralistic society rejects efforts to suppress individual differences through systematic imposition of a static set of "approved" values. On the other hand,

teachers do have a legitimate interest in knowing about students' attitudes toward their course work. Instructional objectives in the affective domain that are designed to provide this information are worthwhile. Information gained about students as a consequence on affective-domain objectives should be regarded as confidential information for the teacher's use alone. Under no circumstances should performance on affective-domain objectives play a role in determination of students' grades.

6. Psychomotor domain objectives focus on behaviors related to students' control of the body's muscular systems. They often are developed to guide instruction in such areas as physical education, crafts, and in other activities where successful performance requires skilled applications of the large and fine muscle systems.

POSTTEST

DIRECTIONS: Using your own paper, answer the following true/false questions. For each correct statement, write the word "true." For each incorrect statement, write the word "false."

_____ 1. All districts provide curriculum guides for teachers to follow.

_____ 2. Instructional objectives that focus on students' attitudes are affective-domain objectives.

_____ 3. Instructional objectives that focus on development of students' fine motor skills are generally classified as psychomotor-domain objectives.

_____ 4. There should be a clear relationship between instructional objectives and what a teacher does in the classroom.

_____ 5. Verbs such as "appreciate," "know," and "understand" are among those that are most recommended for use in instructional objectives.

Bibliography

BLOCK, JAMES H. "Student Learning and the Setting of Mastery Performance Standards." *Educational Horizons* (Summer 1972), pp. 183–191.

BLOOM, BENJAMIN S. (ED.). *Taxonomy of Educational Objectives: Handbook I: The Cognitive Domain.* New York: David McKay Inc., 1956.

FERRE, ALVIN VICTOR. "Effects of Repeated Performance Objectives upon Student Achievement and Attitude." Ed. D. dissertation. New Mexico State University, 1972.

GOOD, THOMAS L. AND BROPHY, JERE. E. *Looking In Classrooms*. 4th ed. New York: Harper and Row, Publishers, 1987.

GRONLUND, NORMAN E. *Stating Objectives for Classroom Instruction*. 3rd ed. New York: Macmillan Publishing Company, 1985.

HARROW, ANITA J. *A Taxonomy of the Psychomotor Domain*. New York: David McKay Company, Inc., 1972.

KRATHWOHL, DAVID; BLOOM, BENJAMIN S.; AND MASIA, BERTRAM B. *Taxonomy of Educational Objectives: Handbook II: Affective Domain*. New York: David McKay Company, Inc., 1964.

MAGER, ROBERT F. *Developing Attitudes toward Learning*. 2nd ed. Belmont, California: David S. Lake, 1984.

MAGER, ROBERT F. *Preparing Instructional Objectives*. 2nd rev. ed. Belmont, California: David S. Lake, 1984.

MORSE, JEAN A. AND TILLMAN, MURRAY H. "Achievement as Affected by Possession of Behavioral Objectives." *Engineering Education* (June 1973), pp. 124–126.

OLSEN, ROBERT C. "The Effects of Behavioral Objectives on Class Performance and Retention in Physical Science." *Journal of Research in Science Teaching*, no. 3 (1973). pp. 271–277.

POPHAM, W. JAMES. "Instructional Objectives Benefit Teaching and Testing." *Momentum* (May 1987), pp. 11–16.

RATHS, LOUIS; HARMIN, MERRILL; AND SIMON, SIDNEY B. *Values and Teaching*, 2nd ed. Columbus, Ohio: Charles E. Merrill Publishing Company, 1978.

ROKEACH, MILTON. *Understanding Values: Human and Societal*. New York: Free Press, 1979.

SIMPSON, E. J. "The Classification of Educational Objectives Psychomotor Domain," *Illinois Teacher of Home Economics* (Winter 1966), pp. 110–144.

TANNER, DAVID E. "Achievement as a Function of Abstractness and Cognitive Level." *Journal of Research and Development in Education* (Winter 1988), pp. 16–21.

TRAVERS, ROBERT M. "Unresolved Issues in Defining Educational Goals." *Educational Theory* (Winter 1987), pp. 29–41.

CHAPTER 6

Motivating Students

AIMS

This chapter provides information to help the reader to:

1. Identify important components of motivation.
2. Point out the motivational role of physiological needs.
3. List psychological needs that must be accommodated in the class-room.
4. Describe how teacher expectations influence students' motivation.
5. Suggest how the identification motive might be used to increase student's motivation.
6. Describe the relationship between students' perceptions of a task's difficulty and their motivation to accomplish the task.
7. List several ways a teacher can utilize success as a means of motivating learners.
8. Point out the relationship between locus of control and the use of success in motivating students.

PRETEST

DIRECTIONS: Using your own paper, answer these true/false questions. For each correct statement, write the word "true." For each incorrect statement, write the word "false."

_____ 1. Teachers 20 or more years ago had few complaints about students' levels of motivation.

_____ 2. As levels of student motivation in a class increase, there is a tendency for the number of misbehavior incidents to decrease.

_____ 3. Students who sense that their needs are being met in the classroom tend not to become discipline problems for teachers.

_____ 4. Successful experiences in the classroom tend to build students' self-esteem and to result in higher levels of motivation to do well in school.

_____ 5. Motivation associated with novelty tends to be short lived.

Introduction

Terry Brown had always wanted to be a teacher. He remembered well those teachers who had inspired him. One or two English teachers had opened his eyes to literature. His appreciation of the world and the human condition had grown tremendously as a result. As a new teacher, he had hoped his enthusiasm would be "catching" and that his students would develop a commitment to literature that was as deep and compelling as his own.

In spite of his enthusiasm, in spite of planning that frequently kept him up beyond midnight, in spite of his high expectations, things were not going well. Many class members simply did not seem to care about learning. Certainly few of them were exhibiting any flashes of insight as they slogged their way through their assignments. Many students seemed to make fun of Terry's interest in English. Some of them openly questioned the relevance of the subject by asking such questions as: "Why do we have to read this stuff? If it's not going to be on the test, why should I read it? How will English help me get a better job? Why can't we just see the movie rather than read the book?"

Terry had envisioned classes filled with students who were stimulated about what they were reading and eager to discuss complex ideas. Instead, he had found a world of indifference where assignments were done reluctantly and without interest. Terry did not remember students being like this when he was in school. Had they changed? Box 6.1 presents some questions for exploring motivation.

Box 6.1

Exploring Motivation

Our own experiences can be a beginning point for understanding motivation. Take a few moments to look over the following questions.

1. What attracted you to the idea of becoming a secondary school teacher?

2. Why do you want to teach the subject you have selected as your major area of interest?

3. Did anyone influence you to want to become a teacher? If so, who was this person? How did he or she influence you?

4. Would you still want to go into teaching if a doctoral degree were required before you could be certified?

5. Would you continue in your teacher preparation program if you learned that only the top 10 percent would be recommended for certification?

Share your answers with others in your class. Drawing on experiences mentioned by class members, try to identify some general variables that seem to be associated with motivation.

The circumstances faced by Terry are not unusual. New teachers frequently complain that today's students are not as motivated as students used to be. This is a mistaken impression. Unmotivated learners have been a concern of educators for generations. Because Terry was a motivated and successful learner when he was a secondary school student, he may not have noticed the large numbers of unmotivated individuals in his classes. This is a common problem among beginning teachers. They tend to believe their experiences in school were "typical." In fact, as individuals who generally performed better than the average student, they probably were not particularly representative members of their classes. New teachers' surprise at students' levels of interest does not result from changes in average students. Rather, it comes about because, for the first time, new teachers are confronted with the entire spectrum of secondary school students.

The label "unmotivated" is misleading because it suggests that the student is unmotivated in a general sense. Everyone is motivated to do something. It is just that many young people are not particularly motivated to do those things required of them in secondary schools. Though most classes have some students who do demonstrate an interest in what they are studying, most teachers wish larger numbers of their students felt this way.

"I'll sure say one thing for that new Economics teacher. He sure lowered *my* interest rate!"

Despite their professed interest in increasing students' motivational levels, research suggests that relatively few teachers take specific steps toward this end (Brophy 1987). For example, in one study investigators found that fewer than five percent of teachers took time to explain the purposes of their presentations to students. Another study found that none of the teachers who were observed did anything to suggest to students that they might derive some personal satisfaction from learning the material. In one long-term investigation that included classroom observations totaling over 100 hours of teaching time, only nine instances were recorded of teachers specifically trying to motivate students as they introduced new learning tasks (Brophy 1987, p. 203).

The lack of attention to motivation is somewhat surprising. There is evidence of an important relationship between motivation and classroom management problems. As motivational levels increase, the incidence of discipline problems tends to decrease. One reason relatively few teachers seem to take direct action to increase motivational levels is that they lack information about variables associated with motivation. In recent years, researchers have identified a number of these variables. This chapter introduces a number of them that successful teachers use to build students' interest in school subjects.

Motivational Variables

Researchers have found that three basic forces influence individuals' willingness to expend effort on a specific task. These include (1) the unique interests and needs of the individual, (2) the perceived difficulty of the task, and (3) the individual's perception of th likelihood of success (Klinger 1977, p. 304).

Needs and interests are important motivational factors because they attract individuals' attention and focus their energies. Learners are attracted to activities that they view as having potential to meet unmet needs or that appear "interesting." People have a limited amount of time and energy. Therefore, they are forced to make decisions about how they commit these scarce personal resources. The economic term "opportunity cost" aptly describes this situation. When people choose one option they give up the opportunity of choosing others. They tend to select alternatives that they see as providing the greatest personal benefit at the least "cost."

What all of this suggests is that teachers need to identify the needs and interests of their students. This information can help them motivate learners. But, motivation does not automatically follow a teacher's discovery that students are interested in a topic. There are many levels of interest. For example, football stadiums fill up on Saturday afternoons in the fall. Fans have sufficient interest in the game to drive from their homes, pay for tickets, and cheer for their favorite team. Relatively few of them, though, have sufficient interest in the game to play it actively. Even young people who are in excellent physical condition often do not care to play football even though they may be avid fans of local teams.

Active participation reflects a motivation that goes well beyond interest. It requires a commitment to expend a level of personal effort.

Some students who are genuinely interested in certain school subjects are not sufficiently motivated to master them because they believe too much effort is required. This suggests that teachers must pay close attention to students' perceptions of task difficulty.

Closely related to students' perceptions of task difficulty is their estimation of their personal probability of success. Many students are convinced that no matter how great an effort they might expend, some learning tasks are too difficult for them to master. Hence, they are reluctant to try. In attempting to overcome this perception, teachers try to assure each learner that he or she has a real opportunity for success. Learners must be convinced that they can do the work. This is especially true with students who have had a long history of failure. School has "taught" them to avoid trying. Their battered self-esteem cannot stand the threat of additional failure.

Typically, motivational levels within a given classroom vary tremendously from student to student. Some students will be both motivated and willing to commit the time and energy required to succeed at assigned tasks. Regardless of what is being taught, some individuals will be convinced that the topic fails to meet any of their personal needs or interests. Others may be mildly interested, but also convinced that

Teachers who seem to "care" and who communicate sincerely tend to be good motivators.

too much effort is needed to learn the new material. Still others may have experienced so much failure during their school years that they are unwilling under almost any circumstances to do the required work. The barriers standing in the way of active student commitment to learning tasks suggest that teachers must pay close attention to motivation. They need to focus concurrently on issues related to students' interests, perceptions of task difficulty, and belief in the likelihood of personal success.

Student Needs and Interests

As noted previously, students tend to feel more positively toward topics and activities that they feel are meeting personal needs or to be intrinsically interesting. There is also a relationship between instruction that is responsive to students' needs and discipline problems. Students who sense their needs are being met in the classroom rarely cause discipline problems. This is true because interfering with something that is meeting a need is not in their own self-interest. Glasser (1986, p. 15) emphasizes this point in his description of a good school:

> A good school could be defined as a place where almost all students believe that if they do some work, they will be able to satisfy their needs enough so that it makes sense to keep working.

Glasser suggests that many school problems arise because educators incorrectly assume that all students want to learn what is taught. This assumption, he argues, is false. It fails to consider whether individual students find the provided instruction to be personally satisfying.

Teachers have a number of options open to them as they consider ways to fit school experiences more closely to students' needs and interests. Among teacher responses are those directed at students' physiological, psychological, and social needs.

Physiological Needs

Physiological needs are so fundamental that they must be accommodated before other needs can be considered. Among physiological needs that must be met are food, rest, physical comfort, freedom from illness, movement, and stimulation of the senses. Teachers are not in a position to accommodate all of these needs. However, they should be familiar with them because, when unmet, students may reflect little interest in their school work. In some instances, these students may be difficult to control.

Many youngsters come to school who have not eaten properly. In some cases, there is insufficient food at home. In others, students have chosen improper foods. In both instances, inadequate nutrition is the result. A lack of a proper diet can result in patterns of classroom behavior characterized by an inability to stay on task. Some research suggests that nutritional variables lay an important role in behavior disorders and violence (Schauss 1985, p. 21). An appreciation of the importance of proper nutrition has led to the establishment of free and reduced-price breakfast and lunch programs in schools.

Physical comfort of students is another important consideration. Modern schools keep interior temperatures at acceptable levels and feature excellent lighting systems. There are other environmental variables that may also contribute to students' comfort. For example, chairs and desks may not be the appropriate size for all students in a class. Such conditions interfere with students' abilities to concentrate. Physical discomfort demands relief. This relief sometimes comes in the form of highly disruptive classroom behavior.

All people have a need for sensory stimulation. Senses of hearing, sight, and feeling must be stimulated for the brain to receive messages that can be translated into information. Sensory deprivation is painful. Headaches and other physical manifestations of deprivation may occur. People who experience severe sensory deprivation may even hallucinate. Above all, sensory deprivation leads to boredom. Bored students seek relief. Often it comes in the form of unacceptable classroom behavior.

In summary, physiological needs of learners must be met before learners' attention can be drawn to the demands of learning tasks. When teachers fail to satisfy basic physiological needs, behavior problems may result. Under these circumstances, students almost always find it difficult to learn. Box 6.2 discusses the issue of meeting students' physiological needs.

Psychological Needs

All people have emotional and psychological needs. People want to feel accepted, loved, and respected. Glasser (1969) pointed out that school is one of the few places where young people have opportunities to feel significant and important. When schools nurture these attitudes, students tend to commit to both the school itself and the instructional programs it offers.

Box 6.2

Physiological Needs

Physiological needs constitute an important motivational variable. Unless these needs are met, students will find it difficult to generate enthusiasm for the school program. Learning is hard when people feel uncomfortable.

What Do You Think?

1. From your own past experiences, can you cite some examples of secondary schools' failure to pay attention to students' physiological needs?

2. Suppose you had students in your classes whose height varied by over two feet. What physiological problems might they face in your classroom? What might you do to resolve them?

3. Do you believe that the typical high school schedule of daily class adequately considers students' physiological needs? Why, or why not?

4. What are some things you as a teacher might do in your own classroom to accommodate students' needs for sensory stimulation?

Security is a major psychological need. People need to feel that they are safe from physical danger. In some schools, students have concerns about their safety. A common cause of absenteeism in junior and senior high schools is fear of physical injury. School leaders are aware of this situation. In some places, rather drastic actions have had to be taken to assure students' safety. For example, a few schools have installed metal detectors at building entrances to eliminate the possibility of students bringing weapons into their classrooms.

Though physical danger to students is a severe problem in a few schools, a much more pervasive difficulty facing students has to do with their psychological serenity. Students need to feel that they are emotionally safe in the school environment. Many students fear failure and ridicule. This can result in psychological intimidation. In its most serious manifestations, this can block learning. Teachers work hard to assure students that they are people of worth. They try to establish a warm supportive classroom environment. In short, they work to build students' self-esteem.

A person's self-esteem consists of a collection of subjective beliefs about who he or she is and what he or she can do. Individuals' self-esteem is influenced by the "mirror of others." The way people respond to us tells us much about what they think. From this information, we develop a self-portrait. Teachers are among individuals to whom young people look for cues as they form their own self-portraits. For this reason, teachers have a special obligation to help students develop images of themselves as worthy, competent people.

Teachers' expectations of what learners can do provide important information to students. Some researchers have found that students are very much aware that teachers have different expectations for different students (Weinstein 1985). Students consider how the teacher seems to be viewing them as they engage in self-analysis. Results of this self analysis can affect how they perform in the classroom. Good and Brophy (1987) have suggested that teachers' expectations of a given student initiate a predictable cycle. Steps in this cycle are as follows:

1. The teacher formulates an opinion about what a given student can do.

2. The teacher proceeds to act toward this student in a manner consistent with this opinion.

3. The teacher's behavior communicates to the student how he or she is expected to act or perform.

4. In time, the achievement, motivation, and classroom conduct of the student begins to conform to the teacher's expectations.

5. The teacher, viewing the student's behavior, becomes convinced that his or her original opinion was correct.

The self-esteem of individuals guides their responses to situations they face in their day-to-day lives. Individuals with high self-esteem tend to approach tasks with more confidence and expectations of success than those with low self-esteem. People with high self-esteem are inclined to take more risks because they are less fearful of failure. Low self-esteem individuals demonstrate more anxiety, stress, and apathy when approaching new tasks than do high self-esteem individuals.

Success experiences tend to improve students' levels of self-esteem. Success breeds feelings of adequacy and competence. A few misinformed teachers believe that students should experience failure because it somehow "prepares them for life." In fact, the best preparation for the challenges of adult living are school experiences that build self-confidence through success. Effective teachers work hard to assure that students in their classes experience success. Successful experiences on one learning task tend to give learners the emotional support to commit their energies to the next one. A series of successes can result in greatly enhanced levels of self-esteem.

Teachers have a particular stake in using school-based experiences to build students' self-esteem. The drive to establish self-worth is very strong. If students can achieve this in connection with their classroom activities, they tend to commit to the agendas of the teacher and the school. If they find that teachers and the school are not supportive of their self-esteem, they may seek other ways to establish their own sense of self worth. In some cases, these alternatives can result in undesirable classroom behaviors.

Social Needs

The classroom is a social setting. Much of what happens here to students relates to their efforts to be accepted by and belong to a group. Dreikurs (1968) pointed out that the need to belong is one of the most basic human needs. Secondary school students spend a good deal of time striving to become part of the "in" group. When young people are frustrated in their attempts to be accepted by their peers, they sometimes manifest behaviors that cause teachers problems. For example, they may seek peer approval by challenging authority figures such as the teacher.

The need to belong is a manifestation of a broader need for love and affection. All people feel better about themselves when they believe others love and care about them. In times past, the extended family provided a strong support network for its members. In today's mobile society, many individuals live at great distances from other family members. A majority of the students in school come from either single-parent homes or homes where both parents work. Many young people do not enjoy the emotional support at home that they would like to have.

Some students look to their teachers for emotional support. This places teachers in a difficult position. They have many roles to play in the school. They cannot serve as substitute parents. However, they can be sensitive to students' needs for support and can provide support, as appropriate.

Interests

All people have certain interests in addition to those related to meeting their basic needs. Students are more motivated when classroom tasks are organized in ways that tie content to these interests. For example, a group of 15-year-olds in a developmental reading class may not get excited about reading material on pistacio nut cultivation in Turkey. On the other hand, members of the group may eagerly consume materials discussing content to be covered on the state's driver's license exam.

There are some general principles that are useful to teachers who wish to organize content to respond to students' interests. One principle is the "identification motive." The identification motive suggests that people generally attempt to increase their similarity to or identification with individuals who are perceived to be "important." Important people are those who are viewed as having desirable characteristics. Among these characteristics are (a) attractive physical features, (b) popularity with others, (c) monetary wealth, (d) athletic competence, and (e) political power. Students who are attracted to people having one or more of these characteristics try to emulate them in some ways. At the secondary school level, this is often seen in students' dress. Styles often imitate those of popular music or film stars.

The identification motive sometimes works to the advantage and sometimes to the disadvantage of teachers. If the person with whom students identify has characteristics consistent with the instructional program, the identification motive may prompt students to study harder. This might occur, for example, if a student identified with a leading astronomer or with someone else whose prominence reflected the importance of sound academic training. On the other hand, the contribution of study and schooling to the success of the leader of a heavy-metal-oriented rock group is less clear. A student identifying with this kind of person may not be inclined to take school work seriously.

In addition to the "affiliation motive," student interest is often prompted by things that are novel and different. Information that is unusual or unexpected will draw the interest of most students; at least it will for a short period of time. Generally, the impact of novelty is short lived. Motivation associated with novelty fades quickly unless other elements in the learning task attract students' interest. (see Box 6.3.)

Accommodating Needs and Interests in the Classroom

Teachers behave in different ways when responding to varying kinds of student needs. Successful teacher actions require time and hard work. However, when needs and interests are accommodated, teachers enjoy a number of benefits. Discipline problems are likely to be reduced. Students' levels of involvement are likely to be greater. In short, the general atmosphere of the classroom may be much more satisfying to both teacher and students.

Accommodating Physiological Needs

A high priority in this area is establishing a safe and comfortable classroom environment. Creating a safe school requires the cooperation of

Box 6.3

Responding to Students' Interests

Students' levels of motivation often increase when teachers are able to relate topics being studied to students' own interests. Some topics are more easily connected to students' interests than others. But some lessons in nearly every content area can be organized in this way.

What Do You Think?

1. Who are some people who are popular among secondary school students? Are there ways students' interests in these people can be tied to school subjects?

2. What are some specific things you might do to tie instruction in your subject area to students' interests?

3. Can you identify some specific ways you could use novelty to prompt students' interest in some aspects of a topic you might teach?

4. How might you use the identification motive to prompt students' interest in what you are teaching?

---

local community members as well as school teachers and administrators. Principals need to exercise leadership to involve parents and other community members. Community participation is especially important in developing plans to assure safe, hassle-free movement of students from their homes to the school.

Teachers and building administrators have primary responsibility for providing a safe, secure environment within the building. One desirable step involves a reduction to a bare minimum of those areas within the school that might be described as "neutral turf." Neutral turf includes parts of the building where no individual or group has a clear sense of ownership or responsibility. These include such places as hallways, restrooms, cafeterias, and open areas outside the main school buildings. Plans need to be implemented to monitor these areas and to stop inappropriate behavior when it occurs. Students need to feel safe when they pass through or use these parts of the school environment.

There is more to the issue of physiological needs than personal safety and security. Individuals have a need for active movement. People need sensory stimulation. They need adequate light to accomplish reading and writing tasks. Chairs should be of the appropriate size. Tables and other work surfaces should be stable. Teachers and administrators can work together to modify classroom environments that do not lend themselves to accommodating these needs.

Accommodating Psychological Needs

A major ingredient in creating a safe a productive psychological environment is the attitude of the teacher. Does the teacher accept and support all of the students in the class? Does the teacher believe that all students are capable of learning? Are high expectations set for all students? Do the teacher's responses to discipline problems reflect a respect for students' dignity? If the answer to questions such as these is "yes," then there is a high probability that the classroom's psychological environment is positive.

Teachers are in a position of leadership. They have major responsibilities for modeling desirable patterns of social behavior. If students are expected to be respectful of one another and of the teacher, then the teacher must be respectful toward students. Teachers who, themselves, are disrespectful set a negative classroom tone. Negative teachers promote negative patterns of student behavior.

The question of teacher expectations deserves special mention. Researchers consistently report that students perform better and feel more personally adequate when teachers set high expectations and hold students to them (Good and Brophy 1987). Some teachers find it useful to bring observers into their classrooms to note the pattern of their interactions with students. They are particularly interested in learning whether they are setting expectations at appropriate levels for all students in their classes. Discussions with the observers and a review of the observation notes provide information that teachers can use to assess the adequacy of their expectations.

Some secondary students do not understand how they should act to become part of a group. Though they may want acceptance, their patterns of behavior sometimes interfere with their goal of gaining acceptance. Teachers have a special responsibility to help these students see the connection between their behavior and the reluctance of other students to welcome them. Sensitive, personal discussions sometimes result in changed behavior patterns that help individual students to be more broadly accepted by others. When students sense they are "part of the group," they feel better about themselves. An improvement in self-concept is often associated with improved behavior and better academic achievement.

Students tend to feel better about teachers and learning when they play a role in making some classroom decisions. Participation in the decision-making process increases their sense of "ownership" in the instructional program. Teachers need to identify areas where student decision-making is appropriate. The specific areas selected will vary greatly, depending on such variables as students' age, nature of the subject being taught, and teachers' personalities. One common area teachers select for student decision-making is assignments. Provision of alternative assignments allows the teacher to retain basic control of the available assignment options. Allowing students to choose from among these alternatives allows them to make judgments, and it promotes a feeling that they have some personal control over their learning.

Accommodating Social Needs and Interests

Cooperative learning approaches represent one way to accommodate students' social needs in the classroom. Cooperative learning approaches provide incentives for students to work together. They encourage students to draw on special abilities of group members. They build students' confidence by strongly supporting their contributions to the overall group effort. A number of models for cooperative learning have been developed. Several of these are discussed in detail in Chapter 8, "Learning in Groups."

As noted previously, the identification motive strongly influences the behavior of many students. It is to be expected that students may emulate behaviors of many different kinds of people. Often this is reflected in how they dress. In general, schools should be quite broad-minded in standards set for dress and grooming. Unless certain kinds of dress and patterns of grooming can be demonstrated to interfere with the learning process or to pose a danger to students, specific regulations on these issues should not be a high priority of educators.

Schools that ignore the strength of the identification motive by imposing extremely strict standards of dress suggest to students that the school is a place that is out of touch with reality. Capricious and arbitrary standards may communicate to students that school authorities are more concerned with exercising their authority than with students' interests and needs.

In addition to using restraint in the area of dress and grooming standards, teachers can respond to the importance of the identification motive by integrating selected aspects of popular culture into their classroom learning tasks. For example, a physics teacher in a unit on sound might focus on the physical properties of the sounds produced by a popular rock star. A social studies teacher might incorporate the study of the biographies of popular young politicians with whom some students might identify. Certainly, teachers have a responsibility to transmit the essential contents of their courses. There is no suggestion here that this obligation be disregarded in an effort to create lessons that only pander to student' affiliation needs. The idea is simply to take advantage of the identification motive when lessons can be developed that focus on legitimate academic content at the same time they respond to important student needs and interests.

Students' interest is often stimulated when teachers introduce a puzzling event. Puzzling situations challenge students' existing ideas and motivate them to fit this new information into their prior understanding of reality. Teachers do not have a ready supply of puzzling events that are suitable for lessons in all subject areas and on all topics. But, when this information is available and relevant to what is being studied, it can be a powerful motivating influence.

Perception of Effort Required

This dimension of motivation poses real challenges for teachers. It forces them to view new content not as they see it, but rather as their students may see it. In their own student days, many teachers were successful learners. Many of them were quite willing to tackle school assignments. As teachers, they find themselves working with many students who have not had a history of success in school. Some of these students may consider an assignment that, in the teacher's mind, is not challenging at all to be beyond their capabilities. To avoid what they perceive to be certain failure, some of these students will be reluctant even to attempt the assigned work.

Students who feel incompetent to complete assigned work have arrived at this conclusion for many reasons. Some students may lack the resources to complete an assignment at the same level of excellence as students who command more resources. For example, suppose a history teacher assigned a class to write a term paper contrasting alternate explanations for the outbreak of World War I. Some students may be in a position to draw on a wealth of information. Other students, who are unable to use information other that that available in the meager holdings of the school library, may perceive themselves to be set up for failure. Some of them may refuse to do the assignment. When teachers make assignments, this situation suggests the importance of considering whether all students will have equal access to needed learning resources.

Perceptions of task difficulty certainly are not limited to concerns about access to needed materials. In a more general sense, students' views about the potential difficulty of an assignment relate to their perceptions of (a) what the basic task is, (b) the adequacy of their preparation for the task, and (c) the expected length of the work to be completed.

In dealing with the first of these concerns, teachers must take care to explain clearly to students what they are to do. A student's view that a given assignment is "impossible" may well be the result of a faulty understanding of the teacher's expectations.

In making an assignment, teachers need to highlight the relevance of previous learning to what is to be done. When students understand that they have the necessary background to complete an assignment successfully, they are much more willing to do it. Teachers' reassurance to students that they have mastered the appropriate prerequisites make them more willing to attempt the assigned work.

The issue of assignment length is a difficult one. Many beginning teachers are surprised to find that assignments they consider to be quite brief are viewed by some students as impossibly long. This is particularly likely to be the case when students are asked to write short papers. For some students, a request that they write two pages is seen as unreasonable.

In responding to the length issue, the teacher needs to help students realize that time required to complete the task will not be excessive. Sometimes students feel better when the teacher takes time to model some of the activities that the assignment will require. For example, in the case of a two-page paper, the teacher might use an overhead projector and a transparency to write a page or so of copy. When the job is complete, the teacher might say something like this: "Notice that it took only about five minutes to write one page. I know it might take you just a little longer. But, you won't need to spend even as much as a half hour to complete the entire assignment."

Perceptions of task difficulty will vary greatly from student to student. Individuals who have generally been successful in school tolerate, even welcome, tasks that require a good deal of work. On the other hand, students with long histories of failure resist doing tasks that are not particularly challenging. In responding to these differences, teachers need to consider the possibility of varying assignments.

The idea is not to let some students off easy. Rather, the objective is to assure that all students actually do the assignments that are assigned. Little benefit accrues to the student who, when confronted with a very difficult assignment, simply fails to do it. Ideally, assignments are pegged at levels that present students with tasks that are legitimately challenging, but not so challenging that they refuse to do them.

Analyzing the Difficulty of Tasks

There are several general steps a teacher can take to help students understand how much effort is required to complete a given task successfully. The first step involves an informal "task analysis." In task analysis, the teacher works to break down an assigned task into its individual parts. Once all relevant sub-tasks have been identified, the teacher arranges them in a logical sequence. This sequence provides a general route to completion of the contemplated assignment.

The next step calls on the teacher to assess individual students' backgrounds. Some students may already have mastered some of the sub-tasks associated with the assignment. Others may have no prior knowledge related to any of them. The purpose of this step is to identify the appropriate entry point for each student.

The third step involves actual presentation of the assignment to the class. The overall assignment is presented as well as the ordered list of sub-tasks. Individual students, based on the teacher's diagnosis of their abilities, are instructed to begin work on sub-tasks that are relevant to their own individual backgrounds. This scheme attempts to fit the assignment to the characteristic of the individual. The idea is to reduce students' perceptions of task difficulty by assigning them to initial sub-tasks that they will be able to complete successfully.

Once students have begun working on an assignment, the teacher needs to provide encouragement. Students should feel free to ask questions. As the assignment is being completed, teachers tend to provide two kinds of feedback. They provide positive support to students who are approaching the task correctly by praising them. Effective praise is not general in nature. It is tied to some specific action that the student has done. ("The first sentence of your paragraph does a fine job of establishing a focus for what follows.")

In addition to supporting appropriate performance, teachers also take care to provide corrective feedback. The purpose of corrective feedback is to draw students' attention to aspects of their work that is not being properly done. Again, the teacher's language needs to be specific. Students must understand exactly what they should do to remedy mistakes.

Probability of Success

This last motivational factor relates to students' personal assessment of their chances of doing a satisfactory job on an assigned task. All people have a need to feel personally competent. Students share this common human psychological condition.

In school settings, competence is likely to be most motivating when it is associated with an area that is highly valued. For example, if a student is fond of athletics and indifferent to auto mechanics, he or she may be more motivated by a newly found ability to climb a rope than by an ability to tune a car engine. In general, achievement in areas that have

Box 6.4

Let Them Fail!

Some critics of secondary education charge that schools coddle students. They condend that "good" high schools are those that are rigorous and difficult. Teachers should not have to motivate students. Students should recognize that they will have to work hard when they come to school. If they are unable to accept the challenges of a rigorous program, they should be prepared to fail. School officials should act quickly to remove such students from school. Their continued presence interferes with the rights of students who *do* want to learn.

What Do You Think?

Read the comments above. Then, respond to these questions.

1. Do you agree that secondary schools tend to "coddle" students?

2. Do you feel that unmotivated students in schools pose a serious threat to quality education?

3. How do you feel about the argument that students should come to school prepared to learn and teachers have no responsibility to motivate them?

4. What do you think would happen if all secondary schools adopted policies consistent with the position reflected in these comments?

---

high status or are associated with individuals students admire are highly motivation. Levels of motivation have a great deal to do with students' willingness to do assigned work. When students sense themselves to be in a situation where they do not trust their own levels of competence, they are not motivated to do the work. Because of unfortunate past academic histories, many secondary school students arrive at school each morning feeling that failure at academic tasks is inevitable.

Students who perceive themselves to have little opportunity for success may "drop out" of any active intellectual engagement with the school program. They may engage in rationalizations for their behavior. Some of them may argue that assignments are "irrelevant." Occasionally students will attempt to discredit the teacher and suggest that he or she has caused their disinterest in the subject. Sometimes these students pose discipline problems for their teachers. (See Box 6.4.)

Psychologists who have studied the impact of success and failure on people's behavior have found that some people have an "internal locus of control" and that others have an "external locus of control." People with an internal locus of control tend to attribute their success or lack of success to their own efforts. Those with an external locus of control tend to believe that success is a matter of luck. If it comes, it is more a matter of chance than of personal action. Factors beyond the control of the individual are thought to determine success or failure.

For people who have a particularly strong external locus of control, success in school may not always be motivating. Such students tend to believe that their own efforts had little to do with their success. They are likely to tell themselves, "I was just lucky this time. There is no use in studying. Next time I may be unlucky." Teachers need to work with these students to help them perceive the connection between their own behavior and their levels of academic success.

Increasing the Probability of Success

Some traditional administrative arrangements in schools are not particularly conducive to motivating students. For example, report card grades rarely are distributed more frequently than once every six weeks. This is too long an interval for good grades to serve a strongly motivating function. Students need more frequent feedback about how they are doing. To some extent, daily and weekly grades and evaluations on projects serve this end. Students need to understand that these short-term evaluations have a logical connection to the longer-term grade that will be awarded at the end of the grading period. If they do not see this connection, they may feel short-term feedback is irrelevant.

Some secondary teachers have found it useful to plot or chart the academic progress of each student. At regular intervals, students have opportunities to see evidence of their progress. These reports provide a continuous record of success. For some students, this is highly motivating information.

It is especially important for students to understand the criteria that will be applied in assessing their progress. Students who understand what they must do to be successful will be more prone to try than those who are uncertain about the requirements. Sometimes these criteria are presented to students in the form of lesson objectives. Sometimes teachers provide students with examples of assigned work that has been completed properly.

Often it is desirable to adjust objectives to meet special student needs. One English teacher had trouble with a student who simply refused to do writing assignments. A discussion with the student revealed a deep-seated fear of failure. The teacher and the student together developed an objective calling on the student to write just five sentences every day. There could be on any topic chosen by the student. It was decided they would be written in a diary.

The teacher examined the diary once a day. Every day, the student saw the teacher award credit for the sentences in the class grade book. Gradually, the student began writing more sentences. By the end of the semester, this person was writing entire pages. One day toward the end of the term, the student asked the teacher, "Do you mind if I start writing more than a page?" This student had learned that it was possible to succeed and that writing could be enjoyable.

The ways teachers mark papers can influence students' feelings about their own levels of competence. It has long been a common practice for teachers to note mistakes when returning student work. Some teachers, with a view to highlighting the positive, mark the correct student answers on true-false, matching, or multiple choice tests. Essay tests are likely to include written praise for especially well written sections.

The nature of the tests, themselves, can influence students' feelings about their probable success. Tests that include trick questions or that focus on minimally important content reinforce some students' perceptions that success is more a matter of luck than of personal effort. Good tests bear a clear relationship to the main points that teachers have introduced. High grades should be a reward for mastery of this material. When they are, test grades can be highly motivating.

Another classroom practice of teachers who recognize the importance of success as a motivator is to summarize what students have learned at the end of the lesson. This procedure helps students to appreciate that they have learned new material and are making good progress.

Key Ideas in Summary

1. Three important variables have been found to be widely associated with levels of student motivation. These are (a) student interests and needs, (b) student perception of the difficulty of a given task, and (c) student expectation of success. Teachers who are good motivators attend carefully to each of these key variables.

2. Students have physiological needs, psychological needs, and social needs. Generally, motivation increases as instruction accommodates one or more of these basic types of needs.

3. The identification motive can be exploited by teachers as they seek to appeal to students' interests. Students want to increase their similarity to people they see as having desirable characteristics or abilities. Sometimes teachers are able to draw important connections between content they are teaching and characteristics of people who serve as models for some of their students.

4. As they seek to motivate students, teachers try to change perceptions of some students that the assigned work is "too difficult."
They remind students of important prerequisite knowledge they
have already acquired, and they take other actions to build students'
feelings of competence.

5. Success is a powerful motivator. This is particularly true when individuals achieve a task that they perceive to be important or relevant.
The importance of success suggests that teachers should strive for
instruction that enables high percentages of students to succeed.

6. These scores and grades can have detrimental effects on motivation
if students see them as being the results of chance rather than of
personal effort. This situation is particularly likely to arise when test
questions fail to focus on major aspects of content that has been
introduced. Test questions that focus on trivial, unimportant points
suggest to students that the testing process is a game, not a serious
attempt to assess what they have learned.

POSTTEST

DIRECTIONS: Using your own paper, answer these true/false questions. For each correct statement, write the word "true." For each incorrect statement, write the word "false."

_____ 1. Researchers have found that most teachers take specific
actions to increase students' levels of motivation.

_____ 2. When students are interested in a given topic, they are always
motivated to do assignments related to the topic.

_____ 3. Some studies have found that improper nutrition plays an
important role in shaping students' behavior at school.

_____ 4. The identification motive suggests that people try to increase
their similarity to others whom they believe to be "important."

_____ 5. Young people who believe their teachers set them up for
failure are not likely to be highly motivated students.

Bibliography

AMES, C. AND AMES, R. (EDS.). *Research on Motivation in Education.* Orlando,
FL: Academic Press, 1985.
BALL, S. *Motivation in Education.* New York: Academic Press, 1977.

BROPHY, JERE. "On Motivating Students." In Berliner, D.C. and Rosenshine, B.V. (eds.). *Talks to Teachers*. New York: Random House, 1987.

DREIKURS, R. *Psychology in the Classroom*. 2nd edition. New York: Harper and Row, 1968.

FANELLI, G. C. "Locus of Control." In Ball, S. (ed.). *Motivation in Education*. New York: Academic Press, 1977.

FEATHER, N. (ED.). *Expectations and Actions*. Hillsdale, NJ: Erlbaum, 1982.

GLASSSER, WILLIAM. *Control Theory in the Classroom*. New York: Harper and Row, 1986.

GLASSER, WILLIAM. *Schools Without Failure*. New York: Harper and Row, 1969.

GOOD, THOMAS AND BROPHY, JERE. *Looking in Classrooms*. 4th edition. New York: Harper and Row, 1987.

KLINGER, E. *Meaning and Void: Inner Experiences and the Incentives in People's Lives*. Minneapolis, MN: University of Minnesota Press, 1977.

MENDLER, A. N. AND CURWIN, R. L. *Taking Charge in the Classroom: A Practical Guide to Effective Discipline*. Reston, VA: Reston Publishing Company, 1983.

SCHAUSS, A. "Research Links Nutrition to Behavior Disorders," School Safety (Winter 1985). pp. 20–28.

WEINER, B. *Human Motivations*. New York: Holt, Rinehart and Winston, 1980.

WEINSTEIN, R. "Student Mediation of Classroom Expectancy Effects." In Dusek, J. (ed.). *Teacher Expectancies*. Hillsdale, NJ: Erlbaum, 1985.

WHITE, M. N. "Effects of Nutrition on Educational Development." In Ball, S. *Motivation in Education*. New York: Academic Press, 1977.

CHAPTER 7

Classroom Management and Control

AIMS

This chapter provides information to help the reader to:

1. Identify the relationship between instruction and classroom management.
2. Suggest some space-management guidelines that should be considered in arranging the classroom.
3. Point out how materials should be organized and managed.
4. Identify routines to promote a smoothly functioning classroom.
5. Describe the basic goal of discipline.
6. Point out the importance of planning for transition points in lessons.
7. List some characteristics of teachers who manage inappropriate behavior effectively.
8. Describe basic principles that might be followed in establishing a plan for discipline.
9. List a range a responses that a teacher might use when responding to inappropriate student behavior.

PRETEST

DIRECTIONS: Using your own paper, answer these true/false questions. For each correct statement, write the word "true." For each incorrect statement, write the word "false."

_____ 1. Though beginning teachers often express concerns about the issue of classroom control, few experienced teachers worry about student misbehavior.

_____ 2. It is always best to place the teacher's desk at the front center of a classroom.

_____ 3. There is evidence that much instructional time is lost in classrooms where teachers have not carefully planned transitions between lesson parts.

_____ 4. Teachers with well established classroom routines are better able to direct their full attention to problem situations than are teachers with poorly established routines.

_____ 5. In responding to a discipline problem, it is important for the teacher to respect the personal dignity of the misbehaving student.

Introduction

One recent student teacher had this initial reaction to the class of ninth graders that trooped into the room at eight o'clock for their English class.

> Many of the them were the antithesis of everything I was raised to believe in. Two of the students were pregnant. Some of them glared at me menacingly. Others put on makeup. I was in a state of shock. This was a totally new scene. It seemed a planet away from the suburban public schools I had attended just a few years before.

Many student teachers are surprised by the tremendous diversity of students with whom they must work. Though they may have had an intellectual appreciation of these differences before, until student teaching begins many fail to appreciate the difficult challenges these differences pose for teachers. As a result, student teachers sometimes experience strong feelings of self-doubt during the first days or weeks of student teaching. Often they have serious concerns about their abilities to manage and control students in their classes.

Issues associated with classroom control are of great concern to experienced teachers as well as beginners. A study commissioned by the National Education Association found that 14.5 percent of the teachers who were surveyed reported that misbehavior interfered to a "great extent" with their ability to teach; 30.4 percent indicated that such misbehavior interfered to a "moderate extent" (Baker 1985, p. 486).

Though problems associated with classroom management and discipline are serious, it is a mistake to conclude that the secondary schools are out of control. Secondary school teachers tend to report less interference with teaching from student misbehavior than do elementary teachers. Kinds of behaviors that secondary teachers are concerned about include some relatively minor problems such as student inattention, talking, tardiness, and missed assignments. More serious behaviors are relatively infrequent. One study reported that only about eight percent of students in high schools were considered to pose severe discipline problems (Baker 1985, p. 486).

Two basic dimensions of classroom management are introduced in this chapter. These are (1) preventing problems through good management and (2) responding to incidents of misbehavior.

Dimensions of Classroom Management

"Classroom management" refers to the way a teacher organizes and manages time, materials, and space to promote smooth and efficient operation of the classroom. It is directed at the prevention of problems. One study revealed that the basic difference between teachers rated as "effective" or "ineffective" in terms of their abilities to control their classrooms was not in their patterns of response to inappropriate behavior, but rather in their methods of organizing and managing their classrooms (Kounin 1970).

Sometimes visitors to classrooms of experienced teachers remark on the excellent deportment of the students and comment that the classroom almost seems the "run itself." In a systematic study of such classrooms, Emmer, Evertson, and Anderson (1980) found that these smooth-functioning classrooms were not chance occurrences. Neither did they stem from teachers' good fortune in drawing groups of students who were "naturally" cooperative. Rather, these well-managed classrooms resulted from careful teacher preparation and planning that began even before the school year began. These teachers developed systematic management procedures and clearly conveyed their expectations to students. Many of these decisions related to the use of space and time.

Space Management

Before students arrive at the beginning of a semester, decisions need to be made about how space in the room can be organized to facilitate both learning and control. Among issues that must be addressed are those related to seating arrangements for students, location of the teacher's desk, storage of instructional materials and supplies, and use of classroom wall space. There is no "ideal" arrangement. Each teacher makes decisions based on such considerations as instructional techniques to be used, movement patterns of students, visual barriers, and other distractions.

In some instances, aspects of the classroom environment cannot be easily changed. For example, a sociology teacher might like to arrange student seats in a circular fashion to facilitate discussion. If chairs are bolted to the floor and arranged in rows, such an arrangement cannot be made. The bottom line is that teachers attempt to modify the classroom environment to the extent possible to make it conform to the kind of instructional program they intend to provide.

A number of specific decisions must be made relating to classroom space. Some of these concern the issue of floor space.

Floor Space

Classroom floor space needs to be arranged to support intended instructional activities. Organization of the floor space can cue students as to what patterns of behavior are expected. Since activities vary in most classrooms, many teachers will alter floor space arrangements depending on the nature of the activity. For example, different arrangements might be considered when students are working in small groups, listening to a lecture, or accomplishing tasks at various learning stations scattered throughout the classroom area.

Consider a situation where the teacher wants to organize the class for some large group instruction. It is important for the teacher to have eye contact with all students. Desks need to be arranged so all students can see the teacher clearly. If the teacher's presentation is to feature writing on a chalkboard or on an overhead transparency, then each student must have a clear view of the chalkboard or of the projection screen.

In large-group instruction, students generally are not asked to interact frequently with one another. Indeed, often such interactions are discouraged. Since this is the case, desks should be arranged to minimize the temptations of unauthorized student-to-student talk. Often arranging desks in rows facing the teacher will accomplish this purpose. To the extent such an arrangement is possible, allowing extra space between individual pairs of desks also tends to inhibit inappropriate student talk.

Often students will be asked to perform an application task of some kind at the conclusion of a large-group lesson. For example, a geometry teacher may introduce a new proof. Students then may be provided with some problems that require them to apply the procedure. The teacher will want to check on each student's work during this phase of the lesson. This suggests a need for the teacher to move smoothly from one area of the classroom to another. Enough space needs to be left between individual student desks to allow for this kind of movement. This arrangement encourages careful monitoring of each student and can decrease the incidence of inappropriate student behavior patterns. Box 7.1 is an exercise in planning student seating arrangements.

Traffic Patterns

Basic traffic patterns must be considered when decisions about floor space are made. High-traffic areas must be identified. These include places of entry into the classroom, areas where lesson supplies are stored, and the teacher's desk. High-traffic areas must be kept free from obstructions. Desks should be arranged so they do not interrupt the flow of students moving to and from these areas. For example, student desks should not be placed too close to the main entry door of the classroom. If they are, students seated at those desks will be disturbed every time some one enters or leaves.

The Teacher's Desk

Placement of the teacher's desk is an important decision. In many classrooms, the desk is at the front of the room. This may not be the best choice. A placement toward the rear of the room has several pluses for teachers.

First of all, such a placement makes it impossible for the teacher to sit at the desk and teach. Generally, this kind of "seated" instruction is not as effective as is instruction delivered by someone who is standing or moving about the classroom. A teacher who is seated communicates a lack of enthusiasm for the lesson. If students perceive the teacher as unenthusiastic, they are likely to develop similar feelings about the lesson's content.

Another advantage for a rear-of-the-room placement of the desk has to do with monitoring. This is especially true when students have been assigned to do independent work at their desks. Students who are facing away from the teacher cannot tell when the teacher is looking at them unless they turn around. As a result, they often assume their behavior is being very closely monitored. This tends to encourage students to stay at their assigned tasks.

Regardless of where the desk is placed, successful classroom managers find that it is useful to have a classroom rule that requires students in need of help to stay seated and raise their hands. Students should not

Box 7.1

Organizing Student Seating Arrangements for Different Instructional Tasks

A seating arrangement that might be appropriate for one kind of instructional activity may not work well at all for another. Think about three different kinds of instructional activities you might include as you teach your subject. Prepare examples of preferred seating arrangements for each. Ask your course instructor to comment on your plans. Be sure to note location of windows, chalkboards, doors, and any other major room features. (Assume that student desks are not bolted to the floor and may be moved to any location in the room).

What Do You Think?

1. Look at each of your arrangements. Would it be possible for you to conduct your planned instructional activity if you were unable to locate student seats as you have suggested?

2. For each arrangement, provide a rationale for your decision to locate student desks as you have recommended.

3. In your view, how important is the issue of seating arrangement? Why do you think so?

---

be encouraged to leave their seats to go to the teacher's desk. When this happens, there are too many opportunities for them to interrupt work of other students on the way. This situation is especially serious when several students have left their seats and a line forms in front of the teacher's desk. It is much better for the teacher to respond to a raised hand by leaving his or her desk and moving quickly to the student's seat.

Wall Space

Constructive use of wall space can contribute to a positive classroom environment. Wall space can be used to display materials that might spark interest in a topic, to provide an example of a procedure students will be asked to follow, to put student's work on view, and to display classroom rules and time schedules.

Before a class begins, many teachers prepare bulletin boards or other wall displays that are designed to promote the development of positive student attitudes. In some cases, this information ties directly to academic topics. In others, there may be more general items, perhaps even cartoons, that will convey to students the idea that the classroom is a place where interesting things can be found. The purpose is to use walls to motivate students to think about the classroom as a place they would like to spend time.

Many teachers use part of their wall space to display classroom rules. Sometimes, students and teachers spend time negotiating these rules at the beginning of the term. Regardless of how they are derived, it usually is not a good idea to post a long, tedious list. An excessive number of rules can give a negative tone to a classroom. Three or four major guidelines for students' behavior in class should suffice.

Another section of wall space often is devoted to information about assignments and about adjustments in the daily schedule. For example, special assemblies and so forth sometimes require a modification of the school day, and classes' meeting times vary from the established routine. Posting of "due dates" for homework is often a feature of this wall display. The information prompts students to complete work on time. Displaying it in a formal way also communicates to students that the teacher is a business-like professional who has not made off-hand decisions about these matters and who has a genuine expectation that the material will be available from students on the date listed.

Equipment Storage

Secondary school teachers use a wide variety of instructional support equipment. Overhead projectors, opaque projectors, microcomputers, and film projectors are among items used by teachers in many subject areas. Teachers in specialized areas, for example the sciences and physical education, also have many items that are unique to their own subject areas. Needed items of equipment need to be stored in areas where they are easily accessible, yet in places where they will not be constantly handled by unauthorized persons. If equipment is not secure, items will be lost and maintenance costs will go up.

One important reason for storing items with a view to providing for ready teacher access is scarce instructional time. Teachers should not have needed support equipment so inaccessible that time required to obtain it and set it up takes valuable minutes away from their lesson presentation.

Decisions must also be made about where students' individual belongings should be stored. In most high schools, there are lockers that allow a good deal of student property to be stored outside of instructional areas. Depending on what is being taught, some teachers may also find it necessary to locate areas within the classroom to store some students' belongings. For example, in a laboratory portion of a chemistry class, perhaps involving a temporary move to an adjoining room, it may be desirable to have a large cabinet with a lock available to store and secure students' purses and other belongings.

Time Management

Teachers who manage classroom time well experience fewer student control problems than teachers who do not. A number of studies have revealed that there is much nonproductive time in many classrooms (Good and Brophy 1987). Effective teachers maximize the amount of time students spend on productive tasks. High levels of student engagement on academic tasks diminish the probability of occurrence of disruptive behaviors. Students also tend to do better academically in such environments. Students who succeed academically are less likely to pose discipline problems for teachers than students who are frustrated by their lack of progress.

Transitions

Transitions are times when students switch from one part of a day's activities to another. In some classrooms, a great deal of productive time is lost to transitions. The teacher may have done a fine job of preparing individual parts of the lesson but failed to consider what should be done during "gaps" between the parts. A concern for transitions needs to be built into the overall planning process.

Returning of student work is an activity that frequently occurs between lesson parts. Procedures can be established to accomplish this task quickly and efficiently. For example, if students are seated in rows, the materials can be organized ahead of time by row. This allows for a very quick distribution. Another approach involves construction of a return-of-student-work wall unit featuring 30 to 40 numbered boxes. Each student is assigned a number at the beginning of the term. His or her work is regularly returned in the appropriate numbered box. Returned work can be placed in the boxes and students requested to look for it there as they come into the classroom. Some teachers also use this arrangement as a method of collecting student assignments. Transitions are discussed further in Box 7.2.

In some classes it is necessary for students to move from one instructional area to another for different parts of the lesson. For example, a science teacher may wish students to go to a laboratory area for a short demonstration. In such a case, the teacher should plan movement patterns in advance and communicate expectations clearly to students. ("All right, we are going to move to the lab now. You people in row one go first. Move quickly. Let's not have any talking. Take your regular lab seats. As soon as the last person in row one has left the room, row 2 can go. We will follow the same procedure until all five rows have gone. Stay in a single file. As soon as you sit down, take out your notebooks. I am going to begin as soon as the last person has taken a seat in the lab.")

Box 7.2

Preparing for Transitions

Classroom discipline problems are particularly likely to arise during periods of inactivity or confusion. Inexperienced teachers often break the flow of their lessons and provide conditions for misbehavior to occur by failing to plan carefully for transitions. Transitions involve changes from one part of the day's program to another. For example, there is a transition at the beginning of each period from administrative activities such as role-taking to beginning academic instruction; there is a transition between parts of a lesson; and there is a transition at the end of the period as students put away materials and prepare to leave.

Some teachers have found it useful to plan in advance what they are going to say to students at each transition point. These instructions are very explicit. They seek to move students quickly and efficiently from one activity to another. Efficient transitions save instructional time, maintain a smooth flow of activity, and minimize opportunities for disruption. For each of the following transition points, prepare a short set of instructions that you would provide to students:

1. Transition between role-taking and initial instruction.

2. Transition involving a move from one location to another.

3. Transition from a demonstration to an application activity.

4. Transition from an application activity to end-of-the-period preparation to put away materials and move.

Careful monitoring of students when they are moving is a must. Students should be encouraged to move quickly and purposefully to the new location. This is not a time for them to engage the teacher in conversation. This will slow down the movement process and nibble away at scarce instructional time.

Beginning Class

Getting classes started promptly can help decrease the number of discipline problems. Plans need to be developed that allow for quick accomplishment of such tasks as roll taking, making special announcements, and distributing needed learning materials. Once the instructional phase has started, the focus should remain on the lesson and not be diverted back to one of these administrative matters. Such digressions interrupt the logical flow of the lesson. They interfere with students' concentration and may divert their attention away from the teacher.

Many teachers have developed a system involving the use of a visual cue that communicates to learners that their undivided attention is required. When the teacher gives the appropriate signal, students are expected to stop what they are doing, look at the teacher, and await instruction. The specific signal chosen must be clearly explained to members of the class. For example, the teacher might say something like this at the beginning of the term: "When I move to this place in the center front of the room with my grade book in hand and look across the class, I want you to stop whatever you are doing. This means I have something that all of you will need to hear. There is to be no talking at this time."

Successful classroom managers have learned not to start the formal instructional phase of lesson until they have the attention of all students. This behavior communicates to all members of a class that the teacher has something to say that is important for all of them to hear. Further, it saves the teacher's voice. Attempting to speak over even the murmured whispers of even a few students is a strain. There is no need to put this kind of stress on the vocal cords.

Lesson Pacing

To prevent control problems, lessons should feature (1) a brisk pace and (2) content that allows learners to achieve high levels of success. Care should be taken to avoid spending too much time on points that most students already know. This can result in diminished levels of attention.

Boredom is an important contributor to classroom control problems. To get a feel for how much time needs to be spent on given portions of a lesson, some teachers identify a "reference" group in each class. Students in this group represent a sampling of individuals who are about in the middle of the class in terms of their academic talent. The teacher carefully monitors levels of understanding of students in the reference group. When these students understand a point, then it is time to move on to something else.

Students finish assignments at different rates. There is a need to plan activities for individuals who finish their work early. Students need to be told what they are to do when they complete their basic assignment at the time the initial assignment is made. This promotes a smooth transition from the basic assigned activity to the back-up provided for early finishers.

Providing Assistance

When teachers provide assistance to individual students, they consume valuable class time. For this reason, providing assistance needs to be considered when planning for time management. Since most teachers deal with classes enrolling 20 or more students (some have classes that are much larger), teachers face real difficulties in responding to the special needs of individual students. Jones (1979) has suggested an interesting approach to providing personal help.

In his research, Jones found that the average teacher spends more time working with individual students than is necessary. He suggests that the teacher adopt this general sequence in working with a student needing help. First of all, to build the individual's self-confidence, the teacher should find something the student has done correctly and mention it. Second, the teacher should provide a direct suggestion as to what the student should do next. It is important that the teacher not do this task for the student. The purpose is to give the student an idea about how to proceed, but to allow him or her to tackle the difficulty personally. Once this suggestion has been made, the teacher should move on immediately to the next student. Jones has estimated that, using this procedure, a teacher need not spend more than about 20 seconds with each learner (Jones 1979).

Assistance does not always have to be provided by the teacher. Peer help is another procedure for assisting individual students. One junior high school teacher developed badges that were awarded weekly to students who had achieved high levels of success on a topic. These badges allowed them to serve as "consultants" to other students who were having difficulty understanding it. This student-to-student assistance worked well, and it allowed the teacher more time to work individually with students experiencing more serious learning difficulties.

Establishing Routines and Procedures

Teachers need to develop routines and procedures for handling recurring events. These routines promote efficiency, and they can yield increased time for important instructional activities. In many secondary classrooms, recurring events include taking attendance, making announcements, recognizing students wishing to make a contribution in a discussion, dealing with students' personal problems, leaving the room, and using specialized equipment. Routines for handling these matters can be planned and shared with students. Teachers who share their expectations with regard to these matters with students and who follow adopted procedures consistently tend to have fewer classroom management problems than teachers who fail to do so.

Planning for routines and working with students to become familiar with them over time can put part of the classroom's activities on "automatic pilot." When unanticipated situations arise, teachers with well-established routines are able to concentrate all of their energies on their resolution.

The classroom management principles introduced in this section, when successfully applied, can help teachers avoid a large number of problems. It should not be assumed that those who apply all of these principles will not experience classroom control problems from time to time. Even the best classroom managers have to deal with occasional episodes of student misbehavior. However those who use sound classroom management principles will experience fewer of them than those who do not.

Building Acceptable Behavior Patterns

As they move through their school programs, students are confronted with many academic and personal challenges. These pressures may lead virtually every student, at one time or another, to misbehave in the classroom. All who teach must recognize this reality.

The probability that they will face occasional discipline problems ought not to lead teachers to conclude that these episodes necessarily detract from their instructional role. One purpose of education is to help young people develop patterns of behavior characterized by self-control and responsibility. Part of the instructional role of all teachers is to help young people behave in socially acceptable ways. Occasional discipline problems can provide teachers opportunities to help students develop more responsible patterns of personal behavior.

There are advantages for teachers who recognize that the goal of their disciplinary actions is to teach students self-control and responsibility. First of all, they look at their disciplinary duties as a part of their basic instructional responsibility, not as something that diverts their attention from it. Second, successful disciplinary programs that result in productive changes in student behavior can be very satisfying. These changes signal to teachers that they are having an impact that will benefit students throughout their adult lives. (See Box 7.3.)

The Importance of a Positive Classroom Atmosphere

Several elements are involved in teaching self-control and responsibility. First, it must be recognized that students' self-control and willingness to accept responsibility are influenced by their levels of trust and fear and by their individual hopes and aspirations. Students who believe their classroom is characterized by a high level of trust, a generally positive atmosphere, and high teacher expectations are more likely to exercise self-control than students in classrooms lacking these qualities.

Students' self-concepts also play a role in their patterns of behavior. Students with good self-concepts typically exhibit more acceptable pat-

Box 7.3

Secondary School Teachers Should Not Have to Discipline Students

Elementary school teachers who deal with immature pupils are expected to discipline students. After all, part of their function is to help these young people learn expected behavior patterns of our society. Secondary teachers, on the other hand, have primary responsibilities for transmitting academic content. By the time students are in the secondary school, they should know which kinds of behaviors are acceptable and which are not. Teachers at this level should not have to teach patterns of behavior that should have been mastered years earlier. Disruptive students should simply be removed. Their continued presence undermines the teacher's abilities to deal with the academic issues that are the primary concern of the secondary school.

What Do You Think?

Read the statement above. Then respond to these questions.

1. What basic difference does the person who made this statement see between the elementary school and the secondary school? Do you share this view? Why, or why not?

2. How do you think secondary teachers should react to the issue of student misbehavior? Is correcting student behavior problems a legitimate part of their role?

3. Suppose you were asked to write a letter to the editor in response to this statement. What would you say?

---

terns of behavior than students with poor self-concepts. Teachers have an important part to play in enhancing the self-concepts of their students. When the instructional program is organized to promote students' academic success, individuals tend to do well. Successful students tend to feel good about themselves.

Allowing Students to Make Choices

Teachers who view promotion of self-control and responsibility as a major dimension of their instructional roles do not assume that students who are not misbehaving are necessarily self-controlled and responsible. It may be that an individual student has rarely been placed into a classroom situation that has called upon him or her to demonstrate self-control or responsibility. For this reason, teachers interested in developing these traits provide opportunities for students to make and experience consequences of personal choices. The attendant frustrations give students opportunities to exercise self-control and demonstrate levels of responsibility.

Kinds of Teacher Leadership in the Classroom

The kind of leadership the teacher exercises in the classroom has an influence on students' likelihood of developing and maintaining acceptable patterns of self-control and responsibility. Secondary school students are striving to establish personal identities and to exercise some independence of adult authority figures. They should not be expected to give unquestioned obedience to every teacher demand. To obtain

This teacher is counseling a student who has had difficulty understanding part of the lesson. This kind of personal attention can help reduce the number of classroom control problems a teacher faces. *Photo courtesy of Barbara Hadley.*

student cooperation and maintain control, teachers need to use their authority wisely.

A framework for identifying different types of power or leadership a teacher might use to promote harmonious working relationships with students was described by French and Raven (1959). They identified these important leadership types: (1) expert power or leadership; (2) referent power or leadership; (3) legitimate power or leadership; (4) reward power or leadership; and, (5) coercive power or leadership.

EXPERT POWER OR LEADERSHIP.   Expert power or leadership is the authority a person gets through superior knowledge. Individuals having this kind of information are accorded leadership authority and some power over group members out of a recognition of the importance of this knowledge. A key here is that members of the group appreciate the worth of the knowledge of the leader. Teachers who attempt to justify their authority on the basis of their superior knowledge assume that students perceive this knowledge to be important. If students do not, this kind of a teacher appeal probably will fail.

REFERENT POWER OF LEADERSHIP.   This kind of power comes to a leader because he or she enjoys positive interpersonal relationships with group members. People in groups tend to cede authority to individuals who are seen as likable, trustworthy, and ethical. Group members feel the leader has their interests at heart. The leader, in turn, acts to communicate his respect for members of the group. Teachers who develop good lines of communication with their students often exert authority that has come to them through referent power.

LEGITIMATE POWER OR LEADERSHIP.   This power comes to individuals who have been placed in an official position of responsibility by our society. For example, the mayor of a city exercises certain legitimate power as a result of his or her election to this office. Teachers have some legitimate authority by virtue of their appointment by the school board. However, successful use of this power depends on students' acceptance of this legitimate authority. Some students tend to reject this kind of teacher power. For this reason, teachers cannot depend exclusively on legitimate power to solve their leadership problems in the classroom. More often, they will need to combine this with referent power and with other kinds of claims to leadership.

REWARD POWER OR LEADERSHIP.   Individuals who are seen as having an ability to reward group members for their compliance with certain prescribed patterns of behavior are given some leadership authority. In some cases, material items such as money or gifts are used as rewards. In other cases, rewards are intangibles. For example, leaders can make decisions that give certain group members more status, recognition, prestige, or privilege.

Teachers exercise some control over rewards. To be effective as a leadership tool, rewards must be something students perceive as important. Not all secondary students respond to grades. Teachers who wish to use reward power must diagnose individual students to determine what works with different members of the class. Intangible as well as tangible rewards need to be considered.

COERCIVE POWER OR LEADERSHIP. Individuals sometimes are given leadership authority because members of the group perceive them to have the ability to punish or coerce other group members. For example, in elementary schools, terrified youngsters may accord leadership authority to the oversized school bully. In general, members of a group tend to resent leadership exercised by individuals whose authority rests on coercive power.

Teachers have some coercive power. The ability to keep students after school, require special additional work, and, in some cases, to administer corporal punishment are examples of their coercive power. Teachers who rely on this source of leadership authority may find their relationships with students to be strained. Coercive power tends to lead to resistance and to a generally negative classroom climate.

An understanding of the various sources of teacher power can be helpful to a newcomer to the profession. Today, many teachers complain that students do not seem to be as respectful as they were in times past. If true, this situation may have come about because of a decline in society's perception of the "legitimate power" of teachers.

In recent years, there has been much criticism of teachers and teaching. One result may be a decline in the social status of teachers. Hence, students in school today may be unwilling to ascribe as much authority to teachers as did students who attended school 10 and 20 years ago.

Probably the most effective kind of teacher leadership authority today is based on expert power and referent power. Teachers who are perceived as experts in their fields and as caring, trustworthy individuals can exercise classroom leadership effectively. Preparation of leadership based on expert power and referent power requires hard work.

For example, expert power demands expertise. To get this, individuals aspiring to teach need a solid academic grounding in their teaching fields and in pedagogy. Expert power will be undermined when teach-

Box 7.4

Developing "Expert" Power Through Rigorous Testing

Recently, a teacher was overheard making these comments:

> Some of these students need a good shaking up. They know so little, but they think they know so much. These arrogant 16-year-olds are just a bit much. I'm going to bring them down to earth. The test I'm preparing is going to provide a much-needed dose of 'reality.' When the low Cs, Ds, and Fs go out to this bunch, they should appreciate that they still have much to learn.

What Do You Think?

Read the statement above. Then respond to these questions.

1. How do you react to this attempt to establish "expert" power?

2. The teacher seems to suggest that the difficult task will have a beneficial impact on students. Do you agree? Why, or why not?

3. What is your general reaction to this teacher's comments?

ers make obvious content mistakes, communicate expectations poorly to students, develop poor examinations, and implement grading practices that students find unfair. Careful planning of instruction is a must for any teacher who seeks authority through expert power. (See Box 7.4.)

Referent power comes to teachers who develop positive classroom climates. Students need to feel that they have a legitimate opportunity to succeed. They need to feel free to ask questions and state opinions without fear or ridicule. In short, they must sense that the teacher cares about them as people.

General Teacher Reactions to Problems

Teachers who have a good record of classroom management and control are themselves self-controlled and responsible. These teachers have the confidence to deal personally with most classroom management problems. They sometimes refer difficult problems to other school officials, but for the most part they respond to student behavior problems without calling on others for professional assistance. They view classroom behavior problems as part of their personal responsibility, not the result of factors that are beyond their control.

Effective classroom managers favor the use of long-term approaches to changing an unacceptable behavior problem as compared to short-term approaches designed to stop a single incidence of the behavior. They seek to eradicate the underlying cause of the behavior rather than simply to eradicate the symptoms. In this connection, these teachers attempt to analyze misbehavior incidents to determine their fundamental causes (Brophy 1983).

Several principles have been identified that teachers find useful in responding to incidents of misbehavior. A number of these are introduced in the next section. These guidelines have potential for helping students develop more self-control and personal responsibility.

Basic Principles of Discipline

Respect the Student's Dignity

Secondary school students are at an age when they are trying to establish their own identities. They tend to react negatively when they sense an adult is not treating them in a respectful manner. Efforts to correct an inappropriate behavior that undermine the basic dignity of the offender may cause more problems than they resolve. Teachers need to communicate their displeasure with the behavior, not their displeasure with the offending student as a human being.

Ridiculing or embarrassing a secondary student often invites a power struggle between the student and the teacher. This does little to resolve a long-term behavior problem, and it can seriously undermine the teacher's efforts to establish a positive climate for learning.

Private Correction Is Better than Public Correction

One way to avoid humiliating offending students is to correct them privately rather than publicly. There are several important advantages to this approach. For one thing, when a teacher speaks quietly to a misbehaving student outside of the hearing range of others in the class, the student saves face. He or she has little incentive to engage in a power struggle with the teacher, because there is no audience to impress.

Additionally, private correction allows the teacher to work for a close, personal relationship with the student. The teacher can communicate his or her concern for the student as a person. This may lead the student to conclude that the teacher is willing to listen and to seek solutions to a problem rather than simply imposing a heavy-handed authoritarian decision.

Misbehaviors' Causes, Not Their Symptoms, Should Be Addressed

A firm response to a misbehavior may solve a problem in the short run. However, many misbehaviors are symptoms of more fundamental difficulties. Teachers need to probe for possible underlying causes of discipline problems.

This kind of investigating is not always easy. For example, it might reveal that some actions of the teacher are causing the problem. Lessons could be poorly planned or delivered. Unknowingly, the teacher may have been doing something to undermine the self-esteem of an offending student.

By no means are all causes likely to be teacher-related. For example, some students may be working long hours and simply be in an ill humor because of lack of sleep. Others may come from homes where there is a great deal of stress. Still others may be having a reaction to medication. Sensitive teachers consider a wide variety of possibilities as they seek to understand causes of student misbehavior. When such causes can be identified, teachers sometimes are able to help students overcome difficulties that result in unproductive patterns of classroom behavior.

Teacher Responses Should Be Consistent and Fair

In working with students who are misbehaving, teachers need to be consistent and fair. Students need to know that there will be a consequence when they misbehave. The teacher's response to a given incident of inappropriate behavior should not be dependent upon his or her mood at the time it occurs. If something was a rule violation on Monday and certain sanctions were imposed on an offending student, the same behavior occurring on Wednesday should also result in similar sanctions for another misbehaving individual.

Sometimes teachers find it particularly difficult to treat misbehaving "A" students in the same way they treat misbehaving "D" or "F" students. "Good" students who misbehave are every bit as much in need of correction that will lead them to a more responsible behavior pattern as are "not-so-good" students. The temptation to hold one set of students to a different set of standards must be resisted. Students will perceive a teacher who treats some students differently than others as unfair, increasing the incidence of misbehavior problems.

Some teachers complain that their students are always "testing the boundaries" of acceptable behavior. Often this pattern develops because students are not sure what the boundaries are. Consistent responses to misbehavior can bring these boundaries into tighter focus and reduce students' inclinations to test teachers' tolerance for unacceptable class-room behaviors.

Students Must Understand that, by Choosing to Misbehave, They Have Also Chosen the Consequences of Their Misbehavior

When students learn responsibility, they come to accept the idea that consequences of their misbehavior have resulted from their own actions, not from arbitrary actions of the teacher. Teachers need to help students recognize the relationship between their own behavior patterns and the attendant consequences. Teachers who experience difficulty in managing their classrooms often overlook this principle. For example, they may allow some students to escape consequences for their actions, or they may impose consequences that seem little connected to the nature of the student's behavior.

"Consequences" should not be meted out to students only when they engage in unacceptable behaviors. Students should realize that pleasing consequences will come their way when they behave appropriately. In some schools, this is not a frequent occurrence. One student in such a school commented to one of the authors, "Everyone in this school knows me because I'm not afraid of teachers. What do you get for being good?" This student had "learned" that there were more rewards associated with inappropriate than appropriate behavior. To prevent students from arriving at such a conclusion, teachers must reward positive behaviors of students as consistently as they apply sanctions to their inappropriate behaviors.

These basic principles provide some general guidelines for responding to incidents of misbehavior. Many teachers, using these guidelines as backdrop for their planning, have found it useful to develop a sequence of intended responses to inappropriate student behavior. Often, responses are scaled in terms of their severity and intrusiveness. That is, the teacher plans rather low-level responses to minor problems and to "first time offenders" and more severe responses to more serious problems and "repeat offenders." The next section introduces an example of a sequenced series of teacher responses to classroom behavior problems.

A Range of Responses to Student Misbehavior

The sequence of responses introduced here includes four basic categories. They are (1) responses supporting self-control, (2) providing situational assistance, (3) implementing punishment, and (4) involving others.

Responses Supporting Self-Control

Teacher responses in this category are designed to help students exercise self-control. They generally do not divert students' attention from the lesson and tend to be quite unobtrusive. There are five types of teacher response associated with this category.

1. REINFORCE PRODUCTIVE BEHAVIOR. To help students maintain self-control, teachers must reinforce desirable patterns of behavior. This can be done by providing rewards for productive behavior. Rewards can be given both to individuals (quiet praise, a written compliment, selection for a leadership role) or to the entire class (provide five minutes free "talking time," allow class to vote on next topic to be studied, and so forth). (See Box 7.5.)

2. USE NON-VERBAL SIGNALS TO INDICATE DISAPPROVAL. Minor episodes of misbehavior should be handled in ways that do not interfere with the flow of the lesson. Non-verbal responses from the teacher permit communication with an offending student that is not disruptive. Non-verbal signals may include eye contact, hand signals, or facial expressions.

3. PROXIMITY CONTROL. Some students in a classroom are less inclined to misbehave when the teacher is standing nearby. A frequently used teacher technique for remedying minor control problems involves nothing more than simply walking to the area of the classroom where the problem is occurring. In many cases, it is possible for a teacher to do this without ever interrupting his or her instructional activities. Proximity control, therefore, has the advantage of providing a response to an unacceptable behavior that will not divert the attention of the class away from the day's instructional program.

Box 7.5

Preparing a List of Rewards for Productive Behavior

Students' self-control improves when they sense that this behavior pattern is rewarded. Rewards sometimes are directed toward individuals, sometimes toward an entire class.

Think about a class you might teach. Then, generate a list of four possible rewards you might provide to individuals and four possible rewards you might provide to a class to encourage controlled individual behavior.

Possible Individual Rewards

1.

2.

3.

4.

Possible Class Rewards

1.

2.

3.

4.

4. USING A STUDENT'S NAME IN THE CONTEXT OF A LESSON. This teacher response is somewhat more intrusive than others that have been suggested. It works like this. If a teacher notices that a student is not paying attention or is engaged in a minor misbehavior, he or she simply inserts the student's name into the discussion. ("If John were a member of the crew sailing for the New World, he might have the responsibility for. . . .")

Use of the student's name engages the student's attention. Very often, the student will become more attentive and cease any inappropriate behavior. The approach has the advantage of communicating directly with a student while, at the same time, maintaining the academic focus of the lesson.

5. SELF-MONITORING.   Some students who have difficulty controlling their own impulses can profit when the teacher provides some direct instruction on self-monitoring skills. The nature of what the students are taught may vary. In some cases, students are advised to implement a specific acceptable alternative behavior whenever they sense themselves to be losing control and on the verge of misbehaving. For example, younger secondary students might be taught to clench their fists or to

count quietly to 20 before doing anything else. Engagement in this alternative behavior gives them an opportunity to work off their frustrations and to think about alternatives to an unacceptable outburst (Brophy 1983).

Providing Situational Assistance

If responses designed to help students become more self-controlled are not effective, teachers may need to try responses that are designed to provide situational assistance. The basic function of teacher actions in this category is to change unacceptable student behavior by modifying the learning environment.

1. A QUIET WORD.   This response to misbehavior calls on the teacher to move to the location of the offending individual and provide a quiet reminder of what behavior is expected. This should be done quickly. The idea is to maintain the basic flow of the lesson and, at the same time, avoid drawing the attention of the class to the misbehaving student.

2. PROVIDING A RULE REMINDER.   Sometimes teachers find it necessary to stop what they are doing and remind an individual or an entire class about a classroom rule that is being violated. For example, a teacher might say something like this: "Angela, what are you supposed to do when you are having a problem with the assignment and need some help?" Often students understand what the rule is and will cease the inappropriate pattern of behavior in responses to a teacher question of this kind. On those instances when students do not recall the rule, the teacher can review it.

3. REMOVING THE STUDENT FROM THE SITUATION.   Sometimes behavior problems can be solved by asking a student to move to another area of the room and continue working there. Teachers who implement this response to misbehavior successfully work hard to avoid a confrontation. Often a nonjudgmental direct statement works well. "Mike, take your material and move to the empty table to continue your work." This statement clearly indicates to the student that the issue is not open to debate. It should be delivered in a calm, matter-of-fact tone of voice.

4. RESPONDING WITH CLARITY AND FIRMNESS.   If other responses have failed to produce a desired change in behavior, the teacher may need to use more direct and intrusive verbal behaviors. A clear and firm statement needs to be made that makes specific references to (a)

the name of the misbehaving student, (b) the nature of the unacceptable behavior, and (c) an acceptable alternative. "Priscilla, now is not the time to be doing your English homework. Close your English book. Take out your lab manual, and read the information of 'parts of the microscope' on page 23." Direct eye contact should be made with the student as the statement is made.

5. CONFERENCING WITH THE STUDENT.   If misbehavior continues, an individual conference with the student might be in order. During a conference of this type, the teacher should emphasize ways of solving the problem and avoid threatening and blaming the student. The teacher might begin by identifying the problem, sharing his or her feelings about it, and asking the student for ideas about how it might be solved.

Sometimes, a teacher and a student will develop a behavior contract as a result of the conference. The contract should suggest what the student intends to do to change an unacceptable pattern of behavior. It should include references to rewards that will come to the student for maintenance of an acceptable pattern and to consequences that will result from continued misbehavior.

6. SOLICITING PARENTAL ASSISTANCE.   At some point, it may become necessary to solicit parental assistance. Most parents are concerned about the progress and behavior of their children in school. Sometimes a call to a parent about a behavior problem will have positive results. In making a call to a parent, the teacher should emphasize his or her personal interest in the student's welfare and should express a desire to help. This kind of an approach frequently will result in a parent's willingness to work cooperatively with the teacher to remedy a problem.

Implementing Punishment

Punishment is an appropriate teacher response only after all actions described under the headings "Responses Supporting Self-Control" and "Providing Situational Assistance" have been tried with no resultant change in a student's inappropriate behavior. Punishment, as a tool of classroom management, is only effective if used infrequently. Severity of punishment must be consistent with the nature of the misbehavior. When teachers overreact to minor offenses by administering serious punishments, levels of student anxiety rise. Over the long run, these can poison a classroom's atmosphere and contribute to the development of additional problems.

1. MAKE-UP OF TIME. This punishment requires students to return to the teacher's classroom after school or during some break during the day to make up time that they wasted while they were misbehaving. Because many students ride buses or work at the end of the school day, this make-up time cannot always be accomplished at the end of the day. Occasionally teachers have students come in early in the morning before classes start. Other options include requiring students to spend time in the teacher's classroom when others may be participating in a pep rally, attending an assembly, or engaging in another enjoyable activity.

When a teacher chooses make-up of time as a punishment option, the student should be required to engage in a serious academic task. The teacher should take care to avoid casual conversation with the student or any other behavior that the student might perceive as "special attention." Some students may enjoy the extra attention and, hence, be inclined to misbehave so they could be sentenced to more of this pleasant "punishment."

2. REMOVAL FROM CLASS. If serious misbehavior persists, it might be appropriate to remove the student from class. This may mean sending the individual to a counselor's office or to an administrative office. When a student is sent out of the room, he or she needs to be given specific directions to report to a supervised area. Serious liability problems may arise if a student is given directions to go to an unsupervised area such as an empty cafeteria.

Once a decision has been made to remove a student, the teacher should phone or otherwise communicate with the school office to which the student has been sent. Professional personnel at that office need to know who has been sent and to be provided very brief information about why the student has been asked to leave. At the end of the period or during the first available planning period, the teacher must go to the office where the student was sent to make a full report on the student's actions.

Corporal Punishment

It should be noted that corporal punishment has not been mentioned as an optional teacher response. Its omission has not been an oversight. First of all, it is illegal in several states for teachers to administer corporal punishment to students. In others, elaborate arrangements involving witnesses, certification of the severity of the offense, and other matters make corporal punishment an unattractive option. Perhaps a more important reason for not recommending corporal punishment is that it often fails to address a long-term problem. While corporal punishment can suppress a given inappropriate behavior, it does nothing to model an appropriate replacement behavior. Hence, it is often the case that the bad behavior suppressed by the corporal punishment may be replaced by a different behavior that is equally as objectionable as the one that resulted in the punishment.

Further, teachers who have reached the point that they wish to administer corporal punishment may be in a high-pitched emotional state themselves. This may lead them to use excessive force. If this occurs and a student or his parents sense that the student suffered unreasonable physical or psychological harm, a lawsuit may result. In short, the risks of corporal punishment heavily outweigh any advantages. Box 7.6 further examines corporal punishment.

Involving Others

This is generally the category of last resort. At this point, the teacher has tried a wide variety of responses without successfully modifying an unacceptable behavior. To deal with the situation, assistance of others is solicited. Among individuals who may be asked to help are other teachers, counselors, administrators, and personnel from outside agencies.

1. FACE-TO-FACE CONFERENCE WITH PARENTS.   Probably there already will have been written or telephone communication with a parent. At this point, a face-to-face meeting should be arranged. The teacher should go into this meeting well prepared. For example, he or she might wish to have some anecdotal records to share that include the nature of the inappropriate behavior, dates and times when it occurred, and resultant teacher responses. The conference should focus on ways to help the student. Every effort should be made to solicit parental cooperation in this effort.

2. PROBLEM-SOLVING CONFERENCE WITH OTHER PROFESSIONALS.   It may become necessary to schedule a conference involving a number of other professionals who have worked with the student. This group might include a school administrator, a school psychologist, a counselor, other teachers, and possibly representatives from outside social agencies. The teacher needs to present a well-documented case to this group including specific references to places and dates of misbehavior, teacher responses, and their results. The group will weigh the evidence and make suggestions. The teacher will attempt to implement these. Generally, the teacher will be asked to report back to a school administrator who may then make a judgment about any additional steps that must be taken.

Box 7.6

Is Corporal Punishment the Only Way?

A parent who was concerned about reports of rowdy behavior made these comments to the school board:

I understand that you people have made it very difficult for teachers to administer corporal punishment to students. That's a shame. Some of these kids come from deplorable home environments. As much as we hate to admit it, the only thing some of them understand is the paddle. Let's give our teachers the tools they need to maintain respect and order in their classrooms.

What Do You Think?

Read the statement above. Then respond to these questions.

1. How much merit does the parent's argument have? Why do you think so?

2. Suppose the school board did authorize broader use of corporal punishment. Would you expect a decrease in problems of misbehavior? Why, or why not?

3. What might lie behind the school district's decision to make corporal punishment an unattractive option for teachers?

Key Ideas in Summary

1. Both experienced and inexperienced teachers are concerned about classroom management issues. Researchers have found that those teachers who do a good job of organizing time, materials, and space face fewer discipline problems than teachers who do less well in these areas.

2. Among areas teachers consider in organizing classroom space are (1) arrangement of student desks, (2) placement of the teacher's desk, (3) identification of storage areas, and (4) use of classroom walls.

3. Efficient time management is a hallmark of a professional teacher. Proficiency in this area results from careful planning of transitions between lesson parts and of procedures to move promptly into the lesson at the beginning of a class session.

4. Successful classroom managers quickly establish procedures for accomplishing routine tasks. Once these routines have been put in

"I agree, Jeffrey, that we haven't been seeing much of each other lately, but that was the idea when I suspended you!"

place, teachers are free to devote undivided attention to unexpected problems that occur as their lessons are taught.

5. Teaching students to become more self-controlled and responsible is an important instructional function of teachers. Teachers who accept this view do not see episodes of student misbehavior as diverting their attention away from major teaching tasks. This is true because the encouragement of acceptable patterns of behavior is seen as a major teaching task in its own right.

6. Several major principles undergird responsible teacher actions to deal with student misbehavior. These principles include (a) a commitment to respect students' personal dignity, (b) an attempt to deal with behavior problems as quietly and unobtrusively as possible, (c) a willingness to distinguish between and to respond differently

to minor and major behavior problems, and (d) a decision to communicate clearly to students that unpleasant consequences they may experience are a direct result of their inappropriate behavior.

7. Successful classroom managers often have developed a planned series of responses to misbehavior. Ordinarily, these are scaled in such a way that reactions to minor problems and to first-time offenders are less severe than reactions to serious problems and repeat offenders. Generally, corporal punishment is not recommended. Its use has the potential to create more problems than it solves.

POSTTEST

DIRECTIONS: Using your own paper, answer these true/false questions. For each correct statement, write the word "true." For each incorrect statement, write the word "false."

_____ 1. Researchers have found that as teachers improve their abilities to organize time, space, and materials, their discipline problems tend to diminish.

_____ 2. To minimize possible classroom management problems, it is best to encourage students to leave their seats and approach the teacher's desk when they have a problem.

_____ 3. Lessons should be paced in such a way that the teacher goes no faster than the ability of the least able student in the class will allow.

_____ 4. Coercive leadership has been found to be the most effective leadership style for classroom teachers.

_____ 5. Corporal punishment generally is not recommended as an approach to maintaining classroom control.

Bibliography

BAKER, KEITH. "Research Evidence of a School Discipline Problem." *Phi Delta Kappan* (March 1985): 482–488

BROPHY, JERE. "Classroom Organization and Management." *The Elementary School Journal* (March 1983): 265–285.

CHARLES, C. M. *Building Classroom Discipline: From Models to Practice.* New York: Longman, Inc., 1985.

CHARLES, C. M. *Elementary Classroom Management.* New York: Longman, Inc., 1983.

DUKE, DANIEL L. AND MECKEL, ADRIENNE M. *Teacher's Guide to Classroom Management*. New York: Random House, 1984.

EMMER, EDMUND T.; EVERTSON, CAROLYN M.; AND ANDERSON L. "Effective Classroom Management at the Beginning of the School Year." *The Elementary School Journal* (May 1980): 219–231.

EMMER, EDMUND T.; EVERSTON, CAROLYN M,; SANFORD, J. P.; CLEMENTS, B. S.; AND WORSHAM, M. E. *Classroom Management for Secondary Teachers*. 2nd edition. Englewood Cliffs, NJ: Prentice-Hall, Inc., 1989.

EVERTSON, CAROLYN M.; EMMER, EDMUND T.; CLEMENTS, B. S.; SANFORD, J. P.; AND WORSHAM, M. E. *Classroom Management for Elementary Teachers*. Englewood Cliffs, NJ: Prentice-Hall, Inc., 1984.

FRENCH, J. R. P., AND RAVEN, B. H. "The Bases of Social Power." In *Studies in Social Power*, D. Cartwright, ed. Ann Arbor, MI: University of Michigan Press, 1959, pp. 118–149.

GOOD, THOMAS L. AND BROPHY, JERE E. *Looking in Classrooms*. 4th edition. New York: Harper & Row, 1987.

JONES, FREDERIC H. "The Gentle Art of Classroom Discipline." *National Elementary Principal* (June 1979): 26–32.

KOUNIN, JEROME. *Discipline and Group Management in Classrooms*. New York: Holt, Rinehart and Winston, 1970.

O'LEARY, SUSAN J. AND DUBEY, D. R. "Application of Self-Control Procedures by Children: A Review." *Journal of Applied Behavior Analysis* (Fall 1979): 449–465.

PRESSLEY, MICHAEL. "Increasing Children's Self-Control through Cognitive Interventions." *Review of Educational Research* (Spring 1979): 319–370.

RINNE, CARL H. *Attention: The Fundamentals of Classroom Control*. Columbus, OH: Charles E. Merrill Publishing Company, 1984.

SWANSON, H. L. AND REINERT, HENRY R. *Teaching Strategies for Children in Conflict*. 2nd edition. St. Louis, MO: Times Mirror/Mosby, 1984.

WOLFGANG, CHARLES H. AND GLICKMAN, CARL D. *Solving Problems: Strategies for Classroom Teachers*. 2nd edition. Boston: Allyn and Bacon, Inc., 1986.

CHAPTER 8

Lecture, Discussion, Demonstration, and Case Study

AIMS

This chapter provides information to help the reader to:

1. Distinguish among selected instructional techniques in terms of the kinds of instructional tasks each can effectively accomplish.
2. Recognize four areas in which planning decisions should be made before selecting and implementing any instructional technique.
3. Identify steps involved in preparing and implementing a good lecture.
4. Describe the importance of the interrelationship between question sequencing and teacher responses to student answers.
5. Point out characteristics and appropriate applications of the demonstration technique.
6. Describe characteristics of a well-planned case study lesson.

PRETEST

DIRECTIONS: Using your own paper, answer these true/false questions. For each correct statement, write the word "true." For each incorrect statement, write the word "false."

_____ 1. Researchers have found little evidence to support the idea that there is any one "best" instructional technique.

_____ 2. One potential problem with the lecture is its capacity for introducing large quantities of new content very quickly.

_____ 3. A lecture of approximately 45 minutes is about the right length for a class of seventh grade students.

_____ 4. Discussions should always begin with a question that requires students to make value judgments.

_____ 5. Often teacher demonstrations are followed by opportunities for students to do what has been demonstrated.

Introduction

Lecture? Discussion? Demonstration? Case Study? Or some other instructional approach? Which is *best*? An astonishing amount of writing has addressed this question. Teachers have debated the issue in faculty lounges for years. From time to time professional speakers have taken to the stump in support of the "excellence" of a particular teaching technique. Though a great deal of noise has been generated by strong-willed partisans of individual instructional approaches, little hard evidence supports the proposition that any single instructional approach can be regarded as best.

Teacher characteristics, student characteristics, learning-task characteristics, and instructional-setting characteristics influence student learning (Good and Brophy 1987). Complex interactions among these variables suggest that a given instructional technique might prove highly successful under some sets of conditions and largely unsuccessful under others. Nevertheless, there are certain kinds of instructional tasks that seem to be more easily accomplished through the use of some techniques than others.

Discussions of the four instructional techniques introduced in this chapter include references to kinds of tasks for which each is well suited. Similar information is provided in other chapters where other techniques are introduced. (See chapters 8, 9, 10, and 11.)

In deciding to use a given technique, teachers make planning decisions in four areas. These involve (a) identifying the topic, (b) preliminary considerations, (c) implementing the technique, and (d) debriefing students.

Identifying the Topic

Topic identification is an important part of the process of selecting an appropriate instructional technique. For example, suppose a physical education teacher planned a three-week unit of instruction on tumbling. This activity would required students to engage in sophisticated psychomotor movements. Exclusive reliance on the lecture as an instructional technique would not be appropriate. The lecture does not require students to develop the kinds of psychomotor abilities required in tumbling. A technique such as demonstration followed by guided practice would make much more sense.

Preliminary Considerations

Successful use of any instructional technique requires students to have adequate preparation. In determining whether to use a particular instructional approach, some effort must be extended to determine students' levels of development. Students need to know exactly what they should do once the instructional technique is implemented. Guidelines for students must be planned in advance and shared with them before the lesson begins.

Implementing the Technique

Different instructional techniques require different kinds of teacher behaviors and student behaviors. These must be planned in advance. Planning may result in a need to organize the classroom in a particular way. For example, if a technique will require students to interact in groups, it makes sense for chairs to be organized around tables or in circles rather than in straight rows. On the other hand, if a lecture is planned, classroom seats need to be arranged in such a way that each student has an unobstructed view of the teacher.

Teachers must plan exactly what they are to be doing as the technique is implemented. They also need to identify what students should be doing and to communicate this information to them.

Debriefing

In a sense, debriefing is part of implementation. It is so important a step, however, that it merits special consideration. Debriefing occurs at the end of the lesson. It is that phase of instruction when the teacher and students recapitulate what has occurred. It provides opportunities for students to ask questions and for teachers to clear up misunderstandings. It serves as the lesson's capstone.

Lecture

Few instructional techniques have been as maligned as the lecture. The lecture's unfortunate reputation results more from *misuse* of the technique than from any inherent weaknesses.

To understand how the lecture can be misused, it is important to recognize a basic characteristic that sets it apart from many other instructional techniques. The lecture has a capability to introduce a tremendous quantity of new information in a short period of time. One category of lecture misuse occurs when teachers overwhelm students with too much unfamiliar content.

A second misuse also concerns students. It relates to their ability to concentrate on what a lecturer is saying. Middle school and junior high school students have great difficulty in listening carefully for more than about 20 minutes at a time. Even older students in the upper high school grades find their attention wanders when lectures last much more than 30 minutes. Even within these rather short time spans, many students who "appear" to be paying attention may not be following the teacher's words closely (Good and Brophy 1987).

A third misuse results when the lecture is poorly organized. If the speaker jumps randomly from point to point, even the best note takers in the class will have difficulty in finding the intended message when they review what they have written.

General Characteristics

The lecture format is versatile. For example, it can be used to remind students of the teacher's objective, to review previously encountered material, and to draw students' attention to specific aspects of a topic. The lecture can be used to convey information about a wide variety of subjects. Its greatest strength is its ability to present new information to students quickly. (As has been mentioned, this "strength" can turn into a weakness if too much new content is introduced too quickly.)

A few teachers are splendid lecturers. They lace their presentations with fascinating anecdotes and excite students about their topics. When used by less skillful teachers, the lecture is not a highly motivating technique. Part of the difficulty in this regard may result from students' exposure through the years to large numbers of untalented lecturers.

The lecture is a poor technique for involving students in application activities. This is true because the technique is heavily dominated by the teacher. Typically students are asked only to take notes on what is being said. Similarly, the lecture is not a technique that teachers favor when

"What kind of lecturer is he? Let me put it this way. Daniel Webster's reputation remains secure."

they are interested in assessing students' grasp of new material. Though skilled teachers watch for frowns and looks of "aha, I've got it" during their lectures, they cannot formally evaluate individuals when they use this technique.

Preparation for Using the Lecture

IDENTIFYING THE TOPIC.   Many topics lend themselves to lectures. Often teachers select topics that introduce basic information students will be required to use as they encounter more sophisticated content later in the course. For example, a mathematics teacher working with younger secondary students might organize a brief lecture around the topic, "Working with Triangles."

PRELIMINARY CONSIDERATIONS.   There are a number of important points to keep in mind in organizing a lecture:

1. *Identify present levels of understanding*. Determine what students already know about the topic. Do not presume they know something they may not know. Some questions to students may give the teacher some insight into students' levels of understanding.

2. *Keep length short*. It is desirable to keep the lecture as short as possible, consistent with the need to cover a reasonable amount of content.

3. *Highlight key points*. Emphasize important points during the lecture. Students can be alerted to important material by changes in voice, pitch, and intonation.

4. *Provide students with a note-taking outline*. A list of major points and spaces for students to take notes can be prepared in advance and distributed to members of the class. This will make it easier for them to follow the lecture. Some teachers find that preparation of such an outline forces them to do a better job of organizing their material.

Implementing the Technique

Provide students with a copy of the note-taking outline. An outline for a lecture on "Working with Triangles" might look something like this:

Topic: Working with Triangles
1.0 What Is a Triangle

2.0 Classifying by Angles
    2.1 Acute Triangles
    2.2 Obtuse Triangles
    2.3 Right Triangles

3.0 Classifying by Sides
    3.1 Equilateral Triangles
    3.2 Isosceles Triangles
    3.3 Scalene Triangles
4.0 Measuring Triangle Perimeters
5.0 Measuring Triangle Areas

Box 8.1

Preparing a Lecture

Select a topic from one of the subject areas you wish to teach. Identify a grade level and school course where this topic would be taught. Do some basic planning for a lecture you might give on some important aspect of this topic. In your planning, make specific reference to the following:

1. Describe your intended audience as carefully as possible (age levels, general ability levels, probable initial interest in the topic, and so forth).
2. Specifically, what do you expect students to know about your topic before you begin?
3. What major ideas do you wish to emphasize?

Continue your planning by:

1. Preparing a note-taking outline for your students.*
2. Preparing a short list of debriefing questions that you will ask students at the end of your lecture. Their answers should help you learn whether they have understood the information you had hoped to convey.

Share your planning scheme with your course instructor and ask for comments.

* Be sure to allow room for students to write their notes.

Provide students with some tips on note taking. Explain that some simple words can be abbreviated. Encourage students to take notes during the lecture. Speak at a rate that allows students to keep up.

Debriefing

Follow the lecture with a classroom discussion. Focus on major points that were introduced. Ask some questions about content related to each major heading on the note-taking outline provided to students. Some specific information about subsequent uses of the content introduced in the lecture may be introduced at this time.

Discussion

Discussion is a popular instructional technique. It is also one that many beginners find difficult to implement. Sometimes inexperienced teachers find that a discussion scheduled for 10 or 15 minutes simply runs out of steam after only 2 or 3 minutes.

Experienced discussion leaders have mastered some basic principles that increase the effectiveness of the technique. Teachers generally engage in two kinds of verbal behavior during a discussion. First, they ask questions to provide a focus for the discussion and to move it along in a productive manner. Second, they respond to what students have said. Teachers with good response skills listen to what students have said and provide comments that encourage additional student participation. Good response skills help to maintain the flow of dialogue from teacher to student, student to teacher, and student to student.

General Characteristics

Discussion is an excellent technique for helping students to recall material they have learned previously. It can be used to highlight key points. Discussion, too, affords opportunities for students to apply information they have learned. Successful application of knowledge in a discussion depends on the teacher's skill in framing good questions. These questions encourage students to move beyond simple recall of what they have learned to more difficult thinking tasks that require them to apply, analyze, and synthesize.

Discussion sessions often reveal a great deal about students' individual levels of understanding of content that has been introduced. Discussions can serve as an informal evaluation and diagnostic tool. Teachers often will have opportunities to clarify misunderstandings as they are brought out in students' comments.

The discussion technique is not often used to inform students about learning objectives or to introduce large amounts of brand new content. Certainly, as part of a discussion, the teacher might take time to inform students about some new learning objectives. More frequently, though, discussions focus on previously introduced material. Efforts to introduce large amounts of completely new information are difficult in a discussion. By its nature, the discussion involves an interchange between teacher and students. This arrangement limits the time the teacher has to present totally new information.

Preparation for Using the Discussion

IDENTIFYING THE TOPIC.   Discussion is a very flexible instructional technique. It can be used successfully in many subject areas and with students of different ages and abilities. A real strength of the discussion technique is the opportunity it provides for students to extend their understanding of previously introduced information.

Discussions are particularly appropriate when students' application-level thinking is best expressed in verbal form. For example, one might expect a longer discussion in a history class on the topic "The causes of World War I" than in a crafts class on the topic "Techniques for raising pots on the potter's wheel." In the latter situation, any discussion would probably be short.

PRELIMINARY CONSIDERATIONS.   Since teacher behavior during a discussion involves both questions and reactions to students' responses, preplanning in each of these two areas can improve a discussion's quality. Good teacher questions are (a) clear, (b) concise, (c) purposeful, and (d) appropriately leveled (Groisser 1964).

Clear Questions. Language used in a question should be sufficiently clear to communicate the teacher's expectations to students. Sometimes, incorrect student answers result from their failure to discern the teacher's intent. Consider these two questions:

1. Who was John Adams?
2. What was the name of the second President of the United States?

There are many logical answers to the first question. (John Adams was a man. John Adams was an American. John Adams was the second President of the United States. John Adams' term preceded that of Thomas Jefferson. And so forth.) The question does not cue students as to the nature of the expected answer.

Question two does a much better job of conveying to students the kind of answer expected by the teacher. Students hearing this question do not have to guess at the teacher's expectation. The clear language of the question signifies that the teacher is expecting to hear a name.

Concise Questions. The issue of brevity is closely related to the issue of clarity. Verbose, long-winded questions often confuse students. They may have difficulty sorting through the various parts of a long question to identify the teacher's expectations. Planning some questions in advance and writing them down are good antidotes to excessive verbiage.

Purposeful Questions. Purposeful questions tie to the content that is the focus of a discussion. Many teachers find it useful to prepare key questions in advance. Planning purposeful questions can greatly reduce the number of off-the-topic, irrelevant questions that the teacher asks (Good and Brophy 1987).

Appropriately Leveled Questions. Questions that are appropriately leveled match learners' levels of sophistication. Experienced discussion leaders recognize that their vocabularies must not be so far beyond those of learners that communication is impaired. When this happens, incorrect student answers may be as much a result of their failure to grasp the language used in the question as it is a result of their lack of information.

This does not mean that teachers should strive to use only words known to be in students' vocabularies. One of the purposes of education is for students to develop larger vocabularies, and listening to teachers model a more sophisticated speaking style may help them learn new words (Good and Brophy 1987). However, teachers who are successful discussion leaders take care not to use so many new terms that students fail to understand what is being said.

Preliminary considerations need to be given also to the issue of teacher responses to student answers. These responses are a type of teacher feedback. A strong body of research suggests that feedback to learners correlates strongly with improved student learning (Zahorik 1987). In discussion, however, there is a need for caution in *how* this feedback is provided.

Some studies have revealed that many teachers' responses communicate to students that they are somehow "deficient" (Young, Arnold, and Watson 1987). This can undermine students' self-confidence and diminish their willingness to participate. In situations where teachers have taken care to seek more clarifications of student answers and make fewer negative evaluations, students have tended to perceive teacher comments in a more positive light.

Implementing the Technique

Teachers' sequencing of questions is influential in any discussion lesson (Good and Brophy 1987). In thinking about this issue, it is important to recognize that many students feel they are very vulnerable when a teacher asks them a question. Though they may feel inclined to say something, some students may hold back out of a fear that they may say something the teacher will not like. Initially, some students may be particularly reluctant to respond to questions that require them to voice an opinion or make a value judgment.

On the other hand, students often are less hesitant to answer when a question is less value-laden. For example, a simple question of fact such as "Who wrote the story?" poses little psychological threat to a student who knows the answer. The student will know what the teacher expects. The answer has little potential for drawing an unfavorable teacher comment. On the other hand, a question such as "What are the major strengths of this painting?" introduces a values issue. The student may be unclear of the teacher's position on this matter. As a result, there may be much less inclination to "take a chance" and respond to this question than to the much simpler, "who wrote-the-story" question.

Concerns about students' levels of anxiety suggest that it makes sense to begin a questioning sequence with simple, easy-to-answer, low-threat questions. Professionals at the Northwest Regional Educational Laboratory developed a questioning sequence composed of three basic categories of questions (Northam 1972). Teachers are advised to begin with category 1 questions, then to move on to category 2 questions, and finally to conclude with category 3 questions. The three categories are as follows:

Category 1: Analysis-of-specifics questions
Category 2: Analysis-of-relationships questions
Category 3: Generalizing or "capstone" questions

ANALYSIS-OF-SPECIFICS QUESTIONS.   It is suggested that questions from this category be used at the beginning of a discussion. Questions in this category are nonthreatening, low-risk questions. Students are asked simply to recall specific pieces of information to which they have been exposed prior to the beginning of the discussion. These are confidence-building questions. Students are not asked to make opinions or judgments. Some examples are:

"What was the occupation of the main character?"

"How many elements were known when radium was discovered?"

"What French word for 'trouble' did the officer use?"

"What is the first step in factoring?"

ANALYSIS-OF-RELATIONSHIPS QUESTIONS.   One purpose of analysis-of-specifics questions is to help students build a sound understanding of basic information. Once this has been accomplished, then more sophisticated analysis-of-relationships questions can be asked. Questions in this category require students to compare, contrast, and analyze. Students are asked to go beyond the basic facts and to make some personal judgments. Some examples are:

"All right, we saw what Hamilton thought about the federal government, and we saw what Jefferson thought. How would you compare their views?"

"What similarities do you see in the rhyme schemes, caesura placements, and beats per line between typical seventeenth century French poetry and this contemporary French poem?"

"How would you explain the reaction that took place after the ammonium nitrate was added?"

GENERALIZING, OR "CAPSTONE," QUESTIONS. Questions in this category are the most sophisticated of all. They require students to go well beyond given information. Further, they require them to make rather sophisticated personal judgments. In short, questions in this category are high-risk questions. However, provided that an appropriate information base has been built through the use of a sequence of questions from analysis of specifics through analysis of relationships, students will be willing to respond to questions of this kind. Some examples are:

"What does the poem mean to you personally?"

"What basic message was the author trying to convey to the reader?"

"How do you feel about nuclear proliferation and why?"

"What consequences do you see for a continuation of the high rate of population increase in Brazil?"

Box 8.2 is an exercise in sequencing.

Productive discussions require more than a proper sequencing of questions. Good discussion leaders must also use other important techniques. One of the most basic of these has to do with the issue of "wait time." "Wait time" refers to the time that elapses after a question has been asked before (a) a student answers the question, (b) the teacher calls on another student to answer the question, (c) the teacher answers the question, or (d) the teacher rephrases the question, abandons the question, or asks an entirely different question. There is evidence that many teachers wait for a student answer for only about one second after they ask a question before calling on someone else, answering the question themselves, or saying something else (Good and Brophy 1987).

Experienced discussion leaders have found it prudent to wait at least seven or eight seconds before rephrasing a question or going on to something else. The basic principle here is that thinking takes time. Particularly when questions are complex, it is illogical to assume students can deliver a reasoned response without the benefit of a few moments of thinking time.

Effective discussion leaders are careful to react to student answers in ways that will maintain the discussion. A number of important reaction skills have been identified by the Northwest Regional Educational Laboratory (Northam 1972).

These skills include the following:

1. Refocusing
2. Clarifying
3. Summarizing
4. Mapping the conceptual field
5. Substantiating

Box 8.2

Sequencing Questions

Suppose that a teacher had just shown a film on modern Japan to his or her class. Following the film, the teacher planned to ask some questions of the students as part of a debriefing exercise. The teacher was considering using one of the following sequences of questions:

SEQUENCE 1

Question 1: What was the man in the factory doing?

Question 2: How were the steel worker and the office worker alike and different?

Question 3: How would you compare the Japanese steel plant with an American steel plant?

Question 4: Should we have a government like Japan's?

Question 5: What did the film mean to you?

SEQUENCE 2

Question 1: What did the film mean to you?

Question 2: Should we have a government like Japan's?

Question 3: What was the man in the factory doing?

Question 4: How would you compare the Japanese steel plant with an American steel plant?

Question 5: How were the steel worker and the office worker alike and different?

What Do You Think?

Look at the two sequences above. Then, respond to these questions.

1. Are there any questions that students might find more threatening than others? If so, which questions are they? Why do you think that they would be higher-threat questions than the others?

2. Do you think you would get more student participation using one of these sequences rather than the other? Why do you think so?

3. Which one of these sequences would you use? Why?

REFOCUSING. This skill is important as a means of keeping the discussion "on track." Certain students are adept at injecting comments that can lead the group away from the main topic of the lesson. To prevent this from happening, skilled discussion leaders listen carefully and make comments to refocus group attention whenever the first signs of drift are noted. Consider this example:

Maria: I was thinking about those trinity symbols in *Crime and Punishment.*

Teacher: Yes?

Maria: I saw this space thing on the late movie last night. People were wearing these strange suits with these three-sided patches. I mean, that might mean something.

Susan: That was a b-a-a-d movie. Wonderfully gross!

Mark: Yeah. Remember when they dumped the head guy into the giant blender? I mean *whoosh*, and he was gone.

Teacher: Maria, let's get back to your point. How do you see trinity symbols in the film related to trinity symbols in *Crime and Punishment*? No, let's go back even a bit more. Tell me what you see as trinity symbols in *Crime and Punishment*.

CLARIFYING. Some students have difficulty expressing themselves. Often the intent of their contributions is unclear. They need help in learning how to express themselves clearly and specifically. Teacher comments can help them do this. Consider this example:

Michael: I heard they're going to make Maple into a one-way street. That makes me mad. They can't do that.

Teacher: Just who are this "they" you're talking about?

Michael: You know, the government.

Teacher: You're saying some government officials have decided to make Maple a one-way street. Now let's get a little more specific. Just what government are you talking about?

Michael: You know, those people who decide about streets and that sort of thing.

Teacher: Well, which people make these decisions?

Michael: My dad said something about a planning commission. I think that's a local outfit, but I'm not sure.

Teacher: Yes, I believe that's right. So, to get back to your point, you're saying you're unhappy because the city planning commission has plans to make Maple a one-way street. Why don't you like this idea?

SUMMARIZING. Unless they are very brief, discussions often deal with a huge quantity of information. At points during the discussion, it is useful for the teacher to pause and help students to reflect on points that have been made. Once this has been done, the discussion can move on to still other issues. Consider this example:

Teacher: Let's stop a moment and think about what we've said so far. Jose pointed out that Dr. Friedman said that the main cause of inflation was the government's printing too much money. LaShandra said that other economists say other factors are important. Renee pointed out that people don't save money like they used to and that this drives up prices. What else? Have I missed any other points that were made?

Donna: Well, Nguyen said the big property tax rebate last year made people spend too much and that all the stores jacked up prices.

Teacher: Thank you, Donna, I forgot about that. Anything else I missed?

MAPPING THE CONCEPTUAL FIELD. Secondary school students tend to seek quick answers to complex problems. Many of them are not comfortable with ambiguity. Consequently, during a discussion they will often rally behind the first solution to a problem that is mentioned. When this happens, they may be reluctant to discuss the problem further. One important task for teachers in their roles as discussion leaders is to keep students from arriving at premature conclusions. Consider this example:

Teacher: Most of you seem to be nodding your heads in agreement with Jay's idea that this writer seems pessimistic because she was an orphan and must have had an unpleasant childhood. Are there some possible problems with this explanation? Are there some other possibilities?

Nora: Just because she was an orphan doesn't mean that she had a bad life. Even if she did, she might not be pessimistic now.

Teacher: That's a good observation, Nora. Kim?

Kim: Maybe she had a bad experience when she was a war correspondent.

Teacher: An interesting idea, Kim. How about you, Domingo?

Domingo: She might have been on drugs and got off. That make some people pessimistic.

Teacher: That's another idea for us to think about. Truan?

Truan: She maybe is afraid of dying. Sometimes that makes people pessimistic.

Teacher: These are all good comments. Anyone else have some ideas?

SUBSTANTIATING. Teachers need to monitor students' statements carefully to assure that they are based upon accurate information. Substantiating helps students to look at the logic of their statements. Consider this example:

> *James:*   So what if Jefferson said it? People in those days didn't know much. Why should we care?
>
> *Teacher:*   That's an interesting comment. Let me ask you a question or two just to help me understand your answer. Do you think an understanding of foreign languages, mathematics, and architecture would indicate somebody who "knew something?"
>
> *James:*   Well, I suppose so.
>
> *Teacher:*   Did Jefferson know anything about languages, mathematics, or architecture?
>
> *James:*   I really don't know.
>
> *Teacher:*   I think you might find an answer to that question interesting. Let's get together at the end of the period. I can tell you where to find out some things about President Jefferson that you would like to know.

Debriefing

The debriefing that occurs at the conclusion of a discussion is quite similar to the summarizing that goes on at various times during the discussion. The basic distinction is that the final debriefing attempts to pull together all of the key points that have been discussed. It provides a general review of the lesson content.

Demonstration

Demonstration generally is used in situations where teachers wish to show students steps involved in completing a learning task. The technique has long been a favorite of science teachers. For example, demonstrations are often used to introduce students to procedures to be used in laboratory exercises. The technique has application to other areas of the school curriculum as well. Crafts teachers, wood-working teachers, auto mechanic teachers, physical education teachers, mathematics teachers, social studies teachers, and English teachers are among those who, from time to time, also use the technique.

General Characteristics

Though demonstrations can be used to introduce entirely new material, they are more frequently used to point out to students how they should apply information to which they have been previously exposed.

During demonstrations, teachers have opportunities to reinforce critical information and key points that have been introduced earlier. Demonstrations also allow them to remind students of the basic objectives or purposes toward which the demonstration is directed.

Many demonstrations require the teacher to manipulate physical objects of some kind. This adds a dimension of reality to learning that often is lacking when content is introduced in the course textbooks. For this reason, good demonstrations are often excellent motivators.

Typically, demonstrations by the teacher are followed by opportunities for students to do what has been demonstrated. This gives the teacher an opportunity to monitor work of individual students. The quality of student work can be assessed and remediation can be provided, as required.

Preparation for Using the Demonstration

IDENTIFYING THE TOPIC. Demonstration is a technique well suited to a wide variety of topics. The technique works especially well with those that will involve students in some application activities once basic procedures have been developed. Additionally, learning activities that can be broken down into a number of steps are particularly well adapted to this technique. When content can be divided in this way, the teacher can emphasize each critical step during the demonstration.

PRELIMINARY CONSIDERATIONS. Ordinarily, successful demonstrations require students to have some basic understanding of the content to be introduced. For example, a junior high school social studies teacher might interested in demonstrating that places on a globe can be found by using latitude and longitude coordinates. Prior to the demonstration, the teacher would expect students to have some basic information about the terms "latitude" and "longitude" and about how they are measured. If students lack this basic information, they will be very confused by the demonstration.

In planning the demonstration, it is important to identify the key information to be transmitted to students. This information needs to be highlighted for students during the demonstration itself. Some teachers find it useful to prepare a few note cards with the key points identified. These prompt them to emphasize the importance of this information during the presentation.

Implementing the Technique

Since demonstrations are often followed by opportunities for students to apply content they have learned, students should be asked to take

Demonstration is often used to familiarize students with the use of specialized equipment.
Photo courtesy of Barbara Hadley.

notes on what they observe. They can refer to these as they participate in the follow-up application activities.

Many teachers who have used the demonstration technique successfully follow a carefully planned sequence. An example of such a sequence follows:

Step 1. Demonstrate to students the steps they must follow to accomplish an assigned task. (Obviously, students must be told the nature of the task and told what constitutes "successful" completion of the task.)

Step 2. Respond to questions students might have about what has been demonstrated. (If no questions arise, the teacher cannot assume no questions exist. Teachers generally ask a few questions on their own initiatives to be sure that students grasp what has been demonstrated.)

Step 3. Review steps that students are to follow. (Clarity is a must. To assure they have left nothing out, some teachers find it useful to write these steps on a note card. By referring to this information, they can be sure all needed information is transmitted to students.)

Step 4. At random, selected students should be called upon to tell the teacher the appropriate steps to be followed in accomplishing the follow-up application activity. The teacher listens to this information and corrects any mistakes.

Step 5. Students are provided an opportunity to practice what they have learned. The teacher checks on individual students to assure they are implementing procedures properly.

Often people who have difficulty with the demonstration technique have failed to do a good job on steps 4 and 5 of the suggested sequence. It is critically important that students have a very clear understanding of what they are to do during the application phase of the lesson. This information should be incorporated as an integral part of the teacher demonstration (see Box 8.3).

Debriefing

During the application phase of the demonstration lesson, the teacher has opportunities to work with individual students and note their progress. At the end of the lesson, the teacher once again works with the class as a whole. The teacher comments on any general problems students seemed to be having during the application exercise. During this time, students are encouraged to raise questions of their own. The debriefing concludes with the teacher recapitulating what was done. Students are reminded of the purpose of the exercise, what they did, and why it was important.

Case Study

The case study technique involves students in an intense study of a specific episode or situation. The topic for the case study must be selected with care. The best cases are those that are illustrative of general problems or conditions. If the case is not representative of the general problem or issue on which it focuses, there is a possibility students will take away understandings that do not generalize well.

General Characteristics

Good case studies can prompt high levels of student interest. Many learners find it easy to identify with characters and situations as they are "brought to life" in a case study.

Case studies are quite flexible. They can be used in a number of content areas. Sometimes, case studies are used to review previously introduced content. More often, they introduce students to new material.

Box 8.3

Preparing a Demonstration

Identify a subject area you would like to teach. From this subject, identify a topic that could be taught using a demonstration technique. Do some partial planning for your demonstration that will include the following information:

1. Title of the focus topic.

2. Identification of each step in the process or procedure to be demonstrated.

3. Specific "trouble spots" you would watch for when students were asked to do this procedure themselves.

4. A short paragraph explaining some specific advantages of using the demonstration technique to teach this content.

Share your information with your instructor, and ask for comments.

Many case studies are developed in a way that requires students to apply information and to engage in other activities requiring use of higher-level thinking skills. The level of student thinking stimulated by a case study is closely related to the quality of the focus questions prepared by the teacher who develops the lesson.

Preparation for Using the Case Study

IDENTIFYING THE TOPIC.   Topics that work best for case studies are those that point out dilemmas, identify critical problems, and highlight controversies. They should be capable of stimulating thought.

The materials available about a given topic also place some limitations on topic selection. Successful case studies require students to have a good deal of information about issues that are addressed. If such information is lacking to teachers who prepare the case studies, then students are not going to have enough background to deal with difficult issues that may be raised.

PRELIMINARY CONSIDERATIONS.   Development of effective case studies requires teachers to have a good understanding of interests and capabilities of their students. A knowledge of students' interests will allow the teacher to select a topic that has some intrinsic appeal. An understanding of students' abilities will assure that developed materials are neither too unsophisticated nor too difficult. For example, many case studies require students to read background information. If the reading difficulty of this material exceeds the reading abilities of large numbers of class members, then many students will not grasp basic information they will need to work through the case.

Though commercially prepared cases exist, it is generally preferable for teachers to develop them on their own. When they do this, there is a much better chance that the material will be appropriate for the students than is the case when commercial materials are used. (See Box 8.4.)

Implementing the Technique

In preparing case studies for classroom use, many teachers have followed these basic steps:

1. Identification of a major lesson purpose.
2. Selection of an appropriate case.
3. Preparation of suitable focus questions.

To illustrate each step, consider this example:

Purpose To illustrate varying perspectives on a controversial issue.

Illustrative Case John Peter Zenger came to the British colonies in North America in 1710. A native of Germany, Zenger settled in New York City. He started a newspaper, *The New York Weekly Journal*. His life was relatively uneventful until 1732.

In that year, William Cosby came to the New York Colony from England as its new governor. Before Cosby arrived, another person had been discharging the duties of the governor pending the new appointee's arrival. When Cosby landed in New York, he discovered this person had been drawing the governor's salary. Though some people felt this was fair because this person had been doing the governor's work, Cosby was outraged. He sued the man for the salary money he had been receiving. By using some questionable tricks, Cosby succeeded in getting a court decision in his favor.

After this happened, John Peter Zenger reported a number of the questionable things Cosby had done to win his case. Furious, Cosby accused Zenger of libel. "Libel" is defined as a publicly disseminated statement that unjustly conveys a negative impression of someone. Zenger was brought to trial.

Cosby was concerned that the colonists might be getting the idea that they had real powers of their own. An attack against the governor, a representative of the King of England, might be regarded as an attack against the crown. Cosby viewed Zenger as a dangerous man, and he was eager for him to get his just due in a court of law.

At this time, it was not the practice of juries to decide whether someone had been libeled. This was a decision made by the judge.

Box 8.4

Are Case Studies Worth the Time?

Nobody questions the motivational value of case studies. Many students really "get into" content that is presented in this way. However, there is a down side to case studies as well. Case-study lessons consume huge quantities of class time.

Sometimes case studies go on for several days. Even though students may be very actively involved, every day spent on a single case study reduces time available to cover other important content. There is a danger that depth of content coverage that the case study makes possible may irresponsibly take away from breadth of content.

What Do You Think?

1. Is it necessarily true that case studies take more instructional time than other techniques? Why do you think so?

2. Some people argue that schools attempt to cover too much content. How would these people react to the statement above? How do you feel about the statement?

3. What should be the appropriate relationship between breadth of coverage and depth of coverage?

If the judge decided that libel had occurred, the only task of the jury was to decide whether the libelous statement had come from the individual accused of the crime.

Zenger's lawyers argued two key points. First, they contended that juries, not the judge, should decide whether libel had occurred. Second, they argued that a person should not be held guilty of libel if the information the person disseminated could be demonstrated to be true. The court case was decided in favor of the views of Zenger's attorneys. It established a common law precedent for freedom of the press. This precedent was recognized in one of the first 10 amendments to the United States Constitution.

Focus questions
1. What kinds of pressures was Cosby under as the new governor of New York? What were the sources of those pressures? What kinds of people might have supported his position?

2. What, specifically, was argued by Zenger's attorneys? What kinds of people in the colony might have been most likely to support these positions?

3. How do you think people in England reacted to the decision in the Zenger case? Why do you think so?

4. How might our country be different today if those deciding the Zenger case had decided against the views of Zenger and his

attorneys? Would we be better off or worse off? Are there people today who would like to restrict freedom of the press? What are their arguments?

Debriefing

The debriefing phase of a case study allows the teacher and the class to review the general process that was followed. It also permits the teacher to extend the range of the lesson. For example, in the sample case involving the Zenger trial, the teacher might wish to cite examples throughout American history of legislative efforts to suspend certain aspects of freedom of the press. The entire issue of national security versus freedom of the press is one that might come up during debriefing.

Key Ideas in Summary

1. There is no single instructional technique that is best for all sets of circumstances. Instructional techniques need to be selected in light of teacher characteristics, learning-task characteristics, student characteristics, and instructional-setting characteristics.

2. In planning to use any instructional technique, teachers make planning decisions in four areas. These include (a) identifying the topic, (b) preliminary considerations, (c) implementing the technique, and (d) debriefing students.

3. Lecture, as a technique, has somewhat of a bad reputation. The problem comes not from its inherent deficiencies, but rather from misuse. Types of misuse involve (a) content overload, (b) excessive length, and (c) poor organization.

4. Successful lecturers often do these things: (a) begin only after they have ascertained existing levels of student understanding; (b) keep presentations short; (c) take care to emphasize key points; and, (d) provide students with a note-taking outline.

5. Discussion is a technique that many beginners find difficult to implement. Often they experience problems in keeping the discussion going for more than a few minutes. Successful discussion leaders have learned the importance of sequencing questions. They tend to begin with simple, non-threatening questions and to build only gradually toward more sophisticated, value-laden questions. These teachers are also careful to respond to students' answers in ways that encourage additional participation.

6. Demonstrations are particularly useful when the intent is to show students how to do some task, process, or procedure. Demonstrations

often begin with a teacher presentation that is followed by opportunities for students to do what is demonstrated. Before students are permitted to apply what they have learned, it is important for the teacher to take time to assure they understand the steps that are to be followed.

7. Teachers often find that many students are motivated to learn when they are exposed to case studies. The case study format can be used to "humanize" issues that, in the context of the textbook, may appear distant and abstract to students. Three basic steps are involved in preparation of a case study for classroom use. These are (a) identification of a major lesson purpose, (b) selection and development of an appropriate case, and (c) preparation of focus questions.

POSTTEST

DIRECTIONS: Using your own paper, answer these true/false questions. For each correct statement, write the word "true." For each incorrect statement, write the word "false."

_____ 1. All instructional techniques are equally suitable for all topics.

_____ 2. During debriefing, teachers often have opportunities to clear up student misunderstandings.

_____ 3. It is a poor practice for teachers to provide students with a lecture outline to follow. This practice undermines development of students' listening skills.

_____ 4. Demonstrations are often used in situations where teachers wish to familiarize students with steps to be followed in implementing a procedure.

_____ 5. For many students, information presented in the form of a case study seems more "real" than content introduced in a textbook.

Bibliography

CLARKE, JOHN H. "Building a Lecture that Really Works." *Language Arts* (December 1987): 890–897.

GOOD, THOMAS L., AND BROPHY, JERE E. *Looking in Classrooms.* 4th edition. New York: Harper & Row, 1987.

GROISSER, PHILIP L. *How to Use the Fine Art of Questioning.* Englewood Cliffs, New Jersey: Prentice-Hall, 1964.

LONG, DONNA R. "A Case for Case Studies." *Foreign Language Annals* (May 1986): 225–229.

NORTHAM, SARALIE B. (ED.). "Instructor's Manual: Development of Higher-Level Thinking Abilities." Portland, OR: Northwest Regional Educational Laboratory, 1972.

SCHUY, ROGER W. "Research Currents: Dialogue as the Heart of Learning." *Language Arts* (December 1987): 890–897.

TAMA, M. CARROL. "How Are Students Responding in Discussion Groups?" *The Social Studies* (May–June 1986): 132–135.

WILL, HOWARD C. "Asking Good Follow-up Questions." *Gifted Child Today.* (July–August 1987): 32–34.

WINGO, ROSE C. "Why Students Won't Discuss." *Business Education Forum* (March 1988): 13–14.

YOUNG, R. E.; ARNOLD, R.; AND WATSON, K. "Linguistic Models." In Michael J. Dunkin (ed.). *The International Encyclopedia of Teaching and Teacher Education.* Oxford: Pergamon Press, 1987. pp. 49–58.

ZAHORIK, J. A. "Reacting." In Michael J. Dunkin (ed.). *The International Encyclopedia of Teaching and Teacher Education.* Oxford: Pergamon Press, 1987. pp. 416–423.

CHAPTER 9

Learning in Groups

AIMS

This chapter provides information to help the reader to:

1. State the importance of group learning.
2. Identify some steps involved in implementing group activities.
3. Describe procedures for preparing students for a class debate.
4. Describe procedures for implementing role playing.
5. Point out characteristics of classroom simulation activities.
6. Distinguish among alternative approaches to cooperative learning.
7. Suggest some planning considerations for a field trip.

PRETEST

DIRECTIONS: Using your own paper, answer these true/false questions. For each correct statement, write the word "true." For each incorrect statement, write the word "false."

_____ 1. The primary purpose of group learning activities is the development of students' socialization skills.

_____ 2. Because classroom debates require little advance preparation, they are excellent "spur of the moment" activities.

_____ 3. Simulations seek to simplify reality for the purposes of enabling students to make choices and to experience the consequences of those choices.

_____ 4. Student Teams-Achievement Divisions is an example of a cooperative learning activity.

_____ 5. In the Jigsaw technique, some group members become "experts" on a certain aspect of the topic being studied and share their learning with other group members.

Introduction

We live in an age of specialization. Though some people are more self-sufficient than others, the complexity of our modern technological society makes it impossible for single individuals to master all of the knowledge necessary for sustaining and extending the quality of their lives. What is required is a large number of people who, individually, have varying talents, understandings, and skills. When individual expertise is exercised in cooperation with others, improved circumstances for all can result.

An important implication for education is that students need opportunities to collaborate as well as opportunities to develop their own unique areas of specialized knowledge. Group learning experiences provide students with insights into the kind of give-and-take that characterizes many social and vocational relationships in the adult world.

Happily for teachers, group learning activities often are an "easy sell" to students. Human beings are social creatures who seek out and enjoy relationships with others. For this reason, group learning often is seen by students as a "natural" organizational pattern.

This chapter introduces a small sample of group learning techniques. Each has its own unique characteristics. However, all of them seek to develop students' appreciation for the benefits of cooperative approaches to problem-solving.

Classroom Debates

Classifying a debate as a technique for promoting cooperation might seem a contradiction. After all, the kinds of debates most people are familiar with involve two people hammering away at one another trying to make a case for the side of the issue they are arguing. The kind of classroom debate suggested here is quite different. It involves teams of individuals on each side of the issue. Members of the teams work together cooperatively.

Selection of a classroom debate as an instructional technique requires a special philosophical orientation to teaching and learning. It presumes

"Learning in groups is a sound approach *in general*. As for this particular lesson, well, . . . ?"

that there are no absolutely "right" or "wrong" answers to selected
focus questions and issues. There is an assumption that students who
participate in the process will be exposed to a variety of evidence and
that, at the end of the debate, individuals may come to very different
conclusions.

General Characteristics

Two key purposes of classroom debate are (1) to involve all members
of the class and (2) to promote a commitment to cooperative decision-
making. The teacher begins by dividing the class into small groups.
Each group may have from four to eight members. These individual
groups or teams are given a basic position on an issue. They are charged
with the task of conducting research to gather evidence to support their

position. Every student in a class is assigned to a team. This may mean that there are several focus issues.

For example, suppose a teacher had 28 students in the class. Two major focus issues would be sufficient to involve every student. One issue might be: "Resolved that every male and female high school graduate in the United States should complete six months of mandatory active duty military service." One group of seven students would be assigned to research the "pro" position. Another team would research the "con."

The second issue might be: "Resolved that people should lose their drivers' licenses permanently after their third conviction for 'driving while intoxicated.'" Again, one team of seven would be assigned to research the "pro" position and another group of seven to research the "con" position.

Classroom debate activities require a substantial amount of class time. Students must do their research, work together with team members to synthesize what they have learned and to formulate positions. Time must be provided, too, for the debate itself and for a follow-up discussion.

Preparation for Classroom Debates

The specific preparation will vary depending on how many topics the teacher has identified and how many students will be assigned to each group. The general example introduced in the last section features just two issues. Fourteen students were assigned to each issue. Seven from each team did research on the "pro" position; the other seven did research on the "con" position.

This model is just one of many that might be selected. The same teacher might be interested in having the class consider four issues rather than two. This would require division of the class into four large groups of seven students each. Some students in each group of seven would research the "pro" position and some would research the "con" position. Notice that dividing a group of seven into two equal parts leaves an extra student. There are several ways this situation can be accommodated. One is to create a special additional role. One possibility is to have the seventh person serve as a "skeptical critic."

The skeptical critic studies information relevant to both the "pro" position and the "con" position. This person seeks to prepare himself or herself to ask probing, even embarrassing questions, as part of the debate exercise. These questions will be directed both at members of the "pro" team and members of the "con" team.

A group of seven students assigned to prepare for a debate on a single topic might be organized as follows:

"Pro" team - 3 students

"Con" team - 3 students

"Skeptical critic" - 1 student

After doing the basic research, the flow of the debate might proceed in this way:

1. Each member of the "pro" team and each member of the "con" team speaks alternately for 2 minutes. (total: 12 minutes.)

2. Each member of the "pro" team may cross-examine any member of the "con" team for two minutes. Each member of the "con" team may cross-examine each member of the "pro" team for two minutes. (total: 12 minutes.)

3. Members of each team alternately make a final statement lasting no more than one minute. (total: 6 minutes.)

4. Skeptical critic asks difficult questions of any member of the "pro" or "con" team. The critic tries to unravel arguments, especially weaker ones, made by both sides. A total of about 8 minutes is allocated for this activity. (time: 8 minutes.)

5. Class as a whole votes to determine whether the "pro" side or the "con" side won.

6. Teacher leads a classroom discussion and completes a debriefing of the exercise.

This particular model results in a judgment that declares either the "pro" or the "con" side to be the winner. Some other organizational schemes result in different final outcomes. For example, Johnson and Johnson (1985) describe a model that asks debate participants to reach a consensus on the issue at the conclusion of the activity.

Identifying the Topic and the Roles

Topics that are selected for debates should be controversial. They should be of high interest to learners. Often issues related to legal constraints on young people (dress codes, curfews, graduation requirements, and so forth) work well. Successful classroom debates require participants to have much information in hand. This requires an abundance of information sources. In selecting debate topics, teachers must assure that necessary information is available for students to use as they prepare for the activity. (See Box 9.1).

Box 9.1

Identifying Learning Resources for a Classroom Debate

Successful classroom debates require participants to have adequate resource materials to draw upon as they prepare their arguments. It is especially critical that approximately equivalent amounts of background information be available to support both "pro" and "con" positions. In preparing for a debate, teachers often find it useful to provide students with lists of learning resources they might wish to consult. Suppose you were planning a classroom debate. Identify the topic. Then, identify some specific resources that you would provide to students as they prepared for the exercise.

DEBATE TOPIC: _____

RELEVANT BOOK TITLES: _____
_____
_____
_____

RELEVANT NEWSPAPER AND JOURNAL ARTICLES _____
_____
_____
_____

OTHER RELEVANT RESOURCES _____
_____
_____
_____

Preliminary Considerations

Students' performance in debates tends to improve with their familiarity with the method. The first debate they experience may well teach them as much about the technique as about the subject matter. It is particularly important that an initial classroom debate experience be a good one. The topic should be one that really excites students. They should have ready access to needed resource materials. The planned flow of the debate should be explained clearly, and the process should be carefully monitored by the teacher as it unfolds. The debriefing for this initial debate needs to be planned carefully. Students should be provided tips related to the process as well as provided with a forum to exchange views about content issues that were raised.

Classroom debates require students to work together in teams. Some students may have had limited experience in cooperative exercises of this kind. Some teachers find it useful to precede classroom debate experiences with some group process activities and games. These can help students develop more positive attitudes toward the idea of working together on a common project.

The nature of group composition needs to be addressed. In selecting members of individual groups, teachers typically consider abilities and motivation levels of individual students. There generally is an attempt to divide talents in such a way that expertise in each group is approximately equal.

Implementing the Technique

When team assignments have been made, the teacher must assure that members of each group understand their task and the time they have available to complete it. It is particularly important that they be informed of locations and availability of resource materials.

As team members prepare, the teacher carefully monitors the progress of each group. Among other things, it is necessary to ensure that each student is making a reasonable contribution to the overall group effort. One or two students should not be allowed to do the work for the entire group.

Teachers often play a "devil's advocate" role during the preparation phase. They ask about information students have found and about arguments they propose to make. A teacher may say something like: "Well, that's an interesting idea. But what would you say if I came back at you with this argument. . . ." The idea is to prevent students from coming to premature closure and to keep them thinking about additional possibilities for arguing their case.

Before the actual debate begins, the teacher shares general procedural guidelines and makes sure that students understand them. During the debate, the teacher arbitrates disputes over procedures and other issues that may arise.

Debriefing

The debriefing that occurs at the end of the exercise is one of the most important parts of a classroom debate. The teacher deals with two major areas of concern at this time. First, the major ideas brought up in the debate are highlighted. Second, the nature of the process itself is considered.

To re-emphasize points made during the debate, teachers ask questions such as:

1. What arguments impressed you?
2. Why were these arguments appealing?
3. What arguments would you have emphasized if you had been a member of the "pro" team? Of the "con" team?
4. What major concerns do people need to consider as they think about resolving this issue?
5. Have any of you faced problems with an issue similar to or related to the one we have just debated? How did you resolve them?
6. Where might we find additional information about this topic?

The following are examples of kinds of questions that might be asked that focus on the process characteristics of the debate:

1. Why did we approach the topic in this way?
2. How might this method of group work be used in other situations?
3. What things did some team members do that was effective in helping their group meet success?
4. What things or activities could have been more effective if they had been done differently?
5. Based on what we have learned, what changes should we make if we were going to prepare to debate another issue?

Role Playing

A "role" is a patterned sequence of thoughts, feelings, actions, and words (Chesler and Fox 1966). The role playing technique requires students to study roles of others carefully and to react to situations in a manner consistent with the roles they have assumed. Role playing helps students sharpen their awareness of self and appreciate varying ways in which others interpret and react to events in life.

At one time, role playing was a technique used primarily in the elementary schools. Today, the method is also widely used in secondary schools. Its acceptance at this level, in part, has resulted from the successful application of role playing in settings involving adult participants. For example, role playing has been successfully imple-

mented in labor relationship disputes to help resolve problems arising
from different perspectives of workers and managers. In some law
offices, it is common for attorneys to use a role playing technique to
prepare for situations they expect to confront during a trial. A form
of the technique called "psychodrama" has been used by counseling
psychologists to help their clients come to grips with emotional and
behavioral problems (Joyce and Weil 1986).

General Characteristics

Role playing calls on individuals to step outside of their personal roles
and to assume the patterns of behavior of others. Several goals might
logically be pursued. Among purposes often sought by teachers who
use role playing are (1) developing of general interpersonal relations
skills; (2) sensitizing students to perspectives of different cultural, social,
or ethnic groups; (3) appreciating perspectives of family members of
different generations; (4) predicting the impact of individual decisions
on people other than the decision-maker; and (5) teaching academic
content by replicating roles of individuals who participated in important
events.

The role playing technique can be applied in many different subject
areas. The duration of a role playing exercise will vary depending on
complexities of the issues it addresses, numbers of roles, and on other
variables. Role playing is discussed further in Box 9.2.

Preparation for Role Playing

IDENTIFYING THE TOPIC AND THE ROLE.   The best role playing
topics are topics that are of high interest to students. Some teachers
find it useful to involve students in the selection of focus issues. The
topic selected for an initial role playing activity should be one that will
not require a large number of roles. Further, it should be an issue
that can be addressed in a relatively short period of time. Part of the
purpose of the initial role playing exercise is to familiarize students with
the technique. Once they have become used to the procedure, more
complex focus topics can be selected that require larger numbers of
roles and additional time.

As the focus for a first role playing experience, a common personal
problem experienced by students often serves well. For example, many
younger secondary school students do not have drivers' licenses. In a
family with several children, several family members may have a need to
be at different places at the same time. The "problem" arises in working
out an arrangement with a parent to assure that everyone's needs are
accommodated. A simple role playing exercise with this focus might be
set up in this way.

Box 9.2

Is Role Playing an Appropriate Activity for Secondary School Students?

Role playing experiences require people to hide their own identities as they take on the characteristics of another person. There is nothing particularly wrong with this exercise *provided* the person who is asked to play the role is a mature adult whose own personality characteristics are firmly established. For younger people, particularly adolescents, role playing may be dangerous.

Many adolescents are still seeking to establish their own personal identities. Role playing may provide a convenient escape from the difficulties of carving out their own unique life roles. It may provide an incentive for them to live in a dream world of fantasy where they continue to "play" the role of someone else rather than work to define their own personalities.

Read the comments above. Then respond to these questions.

1. What major concerns about role playing prompted these comments?

2. What strengths do you see in this argument? What weaknesses?

3. What are your own views about the appropriateness of role playing for secondary school students?

The Problem: Mrs. Smith is a single parent. The family has one car. The three Smith children are Susan, John, and Paul. Susan is 9. John is 12. Paul is 14. On Saturday night, Mrs. Smith has been invited to a dinner party at 7:00 p.m. Susan and her friend Irene have been invited to stay overnight at Nora Jackson's house. (Nora Jackson's family's only car is in the garage and won't be available until Monday.) John won a drawing at the grocery store and has a free ticket to a movie. His ticket is good only for the 7:00 p.m. film on Saturday night. Paul wants to go to an all-day football clinic on Saturday. It will take place on the local university campus. He will be there until 7:00 p.m. and will need to be picked up at that time. The Smith house is 10 miles from the location of Mrs. Smith's dinner party, 5 miles from Nora Jackson's house, 8 miles from the movie theater, and 13 miles from the university campus. What should be done on Saturday night in response to the need of the four Smiths to be transported to different places at the same time?

Needed Roles: Mrs. Smith, Susan Smith, John Smith, Paul Smith

As students become more familiar with the technique, more complex role playing situations can be developed.

Preliminary Considerations

For students who have never encountered role playing, some teachers find it useful to select a small number of students to play roles and to arrange for them to meet with the teacher as a group outside of the regular class time. The teacher explains the focus problem, explains roles, and helps these students understand what they are to do. Then, this group acts out the role playing situation in front of the class. With this kind of advance preparation, participants may feel more comfortable in "performing" in front of the class.

Successful role playing lessons are built on careful preparation. Time must be provided for students to learn enough about the situation and the specific roles they will be playing. The following preparation steps are derived from some suggestions put forward by Joyce and Weil (1986):

1. *Initial Focus.* In this step, the teacher introduces the role playing focus to the class. This problem, which should be something class members recognize as important to them, might be introduced in a variety of ways. The teacher might provide a short lecture. Other possibilities include use of a story, a film, a clipping from a newspaper, or an audio or videorecording.

2. *Establishing an Appropriate Climate.* Role playing can be a psychologically threatening experience for some students. The teacher needs to take time to explain that people playing roles will not necessarily be speaking their own views. The purpose is to identify with likely views of people whose roles they are assuming. Students need to be told that feelings and thoughts they express will be accepted. It is very important for them to understand that they will not be ridiculed for what they say after they have assumed their roles.

3. *Select the Participants.* Sometimes students are allowed to volunteer for roles. At other times, the teacher may wish to make these assignments. ("Bill, will you play the role of the 'environmentalist?' And, Susan, would you like to be the 'landowner' who needs money and wants to sell the property to the real estate developer?") Students should be allowed to refuse to play a role. The role playing exercise will not be successful if students are forced to do something they find particularly distasteful.

4. *Familiarizing Players with Their Roles.* Individuals selected to play the roles need to be provided specific information about their individual roles and to be reminded of the basic "problem" selected for the focus of the activity. They need to be provided with time to become thoroughly familiar with this information.

5. *Assigning Responsibilities to Other Class Members.*   A productive role playing lesson involves the entire class. Students who are not playing roles are assigned to watch for something specific as the role playing enactment occurs. (How realistic were Paul's answers to Mrs. Smith? How else might have Mrs. Smith handled this situation? And so forth.) They are asked to be ready to make some specific comments in the discussion that will follow. Sometimes, too, teachers plan for several enactments of the same situation. When this is done, some of the observers may assume roles and participate as players in a second or third enactment of the same basic situation.

Implementing the Technique

In preparation for the enactment, the teacher reminds the class of the general problem addressed. Sometimes it is also useful to provide class members with a reminder of the specific roles that are being played. These steps have been found useful in implementing role playing (Joyce and Weil 1986):

1. *The Enactment.* Role players are encouraged to act out their responses to the situation as realistically and spontaneously as possible. If students have not participated in role playing before, the teacher may find it necessary to intervene occasionally to stimulate dialogue, to insert a question, or to reestablish the problem focus if the dialogue begins to drift toward irrelevant side issues.

2. *Discuss and Evaluate.* Following the enactment, the teacher leads a discussion. Students who were assigned to look for specific things make their contributions. Individual role players are invited to discuss what they did. The teacher focuses the discussion on the motivations of the characters and the consequences of actions taken and decisions made. Alternative courses of action might also be identified. These can set the stage for lessons where the teacher wishes to follow the initial enactment and follow-up discussion with a re-enactment.

3. *Re-enactment.* Not all role playing lessons feature a re-enactment. When there is time to include one, the re-enactment may suggest some alternative courses of action that might be taken. Often, the entire situation played out in the initial enactment will not be repeated. The re-enactment may begin at some critical point that developed during the enactment. Roles are taken up as they were at the point, but directions taken from that point forward may be very different.

4. *Discuss and Evaluate the Re-enactment.* If there has been a re-enactment, this phase parallels the discussion that followed the initial enactment.

5. *Share Experiences and Generalize.* In this step, the teacher seeks to help students form some generalizations about human relationships or to develop deeper appreciations for the focus content of the role playing exercise. Students are encouraged to apply new learning to their own experiences and to other situations. The purpose of this phase of role playing is to help students transfer what they have learned. This helps establish the relevance of the role playing activity.

Debriefing

Debriefing serves several key purposes. It allows the teacher to summarize major points made during the role playing lesson. Additionally, it provides an opportunity for a discussion of the merits of the role playing process. Students can be involved in a discussion centering on the merits of studying topics this way. At this point, teachers sometimes solicit ideas about focus topics for additional role playing lessons.

Simulations

Simulations seek to place individuals in situations that model real-life environments. This is accomplished by simplifying real situations to highlight aspects that the simulation developer considers to be important. Simulations vary in their complexity from relatively simple board games much like Monopoly to complex computer-based schemes that illustrate how spacecraft will perform under different sets of conditions.

All simulations distort reality to some extent because they are based on versions of the real world that have been greatly simplified. In general, the more the real world has been simplified to facilitate participation in the simulation, the more reality is distorted. For example, although Monopoly is loosely based on real estate markets, no one would argue that mastery of the game should be taken as evidence of proficiency in the intricacies of real-world real estate markets.

The simplification of reality found in simulations has important benefits. Components that are selected for emphasis in a simulation can promote student learning of important information. Further, without simplification, it would be impossible for students to gain some valuable learning experiences. For example, students cannot learn about how legislators work by becoming legislators. They can, however, gain valuable insights by participating in simulations that have been designed to highlight certain features of the legislative process. Box 9.3 discusses evaluating simulations.

Box 9.3

Evaluating Simulations

A large number of simulations are marketed today. The following considerations may be useful to a teacher interested in selecting a simulation for classroom use.

TITLE	_____
SOURCE AND PRICE	_____
	_____
MAJOR PURPOSES	_____
	_____
	_____
CLARITY OF RULES	_____
	_____
	_____
SPECIAL EQUIPMENT NEEDED	_____
	_____
	_____
NUMBER OF PEOPLE WHO CAN BE INVOLVED	_____
SUMMARY COMMENTS	_____
	_____
	_____
	_____

General Characteristics

Simulations may be thought of as sophisticated elaborations of role playing. They require students to assume roles, make decisions, take actions, and face consequences. Most simulations require students to deal with several cycles of decision-making and consequence-facing. Because they are somewhat more complex in their structure than role playing, simulations often require more support material for students and more total class time to complete.

Good simulations feature engaging, lifelike problems that must be confronted and resolved. Some simulations require students to make individual decisions. Others call on them to organize in groups and make collective decisions. Individual simulations lay out important goals or objectives for participants. For example, in the simulation "Democracy," individuals assume the roles of legislators. They are given a list of bills that will be considered. Further, they have information regarding whether the people who elected them favor a given bill, oppose a given bill, or have no strong views regarding a given bill. The goal for each individual participant is to pass the bills his or her constituents favor and defeat the bills they oppose. The idea is for individuals to assure their re-election by putting through a legislative program that will please the voters "back home."

Simulations require high levels of interaction among participants. As a result, they are thought to have value in promoting the development of skills associated with decision-making, problem-solving, and critical thinking.

Preparation for Using Simulations

A general concern related to simulations is the time required to complete them. Some simulations can be completed within a single class period. Others require several days. A few go on for weeks. In preparing to use a particular simulation, the teacher needs to do a time-benefits analysis. This boils down to a decision based on the importance of the content to be taught, the unique capabilities of a given simulation to present the content to students, and the other kinds of content that cannot be treated during the time the simulation is taking place.

Most secondary teachers find they can rarely devote more than a few class periods to a simulation. Though simulations that last longer may provide excellent experiences for learners, they simply take too much time away from other matters that must be addressed in the course.

Identifying the Topic

Similar to other instructional approaches, simulations are best used in combination with other methods. Topics within a course or instructional unit that might be appropriate simulations are those that seem better taught through direct experience. For example, though students can memorize the term "negotiation" and can discuss it without difficulty, they tend to have only a limited appreciation for the concept until they have had opportunities to participate in the negotiation process. A teacher might logically decide to use one of the many simulations featuring negotiation experiences to broaden students' grasp of the negotiation concept.

Implementing the Technique

There are three basic phases involved in implementing simulations in the classroom. These are (1) orientation, (2) training participants, and (3) administration of the simulation activity (Joyce and Weil 1986).

ORIENTATION.   During the orientation phase, the teacher introduces members of the class to the simulation and outlines the basic focus problem. Roles that individuals will play are described, and students are introduced to goals they will be pursuing. The procedures to be followed are described. Individual students are given their role assignments.

It is particularly important that sufficient time be allocated to the orientation phase. Students should be invited to ask questions and to seek clarification about what they will be expected to do.

TRAINING PARTICIPANTS.   Often teachers begin this phase by selecting a few students to model some of the behaviors that class members will be performing once the simulation begins. This is accomplished by having selected students act out certain roles and respond to a certain portion of the simulated activity under the guidance of the teacher. This provides the teacher an opportunity to provide pointers to the students and to clarify any questions about roles, objectives, and procedures. This modeling activity should be brief.

Following the modeling, students should be given a few minutes to review their roles. They should again be given opportunities to ask questions. In general, the training-participants stage should not be allowed to drag on too long. Students will want to get involved in the simulation as quickly as possible. Some minor points of confusion can be cleared up during the implementation phases of the simulation.

ADMINISTRATION OF THE SIMULATION ACTIVITY.   Teachers play several roles during this phase. Among their responsibilities are discussing, coaching, and refereeing. Students will not always grasp what they are learning as a result of their participation. Sometimes, the teacher may find it helpful to stop a group for a moment to ask them to reflect on the decisions they are making. The purpose of this teacher intervention is to raise students' awareness of the concepts and ideas they are applying.

Some students may not know how to respond to certain situations that arise. The teacher may need to coach them. As situations change during the simulation and unexpected events occur, teacher hints and suggestions can diminish levels of participant frustration. As a coach, the teacher is interested in helping each student achieve some success.

Teachers act as referees during a simulation. Quite often unpredictable disputes will arise among participants. When this happens, the teacher must step forward to interpret a simulation guideline or make a rule that will keep the activity moving forward.

Debriefing

Debriefing is critical to the success of a simulation exercise. Because events transpire very quickly during a simulation's implementation phase, students often are not immediately aware of what they have learned from the experience. Debriefing allows the teacher and the class to review the action. Students are encouraged to reflect on their decisions and on the consequences that resulted from them. During debriefing, the teacher can help students focus on some important concepts and generalizations that were illustrated by the activity.

Debriefing also provides an opportunity for the teacher and members of the class to discuss the structure of the simulation. For example, the nature of the reality distortions built into the simulation to make its operation possible might be discussed. Class members might wish to suggest alternative ways for structuring the activity.

Finally, class members are encouraged to critique their own performances during the implementation phase. They might focus on what they learned from the experience and what they might do differently another time.

Cooperative Learning

During the past decade, cooperative learning has emerged as a promising approach to classroom instruction. Some research has indicated that cooperative learning approaches lead to (1) higher academic achievement than competitive or individualistic approaches; (2) better interpersonal relationships among students; and (3) more positive attitudes toward subjects studied and the overall classroom experience (Johnson and Johnson 1985). These benefits have led increasing numbers of teachers to implement cooperative learning approaches in their classrooms.

General Characteristics

There are several approaches to organizing students for cooperative learning activities. Many of them share some characteristics. Typically,

Box 9.4

Should We De-Emphasize Cooperative Learning Activities?

Recently, a concerned citizen made these comments:

> Competition drives economic progress. Everybody knows that we have been losing competitive ground to other nations. One answer is to improve our schools. Among other things, schools need to require increased levels of competition among students. Learning activities that downplay competition should be de-emphasized, if not eliminated entirely.

Look over these comments. Then, answer these questions:

1. How accurately does this citizen describe the characteristics of the "real world"?

2. To what extent should secondary schools promote "competition?" Does "cooperation" have any role? What should be the balance between competitive and cooperative activities?

3. If you were to prepare a written response to this citizen's comments, what would you say?

students are organized into groups or teams. Members of each team work together to accomplish a set of tasks. Rewards to individuals often are based largely on the accomplishment of the team. This builds an incentive for students to work productively together. One important task for the teacher in planning a cooperative learning lesson concerns the issue of reward for performance. The selected reward system needs to encourage cooperation. At the same time, it needs to provide for individual accountability so that contributions of each group member can be properly appreciated.

Most cooperative learning schemes provide students with considerable autonomy. Team members exercise a great deal of freedom as they decide how to deal with the assigned task or problem. Sometimes teams even have the right to determine when members are ready to take a test or present their final product to the teacher. Box 9.4 provides a different view of cooperative learning.

Preparation for Cooperative Learning

IDENTIFYING THE TOPIC.   "Cooperative learning" is a general term. Topic selection for cooperative learning exercises is closely related to the specific cooperative learning procedure the teacher decides to use. Some cooperative learning models require the teacher to provide rewards to groups based on how well they scored on some measure of achievement. Clearly, topics for which there are readily available achievement measures are especially well suited to cooperative learning activities of this type.

On the other hand, some cooperative learning models require each student in a group to accomplish just a small part of a larger task. Topics for cooperative learning of this type must be capable of being broken down into a number of parts that can be assigned to different individuals in each group.

Many cooperative learning models have been developed. Four that have been widely used are (1) Student Teams-Achievement Divisions, (2) Teams-Games-Tournaments, (3) Jigsaw, and (4) Learning Together.

1. Student Teams-Achievement Divisions (STAD). This is an approach developed by the Johns Hopkins Team Learning Project (Slavin 1980). The approach is one of the easiest cooperative learning models to implement. Students are assigned to learning teams consisting of four or five members. Each team has a mix of high-, average- and low-achievers.

Every week, the teacher presents each team with new material that is to be learned. This might be done through a short lecture or a discussion. Team members study resource materials, complete worksheets, and do other assigned tasks as a team. When team members believe they understand the material, they take a test. During testing, team members may not help one another.

A special system of scoring is used to promote cooperation and active participation of all group members. Test scores are provided for each student, but each student's score also plays a role in deriving a total score for the entire team.

An individual team member, depending on how well he or she did on the test, may add from 0 to 10 points to the total team score. This is how the system works. The teacher looks at how well each member of a team did on the previous test. Suppose one student scored 15 points (out of 30 possible) on the previous test and 20 points (out of 30 possible) on this test. The difference between 20 and 15 (new test score minus old test score) is 5. Five points would be added to the team score as a result of this student's performance.

Each student may provide a maximum of 10 points to the overall team score. There are two ways the 10-point maximum can be earned. Ten points are awarded if the student scores 10 or more points on the present test as compared to the last test. Ten points are awarded for any perfect paper regardless of what the student received on the last test. This is an incentive to maintain the active participation of brighter students.

Scoring in Student Teams-Achievement Divisions de-emphasizes competition between individuals. Improvement of all team members becomes the goal as team members strive to increase their overall team scores. Teachers usually arrange for some special recognition to be provided to high scoring teams at the end of grading periods, perhaps once every six or eight weeks.

2. Teams-Games-Tournaments. Teams-Games-Tournaments   is another approach developed by the Johns Hopkins group (Slavin 1980). It requires more time to plan and implement than Student Teams-Achievement Divisions. As a first step, the teacher organizes students into teams. Each team has from four to six students. They are assigned in such a way that there some low ability, average ability, and high ability learners in each group. Similar to the Student Teams-Achievement Divisions approach, members of each team study assigned material together. Team members are encouraged to help each other master the assigned content. Instead of receiving team points based on test performance, members of each team participate in weekly academic tournaments.

The format for the tournaments requires the teacher to organize students into tournament groups. Three students, each from a different team, constitute a group. Each group sits around a table. If there are 24 students in a class, there will be eight tables of tournament-group students. Questions are drawn, and students attempt to respond to them. Points for correct answers are awarded to the team to which each tournament group member belongs. At the end, scores for each student are examined.

When the first tournament is held, the teacher simply assigns students to sit at particular tables based on their past performances. For example, the top three individuals will be assigned to table 1, the next three to table 2, and the next three to table 3. The process continues until the bottom three students are assigned to table 8.

Following the individual week, students are assigned to tables based on their performance at the previous week's tournament. The high-scorer at each table moves up to the next table (e.g., the high scorer at table 3 would move to table 2). The low-scorer moves down one table (e.g., the low scorer at table 3 would move to table 4). The person who came in second at each table retains his or her place at the same table for the next tournament. Over time, this system tends to equalize competition.

The Teams-Games-Tournament approach combines cooperative and competitive activities. The format tends to keep competition among students at approximately the same level. Students find this system to be a fair one. Teachers have reported that even quite reluctant learners have become interested in school when the approach has been used (Slavin 1980).

3. Jigsaw. The Jigsaw model of cooperative learning begins by the teacher assigning students to teams of approximately six persons each. Academic material that is to be studied is broken into a number of parts. For example, a teacher may focus on "Advantages and Disadvantages of the North and the South at the Beginning of the Civil

War." This very large topic could be divided into a number of subordinate topics such as: (a) geographic advantages and disadvantages of the North and South; (b) economic advantages and disadvantages of the North and South; (c) transportation advantages and disadvantages of the North and South; (d) political advantages and disadvantages of the North and South.

If the teacher had organized students into six-person teams, then one or two of the students from each team would be assigned to become "experts" on one of the four subordinate topics.

Once assignments are made, the original or "home" teams break up. Members from each team who have been assigned to become "experts" on a given subordinate topic meet together. For example, all students who have been assigned to work on the subordinate topic "geographic advantages and disadvantages of the North and South" meet together. These regroupings are called "expert" groups in that they consist exclusively of students from each home group who have been selected to become "experts" on the assigned subordinate topic. Members of the expert group are provided with needed learning material. They study and discuss the information.

When students meeting in the expert groups have finished their cooperative study, the original home groups are reconstituted. The "experts" on each subordinate topic teach what they have learned to other members of the "home" group. In this way, members of each home group receive information related to all subordinate topics. Since the criterion test at the end of the lesson will cover the entire topic, there is an incentive for home group members to listen carefully to presentations by "experts" on each topic and for them to insist that "experts" share all of their information.

Not all content lends itself to presentation via a jigsaw approach. For example, some topics do not lend themselves easily to be broken into subordinate parts. The approach requires very careful teacher monitoring of the work of the expert groups. It is necessary that members of each expert group understand all of the necessary information and that each student learns it well enough to pass it on to members of his or her home group.

Jigsaw lessons that are designed to last several days pose problems. If a student from one home team is absent during part of the time he or she is supposed to be attending an assigned expert group, then this person's home group may lack important information. The teacher, in such a case, must step in and provide the missing information to the home group. There are particular difficulties when several students are absent. Generally, there are fewer problems when a topic that can be concluded in a single class session is used as a focus for a jigsaw exercise. Box 9.5 is an exercise in planning a jigsaw lesson.

Box 9.5

Planning a Jigsaw Lesson

Select a topic from a subject you might like to teach. Divide content so that it can be introduced using the jigsaw approach. Assume you will have four "expert" groups. With a class of twenty-four students, this would allow you to have six "home groups."

TOPIC: _____

HOMEGROUPS:
    SUB-TOPIC A: _____
    SUB-TOPIC B: _____
    SUB-TOPIC C: _____
    SUB-TOPIC D: _____

NEEDED LEARNING RESOURCES FOR EXPERT GROUP, SUB-TOPIC A

_____

_____

_____

NEEDED LEARNING RESOURCES FOR EXPERT GROUP, SUB-TOPIC B

_____

_____

_____

NEEDED LEARNING RESOURCES FOR EXPERT GROUP, SUB-TOPIC C

_____

_____

_____

NEEDED LEARNING RESOURCES FOR EXPERT GROUP, SUB-TOPIC D

_____

_____

_____

4. Learning Together. In this approach, developed by David W. Johnson and Roger T. Johnson (1984), students are organized into teams that include a cross-section of ability levels. Each team is given a task or project to complete. The approach works best when the assignment involves a wide variety of talents. Individuals on each team work on a part of the overall project that is compatible with their own interests and abilities. The idea is to maximize strengths of individual students to get a better overall group effect.

Roles of individuals in learning-together teams can be quite varied. For example, if the final product is to be a short play, one or more students might assume roles such as (1) head writer, (2) manuscript editor, (3) manuscript production chief, (4) set designer, (5) and sound and light planner.

Each team is responsible for gathering together information and materials needed to complete its assigned task or project. Final assessment is based on the quality of the team's performance. Each student on a team receives the same grade. This encourages individuals to pool their talents in such a way that the work of each student adds the greatest possible contribution to the effort.

Some teachers have expressed concern about the fairness of giving each team member the same grade. Johnson and Johnson (1985) report that, although students tend to favor competitive grading before they engage in cooperative tasks, after they have completed a cooperative learning project they commit to the idea that awarding every group member the same grade is a fair approach.

Implementing Cooperative Learning

Cooperative learning is new to many secondary students. They have spent most of their academic lives in situations characterized by competition between and among individuals. Teachers need to explain procedures very carefully and to work hard to ensure that students have successful experiences in their initial encounters with cooperative learning approaches.

Specific teacher responsibilities vary depending on which cooperative learning approach is used. In almost every case, particular care must be taken to help students understand exactly what they are to be doing within the groups. Incentives for individuals to work with others in a productive way need to be highlighted. Materials for learning need to be organized and easily accessible, and each group's progress needs to be carefully monitored. This typically requires the teacher to move frequently throughout the room to pinpoint and resolve problems before they interfere with the learning process.

Debriefing

The focus of the debriefing that occurs at the end of a cooperative learning experience should be on the process of working together. Students should be encouraged to analyze the nature of their work in groups and to identify those group-work strategies that were effective and those that were not. Debriefing should help students appreciate the benefits of human diversity and the benefits that accrue when different talents are applied to common problems.

Many students like the interactive nature of group learning activities. *Photo courtesy of Tisara Photography Inc.*

Field Trips

Many learning resources cannot be brought to the school. For students to benefit from them, they must leave the school and travel to some other site. These planned out-of-school activities, or "field trips," can be excellent learning experiences for students.

General Characteristics

A field trip is a trip by the class to a place beyond the school that is made for the purpose of learning. The focus on learning is important. If teachers convey the impression a field trip is simply a break away from the tedium of daily school routine, students often will not take the experience seriously. A field trip that students view as a "holiday" may present the teacher with serious student-control problems.

Preparation for Field Trips

IDENTIFYING THE TOPIC. Field trip topics or purposes should tie closely to content being studied in the classroom. When this is the case, teachers have an easier time convincing students that the field trip has an educational rather than a recreational function. Identification of a specific purpose assists the teacher in additional preparation for the trip. For example, it suggests guidelines to be followed in developing instructions for students regarding what they are to see, do, and learn.

PRELIMINARY CONSIDERATIONS. After the topic and purpose have been identified, school schedules must be checked and approvals received from administrators. It may be necessary to make special arrangements with people at the place to be visited. The trip also needs to be entered into the school's master schedule.

Field trips usually require students to be gone from school for at least half a day. Often they are gone all day. This feature has implications for their work in other classes. It requires field-trip planners to work with other teachers and with school administrators to assure that all understand that students may be missing a class on the day of the field trip.

Additionally, field trips raise certain legal questions. Frequently school district policies require teachers to obtain written permission for their students to go on field trips. If some parents refuse to give such permission, the teacher must make arrangements to accommodate any student or students who will remain at the school when the rest of the class is on the field trip.

If possible, the teacher should visit the field trip site well in advance of the class visit. Personnel at the site need to know when the group will be coming, how long they will stay, and what they will be doing. Specific information should be gathered about restroom facilities, eating facilities, bus-parking areas, and the general layout of the area to be visited.

Box 9.6

Field Trip Ideas

Think about one of the subjects you are preparing to teach. Consider some possibilities for field trips that might enrich your students' learning.

1. Generate a list of possible field trips.
2. For each possibility, indicate
   a. the specific things you would like students to learn and;
   b. how these things tie specifically to what you will be doing in the classroom.

3. Describe what you will do to give students the clear impression that the field trip is a serious part of the school program and not a school holiday.

4. Point out some follow-up activities that you might require of students that would involve use of information learned on one or more of the field trips you have proposed.

After this site visit, the teacher may wish to prepare a learning guide for students. The guide will mention the purpose of the trip and include a number of focus questions students should be able to answer with information obtained from their visit. The guide can be provided to students on the day of the trip, and they can be asked to take notes to be used in a debriefing session after the field trip is over. Provision of a learning guide reinforces the point that the trip has an academic purpose.

Provision needs to be made for adequate adult supervision. Signed forms from parents giving their children permission to go on a field trip do not release the teacher and the school from any responsibility for students' well-being. To avoid the possibility of an unfortunate incident and a possible negligence suit, arrangements need to be made for a sufficient number of parents and other adults (perhaps other teachers) to accompany students as trip chaperones. Additional field trip ideas are presented in Box 9.6.

Implementing the Field-Trip Activity

Prior to leaving the school, the teacher should review rules of conduct for the trip. Any potential hazards and suggested responses to them should be identified. Students need to be reminded about what they are to do and learn. Directions about procedures for gathering and recording information should be reviewed.

Once the group has arrived at the destination, students again need to be reminded about what they are to do. If there are guides at the site, the teacher needs to work closely with them to manage students and to help clarify any misunderstandings.

The group of students needs to be monitored carefully during the visit. The teacher and accompanying chaperones need to assure that no students stray from the group. It is particularly important to have a scheme to take role at the end of the visit when students are preparing to leave the site for the return to school.

Debriefing

Debriefing of a field trip sometimes occurs at the field trip site itself or on the way home. Since there are fewer distractions in a classroom, many teachers prefer to defer the debriefing session until the next class meeting.

Debriefing sometimes begins with questions posed in the learning guide developed for the trip. Students are provided opportunities to share responses and report what they observed and learned. Students often are encouraged to take information learned on the field trip and to incorporate it in other course projects. For example, some students might draw on this material as they write papers, prepare charts, create models, and complete other required course projects.

Key Ideas in Summary

1. Group learning approaches emphasize the importance of collaboration. Many of these techniques contribute to students' understanding that collective work on a common task maximizes the contribution of each individual.

2. Classroom debates involve more people on each side than traditional competitive debates. They are formatted in a way that encourages participation by a wide cross-section of class members. The best focus topics for classroom debates are those for which there are no clearly "right" or "wrong" answers.

3. Role playing is a technique that is designed to teach students the values and perspectives of other people. Individual students are assigned roles and react to provided situations in ways they believe to be consistent with the perspectives of their assigned characters.

4. Simulations are complex role playing situations. They attempt to give students a feel for sophisticated real-life situations. This is done

by simplifying reality and placing participants in situations where they must make difficult decisions and live with the resultant consequences.

5. In recent years, a number of cooperative learning approaches have become popular. Though individual models differ, most are dedicated to developing students' commitment to the view that cooperation is a more productive approach to learning than one-against-one competition. Among popular cooperative learning models are (1) student teams-achievement divisions, (2) teams-games-tournaments, (3) jigsaw, and (4) learning together.

6. Field trips allow students to learn from resources not available to them at school. Good field trips require meticulous preparation. It is particularly critical that students perceive the field trip as a part of their academic training and not as a "holiday" from school.

POSTTEST

DIRECTIONS: Using your own paper, answer these true/false questions. For each correct statement, write the word "true." For each incorrect statement, write the word "false."

_____ 1. Cooperative learning seeks to link individual success and group success.

_____ 2. A student should be assigned a role in a role-playing activity that closely fits his or her normal pattern of behavior.

_____ 3. Because it adds little to what students learn, debriefing should not be considered an integral part of a simulation activity.

_____ 4. In Teams-Games-Tournaments, teams are selected so that each team has approximately the same average level of academic talent.

_____ 5. Field trips are designed to reward students by providing them a break from the daily routines of school.

Bibliography

CHESLER, M. AND FOX, R. *Role-Playing Methods in the Classroom.* Chicago: Science Research Associates, 1966.

JOHNSON, DAVID W. AND JOHNSON, ROGER T. "The Internal Dynamics of Cooperative Learning Groups," In Slavin, R.; Sharan, S.; Kagan, S.; Webb, C.; and, Schmuck, R. (eds.) *Learning to Cooperate, Cooperating to Learn.* New York, N.Y.: Plenum Press, 1985, p. 103–124.

JOHNSON, DAVID W. AND JOHNSON, ROGER T. *Learning Together and Alone*. Englewood Cliffs, NJ: Prentice-Hall, 1975.

JOHNSON, DAVID W.; JOHNSON, ROGER T.; HOLUBEC, E.; ROY, P. *Circles of Learning: Cooperation in the Classroom*. Alexandria, Virginia: Association for Supervision and Curriculum Development, 1984.

JOHNSON, DAVID W.; JOHNSON, ROGER T.; AND MARUYANA, GEOFFREY. "Interdependence and Interpersonal Attraction Among Heterogeneous and Homogeneous Individuals: A Theoretical Formulation and a Meta-analysis of the Research." *Review of Educational Research* (Spring 1983): 5–54.

JOHNSON, ROGER T. AND JOHNSON, DAVID W. "Structuring Conflict in Science Classrooms." Paper presented at the annual meeting of the National Association of Research in Science Teaching. French Lick, IN. April, 1985.

JOYCE, BRUCE AND WEIL, MARSHA. *Models of Teaching*. 3rd ed. Englewood Cliffs, N.J.: Prentice-Hall, 1986.

SLAVIN, ROBERT E. *Using Student Team Learning*. Baltimore, Md.: Johns Hopkins Team Learning Project, Center for Social Organization of the Schools, John Hopkins University, 1980.

SLAVIN, ROBERT E. "Synthesis of Research on Groups in Elementary and Secondary Schools." *Educational Leadership* (September 1988): 67–77.

CHAPTER 10

Teaching for Thinking

AIMS

This chapter provides information to help the reader to:

1. Recognize that teaching for thinking is appropriate for all students, not just for those who are academically talented.
2. Describe the importance of teaching thinking skills directly.
3. Implement approaches designed to increase students' awareness of their own metacognitive processes.
4. Differentiate among emphases of different types of thinking skills.
5. Prepare lessons designed to promote the development of different types of thinking skills.

PRETEST

DIRECTIONS: Using your own paper, answer these true/false questions. For each correct statement, write the word "true." For each incorrect statement, write the word "false."

_____ 1. There is broad agreement on exactly how thinking skills should be taught to students.

_____ 2. "Thinking aloud" is an example of a teacher-modeling approach.

_____ 3. Inquiry teaching is based on induction.

_____ 4. Retrieval charts are not useful when the purpose is to develop students' abilities to compare, contrast, and generalize.

_____ 5. Part of the Suchman approach requires students to ask the teacher questions that can be answered either "yes" or "no."

Introduction

Instruction that emphasizes "how to think" is just as worthy of school time as instruction that focuses on the traditional academic subjects (Beyer 1987, 1988). Not only are sound thinking skills needed for students to benefit fully from school subjects, these thinking skills are also needed as they cope with challenges they will face throughout their adult lives (Ruggiero 1988).

The teaching of thinking skills focuses on two key areas. First, students need to be taught to become aware of their own thinking processes. They must recognize the steps they are following as they think. They must learn how to monitor their own thinking. Processes associated with self-monitoring of thinking are part of an area of learning psychology called *metacognition*.

Second, students need to be introduced to a number of different thinking categories. While no master list exists, a number of categories have been suggested by leading researchers. They tend to be distinguished from one another by the purposes sought and by the patterns of thinking they describe. Among these categories are (1) inquiry thinking, (2) creative thinking, (3) critical thinking, (4) problem solving, and (5) decision making.

Metacognition

Metacognition refers to thought about the process of thinking. It involves bringing to a conscious level the kinds of procedures we follow as we think. Metacognitive processes serve an important monitoring function. When people are aware of the steps they are taking as they think, they can make more conscious choices about whether approaches they have selected for a given task are appropriate.

Instructional experiences can be provided that help students monitor and modify their own patterns of thinking. Several approaches have been designed to achieve these purposes. Two that have been used by a number of teachers are "teacher modeling" and "visualizing thinking" strategies.

Teacher Modeling

Modeling has long been known as a powerful instructional tool. As applied to metacognition, teacher modeling seeks to help students rec-

"Today I'm going to teach you a unique new behavior."

ognize that people who successfully think about challenging issues carefully monitor their own thinking processes. They engage in a type of silent personal dialogue as they confront relevant issues. They may speculate about alternatives, consider numerous responses, evaluate available evidence, weigh the relevance of competing views, and get deeply involved in other considerations pertinent to the issue at hand. To help students understand how such thinking processes operate, it sometimes is helpful for teachers to model these processes by "thinking aloud" as they attack a given issue.

The idea is to cue students to thinking patterns that might be useful when they are called on to perform a similar task. By observing the teacher, they will note general approaches to the issue that have proved to be productive. They will see the importance of thinking carefully about their own approaches to the task. After a teacher has "thought aloud," it often is the case that students will perform better on an assigned task than when the teacher has assumed students already know how the task should be approached.

Suppose a teacher in an English class were teaching a unit on "descriptive writing." Each student might have been asked to write a two-to-three page paper on tourist attractions of a selected world place.

After an initial draft, the teacher might expect students to think about what they had written and to rewrite the material. A simple teacher directive to "rewrite what you have written" would not cue students to the kinds of thought processes that should be used as they approach the task of revision. A more productive way to get students successfully started on the revision task would be for the teacher to model what students should do.

For example, the teacher might prepare an overhead transparency from a first draft of the same assignment prepared by a student from a previous semester. The teacher could "think aloud" with students in this way:

> All right, now look at this draft of a paper on "Easter Island." Now, if this were my paper and I were about to revise it, these are some of the things I would want to do.
>
> First of all, readers are going to be reading lots of literature about lots of different places. They will be turned off by anything that has been written hastily without careful attention to spelling and grammar. The first thing I'll want to look for is spelling errors. Then, I'll want to be sure that verb tenses are correct and consistent throughout.
>
> I will want to hold the attention of my reader. I don't want to lose anyone with long, complicated sentences. As a quick check on this, I'll read the paper aloud. Anytime I run out of breath before I finish a sentence, I am going to mark that sentence. Later, I will go back and cut these long sentences into shorter ones. Also, as I read, I will try to spot any places where I am using the same word too frequently. If I find any excessive repetition, I will write a note to correct this situation in a revision.
>
> As I read through the material, I will mark every sentence that has as its main verb some part of the verb "to be." This tends to be a very weak, dull verb for the reader. I will mark these sentences. As I rewrite the material, I will try to replace these verbs with more action-oriented words.
>
> Look at this sentence: "The giant statues are visited by many tourists." There are two serious problems here. First of all, the verb is in the passive voice, a weak, uninteresting construction. Second, the reference to the statues simply being "visited" is not particularly exciting. I would rewrite the sentence to eliminate the passive voice and to add some color. One possibility might be a sentence something like this: "The giant statues of Easter Island challenge tourists' views of so-called 'primitive' peoples."

Students who listened to this teacher "think aloud" about the thought processes to be followed in revising the sample paper have a model to follow as they begin to work on their own revisions. Modeling can also plant the idea that thinking about what the task requires is an essential prerequisite to beginning to address the task. This perspective is one that teachers hope will take root in students as a result of "thinking aloud" demonstrations. Box 10.1 contains an exercise in designing a thinking-aloud approach.

Box 10.1

Designing a "Thinking-Aloud" Approach

In a thinking-aloud approach, the teacher models a thinking sequence appropriate for a given task. Think about a topic you would like to teach and a particular learning assignment you might develop for students. Briefly outline a thinking-aloud strategy you might use. Begin by identifying the focus for your assignment ("identifying unknown compounds," "writing a position paper," "looking for bias in a political speech," and so forth.) Then, briefly describe steps you would follow in your thinking-aloud approach.

Focus:

Step 1:

Step 2:

Step 3:

Step 4:

Step 5:

Step 6:

(The number of steps needed may be larger or smaller than the six indicated here. Develop as many steps as you will need given your focus.)

Visualizing Thinking

Another technique to encourage students to monitor their own thinking processes is "visualizing thinking." This approach is designed to help students think about the nature of an assigned task, consider the kinds of thinking they will be required to engage in, and identify the nature of the information they will need to gather. Once they have decided on their responses to these issues, students are encouraged to develop diagrams. The diagrams will help them to take and organize notes in ways consistent with the requirements of the assigned task.

Suppose a teacher decided to have class members read the following material from their text:

EARLY SPANISH EXPLORERS OF THE CARIBBEAN

In the year 1492, the Spanish explorer Christopher Columbus landed on San Salvador Island, a rather small island in the West Indies. San Salvador is in the group of islands that we know today as The Bahamas. Columbus later explored many other Caribbean islands. He set up a fort on one of the largest islands in the region, Hispaniola. Today, Hispaniola is occupied by the countries of Haiti and the Dominican Republic.

Another well-known early Spanish explorer was Nicolas de Ovando. In the year 1502, he was sent out from Spain to become Governor of Hispaniola. He brought a large number of colonists with him. These colonists sought to make their fortunes in two ways. Some of them attempted to strike it rich in gold mining. Others started large plantations.

A common problem all of these early Spanish colonists faced was the lack of a large supply of local workers.

In response to this situation, the colonists initially tried to make slaves of the local Indians. This was not successful. The Indians did not take to slavery, and many of them died. Once the local supply of Indians on Hispaniola had been exhausted, the Spanish for a time tried bringing in Indians from other Caribbean islands. They, too, died. Later, slaves from Africa were brought to the island. Though many of these slaves survived, Hispaniola continued to have a need for more workers than could be supplied.

As a result of the labor shortage, many Spanish colonists began moving from Hispaniola to other islands in the region. One of the other large islands that attracted a number of Spanish settlers was Puerto Rico. The first settlers arrived there in 1508 under the leadership of Ponce de Leon. The Spanish moved into Jamaica in 1509 when Juan de Esquivel led a group of settlers there. Cuba, the largest island in the region, was reached by Spanish settlers in 1514. In time, it became the most prosperous of Spain's Caribbean territories.

Because of differences in ability levels of students, the teacher might wish some students to focus on different aspects of this material than others. For example, the teacher might have decided that some students should read for the purpose of accomplishing this learning task:

Task: "Who were four famous Spanish explorers who made discoveries in the Caribbean between 1492 and 1514, and what large islands were occupied by Spain during this period?"

To help the students focus on this task as they read the material and take notes, a visual-thinking diagram something like this might be developed:

Leaders and Islands

Leaders	Islands

Others in the class might be asked to read the material for the purpose of accomplishing this task:

Task: "What actions were taken by the early Spanish settlers of Hispaniola to solve the labor shortage, and what happened as a result?"

To help students focus on this task as they read the material and take notes, a visual-thinking diagram something like this might be developed:

Why Laborers Were Needed

_____

_____

_____

_____

What Was Tried First? _____   What Was Tried Second? _____

_____   _____

_____   _____

What Were the Results? _____   What Were the Results?

_____   _____

_____   _____

_____   _____

Final Outcome

_____

_____

_____

Note that, while all students were asked to read the same material, the thinking task assigned to some students was different from the thinking task assigned to other students. These differences are reflected in the visual-thinking diagrams. Use of such diagrams can help students focus on information that is relevant to a specific assigned task.

When this approach is used for the first time, teachers usually provide students with these diagrams. Once they get used to working with them, students can be asked to develop visual-thinking diagrams of their own. The process of constructing the diagrams forces them to think about the nature of the task and about the nature of thinking that will be required in responding to it.

Use of the diagrams helps students to monitor and adjust their own thinking processes as they work with assigned materials. As a result,

Box 10.2

Preparing Visual-Thinking Diagrams

Visual-thinking diagrams can help students take notes on their reading in such a way that information gathered pertains directly to a given learning task. Categories listed on the diagrams cue students to pay attention to relevant points.

Learning Task 1:
   Related Visual-Thinking Diagram

Think about a topic you would like to teach. Suppose you wished to respond to individual differences in your class by assigning different learning tasks to different students. Identify three separate learning tasks. For each, prepare a visual-thinking diagram that would help students successfully master content associated with each of these assignments.

Learning Task 2:
   Related Visual-Thinking Diagram

Learning Task 3:
   Related Visual-Thinking Diagram

---

their work is likely to be more productive and their levels of achievement and self-satisfaction higher. Preparing visual-thinking diagrams is discussed in Box 10.2.

Inquiry Teaching

Inquiry approaches have been used by teachers for many years, and many models of inquiry teaching have been developed. Nearly all of them introduce content to students inductively. "Inductive learning" proceeds from the general to the specific. A simple example will illustrate the general procedure.

Suppose a teacher wanted to teach a group of learners the concept "fish." He or she might provide them with photographs of different fish. Through a series of questions, students would be led to identify common features of the "things" in the individual photographs. To conclude the exercise, the teacher would urge students to develop their own description of the concept "fish" and would ask them to name its necessary defining characteristics.

Inductive or inquiry thinking involves students in the creation of new knowledge. This is true because students develop their own conclusions after consideration of independent pieces of evidence. The process of knowledge production is thought to be motivating for many students.

Additionally, the basic processes of considering evidence and arriving at reasoned conclusions represent the kind of rational thinking ability students will be called upon to exercise throughout their adult lives. In short, supporters of inquiry thinking are as much interested in students' mastering the *processes* of thinking as in students' mastering the academic content that provides the focus for a given inquiry lesson.

Basic Steps in Inquiry Teaching

Inquiry teaching in American schools traces back to a famous book published by the eminent American educational philosopher, John Dewey. In *How We Think*, originally published in 1910, Dewey suggested basic steps for sequencing inquiry instruction. With some variation, the following steps, derived from Dewey's work, are featured in many inquiry lessons:

1. Identify and describe the essential dimensions of a problem or situation.
2. Suggest possible solutions to the problem or explanations of the problem or situation.
3. Gather evidence related to these solutions or explanations.
4. Evaluate possible solutions or explanations of the problem in light of evidence.
5. Develop a conclusion that is best supported by the evidence.

The basic steps of inquiry involve nothing more than the application of the scientific method to a wide variety of problems. Inquiry lessons can be developed in many subject areas.

Suppose a high school humanities teacher were interested in probing the relationship between urbanization and life expectancies of American women. An inquiry lesson with this focus might develop along these lines:

Step One
Focus: The teacher might begin by writing the following statistics on the board:

Percentages of Females in Three Age Groups

Year	Under 30	30 to 50	51 or Older
1850	71	20	9
1910	61	25	14
1970	50	23	27

Inquiry lessons, such as those featured in many laboratory science classrooms, encourage students to arrive at conclusions that are based on a careful consideration of evidence. *Photo courtesy of National Science Teachers Association.*

Median Age of U.S. Females in Three Years

1850	18.8 years
1910	23.9 years
1970	27.6 years

Percentages of U.S. Urban and Rural Population in Three Years

Year	Rural	Urban
1850	84.7	15.3
1910	54.3	45.7
1970	26.5	73.5

Teacher: Look at this information. What trends do you see? Notice that women seem to be living longer in each of the three years. Notice, too, that more people seem to be living in cities. Now, I want you think about two questions. First, what might be the connection between longer lives for women and the trend toward living in cities? Second, are there other possible explanations for women living longer in the later years?

Step Two
Students provide answers to each question.

Question 1: What might be the connection between longer lives for women and the trend toward living in cities?

A Sample of Possible Student Responses:

- People in cities might have earned more. Women may have eaten better and stayed healthier in the cities.
- Women in cities may have had better access to newspapers. They may have read more about good health standards.
- There may have been better access to doctors in the cities. Thus, women may have begun to live longer because they were more likely to get treated when they were sick in cities than when they were sick in rural areas.
- Cities tended to bring more medical scholars and researchers together. This resulted in an explosion of new information about health and medicine. This new information increased the life spans of all people in the later years.

Question 2: Other than the move from rural areas to the cities, what other things might have led to higher percentages of women being in older age groups in the later years?

A Sample of Possible Student Responses:

- Women could have started having fewer children. If this happened, fewer would have died in childbirth, and more would have lived to an older age.
- In the earlier years, a high percentage of women could have been immigrants. Immigrants tend to be younger. This would account for higher percentages of younger women in the earlier years.
- There could have been some fatal diseases that killed women in their twenties and thirties for which cures became available in later years.
- In earlier years, society may not have cared as much for older women as it did in later years. There could have been a deliberate failure to care for older women in the earlier years.

Step Three

During this phase of the lesson, the teacher would direct students to gather evidence supporting or refuting each of the possible explanations they had generated in response to two questions. They would be directed to additional resource materials containing information. Students would be told to gather as much relevant information as possible.

It is important to have specific sources of information readily available for student use. Directions to students to "go to the library and find it" are a sure prescription for failure. Many students will give up. Even those who do not will be frustrated. These kind of negative attitudes can undermine the motivational value that accrues to a well-planned inquiry lesson.

Step Four

During this phase, the responses to the focus questions are re-examined in light of the additional information that has been gathered. The nature of the evidence and the reliability of the evidence is discussed. Once all information related to a given explanation has been considered, the class decides whether to accept, reject, or revise the explanation.

The teacher concludes this phase of the activity by writing on the board those explanations for which the most evidential support has been found.

Step Five

Students are asked to look at the explanations for which they have found good support. The teacher may ask questions such as these:

> Given all of the evidence you have seen supporting these explanations, what do you think is the single best explanation for more women living longer in 1910 than in 1850 and in 1970 than in 1910?

> Why do you make this choice? How confident are you that it is correct?

When the students make a final choice, the teacher reviews the evidence supporting it. He or she points out that this conclusion should not be regarded as final. It should be held open to revision should additional information become available.

This description has been compressed for purposes of illustration. Good inquiry lessons require time. Issues to be addressed are often complex. It takes time for students to master skills associated with logical thinking. If time is at a premium and the primary objective is content coverage rather than teaching the inquiry process, an inquiry approach may not be the best choice. (See Box 10.3.)

Box 10.3

Is Inquiry Teaching Worth the Time?

I would like to do more inquiry teaching. When I've tried it, students have enjoyed it. But, I find I just can't get through my material this way. We face these standardized tests at the end of the year. The school will look bad if my people don't do well. Those tests don't measure thinking skills. They go after content knowledge. Until there is a better payoff for teaching thinking processes, I simply can't make a case for using valuable class time for inquiry teaching.

What Do You Think?

Read the comments above. Then answer these questions.

1. What major concerns about inquiry teaching are reflected in these comments?

2. Do you think these concerns are common or do they reflect reactions of a teacher whose situation is unusual?

3. Why do you think so few standardized tests emphasize higher-level thinking skills?

4. How would you personally respond to these comments?

Comparing, Contrasting, Generalizing

Many inquiry lessons seek to improve students' abilities to compare, contrast, and generalize. Organization of the data into a format that students can easily understand can help students accomplish tasks requiring these complex thinking processes.

One approach to organizing data for learning activities requiring students to compare, contrast, and generalize is the retrieval chart. A retrieval chart is basically a matrix that includes basic concept categories under which relevant information can be listed.

A lesson using a retrieval chart might develop along these lines. Suppose an English teacher had had students read a novel called *Mines and Dreamers* that featured many interactions among the five major characters: Joe Carmody, Luella McPhee, Tony Marino, Gordon Duffy, and Selma Steele. In planning a lesson designed to promote students' abilities to compare, contrast, and generalize, the teacher might develop a chart that students could use to organize basic information from the novel. The chart could require them to organize information about each character under these major headings: (1) family background, (2) education, (3) occupation, (4) basic motives.

Students might be asked to gather information individually. Or members of the class might develop the information as part of a group discussion focusing on the novel. In either case, the result would be a completed data chart. This might take the form of a large chart in the front of the room, a chart prepared on an overhead transparency and projected on a screen, or individual charts that would be printed and distributed to each student. An example of such a chart with data filled in might look something like this:

	Family Background	Education	Occupation	Basic Motives
Joe Carmody	divorced parents; reared by mother	Grade 8	union organizer; former coal miner	improving of lives of the working poor
Luella McPhee	divorced parents; reared by mother	Grade 10	owner of successful real estate firm	personal social advancement; wants to hide nature of her family background
Tony Marino	upper middle class; reared by both parents	college graduate	attorney	betterment of conditions of the working poor
Gordon Duffy	upper middle class; divorced parents; reared by father	college graduate	attorney	promotion of his own economic self-interest; insensitive to needs of others
Selma Steele	upper class; reared by both parents	college graduate	business manager	believes that what is good for her business is, in the long run, good for everyone else too

The completed chart can be used as a basis for a discussion designed to prompt students to compare, contrast, and generalize. The teacher would begin such an exercise by asking students to look carefully at the information on the chart and to respond to this sequence of questions:

1. What are some similarities you see among these characters?
   Possible responses:
   • Joe Carmody, Luella McPhee, and Gordon Duffy were reared in one-parent homes.

- Joe Carmody and Luella McPhee have less than a high school education.
- Tony Marino and Gordon Duffy are attorneys.
- Joe Carmody and Tony Marino are both interested in improving the lot of the working poor.

(These are simply examples. Students may identify additional and different responses.)

2. What are some differences you see among these characters?

- Their educational levels are different.
- They come from a variety of home backgrounds.
- Some of them are basically out for their own interests.
- Some of them are interested in improving the lot of others.

(These are simply examples. Students may identify additional and different responses.)

3. From looking at this information, are there some general statements you can make about what this author may believe to be true?

- There is not necessarily a connection between a person's occupation and his or her sensitivity to the needs of others.
- The kind of home a person grows up in as a child does not necessarily predict the kinds of attitudes toward others he or she will have as an adult.

(These are simply examples. Students may develop different and additional generalizations from the information in the chart.)

The generalizations developed in this exercise are developed from consideration of a very limited amount of information. The teacher should remind students that they should be regarded as only tentatively true. As students study other material, they can be urged to test the accuracy of these generalizations in the light of new information.

Building a Basis for Sophisticated Thinking Through Delimiting and Focusing

Students sometimes find themselves overwhelmed with the volume of available information when they confront a task demanding higher-level thinking. They need a way of sorting through all of the available data to get to the relevant information. Part of an inquiry strategy developed by J. Richard Suchman (1962) can be used to help students develop their abilities to delimit the amount of information they need as they think about a given issue.

Suchman had several major concerns as he developed his approach. First of all, he wanted a system that would prevent students from arriving at premature conclusions. Indeed, he wished to promote the view that knowledge is tentative, and that even the best grounded generalizations can be revised in the light of new and better information.

Suchman's approach builds on students' natural curiosity about puzzling situations. He called these puzzling situations "discrepant events." These can be prepared in many secondary school subject areas. One that has been used in many science classrooms uses a short film to introduce the discrepant event. The film features a man who is looking inside a bell jar. In the middle of the bell jar, there is a beaker of water that is boiling furiously. The man makes a show of putting on elbow-length asbestos gloves. He removes the bell jar, gingerly lifts the beaker with the boiling liquid, and slowly drinks it, showing no evidence of any discomfort. The film stops at this point. Students are asked how the man was able to do this. (Good luck. You figure it out.) Box 10.4 is an exercise in identifying discrepant events.

The following steps are modified from those developed by Suchman:

1. Students are presented with a puzzling or perplexing situation (a "discrepant event").
2. They are encouraged to try to explain it by asking the teacher questions about it.
3. They are told the questions they ask must be framed in such a way that they can be answered by a "yes" or a "no."
4. The exercise ends with a general discussion of explanations that have been suggested and of the processes students followed in arriving at them.

With practice, students come to understand that, by asking large and broad questions, they can eliminate enormous categories of information. (For example, a question such as "Is this a chemical substance?" regardless of whether the teacher answers "yes" or "no" provides students with much more information than a narrow question such as "Is this fluorine?") Students who have had a little experience with the Suchman approach tend to develop a strategy of beginning with broad questions that delimit the range of content they must consider. This provides a focus for their thinking that allows them to disregard information that, early on, is identified as irrelevant.

Box 10.4

Identifying Discrepant Events

"Discrepant events" are puzzling situations that are used as foci for an inquiry procedure developed by J. Richard Suchman. Think about a subject you are preparing to teach. Then, identify six different discrepant events that you could use in lessons based on Suchman's approach.

Discrepant Event 1:

Discrepant Event 2:

Discrepant Event 3:

Discrepant Event 4:

Discrepant Event 5:

Discrepant Event 6:

Creative Thinking

The world confronts people with a never-ending supply of serious problems. Throughout history, solutions often have come from people who have responded to them in unusual, creative ways. Problems would not be "problems" if conventional solutions could be easily applied. It takes a person who has the curiosity, insight, and emotional security to try a novel approach. Often, creative solutions have resulted when people have made unusual associations between very different kinds of things.

For example, Ruggiero (1988) points out the inventor of the forklift truck got the idea from watching mechanical fingers lift donuts out of an oven. He goes on to note that Gutenberg's invention of the printing press resulted, in part, from his observation of a wine press.

Creative thinking is stimulated when people are able to defer final judgment and when they do not have fear of failure (Ruggiero 1988). The ability to generate creative new information is not widespread among students (Perkins 1981). Part of the problem may well be that students experience little systematic instruction designed to develop their creative thinking skills.

A number of instructional techniques have been developed to enhance students' creative thinking powers. One that is widely used is brainstorming.

Brainstorming is designed to stimulate original solutions to problems. It seeks to unleash mental power in ways that discourage students from relying on ordinary and conventional responses. It places a premium on the ability to generate large numbers of creative responses.

Brainstorming developed in the world of business. Concerned leaders noticed that junior-level managers tended to shy away from proposing novel solutions to problems. Often, they simply parroted positions of senior executives. As a result, insights of these younger executives rarely got a hearing. The brainstorming technique was developed to provide a vehicle that would encourage a broad sharing of innovative ideas. The technique ensures that all ideas will be heard and considered.

Rules for conducting a brainstorming exercise are simple:

1. Students are provided with a problem to consider. ("Suppose all books were printed with an ink that would disappear after six months. What would happen if that were true?")

2. Students are invited to call out their ideas as rapidly as possible. A student is free to speak whenever an opening of silence occurs. The idea is to generate a very rapid outpouring of ideas. Students are told to say whatever comes to their minds so long as it is relevant to the problem.

3. Students are cautioned not to comment positively or negatively on any ideas suggested by others. All ideas are accepted. This rule helps break down students' fear of "saying something stupid."

4. The teacher or a designated record keeper writes down every idea. This person should not be concerned about neatness. He or she needs to be someone who can write fast. Student ideas come at a very rapid rate.

5. The exercise should be stopped when there is a noticeable decline in the rate of presentation of new ideas.

6. A general discussion of the ideas concludes the exercise.

Brainstorming can be applied in a number of secondary curriculum areas. It is an effective technique for stimulating students to produce new ideas rather than rehash old ones or react to views of others.

Critical Thinking

Whereas the primary function of creative thinking is to generate ideas, the primary function of critical thinking is to evaluate ideas. Critical thinking always involves judgment. Critical thinking judgments are more than simple exchanges of uninformed opinion. Properly, judgments are made in terms of defensible criteria (Lipman 1988).

Sometimes teachers link activities calling for creative thinking and critical thinking. When this is done, the creative thinking activity takes place first. During this phase of the lesson, students produce ideas. During the second phase, they use critical thinking approaches to evaluate these ideas.

A basic procedure for brainstorming was introduced in the section introducing creative thinking. An analytic brainstorming approach has been developed by Dunn and Dunn (1972). This procedure applies critical thinking to the initial creative results of the first part of a brainstorming activity. An analytic brainstorming lesson might develop along these lines:

1. The teacher poses a problem in the form of a statement about what an "ideal" solution to a problem might be. (Students brainstorm responses. Their answers are written so they can be easily seen by all students.)

   "The best thing we could do to prevent pollution of Gulf Coast beaches would be to. . . ." (Students brainstorm responses.)

2. With step 1 responses in full view, the teacher asks students why the "best things" mentioned have not already taken place. (Students brainstorm appropriate responses. These responses again are written so all students can see them easily.)

   "What things are getting in the way of those 'best things' we could do to prevent pollution of Gulf Coast beaches?" (Students brainstorm responses.)

3. The third phase features a question about what might be done to overcome obstacles noted in responses to the question posed in step 2. (Students brainstorm appropriate responses. These responses are written so all can see them easily.)

   "How could we overcome difficulties that keep us from doing what we have to do to prevent pollution of Gulf Coast beaches?" (Students brainstorm appropriate responses.)

4. In step 4, the teacher asks students to point out difficulties of implementing ideas noted in step 3 responses. (Students brainstorm responses to the step 4 question. These responses are written where all can see them.)

   "What might stand in the way of our efforts to overcome difficulties that keep us from taking necessary action to prevent pollution of Gulf Coast beaches?" (Students brainstorm appropriate responses.)

5. In step 5, the teacher asks students to decide what should be done first to begin a realistic solution to the problem. (Students brainstorm appropriate responses.)

   "Considering all of our thinking, what steps should we take first? Be prepared to explain your choices." (Students respond and defend their choices by reference to appropriate criteria.)

In general, critical thinking involves approaches to making evaluative judgments that are based on logical consideration of evidence and application of appropriate criteria. Barry Beyer, a leading proponent of teaching thinking skills to students in the schools, points out that critical thinking does not result from following a specific sequence of steps. Rather, critical thinking involves the use of a number of mental operations including the following:

1. Distinguishing between statements of verifiable fact and value claims.
2. Distinguishing relevant from irrelevant information, claims, or reasons.
3. Determining the factual accuracy of a statement.
4. Determining the credibility of a written source.
5. Identifying ambiguous claims or arguments.
6. Identifying unstated assumptions.
7. Detecting bias.
8. Identifying logical fallacies.
9. Recognizing logical inconsistencies in a line of reasoning.
10. Determining the strength of an argument or claim.

Box 10.5 discusses using diagrams to help students visualize their thinking.

Problem Solving

Problem solving approaches are used when students are asked to think about problems for which there is likely to be a "best" or "correct" solution. This does not necessarily mean that, in every case, these solutions may not at some future time be held up to question. However, they are considered "best," "correct," "right," or "appropriate," given the evidence that is available at the time the problem is considered. These are some examples of issues that might be addressed using a problem solving approach:

• What is causing the leaves on my house plants to turn yellow and fall off?
• Why is it colder in the winter months in Minneapolis than in Juneau, even though Juneau is much farther north?

- Why do people in Maine and Alabama speak with different accents?

- Why don't armadillos live in California?

- What has caused 20th century English to differ more from 17th century English than 20th century French differs from 17th century French?

When students are introduced to problem-solving, they are often taught to follow certain steps. The following four-part sequence includes steps similar to those found in many problem-solving models.

Step 1: Identify the problem.

Step 2: Consider possible approaches to its solution.

Step 3: Select and apply approaches.

Step 4: Evaluate the adequacy of the conclusion.

Suppose a high-school algebra teacher wished to apply this model. This is how a lesson following these steps might unfold.

Step One

Teacher: "All right, class, I want each of you to solve this equation." [On the board, the teacher writes this equation: $2X^2 - 46 = 116$.]
"Now does everybody understand what I want you to do? [Student raises a hand.] Ruby?"

Ruby: "You want us to solve for X, right?"

Teacher: "Right."

Step Two

Teacher: "Now, before you start, I want someone to tell me how you're going to go about it. John, how about you?"

John: "Well, we're going to have to get this thing boiled down to a simpler form. The first thing I would do is get rid of the $2X^2$ by dividing both sides by 2."

Teacher: "O.K. That makes sense. What would need to be done next? Gabriella?"

Gabriella: "I think we'll need to arrange it so we'll have the X^2 on one side and all of the other numbers on the other."

Teacher: "Fine. Now what do we need to remember about the sign of a number when we move it from one side of an equation to the other? I mean, if I had the equation $X - 3 = 4$, what

Box 10.5

Using Diagrams to Help Students Visualize Their Reasoning

One task of critical thinking is to help students recognize logical fallacies. Sometimes students are taught to use *syllogisms* as they analyze phenomena of various kinds. A syllogism is a formal argument that consists of a major premise, a minor premise, and a conclusion.

Sometimes students master the forms but make errors because their premises are faulty. This can lead to inaccurate conclusions. Natalie Yeager (1987) suggests using diagrams to help students visualize their logic.

The media has made much of Japan's technological excellence and the proficiency of Japanese students in mathematics. An unsophisticated student who meets an exchange student from Japan named Toshi Nakimura might use the following syllogism to conclude that Toshi is a strong mathematics student.

Major premise: All Japanese students are good at mathematics.

Minor premise: Toshi is a Japanese student.

Conclusion: Toshi is good at mathematics.

This relationship can be diagrammed as follows. In the diagram, the largest circle, "a," includes all people who are good at mathematics. The second circle, "b," includes all Japanese. It is totally within the "a" circle because the assumption is that all Japanese are good at mathematics. The third circle, "c," indicates Toshi. It suggests that Toshi is Japanese and, hence, good at mathematics.

would happen if I moved the minus three to the other side? Kim?"

Kim: "The minus three would become a plus three. So you would end up with $X = 4 + 3$ or 7."

Teacher: "Excellent. Remember the sign changes when we move from one side to the other. Now, once you had moved all the numbers to one side, what would you have to do to solve for X? Jean?"

Jean: "You would need to add all of the numbers together and then take the square root of the total."

Step Three

Teacher: "We seem to have the basic procedures well in mind. Now I want each of you to solve the problem. If you get stuck, raise

Box 10.5 *cont.*

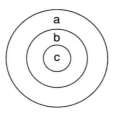

In time, it may become evident that Toshi finds mathematics difficult. This information would suggest a flaw in the original argument. A new argument that takes into account the new information about Toshi might be diagrammed in this way:

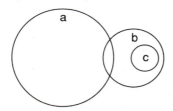

Circle "a" still denotes all people who are good at mathematics. Circle "b" continues to identify all Japanese students. Note, though, that now some Japanese students are among those who are good at mathematics and some are among those who are not. The circle "c" continues to identify Toshi. He is represented now as one of those Japanese students who are not good at mathematics.

Encouraging students to diagram their arguments helps them to understand the flow of their logic. The exercise is particularly useful when new information challenges an erroneous assumption. A comparison of diagrams helps to clarify differences separating the initial line of logic from the line of logic developed once initial errors have been corrected.

your hand, and I will try to help you." [Students individually begin working on the problem.]

Step Four

Teacher: "I see that everybody has come up with an answer. Now let's check our work to see whether the answers are correct. Jennifer, tell me how we might do that."

Jennifer: "I'm not sure."

Teacher: "Anyone have an idea? Raoul?"

Raoul: "We could substitute our answer for X in the original equation to see if it works."

Teacher: "Good idea. Let's try that. Raoul, what did you get as your answer?"

Raoul: "Nine."

Teacher: "Fine, now let's substitute 9 for *X* in our original equation." [Teacher writes following sequence of substitutions on the board:]

$$2X^2 - 46 = 116$$

$$2(9 \times 9) - 46 = 116$$

$$2(81) - 46 = 116$$

$$162 - 46 = 116$$

$$116 = 116$$

Your answer seems to be correct. Does everybody see what I have done here?" [Teacher goes on to answer questions and to emphasize the importance of checking the accuracy of answers to problems.] Box 10.6 discusses the issue of short-lived solutions.

Decision Making

Not all problems have answers that are clearly "right," "correct," or "appropriate." They are questions for which there are no necessarily "best" alternatives. In this situation, people often must make choices from among a variety of acceptable alternatives. This process involves a thinking skill known as "decision making" (Beyer 1988). Because it involves choices from among a number of competing appropriate responses, decision making involves consideration of personal values as well as of relevant evidence.

The thinking model for decision making varies from that used in problem solving. The major reason for this difference is that value judgments play a much more important role in decision making than in problem solving. The following seven-step model is an example of an approach used in decision-making lessons:

1. Describe the basic issue or problem.
2. Point out alternative responses.
3. Identify evidence supporting each alternative.
4. Identify values reflected in each alternative.
5. Point out possible consequences of each alternative.

Box 10.6

Sometimes Solutions to Problems Are Short-Lived

Students need to understand that solutions to problems that are based on excellent evidence and careful thought may not always be "permanently correct" answers. New information may come to light, and there may be unforeseen consequences of a solution that seems impeccable at the time it is adopted.

For example, in the 1870s, planters in Jamaica were desperately searching for a way to control hordes of rats in their sugar cane fields. They tried many approaches without success before, in 1872, introducing nine mongooses from India into the sugar cane fields. The mongooses prospered. Within just a few years, rats ceased to be a problem. But, there was an unintended consequence.

The mongooses continued to increase in numbers. They began attacking chickens. In time they became a real threat to the agricultural economy of Jamaica. Today, the decision to bring the mongoose to the West Indies as a "solution" to a problem is widely regarded as a disaster.

Think about other "solutions" to problems that, in the short run, made perfectly good sense but, in the long run, proved not to be desirable. Prepare to share two or three examples with your class.

Example 1:

Example 2:

Example 3:

---

6. Make a choice from among available alternatives.
7. Identify evidence and values considered in making this choice.

The following example illustrates an application of this seven step model.

Step One

A local school board has taken under consideration a proposal to require every student to take four years of mathematics. The issue or problem might be framed something like this: "Should students be required to take four years of mathematics in high school?"

Step Two

In this case, there are just two basic alternatives. Alternative one is to support a requirement for all students to take four years of mathematics in high school. Alternative two is to oppose such a requirement.

Step Three
Some of the following evidence might be gathered to **support** a four-year mathematics requirement:

- SAT scores in mathematics have failed to reach levels achieved by students in the 1960s.
- The nation is facing an impending shortage of engineers and other technical people who must have sound backgrounds in mathematics.
- Students will begin college-level mathematics instruction at higher levels because of better high-school backgrounds.
- The requirement will improve the general quality of the high-school curriculum by making the whole program more rigorous.

Some of the following evidence might be gathered to **oppose** a four-year mathematics requirement:

- The requirement will weaken existing math courses. This is true because all high school students do not have the talent to do math courses which, given the new requirements, they will be required to take.
- The requirement will result in an unfortunate reduction in the number of available electives.
- Not all high school graduates go to college.
- Not all occupational fields, even for college graduates, demand an extensive background in mathematics.

Step Four
The following values might be among those cited by individuals who **support** a four-year mathematics requirement:

- Mathematics courses are difficult, and they provide a needed element of rigor to the high school program.
- Too much electivity in high school is not good.
- Society needs more technically trained people, and it is the ·school's job to provide them.

The following values might be among those cited by individuals who **oppose** a four-year mathematics requirement:

- Individual choice is an important part of the high school experience.
- Mathematics is not necessarily more rigorous than other subjects it might displace.
- The society should not go overboard in imposing its priorities on individuals.

Step Five

The following consequences might be cited by a **supporter** of a four-year mathematics requirement as logically resulting from implementation of such a policy:

- Quantitative SAT scores may be expected to rise.
- High school graduates will be better prepared for college.
- The nation will be better able to compete with such technologically oriented nations as Japan.

The following consequences might be cited by an **opponent** of a four-year mathematics requirement as logically resulting from implementation of such a policy:

- The dropout rate among high school students will increase as academic frustrations become too much for some students.
- Discipline problems will increase among students who remain because many who are not talented in mathematics will sense themselves to have been put in a "no win" situation.
- Because vocationally oriented electives will decrease in number, some employers will begin to attack the schools for failing to provide "relevant" instruction.

Step Six

At this point, a decision is made. In this case, since there are only two alternatives, a choice would be made either to (1) support the decision to require four years of mathematics or (2) oppose this decision.

Step Seven

A person **supporting** the decision might identify the pieces of information and values relevant to his or her conclusion in this way:

> I was impressed by the data showing the decline in quantitative SAT scores since the early 1960s. The growing shortage of engineers and technicians also impressed me. Thinking back on my own high school experience, I concluded that high school students lack the maturity to choose electives wisely. In the long

run, they would be better served by a more prescriptive curriculum. Finally, I think the schools *do* have a responsibility to require students to take courses in areas where we have a critical national shortage.

A person **opposing** the decision might identify the pieces of information and values relevant to his or her conclusion in this way:

> It is clear to me that requiring four years of mathematics will reduce the number of electives available to students. Many vacational electives in the high school program do a fine job of responding to needs of students who will go to work once they graduate. We need to preserve these programs. Finally, I don't think we should allow needs articulated by bureaucratic federal agencies to force content on students in the schools. Local control and freedom of choice are a cherished part of our educational heritage. (See Box 10.7.)

Key Ideas in Summary

1. At one time it was assumed that students came to school basically knowing how to think. The school's task was seen as that of providing them with appropriate content with which to refine these skills. Today, it is broadly recognized that students need specific instruction in how to think. A number of thinking skills have been identified that can be taught directly to students in schools.

2. Metacognitive processes are used to monitor thinking patterns. Experiences designed to make students more aware of their own metacognitive processes can help them choose thinking strategies that are appropriate for a given task. Teacher modeling and visual-thinking diagrams are sometimes used to help students become more aware of their metacognitive processes.

3. Inquiry instruction is largely based on an inductive approach to teaching. The basic steps of inquiry basically represent an application of the scientific method to a broad array of problems. Inquiry instruction can help develop students' higher-level thinking skills.

4. Retrieval charts are often used to help students grow in their abilities to compare, contrast, and generalize. They provide valuable assistance to students in organizing data into a limited number of coherent categories.

5. J. Richard Suchman developed a strategy that helps students to focus on content that is really relevant to a given learning task. It promotes

Box 10.7

Providing Students with an Example of a Problem Requiring Decision Making

If students have not worked much with problems requiring decision making, it is useful to introduce an example of how such a problem is attacked. Identify a problem in a subject area you might like to teach for which decision making would be a good approach. For each of the first five steps of the seven-step decision making sequence, provide material that you can use in explaining the procedure to students. (Since steps six and seven involve student decisions, it will not be necessary to include material related to these steps in your example. If you wish, you could have students respond to these steps in terms of their own interpretation of the evidence and values.)

1. Basic issue (identify it).
2. Point out alternative responses (list several).
3. Identify evidence supporting each alternative (do this for each alternative).
4. Identify values reflected in each alternative (do this for each alternative).
5. Point out possible consequences of each alternative (do this for each alternative).

At this point, explain to students that their task would be to make a choice from among available alternatives (step 6 in the sequence) and to identify evidence and values they considered in making their choice (step 7 in the sequence).

active student involvement through a system that requires students to interrogate the teacher.

6. Creative thinking approaches attempt to unleash brainpower to solve difficult problems in imaginative new ways. Brainstorming is an example of an instructional technique that has been used to develop students' creative-thinking abilities.

7. Critical thinking has as its primary function the evaluation of ideas. It always involves judgments that are made in light of defensible criteria. Many critical thinking models introduce students to logical-thinking processes of various types.

8. Problem-solving approaches are used when the purpose is to help students arrive at a conclusion for which a "correct," "right," or "appropriate" answer is likely to exist. Steps in problem solving include (a) identifying the problem; (b) considering possible approaches to its solution; (c) selecting and applying approaches; and (d) evaluating the adequacy of the conclusion.

9. Decision-making is a thinking process that is required when a given problem has no clearly "correct" answer. It is used when a number of alternative answers may be suitable. The one that a person chooses depends not only on the available evidence, but also on his or her personal values. Hence, values play an important role in the decision-making process.

POSTTEST

DIRECTIONS: Using your own paper, answer these true/false questions. For each correct statement, write the word "true." For each incorrect statement, write the world "false."

_____ 1. Metacognitive processes refer to those people use to monitor their own patterns of thinking.

_____ 2. Visual-thinking diagrams can be used by students as they take notes on their reading.

_____ 3. Inquiry begins by providing students with a broad general explanation that is followed with information about more specific items of content.

_____ 4. "Problem solving" and "decision making" are different names for the same thing.

_____ 5. Values play no role in "decision making."

Bibliography

BEYER, BARRY K. *Developing a Thinking Skills Program.* Boston: Allyn and Bacon, 1988.

BEYER, BARRY K. "Practice is Not Enough." In Marcia Heiman and Joshua Slomianko (eds.). *Thinking Skills: Concepts and Techniques.* Washington, D.C.: National Education Association, 1987. pp. 77–86.

BRUNER, JEROME; GOODNOW, JACQUELINE J.; AND AUSTIN, GEORGE A. *A Study of Thinking.* New York: John Wiley, 1977.

COSTA, ARTHUR L. "Teaching Skills: Neither an Add-On Nor a Quick Fix." In Marcia Heiman and Joshua Slomianko (eds.). *Thinking Skills: Concepts and Techniques.* Washington, D.C.: National Education Association, 1987. pp. 16–23.

DEWEY, JOHN. *How We Think.* Boston: D.C. Heath, 1910.

DUNN, RITA AND DUNN, KENNETH. *Practical Approaches to Individualizing Instruction.* New York: Parker Publishing Company, 1972.

HALPERN, DIANE F. "Thinking Across the Disciplines: Methods and Strategies to Promote Higher-Order Thinking in Every Classroom." In Marcia

Heiman and Joshua Slomianko (eds.). *Thinking Skills: Concepts and Techniques*. Washington, D.C.: National Education Association, 1987. pp. 69–76.

HEIMAN, MARCIA AND SLOMIANKO, JOSHUA(EDS.). *Thinking Skills Instruction: Concepts and Techniques*. Washington, D.C.: National Education Association, 1987.

Historical Statistics of the United States: Colonial Times to 1970. Washington, D.C.: U.S. Department of Commerce, Bureau of the Census, 1975.

JOYCE, BRUCE AND WEIL, MARSHA. *Models of Teaching*. 2nd edition. Englewood Cliffs, NJ: Prentice-Hall, Inc., 1980.

LIPMAN, MATTHEW. "Critical Thinking—What Can it Be?" *Educational Leadership* (September, 1988): 38–39.

LOCHHEAD, JACK AND CLEMENT, JOHN (EDS.). *Cognitive Process Instruction*. Philadelphia: The Franklin Institute Press, 1979.

PERKINS, DAVID. *The Mind's Best Work*. Cambridge, MA: Harvard University Press, 1981.

RATHS, LOUIS E.; WASSERMANN, SELMA; JONAS, ARTHUR; AND ROTHSTEIN, ARNOLD. *Teaching for Thinking: Theory, Strategies, and Activities for the Classroom*. 2nd edition. New York: Teachers College Press, 1986.

RUGGIERO, VINCENT RYAN. *Teaching Thinking Across the Curriculum*. New York: Harper and Row, Publishers, 1988.

SCHOENFELD, ALAN H. "Can Heuristics Be Taught?" In Jack Lochhead and John Clement (eds.). *Cognitive Process Instruction*. Philadelphia: The Franklin Institute Press, 1979. pp. 315–338.

SUCHMAN, J. RICHARD. *The Elementary School Training Program in Scientific Inquiry*. Report to the U.S. Office of Education, Project Title VII, Project 216. Urbana, Illinois: University of Illinois, 1962.

TABA, HILDA. *Curriculum Development: Theory and Practice*. New York Harcourt, Brace and World, 1962.

TABA, HILDA; DURKIN, MARY C.; FRAENKEL, JACK R.; AND MCNAUGHTON, ANTHONY H. *A Teacher's Handbook to Elementary Social Studies: An Inductive Approach*. Reading, Massachusetts: Addison-Wesley Publishing Company, 1971.

U.S. BUREAU OF THE CENSUS. *Historical Statistics of the United States, Colonial Times to 1970*. Bicentennial Edition, Washington, D.C.: U.S. Bureau of the Census, 1975.

YEAGER, NATALIE C. "Teaching Thinking to Teach Literature while Teaching Literature to Teach Thinking." In Marcia Heiman an Joshua Slomianko (eds.). *Thinking Skills: Concepts and Techniques*. Washington, D.C.: National Education Association, 1987. pp. 134–144.

CHAPTER 11

Individualized Approaches

AIMS

This chapter provides information to help the reader to:

1. State reasons for using individualized approaches in secondary schools.
2. Define variables that can be altered when accommodating individual differences.
3. Provide examples of how the pace of instruction can be changed.
4. Identify basic assumptions of the mastery learning approach to teaching.
5. Describe the content-of-learning variable.
6. Point out some specific ways a teacher might respond to students having different learning styles.
7. State how contracts might be used to modify the goals of learning.
8. List typical components of a "learning activity package."
9. Describe differences between "learning centers" and "learning stations."
10. Point out ways new technologies might affect individualized instruction.

PRETEST

DIRECTIONS: Using your own paper, answer these true/false questions. For each correct statement, write the word "true." For each incorrect statement, write the word "false."

—— 1. Accommodating individual differences is less of a problem in secondary schools than in elementary schools.

—— 2. Mastery learning approaches are based on the idea that differences in school achievement are related more to the time individuals need to learn than to differences in intelligence or aptitude.

—— 3. Adaptive Instruction is an attempt to match instructional aptitudes, abilities, and learning styles of students with instructional methods.

—— 4. The terms "learning activity package" and "learning contract" refer to precisely the same approaches to individualizing instruction.

—— 5. "Learning center" and "learning station" are two terms for the same thing.

Introduction

Teachers have long puzzled over how to provide meaningful instruction for all of the students in their classes. Secondary students are a very diverse group. In fact, differences among secondary students are more profound than those among elementary students. As learners progress through school, bright and motivated students increase their distance from less able and less motivated students. Differences among 12th graders are more pronounced than among students at any other grade level in the K-to-12 program.

Differences among secondary school students seem to make an iron-clad case in support of tailoring instructional practices to meet needs of individual learners. Yet, surprisingly, much more individualized instruction goes on at the elementary school level than at the secondary level. Thomas Good and Jere Brophy (1987), two well known educational researchers, found that about one-third of elementary school teachers make some attempts to individualize instruction as compared to only about one-fifth of secondary school teachers (p. 361).

Few question the theoretical merit of individualizing instruction. The reality, however, as Good and Brophy (1987) have pointed out, is a compromise between the desire to accommodate individual differences and pressures to deliver educational services inexpensively. Over time, the latter concern has resulted in the traditional practice of assigning teachers 20 to 40 students per class period. When groups this large are formed, it is inevitable that there will be great differences in abilities and attitudes of individual students.

Instruction that is geared to a class average may reach some of the students, perhaps even a majority; but, it will not reach all of them. Exceptionally bright students have the potential to become bored. Slower learners who are unable to maintain the pace established by the teacher may become frustrated and present teachers with discipline problems. Students from culturally different backgrounds may challenge the relevance of what the teacher is offering. All of these difficulties build a case in support of the idea that teachers should give some attention to individualizing their teaching.

This does not mean that all classroom instruction should be individualized. There are times when whole-group instruction makes sense. Professional teachers need to know when to individualize and how to individualize. Teachers who have these abilities are more likely to help their students reach their potentials than are teachers who lack these skills. Some approaches to individualizing instruction are introduced in the sections that follow.

Altering Variables to Accommodate Individual Differences

The term "individualized instruction" is a slippery one. It has been used in so many ways that the term sometimes communicates very different things to some individuals than to others. For example, for some people "individualization" suggests a program where all students are working independently on the same assignment. They are doing the same thing; only their rate of progress varies. This kind of individualization is sometimes called "continuous progress learning." The phrase "continuous progress" implies that the rate of academic development of one learner will not be held up because others in the class may learn at a slower rate than he or she does.

Others see individualization focusing not on the rate of learning but on the content of instruction. These people define individualized programs as those in which individual students study different topics, with the teacher acting as an overall learning manager. Individualized programs of this kind place a great deal of responsibility in the hands of individual students. The teacher functions as a facilitator and monitor.

Still other conceptions of individualization focus on issues such as the method of learning and the goals of learning. To appreciate the array of concerns that are implied by the general term "individualized instruction," it is useful to consider each of the variables that can be

"I know you're all for individualizing, but Lorton can't play his boom box here. Let's take a chance on the possibility that his psyche can take this kind of repression."

changed to accommodate individual differences. Again, these variables are (1) the rate of learning, (2) the content of learning, (3) the method of learning, and (4) the goals of learning.

Altering the Rate of Learning

The term "rate of learning" refers to the pace at which instruction occurs. In a class where all students are exposed to exactly the same instructional program, there is an assumption that all of them are capable of learning at the same rate. Proponents of individualized instruction point out that this assumption is false. Students vary tremendously in terms of the rate at which they can learn new material.

When the learning-rate or pacing variable is manipulated, the basic content remains the same as do basic assignments for students. What is altered is the time teachers allow for the completion of the tasks. Arrangements are made that allow brighter students to move quickly through the material, while less able learners are allowed more time. Altering the learning rate makes most sense in situations where it is essential for all learners to master a given body of content. This form of individualization is reflected in a number of instructional approaches. One of these is mastery learning. Mastery learning presumes that differences in students' levels of achievement are not the result of differences in their intelligence or aptitudes (Bloom 1976, 1980). Rather they result from variations in time required by individual students to learn. Provided the learning task is appropriate, Bloom (1976, 1980) suggests that nearly all students can achieve success on school tasks if they are provided with sufficient time. Box 11.1 provides further discussion of mastery learning.

The Personalized System of Instruction (PSI) represents an example of an application of mastery learning to individualized instruction (Guskey 1985, p. 9). Similar to other mastery learning programs, it features (1) clearly specified learning objectives; (2) diagnoses of students' entry-level capabilities; (3) numerous and frequent assessment measures; (4) specification of mastery levels to be attained; (5) a structured sequence of facts, principles, and skills to be learned; (6) frequent feedback to learners about their progress; and (7) provisions of additional time that allows students who fail to achieve mastery to study some more and master the content.

Mastery learning approaches such as PSI have drawn some criticism. For example, use of these programs does not always result in increased student motivation and achievement. In some applications in higher education settings, students have expressed a dislike of the format. Some have complained about the lack of opportunities to work with other students in the class. Sometimes monitoring has been lax, and progress has been slowed because students have procrastinated. Some teachers have resisted mastery learning approaches because preparation is very time-consuming (Good and Brophy 1987, p. 359).

Other criticisms have focused on procedural matters. Because mastery learning programs often divide large tasks into small pieces, sometimes a great deal of paperwork is involved. This feature along with the frequent testing that goes on often creates work for teachers that, in the view of some, goes beyond what they face in more traditional instructional programs (Good and Brophy 1987).

Frequency of testing, a common characterstic of mastery learning programs, has also been attacked. Some critics charge that frequent testing results in assessments that focus on isolated pieces of content. Such tests may encourage students to lose sight of larger dimensions of the subject. Some teachers have found that students may do well on mastery tests but experience difficulty in applying what they have learned to different settings (Good and Brophy 1987).

In summary, mastery learning programs seem to work best when they focus on a relatively narrow band of content that is required of

Box 11.1

Is Mastery Learning Unrealistic?

Supporters of mastery learning point out that many more students would master content taught in school if only they were given sufficient time. This may be true, but one might well ask, "so what?" The reality with which we all live is that time is limited. Students need to be taught to become more efficient. One way to do this is to insist that work be completed within a strictly limited time period. To do otherwise encourages students to be lazy, knowing that they have unlimited amounts of time to complete their work.

Further, taking too much time on some content automatically results in less time being available to study other topics. Mastery learning would seem to encourage a school program that allowed students to be cut off from exposure to some subjects simply because they had used the available time to study others. Is this realistic or wise?

What Do You Think?

Read the comments above. Then answer these questions.

1. **Is** it unrealistic to vary the time students take to master content in terms of how much time they individually require?

2. How do you feel about the contention that mastery learning has the potential to restrict the number of topics to which some students are exposed?

3. In general, how would you respond to the points made in this statement?

all students. They function better when the content lends itself easily to division into numerous smaller pieces that can be organized for purposes of teaching and testing. Under these circumstances, mastery learning programs can motivate some students who have developed chronic failure patterns in more traditional instructional programs. Success depends on careful teacher monitoring of students to assess levels of progress and to provide encouragement to stay on task. It is particularly important that students who have experienced few instances of success develop confidence in their own abilities to succeed. Teachers in mastery-learning programs work hard to assure that this happens.

Altering the Content of Learning

Instead of focusing on the issue of pacing, some programs try to individualize instruction by altering the content studied by different students. Students may be pursuing common goals and objectives, but they may work with very different learning materials. For example, a mathemat-

Some individualized learning programs alter the content of learning. This student is working with material that has been assigned to him because of his special interests and aptitudes. *Photo courtesy of Elizabeth Crews.*

ics teacher may allow students interested in automobiles to study mathematics concepts in the context of car design. Students in the same class with interests in farming might study the same concepts in the context of agriculture.

A basic premise of programs that focus on changing the content of learning is that students will be more motivated when they study material that interests them. Supporters of this approach point out that many traditional programs fail to consider students' interests. For example, a textbook written by an author in New York City may contain examples and explanations that are not of interest at all to students in Missoula, Montana or Laredo, Texas. To accommodate this problem, supporters of altering the content urge teachers to provide learning options for students that do take into consideration individual interests.

When this approach to individualizing instruction is used, students often are given some flexibility in choosing the specific content they will study to meet goals and objectives of the teacher. The nature of student choice will vary from setting to setting. In some places, this basic concept has been extended so far as to create magnet high schools with unique emphases.

Each magnet high school has a special theme or special focus. For example, there may be a high school for mathematics and science, another one for music and the performing arts, and another one for classical studies. Students attend a given magnet high school by choice. Though each school teaches a number of required basic courses, instruction tends to be "flavored" in accordance with the theme of the school. Hence, students attending a high school for music and the performing arts might study mathematics in terms of its application to musical harmonies.

Magnet high schools are features of the nation's largest urban areas. These kinds of learning environments are not open to most of the nation's secondary students. However, this does not mean that many high schools deny students opportunities to learn in settings where the content is varied to meet individual interests. Many teachers make serious attempts to diagnose student interests and to make assignments consistent with them. The approach, however, is not without its difficulties.

One obvious problem has to do with the availability of learning materials and the diversity of student interests. Materials that would meet the interests of every student in a class would require an investment beyond what many school districts can afford.

Traditional teacher programs rarely spend a great deal of time preparing people to develop extensive sets of materials to accommodate individual student needs. Though prospective teachers are admonished to use instructional resources other than texts, there usually is an assumption that many students will be working with similar learning materials.

Another force militating against individualized programs that vary content is standardized testing. There is a trend for school quality to be assessed in terms of students' scores on standardized tests. When students study different kinds of learning material, there is a danger that at least some students may not come into contact with the kinds of content likely to be sampled on the test. Standardized tests act to encourage teachers to prepare instructional programs that expose all students to learning materials that closely parallel those that will be included on test items.

Though there are many problems in organizing and delivering individualized programs that are based on varying kinds of content studied by each student, there are teachers who use this approach successfully. When such programs are carefully planned, delivered, and monitored, they can greatly enhance students' levels of motivation. Box 11.2 is an exercise in planning an individualized learning program.

Box 11.2

Altering What Students Study to Master Objectives

One variable that is manipulated in some individualized instructional programs is the content-studied variable. When this is done, all students are seeking to master a common set of objectives. But, teachers provide them with alternative materials to study. The idea is to select materials that are well matched to individual student interest.

As an exercise, identify a specific learning objective for a subject you would like to teach. Identify three separate "interests" represented among students in your class. Suggest kinds of learning experience that might help students with each of these interests master the material.

OBJECTIVE: _____

_____

INTEREST *A* _____
    Suggested Learning Experiences: _____

_____

_____

INTEREST *B* _____
    Suggested Learning Experiences: _____

_____

_____

INTEREST *C* _____
    Suggested Learning Experiences: _____

_____

_____

Altering the Method of Learning

Individualized programs that focus on varying the method of learning attempt to respond to different learning styles or aptitudes of students. These programs presume that people vary in their aptitudes for specific tasks and in their preferred modes of learning. To maximize learning, it is necessary for teachers to take these differences into account and to respond to them.

In programs of this kind, the objectives and content of learning remain the same for all students. The teacher directs students to learn the material by a means that is compatible with their aptitudes and learning styles. Sometimes teachers offer students several options and allow them to select the one they would prefer (the assumption being they will choose one that comports well with their own preferences). For example, some students in a class might choose to read information from a textbook, while others might choose to view a filmstrip covering the same topic.

"Adaptive instruction" has been used as a general term to refer to approaches that attempt to alter the variable of instructional method to meet individual student needs (Glaser 1980). Students are matched to instructional methods based on initial diagnoses of their needs and subsequent monitoring of their progress. Sometimes students who are initially matched to one instructional approach are switched to another based on teacher observation of their performance.

Altering the method of instruction poses a number of problems for teachers. For one thing, teachers must be familiar with a number of methods. For another, they need a variety of support materials and equipment to deliver the alternatives. Finally, they must be capable of diagnosing a wide variety of student needs. These constraints tend to put some limits on the number of instructional options that teachers can make available to students. Whatever options are selected must be delivered well. Abundant evidence supports the proposition that student learning correlates highly with well-designed and well-delivered instruction (Good and Brophy 1987).

Research focusing on matching instructional methods to individual student characteristics is still in its infancy. The theoretical rationale for this practice is well grounded. However, there are practical issues to be addressed and resolved before altering the mode of instruction to fit individual student characteristics becomes a common feature of secondary school programs.

Altering the Goals of Learning

Instructional programs that alter learning goals to individualize are controversial. Perhaps for this reason, they also are rare. Much of the debate about the approach results from the great latitude given to students. In some programs of this type, students are permitted to make many decisions about what they want to learn. Teachers function as facilitators. They listen to students and help them clarify their personal goals. This approach presumes that each student is the best judge of his or her educational needs. There also is an assumption that, when given the freedom to do so, students will make intelligent choices.

A few examples of highly student-controlled programs of this type were implemented in a small number of schools during the late 1960s and 1970s in response to critics who charged that schools were impos-ing too many limitations on students. More recently, educational critics have been making quite a different argument. Many of them have sug-gested that schools have provided students with too many electives and that authorities should require a larger number of core courses of all students. These recommendations have acted to eliminate most of the highly student-controlled individualized learning programs of the type that appeared in some schools twenty or so years ago.

Some more common examples of altering-the-goals-of-learning approaches to individualized instruction are those where the goals are negotiated between teacher and students. One scheme of this type that has been used by many teachers is the learning contract. A learning contract is an agreement betwen the teacher and student. Its terms are somewhat negotiable. In most cases, the teacher has the final word as to what the contract will include. In general, a learning contract specifies what an individual student will do to satisfy a given learning requirement.

Among items often referenced in a learning contract are:

- a description of what steps the student will take to accomplish the learning objective
- a list of learning resources that will be used
- a description of any product(s) the student will be required to produce
- an explanation of criteria that will be used in evaluating the student's work
- a list of dates when different tasks are to be completed and submitted to the teacher for review.

Both the teacher and the student sign the contract. Its provisions become the curriculum for the student. When its terms are satisfied, a new contract is developed. Completed contracts document what the student has done and learned.

Though many teachers have had great success in using learning con-tracts, other teachers are not so enthusiastic. Part of their resistance may stem from teacher preparation programs' failure to focus heavily on skills related to negotiating curriculum issues with students. Teachers who use contracts must be very good diagnosticians. They need to know the appropriate learning experiences for individual students, and they need to be aware of the kinds of support materials that are available for them to use. Unquestionably, contract approaches require a great commitment of teacher time. In addition to preparing and monitoring a large number of individual instructional programs, teachers must man-age a huge volume of paperwork. The daunting prospect of maintaining records on large numbers of students working on individual contracts has made some teachers shy away from the approach. Box 11.3 contains an exercise in preparing a learning contract.

The discussions in the preceding subsections have focused on issues related to individualized programs organized around variables associated with (a) the rate of learning, (b) the content of learning, (c) the method of learning, and (d) the goals of learning. Some individualized programs may alter several of these variables at the same time. Decisions about which variables are altered tend to reflect the values and priorities of the teacher, the nature of the subject being taught, the characteristics of the students, and the nature of the school and community.

There are many problems associated with attempts to individualize all aspects of instructional programs for all students. Issues such as availability of learning resources, teacher planning time, and record keeping are among some that have already been noted. Additionally, there are some difficulties for students of a psychological nature when they are asked to work independently for long periods of time. Secondary students are peer-oriented. They enjoy opportunities to work together on projects.

In our view, the term "individualized instruction" ought not to be thought of as synonymous with "independent learning." We believe that "individualized instruction" represents an attempt by the teacher to respond to individual students in ways that recognize limitations of resources and planning time. Further, we suggest that careful analyses of students' individual needs often will result in a decision that these needs can best be met in a group setting of some kind, rather than by independent study. The key to successful individualized instruction is careful diagnosis of needs. Analyses of these needs may well lead to the development of programs for a given student that feature a good deal of large-group instruction, some small-group instruction, and, perhaps, a limited amount of independent study. Sections that follow introduce some approaches to individualized instruction that view the approach as broader than independent learning.

Learning Activity Packages

Learning Activity Packages (LAPs) are highly structured, self-contained guides to learning. Typically they are developed by teachers to meet the needs of specific groups of learners. LAPs break content into a series of small steps. Students accomplish each step and are tested on mastery of this material before they go on to the next step. Usually there is a summary test at the end covering all content that has been introduced.

Most often LAPs are used to supplement the regular instructional program. Ray Latta (1974), who has worked extensively with LAPS,

Box 11.3

Preparing a Learning Contract

Suppose you had a student who was not doing well in a subject you were teaching. You might decide to try a learning-contract approach. Identify a subject and a topic of your own choice. Then, give an example of a learning contract that you might develop. Your learning contract should include each of the following components:

1. The overall learning objective.

2. A description of what steps the student must take to master the objective.

3. A list of learning resources the student will use.

4. A description of any work the student will be required to complete for your review.

5. An indication of any "due dates."

6. An explanation of how the student's work will be evaluated.

---

has suggested three basic uses of this scheme for individualizing instruction. First, they may be appropriate for students who, for one reason or another, are not able to profit from instruction delivered in more conventional ways. Second, they may feature content that goes beyond what is introduced to every student in the class. LAPs of this kind are directed toward brighter learners. Finally, on some occasions, teachers may choose the LAP format as a vehicle for delivering instruction on a certain topic to all students in a class.

LAPs typically allow students to work at their own pace. Teachers do need to monitor students to assure that they are staying on task. Some LAPs provide alternatives from which students may choose in learning specific kinds of content. Others contain some open-ended sections that encourage students to pursue issues of personal interest. In short, the LAP format is extremely flexible. This feature makes them an attractive instructional option for many teachers.

LAPs vary somewhat in terms of their format. The following components are found in large numbers of them (Latta 1974): (1) title page, (2) overview, (3) rationale, (4) objectives, (5) pretest, (6) instructional program, and (7) posttest.

Title Page

The title page reflects the general theme of the LAP. For example, if the LAP is designed to teach the student content related to music theory, the title should make some reference to "music theory. " Developers of LAPs often try to create a title that prompts student interest. For example, the music theory LAP might be called something like: "Beethoven vs. The Beatles: Explorations in Music Theory. "

Overview

The overview provides a general description of what the student will be expected to do to complete the LAP. There often is an indication of the approximate time required to complete the work. The overview, further, will identify major concepts and principles to be introduced. The overview serves as an advance organizer—something that helps students develop a mental framework that will prove useful to them as they begin completing tasks associated with the LAP.

Rationale

The rationale is a brief statement that indicates why the LAP is important. Good rationales give students a "need to know" the information they will be studying. They help students see how new content fits in with what they have already learned. Additionally, the rationale points ahead to what students will be learning later. The latter feature helps students understand the future relevance of the material they will be studying in the LAP.

Objectives

The purpose of the LAP objectives is to provide students with a sense of direction. They indicate in specific language what they are expected to learn. Further, the objectives inform students about what will be done to assure them that their learning has been successful. Good objectives remove a good deal of ambiguity for students. When objectives are well written, students tend to have relatively high levels of motivation as they begin working through their LAPs.

Pretest

Students complete the LAP pretest before they begin work on the material that introduces new content. The pretest has two functions. First, it is designed to determine whether students have the prerequisites necessary to begin the academic work associated with the LAP. Second, it seeks to point out any information introduced in the LAP that the students might already know. When pretest scores reveal that students have already mastered some of the content that is to be introduced, the teacher usually will ask these individuals some questions to assure they really do have this content mastered. If they do, they will be encouraged to skip some of the instructional material in the LAP and begin at a point where they begin to encounter information that they do not know.

Instructional Program

The heart of the LAP is the instructional program. Often it is divided into a number of sections. Students are provided with explicit instructions about what they must do to complete each section. The instructional program includes very explicit directions for students to follow. There may be references to pages to be read, films to be viewed, audio tapes to be heard, and papers to be written. If students are to complete forms of any kind, they will be included.

Often the instructional program of a LAP will present students with several alternatives from which they can choose to complete work in each section. This allows students to choose an option that interests them. Teachers find that providing alternatives motivates students to complete the LAPs.

Often there are assessment activities at the conclusion of each section. Sometimes, there are practice tests for students to take as part of their review for the section tests. When students do well on the practice test, they usually will do well on the section tests themselves. When they do poorly, they are encouraged to review the material that has been introduced and retake the practice test until they achieve a higher score. This general procedure tends to result in fairly high levels of success on the section tests.

Posttest

The posttest is administered at the conclusion of the instructional program. It is given only after all sections have been completed. Scores provide an overall measure of student learning regarding the content introduced in the LAP. The best LAP posttests are constructed in such a way that individual questions are tied to each of the content sections that have been introduced. This allows teachers and students to pinpoint particular areas of weakness. For example, if a student's overall posttest score was relatively good but his or her score on items associated with the second section of content was low, this suggests a need for the student to review information related to the second section. It also might prompt the teacher to look at the way information was presented in this section. A low student score could be a reflection of an inadequate instructional design in the LAP's second section.

LAPs were more widely used in schools a decade ago than they are today. The decline in their popularity can be attributed to several factors. LAPs require the availability of a fairly wide range of instructional resources. Where school budgets have been tight, these resources have not been available. LAPs also require a good deal of time to develop. Heavy teaching loads and a lack of money to hire teachers to develop LAPs during the summer months have also contributed to a decline in their popularity.

Some teachers have become discouraged by the record keeping required when large numbers of students are working with LAPs. Further, monitoring can take a heavy toll. A teacher may find that 20 students working on 10 different topics all require help at the same time. This kind of situation can place a heavy drain on a teacher's emotional resources. For some, it has resulted in a diminished enthusiasm for LAPs as an instructional approach.

Despite some problems associated with their use, LAPs provide a worthwhile alternative to group-paced instruction for some students. Students who use them may sense more control over their own learning. They may feel less pressed for time. And, provision of some alternative methods of accomplishing given tasks may suggest to them that their teachers are sensitive to their individual needs and interests. For these reasons, some teachers feel that the results that can be obtained with LAPs for some students are ample compensation for the difficulties associated with their use.

Learning Centers and Learning Stations

Traditionally, learning centers and learning stations have been more associated with elementary than with secondary programs. However, they do offer the secondary teacher some methods for dealing with difficult instructional problems. A learning-center approach and a learning-station approach share a number of common features. However, each also has some unique characteristics.

A learning center is a designated place within the classroom where a student goes to pursue either required or optional activities related to a single topic. A learning center provides a self-contained environment for learning all required information about a given subject. Centers typically will feature general information about the topic, a list of options students may pursue in mastering the material, needed materials, and information about tests or other assessment alternatives. (See Box 11.4.)

Box 11.4

Layout of a Simple Learning Center with Directions for Users

This learning center has been designed to be set up on top of a table. Note that there are two alternatives for learning the material that students may select. One is in the box labeled "yellow." The other is in the box labeled "blue. " In this learning center, the teacher assigns students either to work with the yellow materials or the blue materials. Assignments are based on diagnoses of individual student characteristics.

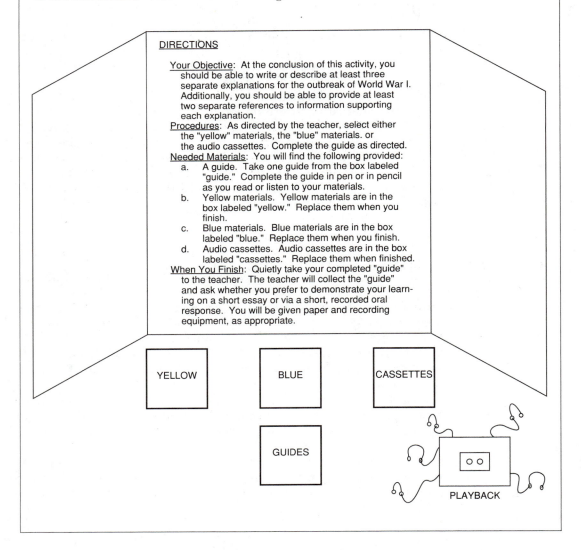

DIRECTIONS

Your Objective: At the conclusion of this activity, you
  should be able to write or describe at least three
  separate explanations for the outbreak of World War I.
  Additionally, you should be able to provide at least
  two separate references to information supporting
  each explanation.
Procedures: As directed by the teacher, select either
  the "yellow" materials, the "blue" materials. or
  the audio cassettes. Complete the guide as directed.
Needed Materials: You will find the following provided:
  a.   A guide. Take one guide from the box labeled
       "guide." Complete the guide in pen or in pencil
       as you read or listen to your materials.
  b.   Yellow materials. Yellow materials are in the
       box labeled "yellow." Replace them when you
       finish.
  c.   Blue materials. Blue materials are in the box
       labeled "blue." Replace them when you finish.
  d.   Audio cassettes. Audio cassettes are in the box
       labeled "cassettes." Replace them when finished.
When You Finish: Quietly take your completed "guide"
  to the teacher. The teacher will collect the "guide"
  and ask whether you prefer to demonstrate your learning on a short essay or via a short, recorded oral
  response. You will be given paper and recording
  equipment, as appropriate.

YELLOW   BLUE   CASSETTES

GUIDES

PLAYBACK

In response to the need to provide learning options for students, a center focusing on "Reasons for the Outbreak of World War I" might allow students to gain information either by (a) reading some material from one or two textbooks; (b) reading a transcript of a lecture on this topic; (c) viewing a filmstrip; or (d) listening through headphones to a discussion of this issue on a cassette tape. Sometimes classrooms feature several centers. However, each center is independent of all of the others. Completion of work at one center is not prerequisite for work at another.

Learning stations, unlike learning centers, tend to divide a single topic into several parts. Each learning station provides experiences for students related to one part of a more general topic. Individual stations are very much interrelated.

In terms of their basic organizational features, individual learning stations are very much like learning centers. They typically will include general information, learning alternatives, needed materials, and details about what a student must do to demonstrate what he or she has learned. Depending on the nature of the focus content, it may be necessary to work through learning stations in a prescribed sequence. Where this is done, teachers often will assign numbers to each station and instruct students to work through them in numerical order. In other cases, where the material does not have to be presented in a sequential fashion, students can be assigned randomly to stations and told to work through them in any order.

Using Learning Centers

Learning centers vary enormously in their complexity. Some may involve little more than a corner of a room featuring a bulletin board display, an instruction sheet, and descriptions of activities students will complete prior to taking a test on the content. More complex centers may require space for media equipment such as filmstrip projectors, video or audio tape players, overhead projectors, and computers. There may have been a need for shelving to hold books, pamphlets, newspapers, filmstrips, audio and video tapes, and software. These elaborate centers may require a good deal of classroom space.

In general, learning centers are used for several rather different purposes. Several of the more frequently encountered learning center types are introduced in the subsections that follow.

The Alternate-Materials Center

The alternate-materials center focuses on content that is required of all students in the class. It responds to individual student needs by including a wide variety of learning materials related to the same topic. Students are allowed to select materials that are consistent with their own interests and abilities.

A problem faced by many secondary school teachers is that some students lack reading skills sufficient for them to profit from information in the course textbook. At an alternate-materials center, teachers can respond to this dilemma by introducing some other options for students with reading problems. These might include less difficult reading materials, audio cassettes, filmstrips, and other alternatives that would convey information similar to that in the course text.

The Enrichment Center

The enrichment center is designed to challenge students who are capable of doing more sophisticated work than many of their classmates. Enrichment centers maintain a focus on a single topic that is being studied by the entire class. However, only more able students are assigned to work at centers of this type, and assignments are designed to motivate them and to "stretch" their mental powers. Sometimes teachers use enrichment centers to maintain the interest of brighter students who finish regular assignments much more quickly than others in the classroom and who need to be assigned to an additional productive learning activity.

The Reinforcement Center

Reinforcement centers focus on a topic all students in a class have been studying. Their primary purpose is to provide students opportunities to review what they have learned. Hence, teachers typically set up reinforcement centers toward the end of a given instructional unit. Activities in the reinforcement centers provide students opportunities to work again with difficult concepts that have been introduced and to practice new skills.

In preparing reinforcement centers, teachers tend to focus on areas that have typically proved difficult for students. Sometimes, when a particularly large and difficult topic has been taught, teachers will develop several reinforcement centers. Each will focus on a particular dimension of what has been taught.

Using Learning Stations

Because a learning-stations approach always requires development of several interrelated stations, preparation typically requires more teacher time than does development of a single learning center. In addition to deciding on which elements of a larger topic will be featureed in each station, teachers also must think about how to manage student movement from station to station.

In planning a series of learning stations, the teacher's first task is to divide a proposed unit of work into a number of sub-topics. Each of these becomes the focus for an individual station. Next, physical locations for the stations need to be identified. For each station, sets of student instructions must be developed, equipment and materials must be provided, and tests and other assessment procedures must be prepared. Additionally, guidelines must be developed regarding what students should do to indicate to the teacher they need help or are ready to leave the station. (See Box 11.5.)

Planning for this last issue is important. Rules need to be established that prevent individual stations from becoming overloaded with students. Sometimes teachers establish a rule such as "no more than four students at a station at a given time. " To make such a rule practical, students who have finished work at one station and who are waiting for someone to vacate a "filled" station must be given something productive to do. Some teachers handle this by developing guidelines at each station beginning with this phrase, "If you have finished all work at this station and there are too many people at the next station, do this until there is a vacancy at the next staton: (specific instructions follow)."

Teachers who use learning stations must develop good record keeping schemes. These allow them to keep track of the progress of individual students' progress through the various stations. This information helps them pinpoint problems of individual students or to identify general design deficiencies of a station that may be causing difficulties for a large number of learners.

Properly designed and managed learning centers and learning stations represent good responses to some chronic difficulties faced by secondary teachers. They provide reasonable alternatives for providing enrichment experiences for brighter students. They can assist problem readers and other slower students. They give students some control over the pace of their learning. They provide opportunities to review materials in a more interesting way than the traditional classroom discussion.

These benefits do not come free. Preparation of good learning centers and learning stations requires a tremendous time investment. It may also require commitment of funds for extra learning resources. Further, centers and stations, once in operation, require intensive teacher monitoring. Even with these difficulties, the benefits for students have led many teachers to be attracted to centers and stations as workable options for tailoring instruction to meet individual student needs.

Box 11.5

Example of General Student Instructions for Using Learning Stations

At the beginning of this unit, you will be assigned to work at one of the eight learning stations. Go directly to that station and begin. You will find instructions at that station telling you what to do. DO NOT GO TO ANY OTHER LEARNING STATION UNLESS SPECIFICALLY INSTRUCTED TO DO SO BY THE TEACHER.

When you complete each assignment at each station, secure it in this notebook. Place the notebook in the box for your period on the shelf along the west wall of the room.

When you have completed the work at the station to which you have been assigned, raise your hand. The teacher will come to you and check your work. If everything is in order you will be directed to go to another station. Please do *not* go to another station until you have been directed to do so by the teacher.

As you work through each of the stations, you may wish to keep track of your own progress. If that is the case, fill in information on the form below as you complete your work:

		Date Completed	*Score* (if appropriate)
Station 1:	Test on "Sinking of PT 109"	_____	_____
Station 2:	Vocabulary Test	_____	_____
Station 3:	Short paper on imagery	_____	_____
Station 4:	Short story I wrote	_____	_____
Station 5:	Six examples of personification I found	_____	_____
Station 6:	Completed crossword puzzles	_____	_____
Station 7:	Vocabulary Test	_____	_____
Station 8:	Six poems I wrote	_____	_____

Computers and New Technologies

One of the fast-growing approaches to individualizing instruction in secondary schools is computer-based instruction. Over the past 10 years, numbers of computers in schools have grown at an explosive rate.

Today, some personal computers are available in nearly every middle school, junior high school, and high school in the nation.

Increasing numbers of quality software packages are coming on the market. The better of these programs allow teachers to alter most of the important variables associated with individualized instruction to provide a learning experience that "fits" the needs of the individual student. For example, programs can be modified to allow students to work at their own pace. Some programs allow for variations in how new content is introduced. Many provide alternative ways for students to review content.

A problem that continues to plague teachers in many schools who wish to make more extensive use of computers is that of hardware availability. Optimally, there should be computers for every student. Many schools do not meet this standard. Consequently, availability of equipment continues to limit numbers of individualized instructional programs that depend on the use of personal computers.

Computers represent just one of the new technologies that have the potential to help teachers individualize. Optical disc technologies are just beginning to enter the mainstream of public school use. Some of the more sophisticated optical disc applications allow for storage and retrieval of vast quantities of information and for highly flexible teacher control over the organization of learning experiences. A more comprehensive review of optical discs and other emerging technologies is provided in Chapter 18, "Technology and the Secondary Schools."

Key Ideas in Summary

1. Differences among students in a typical class increase as students progress through the school program. Differences among individuals in a 12th grade class are much more profound than those among youngsters in a 1st grade class.

2. Individualized instruction involves varying one or more variables of instruction to accommodate specific learner differences. Variables that are commonly altered are (a) rate of learning, (b) content of learning, (c) method of learning, and (d) goals of learning.

3. Advocates of mastery learning contend that differences in the educational performance of people is more a factor of time provided to learn the content than in differences in intelligence or aptitude. When people are provided sufficient time, many will achieve who would not ordinarily achieve given time limitations.

4. Recent advances in educational research have begun to suggest that individuals have different learning styles. To the extent possible,

designers of individualized instructional programs often try to prepare learning experiences that respond to unique styles of particular students.

5. Some individuals have approached individualized instruction out of a conviction that students learn best when they see the goals of instruction as consistent with their own personal goals. This kind of student-directed learning has diminished in its application in recent years. It has fallen victim to a trend to hold all students accountable for a common body of knowledge which is assessed through periodic application of standardized tests.

6. Learning Activity Packages (LAPs) represent one approach to accommodating individual differences in the classroom. LAPs are self-contained booklets that allow students to vary the pace of the learning and that often provide them with some alternative methods to master the prescribed content.

7. Learning Centers are areas in the classroom where resources are gathered together for students to use as they study a single topic. They typically will include a set of student directions, explanations of alternative activities that can be pursued, and needed resource materials.

8. Learning Stations divide topics into a number of parts. A separate station is prepared for each part. Each station includes directions for students, suggestions about ways the content can be learned, needed learning material, and assessment-of-learning materials. After a student completes work at one station, he or she moves on to another. Sometimes it is essential for students to work through stations in a prescribed sequence.

9. Computers and other new technologies promise to make it easier for teachers to respond to individual student differences in the future. Today's computer programs are making it increasingly possible for teachers to develop learning experiences that vary the pace of instruction, the mode of presentation, and the sophistication of the material. A continuing problem facing teachers wishing to use computers and other new technologies is that of equipment availability. This situation may ease in the years ahead as schools increase their inventories of needed equipment.

POSTTEST

DIRECTIONS: Using your own paper, answer these true/false questions. For each correct statement, write the word "true." For each incorrect statement, write the word "false."

_____ 1. Individualized instruction primarily refers to situations when students work independently at their own pace.

_____ 2. Standardized testing is a force that has tended to reduce the number of individualized instructional programs that vary the goals of learning.

_____ 3. Many individualized instructional programs are partially dependent for their success on the availability of a wide range of learning resources.

_____ 4. When teachers adopt an individualized instructional program, they frequently find that they have much less work to do than they did before.

_____ 5. The major focus of an enrichment center is to challenge brighter students by allowing them to go beyond the content introduced to less talented class members.

Bibliography

BLOOM, BENJAMIN S. *All Our Children Learning.* New York: McGraw-Hill, 1980.

BLOOM, BENJAMIN S. *Human Characteristics and School Learning.* New York: McGraw-Hill, 1976.

GLASER, ROBERT. "General Discussion: Relationships Between Aptitude, Learning, and Instruction," In Snow, R.; Federico, T. and Montague, W. (eds.). *Aptitude, Learning, and Instruction.* Volume 2. Hillsdale, NJ: Lawrence Erlbaum Associates, 1980.

GOOD, THOMAS L. AND BROPHY, JERE E. *Looking in Classrooms.* 4th edition. New York: Harper and Row, 1987.

GUSKEY, T. *Implementing Mastery Learning.* Belmont, CA: Wadsworth Publishing Company, 1985.

LATTA, RAY. *A Practical Guide to Writing and Using Learning Activity Packages.* Bellingham, WA: Western Media Printing, Inc., 1974.

SNOW, R. "Aptitude-Treatment Interaction Models. " In M. Dunkin (ed.). *The International Encyclopedia of Teaching and Teacher Education.* New York: Pergamon Press, 1987. pp. 28–32.

CHAPTER 12

Teaching for Affect

AIMS

This chapter provides information to help the reader to:

1. Point out the importance of including the affective dimension in instructional programming.
2. State several reasons that lead some teachers to avoid dealing with the affective dimension in their classrooms.
3. Describe several techniques for helping students to develop more positive attitudes toward school.
4. Cite some basic issues associated with dealing with values in the classroom.
5. Describe some methods that can be used to deal with values issues in secondary school classes.
6. Describe differences involved in dealing with values issues and with moral issues.
7. Describe a framework that can be used in dealing with issues of morality in the classroom.
8. Define and describe several types of "moral discourse."
9. Describe each of Kohlberg's stages of moral development.
10. Point out how moral-dilemma discussions can lead students to higher levels of moral reasoning.

PRETEST

DIRECTIONS: Using your own paper, answer these true/false questions. For each correct statement, write the word "true."   For each incorrect statement, write the word "false."

_____ 1. The public generally does not favor inclusion of issues related to values and morals in the school curriculum.

_____ 2. Though there are some good social outcomes when students develop positive attitudes toward school, these positive attitudes have been found to cause students to do more poorly in their academic subjects.

_____ 3. Classroom meetings are simply simulated versions of the kind of decision-making process that occurs regularly in state legislatures.

_____ 4. Values clarification presumes that teachers have no right to impose their values on students.

_____ 5. Lawrence Kohlberg contends that people pass through the various stages of moral reasoning at about the same rate.

Introduction

Education involves more than transmission of knowledge. Emotional or affective components are important as well. Teachers' interests in the affective dimension of education are concentrated in three basic areas. First of all, they are interested in students' attitudes toward their subjects and toward school in general. Second, they have concerns related to the personal values students learn as they progress through the program. Finally, they are interested in the general issue of developing in students a general sense of morality.

Attitudes Toward Subject and School

Development of positive attitudes toward learning is especially critical today. Knowledge is changing more rapidly than ever before. This means that individuals must become lifelong learners if they are to keep abreast of new developments and compete successfully. Schools have a responsibility to help students commit to the idea that they will need to continue studying and learning throughout their lives.

At a more personal level, most teachers are sincerely interested in what they teach. They appreciate the power that mastery of their subjects has given them to appreciate and understand some of life's complexities. Most teachers would feel a strong sense of personal failure if large numbers of their students left their classrooms with an intense dislike of the subjects they studied.

Personal Values

Personal values and attitudes are important parts of the lives of all people. Values are those bedrock beliefs that give direction to a person's life. Individuals prize, cherish, and act in ways that are congruent with these deeply rooted convictions. Values help people make decisions about how to choose among competing demands for their time, talent, and money.

Values serve as guideposts that help people find meaning in their lives. A person who is confused about his personal values may be confused and inclined to act in inconsistent or self-destructive ways. An awareness of personal values helps us to recognize who we are and what is important in life. Because of their importance, secondary schools have an obligation to deal with the issue of personal values. Students need to be confronted with values decisions and value choices. They need opportunities to reflect on the values they hold and to develop an awareness of how these values affect their decisions.

Morality

Although the values a person holds are related to morality, moral behavior involves more than just values considerations. Morality focuses on questions of "right" and "wrong" as they are viewed by the society in which a person lives. "Moral" questions often focus on such broad issues as justice, equality, fairness, compassion, responsibility, and truth. Rest (1983) has suggested that morality includes those behaviors that help others, conform with social norms, arouse empathy and guilt, stimulate thought about social justice, and lead people to put the interests of others ahead of their own. Preparing individuals for life in their society is an important mission of the schools. Hence, issues relating to morality, which influence patterns of social behavior, have a place in secondary school classrooms.

Growing Interest in Education's Affective Dimension

In recent years, interest in affective dimensions of education has been increasing. For example, one survey found that 68 percent of the parents of public school students felt that a major goal of education should be helping young people to develop a sense of right and wrong. This concern ranked second only to a belief that schools should teach children how to read and write (Gallup 1984, p. 37).

In spite of evidence that the public is interested in this area of education, many teachers are reluctant to deal with affective issues. Some fear they will be accused of inappropriately imposing their own values and standards of morality on impressionable students (Oser 1986, p. 917).

"Mirror, mirror on the wall, who's the most sensitive, open, student-oriented and innovative teacher of all?"

One aspect of this fear is a concern that discussing values issues may intentionally or unintentionally assault the values of people whose lifestyles are inconsistent with local standards. Some teachers are concerned that instruction in the affective area can prompt controversy which may cause general problems for them in their professional roles.

Developing Positive Attitudes Toward Subjects and the School

Successful schools engender positive student attitudes toward school subjects and toward the general school experience. These attitudes tend to develop when schools feature an accepting, supportive environment, encourage students to accept responsibility for school affairs, and direct personal attention toward students (Stedman 1987).

Creation of a positive school environment is important for more than just ethical reasons. Such environments also have a positive influence on students' levels of achievement. Some experts believe that many current school reform efforts have failed to appreciate the importance of a positive school environment. Suggested reforms may have little impact on achievement levels unless careful consideration is also given to making school environments more positive (Glasser 1986).

William Glasser (1986) has pointed out that students are social beings. They have important social needs that must be met. These include needs for love, power, belonging, acceptance, and fun. Glasser suggests that many secondary schools have failed to meet these needs. When they are ignored, students tend to develop a sense of apathy or even of hostility toward their school and their teachers (Glasser 1986, p. 15). Subsections that follow introduce some approaches to creating positive school environments. Box 12.1 discusses sharing power with students.

Non-directive Teaching

Carl Rogers' non-directive teaching model is an extension of this famous educator's perspectives on counseling (Rogers 1981). Non-directive teaching requires teachers to accept the proposition that students are capable of understanding and of coping with their own problems. It requires teachers to yield some power to students and to respect their feelings and attitudes. In non-directive teaching, teachers try to view the world through the perspective of the student. Learning is viewed as an activity involving teacher-student partnership.

Box 12.1

Sharing Power with Students

Authorities such as Glasser and Stedman have suggested that school environments are more positive when students have a sense of power. This means that teachers and administrators must be willing to yield some authority to students. Think about a subject you would like to teach. You are interested in providing your students with a feeling that they exercise real control in some areas. Make a list of five kinds of decisions you might allow students to make.

1. _____
   _____

2. _____
   _____

3. _____
   _____

4. _____
   _____

5. _____
   _____

These general steps are followed in non-directive teaching:

1. Defining the situation.
2. Exploring the problem.
3. Developing insight.
4. Planning and decision-making.
5. Integration.

Defining the Situation

The first step in non-directive teaching is defining the situation. This step is designed to focus the discussion on pressing issues or concerns. The teacher plays an important role during this step. He or she must work with students to help them clearly understand critical issues, key terms, and ground rules for participating in the discussion. During this phase, teachers typically make a special effort to assure students that they will be free to express their genuine feelings throughout the discussion.

Exploring the Problem

During this phase, students are encouraged to share their own ideas about the issues under discussion. The teacher encourages all students to participate. The intent is to bring out into the open all perspectives and feelings held by students in the group.

Developing Insight

During this phase, teachers seek to help students develop new insights about the issue under discussion and about their own feelings regarding the issue. The teacher attempts to do this by using non-directive, non-threatening kinds of questions. ("What do you think about that reaction?" "What do you feel when that happens?" "Why do you think you feel that way?") The teacher is careful not to make judgments about students' answers. The idea is to get students to clarify and reflect on their own feelings.

Sometimes teachers may need to provide some guidance and to render interpretations for the purpose of keeping the discussion moving. In taking these actions, the teacher works to avoid suggesting that a given student answer is "right," "wrong," "good," or "bad." Interpretations often are provided to students in the form of tentative hypotheses. ("Are you saying that the reason you feel this way is . . . ?" "Do I understand you to be saying . . . ?" Is it fair to say that you are doing this because you don't believe anyone listens to you?")

The purpose of these interpretive statements is to elicit additional responses from students. Students are the ones who must develop insights into their own feelings and behaviors. Thus, the teacher works hard to avoid making judgments. He or she must have confidence in students' abilities to work out their own views on issues and problems.

Planning and Decision-Making

In the fourth step, the teacher tries to move students toward developing a plan of action or toward making decisions. The students should do the actual planning, not the teacher. The teacher prompts students by asking them what actions they might take. As students make tentative decisions, the teacher asks probing questions to assure that they adequately understand the issues to which they are responding. Further, the teacher tries to keep them from arriving at decisions prematurely. He or she works to get students to consider alternative courses of action before they commit to a final plan.

Integration

The integration step occurs when the students implement their decision and reflect on their feelings and on the consequences of their decision. They report on actions taken and try to develop additional insights as they analyze what has occurred. In light of these analyses, they plan additional actions.

The integration-phase of non-directive teaching is a particularly delicate one. If it is to succeed, the teacher must be sure that students sense the emotional climate to be safe. They must feel free to report mistakes in judgments as well as decisions that worked out well. Students need to understand and accept the idea that a certain amount of failure is a part of life. It is not the failure that is critical but rather what one does in response to it that is the key issue. A successful integration phase can help students grow emotionally. They can develop more confidence in their abilities to develop long-term solutions to difficulties that, in the short run, appear to be particularly intractable.

In summary, the non-directive teaching model suggests a pattern teachers can follow in dealing with issues involving students' emotions and feelings. The procedure can help students cope with their feelings and to grow in self-confidence. It builds their ability to express their feelings and to develop their own solutions to problems of all kinds. This kind of personal "empowerment" associates with the development more positive student attitudes toward teachers and schools. Some further discussion of building students' self-images is found in Box 12.2.

Classroom Meetings

Classroom meetings have great potential for improving students' attitudes toward school, themselves, and others (Glasser 1969). William Glasser believes that regular use of classroom meetings can help students learn how to accept social responsibility. Glasser says students have a need to develop a "success identity," a perception of themselves as competent individuals. He points out that the home and the school are the only places students can acquire this perspective. He suggests that education for social responsibility should be part of every school program (Glasser 1969, p. 17).

The classroom meeting features a discussion of something important that takes place with the teacher and students grouped in a circle. Glasser (1969) identifies three basic types of classroom meetings. The "social-problem-solving meeting" focuses on behavioral or social issues that are facing class members. The "educational-diagnostic meeting" centers on curriculum content and its meaning for students. The "open-

Box 12.2

Is There Time to Build Students' Self-Images?

Recently, a teacher was overheard making these comments:

> I feel that I am absolutely pushed to the wall to cover the academic content. And I *do* have to cover it. Our district has become very concerned about standardized test scores. These scores reflect on me and my teaching. The tests don't care a whit about how students feel about themselves. Special lessons designed to help students develop more positive images are great in theory. But the realities I face in the classroom just don't allow time for this kind of thing.

What Do You Think?

Read the comments above. Then respond to these questions.

1. Is this teacher philosophically opposed to lessons that are designed to improve students' sense of competence and self-worth?

2. How real are the constraints this teacher mentions?

3. Why have test scores become so important?

4. What are your own feelings about the issues raised by this teacher?

---

ended meeting" encourages students to bring up and discuss any issues that are bothering them.

Successful classroom meetings require a warm and trusting classroom climate. Students must sense that the teacher accepts and is genuinely concerned about them. They must feel completely free to express their own views without fears of eliciting negative teacher judgments.

In making the physical arrangement for a classroom meeting, chairs should be arranged in a tight circle. The idea is to make face-to-face discussion possible and to decrease space separating individual students. The teacher occupies one of the seats in the circle. His or her role is to act as a facilitator of the discussion, but a facilitator who is also an active group member and participant. Meetings should not go on to long. Thirty minutes should be viewed as an outside limit.

These are some basic steps followed by many teachers as they conduct classroom meetings:

1. Establishing the focus for the discussion.
2. Making a personal choice or value decision.
3. Identifying alternative courses of action.
4. Making a public commitment.
5. Following-up.

Establishing the Focus for the Discussion

This step is designed to direct the group's attention on the issue or issues to be discussed. This step, depending on the type of classroom meeting, may be initiated either by the teacher or by the students. For example, if an "educational-diagnostic meeting" is planned, the teacher may seek to establish the focus through use of a question, introduction of an example, description of a problem, or explanation of an event. Students may well initiate the focus in "open-ended meetings."

During this phase of the meeting, one task of the teacher, who acts as a facilitator, is to make certain that the basic issue or problem is described completely. All students need to understand what is to be discussed. This might necessitate explanation of specific information, such as the meanings of certain terms. Once students understand the issue, the teacher encourages group members to state their individual reactions and views. All reactions are welcome. The teacher should intervene if some students begin to criticize the opinions of others. These students need to be reminded that all views are welcome.

Another task of the teacher is to help students recognize their own relationship to a situation or problem. Students need to learn to identify ways in which their personal behaviors may have contributed to the development of a problem. The idea is to promote the idea that socially responsible people recognize the consequences of their behavior and are willing to be accountable for it.

Making a Personal Choice or Value Decision

Specific teacher actions during this phase of a classroom meeting will vary depending on the type of meeting that is taking place. For example, during social-problem-solving meetings focusing on problem behaviors, the teacher may solicit information from students about the personal values that led them to act as they did. The group may discuss social norms governing this kind of behavior and may consider the degree to which individual group members accept these norms.

In educational-diagnostic meetings, the teacher may have students identify values issues related to academic content that has been discussed. The discussion may move on to consider the general value or worth of content that is being taught. The idea is to engage students in an active consideration of the values choices that have given shape to individual lessons and to the general school program.

Identifying Alternative Courses of Action

During this phase, the teacher encourages students to explore alternative courses of action. One responsibility of the teacher is to prevent students from making judgments too quickly. They should be encouraged to give sincere consideration to a number of alternatives.

Suppose a group of students had been involved in a social-problem-solving meeting. The teacher might ask questions designed to help them identify alternative behaviors that might avoid similar problems in the future. As a result of an educational-diagnostic meeting, members of the group may come to the conclusion that parts of the school curriculum are "irrelevant." The teacher might ask probing questions designed to elicit from students ideas about what might be done to make the program relevant. If, in an open-ended meeting, students expressed concern about a political issue, the teacher might work to get students to identify specific actions they might take as citizens to influence this issue in a desired direction.

Making a Public Commitment

During this step, the teacher seeks to move the discussion to the level of seeking a personal commitment to act from participants. The attempt is to bridge the gap between talk and performance. The purpose of this step is to keep the responsibility on the student. It seeks to prevent students from giving facile, insincere answers that simply "sound good." During this phase, teachers might ask questions such as "What are you going to do about it?" and "What are you willing to commit to personally?"

Following Up

This step does not occur immediately following the preceding three. It takes place several days, perhaps even longer, after the conclusion of the classroom meeting. At this time, the teacher asks individual students if they have taken the actions they had stated they were prepared to take. They are asked to reflect on the consequences of these actions. Sometimes, a discussion of these consequences provides the basis for another classroom meeting.

Glasser (1969) sees a number of advantages for regular classroom meetings. They help students feel important. They provide them with a sense that they exercise some power over what goes on in the classroom and over their personal lives. They provide opportunities for teachers to bridge the gap between life at school and life in the "real world." They develop students' abilities to express themselves and encourage the development of higher-level thinking skills. They have potential for building positive attitudes toward schools and teachers.

Values and Value Analysis

The teaching of personal values in schools is controversial. Some critics argue that, since values are deeply held personal beliefs, schools should not intrude in this area. Others have argued that some personal beliefs are socially destructive. Hence, the schools have an important role to play in assuring that certain basic acceptable social values become part of the values repertoire of each student.

Few disagree that some personal values that an individual might hold are socially destructive and should be countered by instruction in the school. (For example, no influential group in our society supports the freedom of one citizen to murder another citizen simply because he or she has committed to a personal value that sanctions killing.) The real problem for the secondary teacher is identifying those common values that should be taught. While a majority of people in this country generally support the idea that some values should be promoted by the school, there are violent disagreements about the list of values that should be taught.

In addition to debates about which values should be taught, controversy also rages about how they should be taught. Should teachers provide experiences that are specifically designed to teach values directly? Or, should lessons focus on helping students to acquire them indirectly by helping them clarify the values they do hold and providing them with opportunities to freely reject or accept specific values?

We believe that the most responsible approach for a teacher in a democratic society is the second approach. Any effort to impose a rigid set of values smacks of indoctrination. This is inconsistent with core American beliefs and with the need for students to recognize that they have broad personal responsibility for the values to which they have committed.

Issues, Values, and Consequences Analysis

The technique of Issues, Values, and Consequences Analysis is designed to help students appreciate that decisions individuals make reflect their values. These are the general steps typically followed in an Issues, Values, and Consequences Analysis lesson:

1. Identifying the general issue.
2. Describing Faction A.

Box 12.3

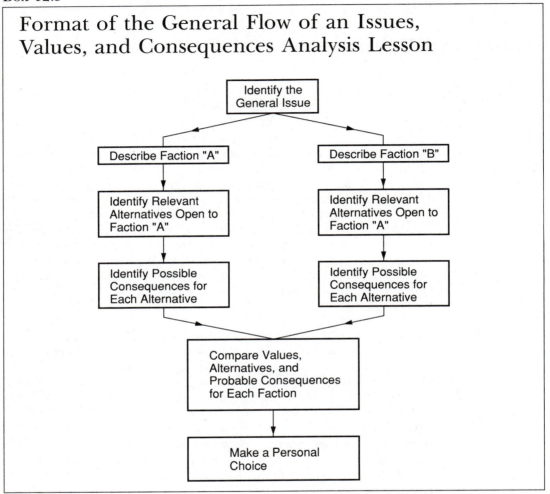

Format of the General Flow of an Issues, Values, and Consequences Analysis Lesson

Identify the General Issue

Describe Faction "A"

Describe Faction "B"

Identify Relevant Alternatives Open to Faction "A"

Identify Relevant Alternatives Open to Faction "A"

Identify Possible Consequences for Each Alternative

Identify Possible Consequences for Each Alternative

Compare Values, Alternatives, and Probable Consequences for Each Faction

Make a Personal Choice

3. Identifying relevant alternatives open to Faction A.

4. Identifying possible consequences for each alternative.

5. Repeating steps 2, 3, and 4 for Faction B (and for other factions should there be more than two).

6. Comparing the values, alternatives, and probable consequences of all factions.

7. Making a choice.

(See Box 12.3.)

STEP ONE: IDENTIFYING THE GENERAL ISSUE.   During this step, the teacher works with the entire class to assure that all students understand the issue. The teacher may do this by introducing students to a problem. ("During the 1950s China was not a member of the United Nations. Some people thought it was strange that the world's most populous nation was not a member. Others feared that admitting China would give additional voting power to nations with communist governments. There was much debate over whether China should be admitted to the U.N. We are going to be working with this issue today.")

STEP TWO: DESCRIBING FACTION A.   Controversial issues used as a focus for lessons of this kind are controversial because different individuals or groups have different opinions about what should be done. Every controversial issue has at least two contending factions associated with it. Some have more.

During this phase, students are assigned to work in groups. They are asked to gain as much information as possible about the people supporting one of the factions. ("All right, I want John's group to think about the motives of people who wanted to admit China to the U.N. What did they see as potential benefits to China? To the United States? To the world? What kinds of things seemed to have been very important to these people? What values did them esteem?" And so forth.)

STEP THREE: IDENTIFYING RELEVANT ALTERNATIVES OPEN TO FACTION A.   During this phase of the lesson, students are asked to think about alternative courses of action open to members of the faction they are considering. Sometimes teachers have students brainstorm their ideas. This tends to open up a number of possibilities, and it tends to prevent all students from restricting their thinking to an extremely limited number of alternatives. ("What are some kinds of things that supporters of China's admission to the U.N. might have done? Let's develop a long list of plausible possibilities.)

STEP FOUR: IDENTIFYING POSSIBLE CONSEQUENCES FOR EACH ALTERNATIVE.   Alternative courses of action may produce different results or consequences. During this step, the teacher encourages students to look at each alternative course of action with a view to identifying consequences that might have followed a commitment to this option. ("We have identified seven distinct possible courses of action for people who supported China's admission to the U.N. Let's look at these one at a time. What might have happened if these people had decided to follow this first alternative?" The same pattern continues for each of the remaining listed options.)

STEP FIVE: REPEAT STEPS TWO, THREE, AND FOUR FOR FAC-
TION B (AND ANY OTHER REMAINING FACTIONS).   The teacher
takes students through the same sequence of activities for each of the
remaining factions. For example, students might be instructed to consider the motives of people opposed to admitting China to the U.N.,
the action alternatives open to these individuals, and the probable consequences of each option.

STEP SIX: COMPARING THE VALUES, ALTERNATIVES, AND
PROBABLE CONSEQUENCES OF ALL FACTIONS.   The purpose of
this step is to help students grasp the point that many policy arguments
involve values conflicts. To help students see differences in values priorities, the teacher helps students review differences that have come
to light during previous phases of the lessons. ("What are similarities
and differences in action alternatives that were open to people favoring
and opposing China's admission to the U.N.? What things were considered to be especially important to those favoring China's admission? To
those people opposing China's admission? How would you summarize
the values that were most important to people in each faction?")

STEP SEVEN: MAKING A CHOICE.   At this point in the exercise, the
teacher challenges students to make a personal decision about the issue
that has been considered. Students are encouraged to consider values
of individuals associated with each faction as well as their own values.
("What should have been done in the 1950s about admitting China to
the U.N.? I want you to let me know your decisions. Then, I am going
to ask you what your decisions tell us about the values you consider to
be especially important. We will want to compare your values to those
of people associated with each of the factions we have studied.")

   In summary, Issues, Values, and Consequences Analysis is designed
to help students appreciate that decisions are not made just by dispas-
sionate consideration of evidence. Students are taught that individual
values also play an important role. The technique helps students to
examine carefully the values that are reflected in decisions of others.
Additionally, students come to appreciate relationships between their
own values' priorities and those of others.

Values Clarification

Values clarification is an approach developed during the 1960s by Louis
Raths, Merrill Harmin, and Sidney Simon (1966). A basic premise of this
approach is that teachers have no right to impose values on students.
Rather, teachers are urged to use an approach that helps students

These students are receiving background information about a topic as part of an issues, values, and consequence-analysis lesson. *Photo courtesy of Barbara Hadley.*

to clarify or recognize their own values, think about alternative value positions, and act on those values that are highly prized.

Raths, Harmin, and Simon suggest that the valuing process has three major components: (a) choosing a value, (b) affirming or prizing a value, and (c) acting on a value. There are criteria associated with each of these major components. "Choosing a value" requires that the person (a) choose the value freely; (b) choose the value with full knowledge of the alternatives; and (c) choose the value with knowledge of the consequences.

"Affirming or prizing a value" requires that the individual be (a) glad about the choice and (b) willing to affirm the choice publicly. "Acting on a value" requires that the individual (a) do something with the chosen value and (b) act repeatedly in a manner consistent with the value until it becomes a permanent part of his or her behavior pattern.

Proponents of values clarification have developed large numbers of teaching activities. One of them is "values ranking." This simple procedure is designed to help students recognize their own values priorities. It requires the teacher to provide members of the class with a situation with a number of alternative responses. Each response tends to reflect a different value. Students are asked to rank the listed responses in terms of their personal preference. Note this example:

Teacher: "Read over the explanation of the general situation. Then, rank each option in terms of your own preference. Place a "1" in the blank before your favorite choice, a "2" in the blank before your next favorite choice, and so forth. Conclude with a "9" in the blank before your least favorite choice.

The Situation: You have just discovered that you have inherited one million dollars (tax free). The same day, you learn that you have an incurable disease. You will die within the next six months. How will you spend your time?
___ Going to church or synagogue
___ Identifying and giving money to worthy charities
___ Traveling to places I always wanted to visit
___ Establishing scholarships for the urban poor
___ Giving lavish parties
___ Building new homes for my relatives
___ Buying an expensive wardrobe of designer clothes
___ Having a car custom-built just for me
___ Reading all the books I always meant to read

Students rank these items independently. In the follow-up discussion, the teacher and students work to identify values associated with the various options on the list. The teacher takes care to assure students that there is no "right" or "wrong" way to prioritize items on the list. The purpose is to get students to think about what they personally value. As part of the exercise, the teacher may wish to invite students to share and talk about their personal rankings, but this must be a completely optional decision. Students' rights to privacy must be respected. Those students who are willing to talk about their own values and choices provide additional information that can help sensitize students to values commitments different from their own.

Box 12.4

Is Values Clarification Immoral?

Schools should not allow teachers to use values clarification lessons. The technique assumes that *any* value a student may have is acceptable so long as he or she accepts it freely, with no coercion from the teacher or anyone else. This idea is simply unacceptable.

What if a student developed a system of values that sanctioned the murder of certain people? Wouldn't this be dangerous? Shouldn't the schools work to oppose such socially destructive values? I believe most people think so, but not those who champion the values clarification approach.

What Do You Think?

Read the comments on the left. Then respond to these questions.

1. What are the primary concerns this person has about the values clarification approach?

2. If you were to write an editorial expanding on this position, what would you say?

3. What counter-arguments might be made to the person who made this statement?

4. What are your personal views about issues raised in the statement?

Many examples of lessons associated with values clarification are available in education's professional literature. Two books widely held in college and university libraries that discuss a number of techniques are Raths, Harmin, and Simon, *Values and Teaching*; and Simon, Howe, and Kirschenbaum, *Values Clarification*. Box 12.4 further discusses values clarification.

Morality

Morality focuses on "right" and "wrong." It concerns such ideas as justice, equality, fairness, compassion, and responsibility. Individuals' values play a role in their understandings of what constitutes moral behavior.

Some of these values are very widely shared. For example, all world cultures hold human life to be sacred. Murder is considered an immoral act everywhere. Many widely held values tend to be of a type that are called "prosocial values." These values relate to patterns of behavior that members of a culture must endorse if their society is to survive.

James Rest's Framework

James Rest (1983) has developed a four-level framework that can be used in preparing lessons that focus on morality. The four levels of Rest's approach are:

1. Moral sensitivity.
2. Moral judgment.
3. Moral decision-making.
4. Moral action.

MORAL SENSITIVITY.   At this level of moral awareness, individuals begin to appreciate that issues under discussion have a moral dimension. Teachers attempt to help students understand that moral considerations may lead to decisions different from what they might be were people only to consider "the facts." For example, some evidence may suggest that wiretaps can assist law enforcement officials in their efforts to apprehend criminals. But, there is also a moral issue involving invasion of privacy that must be considered.

At this level, teachers' actions generally involve asking students questions that are designed to help them focus on moral dimensions of issues. ("Jose correctly points out that tripling fees on the turnpike will reduce the volume of traffic. This, as he mentions, will reduce wear and tear on the roadway, will reduce the number of accidents, and will save lives. Before we commit to Jose's solution to the problem of the deteriorating turnpike roadbed and the high accident rate, are there some moral issues we need to look at?")

MORAL JUDGMENT.   The second level in Rest's model flows logically from the first. Moral sensitivity seeks to plant the idea that issues have a moral dimension that must be considered. Moral judgment requires individuals to think of the moral consequences that might flow once a decision about a given issue has been made.

During this phase of a lesson, teachers take care to help students understand that people may have different value priorities and, hence, different conceptions of morality. ("Let's suppose that the state adopted Jose's solution to triple users' fees on the turnpike. What sorts of things might be most important to people supporting this decision? How might they defend the action on moral grounds? What sorts of things might be most important to people opposing this decision? How might they support their opposition to decision on moral grounds?")

MORAL DECISION-MAKING.   At this level, students are asked to make decisions of their own. Facts relevant to a given issues are reviewed.

Values positions of a number of factions posing alternative solutions are reviewed. Then, students are asked to make their own decisions and to comment on the possible consequences of the choices they make.

("We have talked about several solutions to the problem of turnpike wear and the high accident rate. We have also thought about the values reflected in the positions of a number of alternative solutions. Among these solutions were (a) tripling users' fees; (b) 'rationing' turnpike use by allowing cars with even-numbered license plates to use it on even-numbered days and cars with odd-numbered license plates to use it on odd-numbered days; (c) committing funds to add additional turnpike lanes and to resurface the entire highway; and (d) to require all cars to carry a minimum of four passengers. Now, I want each of you to think about these ideas and about any other solutions that occur to you. I want you to be able to make a decision, point out some possible consequences of the decision, and explain the personal values you hold that led to the decision you chose.")

MORAL ACTION.   During this phase, students are asked to go beyond verbalization of their decision to action. The moral action level calls for a considerable depth of commitment. The purpose of lesson components directed at moral action is to help students recognize that it is easier for people to talk about their conceptions of morality than to act upon them. During this phase, teachers take care not to coerce students to act. The purpose is not the action itself but rather the recognition that different people have different levels of commitment to moral issues they support.

("Let's think about the decisions you have made about this issue. I don't want you to feel a need to answer 'yes' to these questions unless you really want to. Now, how many of you would be willing to write a letter to the editor supporting your decision? How many of you would write a letter to the director of the Turnpike Authority? How many of you would come to a meeting after school to start a pressure group? Now why do you think some of you were willing to do these things and others weren't? Can you think of examples where people sometimes talk about their support for something but aren't too interested in acting on their convictions? Why is it that we humans are like this?")

Moral Discourse

The term "moral discourse" refers to a discussion focusing on issues having a moral dimension (Oser 1986). A wide variety of topical areas can be used as subjects of moral-discourse lessons. Fritz Oser (1986) suggests that such discussions might focus on such issues as (a) moral role-taking and moral empathy, (b) taking "right" moral action, (c) norms of the group, (d) moral values in relationship to school programs, (e) changing personal values, (f) theoretical moral knowledge, and (g) moral conflict and moral judgment.

Lessons directed at moral role-taking and moral empathy encourage students to see issues from the perspectives of others. They are encouraged to analyze both issues and values commitments of individuals whose perspectives they attempt to reflect. Often lessons take the form of role-playing activities.

Taking right moral action lessons focus on the gap that sometimes exists between what people say and what they do. The focus is very much on the word "action." Lessons help students to identify what people say is "good and moral" and compare their actions to these statements. Students consider causes of inconsistencies between verbalized commitments and actual behaviors.

Lessons focusing on "norms of the group" issues focus on the broadly accepted moral principles that guide individuals' behavior in their society. Society-wide principles as well as those of local communities and peer groups may be investigated. Sometimes moral discourse of this type focuses on changing community standards over time.

Moral-values-in-relation-to-school-programs discussions help students to focus on moral dilemmas raised in such areas as literature, government, and history. Sometimes a study of these moral conflicts can help students to clarify their own values. Sometimes moral discourse lessons of this type also focus on the content of the school program. Students and teachers may wish to consider the implicit moral messages embedded in what authorities have decided students should study in school.

Moral discussions focusing on changing personal values help students to reflect on their own values and views of morality, particularly as they may change over time. Students need to understand that all individual values are not rigidly fixed. Changing conditions may modify personal perspectives and alter conceptions of what constitutes a "moral" act or decision.

Occasionally, moral-discussion lessons focus on theoretical moral knowledge. These lessons are designed to help students identify and apply varying theories of moral philosophy. The intent of such lessons is to help students discover relationships between differing value systems. For example, they might be taught to recognize conflicts between ethical relativism and universal principles of morality. The goal is to help them understand premises of people making moral arguments on one side or the other of an issue.

Lessons focusing on moral conflict and moral judgment focus students' attention on issues where two or more value and moral positions might be taken. The idea is to familiarize them with alternative moral orientations and to help them articulate the values and moral principles that undergird their own judgment. Lawrence Kohlberg (1980) has developed a scheme for engaging students in this kind of learning.

Kohlberg's Moral Reasoning

Lawrence Kohlberg argues that individuals' responses to issues vary in terms of their stages of moral development. He has developed a theory that includes six stages of moral development. According to the theory, individuals progress sequentially through these stages. This means, for example, that a person cannot be at stage three without at some earlier time having been at stage one and stage two. Further, people vary in terms of where their moral development stops. Some stop at lower stages; only a few progress to the very highest stage. These are the six stages Kohlberg's scheme:

1. Stage One: Punishment and Obedience Orientation.
2. Stage Two: Instrumental Relativism.
3. Stage Three: Interpersonal Concordance.
4. Stage Four: Law and Order Orientation.
5. Stage Five: Social-Contract, Legalistic Orientation.
6. Stage Six: Universal Ethical Principle Orientation.

STAGE ONE: PUNISHMENT AND OBEDIENCE ORIENTATION. A person at the "punishment and obedience orientation" stage makes decisions about what is right and wrong based on respect for power. The individual makes a choice out of a fear that an inappropriate decision will result in punishment for this action. Logic used by people at this stage is very egocentric. They do not take into account consequences of their actions for others. They worry only about whether punishment will be directed at them personally.

STAGE TWO: INSTRUMENTAL RELATIVISM. Reasoning of people at the "instrumental relativism" stage is also very egocentric. The basis for decisions, though, is different from that of people at the punishment and obedience orientation stage. Instead of fear of punishment, people at the instrumental relativism stage make decisions after they have calculated the likely personal benefits of the alternatives. The "rightness" or "wrongness" of a decision depends on whether it will bring personal benefits to the decision-maker.

Logic at this level often reflects a "you-scratch-my-back-and-I'll-scratch-your-back " mentality. Sometimes people at this level do things that may *appear* to be very altruistic in nature. On closer examination, their decisions always are calculated to provide a personal benefit. For example, a wealthy business owner might give money to a worthy cause. The action may not be taken out of a commitment to the cause but rather out of a conviction that resultant publicity will increase his or her personal profits.

STAGE THREE: INTERPERSONAL CONCORDANCE. Individuals at this stage make decisions based on their assumptions about what others in their group believe to be "right" and "wrong." Many parents of secondary-school-aged children have encountered this kind of logic from their children. ("Mom, *nobody* else has to be in at 11.00. The other parents think 1.30 a.m. is just fine.") Standards of the peer group strongly influence patterns of behavior of people at this stage of moral development.

STAGE FOUR: LAW AND ORDER ORIENTATION. People at this stage base their decisions on respect for established rules and regulations and long-standing traditional social practices. They are strongly influenced by formal authority. What the law says tends to dictate their behavior, even though they may not always agree that the law is correct. If there is a conflict between legal authority and other considerations, they will reject the other considerations. An example of this kind of thinking was reflected in the trials at Nuremberg following World War II. When asked about atrocities against the Jews, many former Nazis simply stated that they were just "obeying orders."

STAGE FIVE: SOCIAL-CONTRACT, LEGALISTIC ORIENTATION. At this stage, reasoning about moral issues moves beyond a simple consideration of the dictates of established authority. Legal authority is considered, but so are some general, less formal guidelines and some personal values. Authority is not always perceived as "right." There is presumed to be a kind of social contract between those in power and the individuals in the society. There are times when those in power may exercise control in ways that violate the social contract. In such cases, people may determine that a decision of constituted authority is "wrong."

   At this stage, people take action to change laws, regulations, and other practices of constituted authorities that they believe may violate the social contract that should govern relations between leaders and citizens. Conceptions of "right" and "wrong" are often based on what individuals see as good for the society as opposed to what is consistent with the views of those in power.

STAGE SIX: UNIVERSAL ETHICAL PRINCIPLE ORIENTATION. At this stage of moral development, individuals base decisions on certain universal principles to which they have decided to commit. Among these

Box 12.5

Recognizing Differences in Logic Used by People at Different Stages of Moral Development

Students often present their teachers with a variety of excuses when they are caught cheating. Look at these examples. Then, decide what level of moral reasoning the student is using to defend his action to a school counselor.

1. "I really shouldn't have done it, but my dad said he would whip me if I flunked another test."

2. "I'm trying to get into this special club. To get in, I have to have cheated on a test."

3. "I just knew the test was going to be unfair. I mean, I don't mind studying for a fair test, but not for one where the cards are stacked against me at the beginning. I've been a pretty good student. I thought if word got around that I was so frustrated that I had to resort to cheating somebody might take action. The teacher really needs to be told to prepare tests that have something to do with the content we've studied."

are respect for justice, freedom, personal dignity, and the sanctity of human life. Decisions of "right" and "wrong" are based on the dictates of individual conscience. Decisions of conscience take precedence over formal rules, wishes of the peer group, and legal frameworks for altering rules. An example of someone at this stage of moral development would be a conscientious objector who chooses not to serve in the military in time of war out of a personal conviction that taking human life is wrong under all circumstances. Further discussion of stages of moral development is found in Box 12.5.

The movement of individuals from a lower stage of moral development to a higher stage is thought to be influenced by the nature of their experiences. When a person comes into contact with others who make decisions based on a conception of morality consistent with a moral stage one stage higher than his or her own, then this individual may begin to move toward this next higher stage. If, however, this same person is exposed to people whose reasoning is based on logic consistent with moral stages two or more stages higher than his or her own, he or she may have great difficulty understanding the logic of these people. To create an environment that will systematically expose individuals to logic at levels one step higher than their own, Kohlberg has developed a "moral dilemma discussion" approach.

Moral Dilemma Discussion

There are four basic steps to the approach, as follows (Kohlberg 1975): (a) introducing the moral dilemma, (b) asking students to suggest tentative responses, (c) dividing students into groups to discuss reasoning, and (d) discussing reasoning and formulating decisions.

Step One: Introducing the Moral Dilemma. This first step requires the teacher to identify an issue that poses a clear moral dilemma. The best issues are those that are of high concern to students. (Should students inform their parents about another student's attempt to provide them with illegal substances at a party? Should a student skip school to help a worried friend 'talk through' a serious personal problem? Should a student who finds a wad of one-hundred dollar bills report this find to the police? And so forth.)

Dilemmas can be introduced in a variety of ways. The teacher might provide students with a written scenario that highlights key aspects of the situation. Films or cassette tapes might be used. Role-playing a situation represents another useful approach. Once the dilemma is introduced, the teacher takes time to conduct a short discussion for the purpose of highlighting key issues.

Step Two: Asking Students to Suggest Tentative Responses. This step begins with a teacher request to the students to write short summaries of what they would do if faced with a similar situation. They are asked to specify reasons that would lead them to respond in this way. The reasons will provide cues as to students' individual stages of moral development. The specific decisions are not nearly so important as the kinds of logic individual students use to defend them.

Step Three: Dividing Students into Groups to Discuss Reasoning. At this time, students are divided into a number of small groups. Members of each group are asked to share the course of action they would take and the reasons for their choices. Chances are that reasons will reflect several levels of moral reasoning. Possibilities are excellent that many students will hear arguments based on moral reasoning that is just one stage higher than their own. This exposure, according to Kohlberg, can facilitate their growth toward this higher stage.

These discussions should be kept fairly brief. The teacher should take action to assure that students engage in open exchanges of ideas, not confrontational debates about the merits of the various positions that are taken. As a concluding part of this step, members of each group should try to come to a collective decision about what action should be taken. Next, group members should identify two or three of the best reasons that were brought up in support of this action.

Step Four: Discussing Reasoning and Formulating a Conclusion. During this step, the teacher asks a spokesperson from each group to share its decision and supporting logic. The decisions and the supporting logic should be written on the chalkboard, on a large chart, or on an overhead-projector transparency. After all information has been recorded, the teacher leads a discussion focusing on reasons and actions chosen by the different groups.

After students have shared ideas during the discussion, the teacher asks each person to write down the best reasons supporting a decision he or she does not personally endorse. Then, students are asked to write down the strongest reasons supporting a decision they do support. These activities require students to carefully consider the logic of others.

In summary, moral reasoning discussions help students consider the logic and moral reasoning of others. By exposing them to the logic of people operating one moral stage higher than their own, there is a good possibility that their move to the next higher moral-reasoning stage will be facilitated. Such movement is unlikely to occur after participation in only a single moral reasoning discussion. Growth in moral reasoning may require many other experiences and a good deal of personal introspection.

Kohlberg himself is cautious on the issue of how much moral development can be expected of students in schools. He suggests that, as a realistic goal, schools might strive to develop students to the law and order stage of moral development (Kohlberg 1980, p. 463). Others may move higher. Certainly, it is hoped that as they grow to adulthood and have broad ranging experiences, many will become higher-stage moral reasoners.

Key Ideas in Summary

1. Teachers have two kinds of basic interests with respect to students' attitudes. They are interested in (a) students attitudes toward the school and school courses and (b) in the kinds of personal values students acquire as they go through the instructional program.

2. Non-directive teaching, as outlined by Carl Rogers, represents an approach to creating a positive school environment. It involves teachers and students in discussions designed to help students develop insights into their own feelings and to make personal judgments about their own behaviors. It helps students develop confidence in their abilities to respond to problems.

3. William Glasser has suggested that a classroom-meetings technique can improve students' attitudes toward school, themselves, and others. The teacher acts as both a facilitator and a participant during the classroom meeting. Participants are organized in tight circles to allow for easy and comfortable communication. Classroom meetings

sort into three major categories: (a) social-problem-solving meetings, (b) educational-diagnostic meetings, and (c) open-ended meetings.

4. Teaching of values in schools is controversial. Some people argue that some values, such as the sanctity of human life, are so important to social survival that schools should teach them directly. Others argue that values should not be taught directly because there is a danger of indoctrinating, a practice that is incompatible with fundamental American beliefs.

5. The technique of Issues, Values, and Consequences Analysis seeks to help students understand that people make decisions not only on the basis of evidence but also after consideration of personal values. There are a number of steps that require students to identify decision alternatives and related values. Students' own values are examined in terms of their comparison to those reflected in decision alternatives.

6. Values clarification developed during the 1960s. It presumes that teachers do not have a right to impose values on students. Rather, teachers are urged to engage students in learning experiences that will help them to identify and clarify their own personal values. The three major components of value clarification are (a) choosing a value, (b) affirming or prizing a value, and (c) acting on a value.

7. Morality focuses on questions of "right" and "wrong." James Rest developed a framework for preparing lessons that focus on morality. The four levels of Rest's approach are (a) moral sensitivity, (b) moral judgment, (c) moral decision-making, and (d) moral action.

8. Moral discourse refers to a discussion that focuses on issues that have a moral dimension. Fritz Oser has identified a number of focuses for such discussions including (a) moral role-taking and moral empathy, (b) taking "right" moral action, (c) norms of the group, (d) moral values in relationship to school programs, (e) changing personal values, (f) theoretical moral knowledge, and (g) moral conflict and moral judgment.

9. Lawrence Kohlberg argues that the logic people use to respond to moral issues varies depending on the levels of moral development. According to his theory, people pass sequentially through these moral stages: (a) punishment and obedience orientation, (b) instrumental relativism, (c) interpersonal concordance, (d) law and order orientation, (e) social-contract, legalistic orientation, (f) universal ethical principle orientation. People's moral development stops at different levels. Kohlberg believes it is desirable for schools to provide programs designed to help students move to higher moral reasoning stages. He has proposed a "moral dilemma discussion" technique as an approach to accomplishing this objective.

POSTTEST

DIRECTIONS: Using your own paper, answer these true/false questions. For each correct statement, write the word "true." For each incorrect statement, write the word "false."

_____ 1. When teachers encourage students to develop a sense of power and of "belongingness," students tend to have more positive attitudes toward school.

_____ 2. Non-directive teaching usually can be productively implemented in classrooms where there are few feelings of warmth or respect between the teacher and the students.

_____ 3. Issues, Values, and Consequences Analysis can help students recognize the relationship between decisions and values.

_____ 4. Moral discourse is commonly used in lessons that focus on morality and moral decision-making.

_____ 5. Moral-dilemma discussions are thought to help students move to higher levels of moral reasoning by exposing them to the logic of individuals who are reasoning at the higher levels.

Bibliography

BENNINGA, J. "An Emerging Synthesis in Moral Education." *Phi Delta Kappan* (February 1988): 415–418.

GALLUP, GEORGE. *"The 16th Gallup Poll of the Public's Attitudes Toward the Schools"* (September 1984): 23–38.

GLASSER, WILLIAM. *Control Theory in the Classroom.* New York: Harper and Row, Publishers, 1986.

GLASSER, WILLIAM. *Schools Without Failure.* New York: Harper and Row, Publishers, 1969.

JOYCE, BRUCE AND WEIL, MARSHA. *Models of Teaching.* 3rd Edition. Englewood Cliffs, NJ: Prentice-Hall, Inc., 1986.

KOHLBERG, LAWRENCE. "The Cognitive-Developmental Approach to Moral Education." *Phi Delta Kappan* (June 1975): 670–675.

KOHLBERG, LAWRENCE. "Education for a Just Society: An Updated and Revised Statement." In B. Munsey (ed.). *Moral Development, Moral Education, and Kohlberg.* Birmingham, Alabama: Religious Education Press, 1980. pp. 455–470.

OSER, FRITZ. "Moral Education and Values Education: The Discourse Perspective." In Wittrock, M. (ed.). *Handbook of Research on Teaching.* 3rd edition. New York: Macmillan Publishing Company, Inc., 1986. pp. 917–914.

RATHS, LOUIS; HARMIN, MERRILL; AND SIMON, SIDNEY. *Values and Teaching.* Columbus, Ohio: Charles E. Merrill Publishing Company, 1966.

REST, JAMES. "Morality." In Hussen, P. (ed.). *Handbook of Child Psychology.* Volume 4. New York: John Wiley, 1983.

ROGERS, CARL. *Freedom to Learn for the 80s.* Columbus, Ohio: Charles E. Merrill Publishing Company, 1981.

SIMON, SIDNEY B.; HOWE, LELAND B.; AND KIRSCHENBAUM, HOWARD. *Values Clarification.* New York: Hart Publishing Company, 1972.

STEDMAN, LAWRENCE. "It's Time We Changed the Effective Schools Formula." *Phi Delta Kappan* (November 1987): 215–224.

CHAPTER 13

Measuring and Evaluating Learning

AIMS

This chapter provides information to help the reader to:

1. Distinguish between measurement and evaluation.
2. Recognize a selection of informal evaluation techniques.
3. Implement a variety of formal student evaluation procedures.
4. Note the relationship between the cognitive level of learning that is sought and the kind of procedure used to assess this learning.
5. Distinguish among several alternative schemes for awarding grades to students.
6. Suggest some general approaches to the evaluation of an entire instructional program.

PRETEST

DIRECTIONS: Using your own paper, answer these true/false questions. For each correct statement, write the word "true." For each incorrect statement, write the word "false."

_____ 1. "Measurement" and "evaluation" are two terms that share a common meaning.

_____ 2. The kind of an assessment procedure selected by a teacher often is determined by the specific information about a student that the teacher needs.

_____ 3. Student-produced tests can provide teachers with a good indirect measure of what students have learned.

_____ 4. Test types differ in terms of the kinds of cognitive thinking each is able to assess.

_____ 5. In norm-referenced grading, a student's grade is determined by his or her performance as it compares with scores of other students in the group.

Introduction

"Is my program working well?" "Are my students learning anything?" These questions are of great interest to teachers. As professionals, they want to know about the impact of their teaching. Students often have a related set of questions. "How am I doing in this course?" "What are my areas of strength and weakness?" "Am I doing as well as others?" Students' parents often share many of these same concerns.

To get information about the general impact of their programs and to provide information to students and parents, teachers use measurement and evaluation techniques. Though the terms "measurement" and "evaluation" are closely related, they are not synonyms. Measurement refers to the process of gathering information. Measurement is nonjudgmental. When the term is applied to instruction, information that is collected generally relates to student performance.

Evaluation refers to the process of drawing conclusions from a study of data gathered as a result of measurement. Evaluation, unlike measurement, is judgmental (Scriven 1967). Evaluation requires interpretation. The measurements almost never "speak for themselves."

How individuals interpret measurements is closely related to their views about standards of student performance. For example, teachers favoring norm-referenced evaluation prefer to evaluate students in terms of how their work compares to that of others in the class. Teachers favoring criterion-referenced evaluation believe students' work should be evaluated in terms of a pre-established standard of performance. A subsequent section of this chapter discusses the issue of assigning grades in both norm-referenced and criterion-referenced systems.

Today, evaluation activities occur more frequently in schools than they did forty and more years ago. Early measurement specialists placed a heavy emphasis on assessing students only at the end of an extended unit of instruction (Tyler 1949). The idea was simply to determine whether or not the students had mastered the content.

More recent thought on evaluation has modified this approach. Michael Scriven (1967), a leading thinker on issues related to measurement and evaluation, pointed out that summary evaluation at the end of a block of instruction provided little information that could help students learn the content. The content had already been taught. By the time the test was given, the teacher was preparing to introduce new material.

Scriven (1967) proposed that teachers should assess students not only at the conclusion of a unit of instruction but also at various times while the unit was being taught. He used the term "formative evaluation" to describe the periodic evaluation that takes place while new material is being taught. This evaluation is designed to provide ongoing feedback to students. It seeks to identify and remediate learning problems as the instructional sequence is being taught. Scriven (1967) used the term "summative evaluation" to refer to the traditional testing at the conclusion of an instructional sequence. Today, evaluation experts support instructional programs that include both formative evaluation and summative evaluation.

Teachers have many options as they prepare to gather information about students for the purpose of evaluation. Some assessment techniques are flexible and informal. Others involve formal testing procedures. Teachers are also faced with the need to provide grade reports to students and parents. Sections that follow introduce selections of formal and informal evaluation techniques and approaches to student grading.

Informal Evaluation

When they hear references to "measurement and evaluation," many people immediately think of formal tests. Certainly pencil-and-paper tests are important. But by no means are they the only available alternatives. For example, depending on what they are teaching, some teachers might wish their students to demonstrate their proficiencies by doing things as diverse as baking a cake, playing a difficult selection on a French horn, or rebuilding a carburetor and installing it in an automobile.

The choice of the assessment procedure depends largely on what kind of information about the student the teacher is seeking. Often, informal procedures provide valuable insights regarding students' attitudes and levels of proficiency. Informal techniques tend to be used more for the purpose of formative evaluation than summative evaluation. They yield information teachers can use to identify and respond to problems learners may be experiencing as they are attempting to master new content.

There are many kinds of informal evaluations. Those included here represent just a small sample of the many kinds of things that teachers do to keep track of students' progress. (See Box 13.1.)

Teacher Observation

Teacher observation is a term that refers to a number of things teachers do to assure students are performing assigned tasks properly. For example, a geometry teacher may walk systematically through a classroom once assignments have been made to identify students having problems and to clarify misunderstandings. An art teacher may observe students who are learning to use the potter's wheel and make helpful comments as they try to center the clay properly. An English teacher may listen to the words used by a student during an oral presentation to determine the extent of his or her vocabulary. A physical education teacher may watch students carefully to assure that required exercises are being done correctly.

Often informal observation results in a teacher giving specific directions to a student about what needs to be done to complete a task successfully. Sometimes, teachers make notes about specific difficulties individual students have been experiencing. These observation notes serve several purposes. For example, they provide a continuing record to which the teacher can refer to see whether a given student is improving over time. A review of observation notes can also help a teacher identify problems being experienced by a number of students. When several students have failed to understand, the teacher may decide that instructions were not well understood and that some additional effort to clarify expectations with the entire class is in order.

Headlines and Articles

This informal technique is appropriate as a procedure for assessing students' abilities to describe essential features of a large body of information. A good newspaper headline provides a concise summary of the article that follows. A writer of effective headlines must be thoroughly familiar with the article's content.

In the secondary school classroom, some teachers assign students to write headlines for a hypothetical article focusing on content they have studied. The headlines provide an informal assessment of students' understanding of general points raised in materials that have been studied. For example, a member of a social studies class that had

Box 13.1

Matching Informal Assessment Procedures to Your Own Information Needs

Suppose you are about to begin teaching a given topic. Make a list of four things you would like to know about what students are taking away from your instruction throughout the period you are teaching this material. For each item on your list, suggest an informal evaluation approach you might use to gather the information you would like to have.

1. Desired Information: _____
   _____
   _____

   Possible Informal Evaluation Approach
   _____

2. Desired Information: _____
   _____
   _____

   Possible Informal Evaluation Approach
   _____

3. Desired Information: _____
   _____
   _____

   Possible Informal Evaluation Approach
   _____

4. Desired Information: _____
   _____
   _____

   Possible Informal Evaluation Approach
   _____

---

been studying the coming end of Britain's Hong Kong lease might write a headline such as: "Brits Out – Chinese In: Hong Kong's Uncertain Future." Or, a student in a biology class might write: "Keeping Fit: Darwin's Theory a Survivor in Scientific World."

Student-produced headlines provide only general indications that basic information has been understood. They are not intended to provide teachers with insights about students' grasp of content specifics. However a headline-writing activity can be a good choice for the limited purpose of informally assessing students' abilities to summarize information accurately.

Some teachers find it useful to require students to prepare short articles to accompany their headlines. These articles provide additional opportunities for them to summarize what they have learned.

Teacher-Student Discussion

Teachers often make informal judgments based on information gleaned from personal discussions with students. These conversations sometimes reveal a great deal about students' understandings, interests, and feelings. Such information can provide teachers with valuable insights. These discussions provide teachers with opportunities to check the accuracy of their assumptions about how well individual learners are understanding content that is being introduced.

There are some important limitations to the teacher-student discussion approach. As a practical matter, it is difficult for teachers to engage in frequent one-on-one conversations with each student regarding all issues that are raised in class. There simply is not enough time. As a result, levels of understanding of individual students cannot be sampled frequently. Therefore, informal evaluations resulting from teacher-student discussions need to be augmented by evaluations based on information gathered in other ways.

Student-Produced Tests

By the time students begin their secondary school years, they will have taken hundreds of teacher-prepared tests. Few of them will ever have had the opportunity to prepare a test of their own. Some teachers find that students enjoy assuming the role of the teacher and preparing test items over what they have been studying. Often teachers who ask their students to prepare tests agree to use a selection of these student-produced items on a "real" test over the material. These teachers usually retain the right to add and modify items to assure the test adequately samples the content.

Student-produced tests provide a good indirect measure of what students have learned. Such tests also reveal which elements of content different members of a class have deemed important. This information can help the teacher to pinpoint students who need additional help with some content areas and others who may have faulty understandings of material that has been introduced.

Other Techniques

The informal procedures introduced here represent only a few that teachers use. Among others that are widely used are sorting activities of all kinds. Frequently, these activities provide opportunities for students to identify major content categories and to point out elements of content properly associated with each category. Observation of students during a classroom debate can be used as an informal evaluation technique. Positions taken by individual students and their skill in using evidence to support points can reveal much about what they have learned. Crossword puzzles and other simple vocabulary exercises sometimes are used to provide general information about students' grasp of key concepts.

The great majority of teachers make some use of informal evaluation techniques. The specific procedures they use vary. Selection depends on the kinds of information about a student's progress that the teacher wants and on the capacity of a given informal technique to provide it.

Formal Evaluation

Formal evaluation refers to the process of making judgments about students' progress based on evidence gathered through the use of carefully planned measurement devices. Formal evaluation techniques take many forms. Multiple-choice tests, true-false tests, matching tests, completion tests, essay tests, rating scales, and checklists are among types commonly used in secondary schools.

Formal evaluation tests fall into two broad categories. These are (a) standardized tests, and (b) teacher-made tests. Standardized tests are prepared by professional evaluation specialists for use with large numbers of students. Some of them are designed to assess general aptitudes of students. Others test their understandings of content related to subjects, for example United States history.

The Scholastic Aptitude Test (S.A.T.) that is taken by many high school seniors and used by colleges and universities as part of their admissions screening process is a well-known example of a standardized test. The National Assessment of Educational Progress administers standardized tests throughout the country to determine average levels of subject matter of students at different grade levels. Some states require teachers to administer standardized tests that focus on basic skills and, in some cases, on individual academic skills. Results provide general indications of effectiveness of school programs and sometimes point to curricular areas that need special attention.

Standardized tests are designed to measure the performance of an individual as it compares to performances of all other individuals in similar circumstances. For example, a standardized reading test given at the seventh-grade level would provide a score for each student that would indicate how the student's performance compared with reading achievement of a national group of seventh graders.

Testing is a familiar feature of life in secondary schools. *Photo courtesy of Mimi Forsyth/Monkmeyer Press Photo Service.*

Students' scores on standardized scores are rarely used for grading purposes by teachers. This is true because items on these tests often do not accurately sample the content that individual teachers have introduced in their own classrooms. Teacher-prepared tests are much more likely to have test items that tie closely to the content to which students have been introduced. Box 13.2 contains further discussion of standardized tests.

Because most teacher evaluation uses teacher-prepared rather than standardized tests as data sources, prospective teachers need to understand techniques for preparing these materials. Guidelines for using a number of teacher-prepared assessment techniques are introduced in the following section.

Rating Scales

Some instructional objectives require students to engage in certain kinds of physical tasks that preclude assessing proficiency using a paper-and-pencil test. Objectives relating to such things as using laboratory equip-

Box 13.2

Debating the Value of Standardized Tests

Standardized tests have engendered a great deal of public debate. Supporters claim that these tests provide a means of gathering important baseline data about performances of large numbers of students. Scores, they suggest, can be used to pinpoint and remediate general weaknesses in the curriculum. They also foster accountability by providing the public with a means of identifying particular schools where performance levels are dramatically above or below national averages.

Some critics suggest that standardized tests often examine students over content they have not studied. Further, it is alleged that standardized test scores fail to differentiate among the capabilities of individual schools to provide instruction. For example, wealthy schools may have sophisticated science laboratories. Poorer schools may have woefully inadequate facilities. Finally, some opponents of standardized tests say they encourage teachers to "teach for the test." This may result in emphasis on memorization of content likely to be sampled on the test rather than on more complex thinking skills.

What Do You Think?

1. What are the greatest strengths of arguments of individuals who support standardized testing?
2. What are the greatest strengths of arguments of individuals who oppose standardized testing?
3. What are your own feelings about standardized testing?

ment, delivering speeches, completing art projects, and turning finials on a lathe are examples. A rating scale is a measurement tool that can be used to gather information about student proficiency on tasks of this type.

Typically, a rating scale identifies a specific set of characteristics or qualities. Indications are made along the scale in such a way that a judgment is made about the degree to which the identified quality (or qualities) is (are) present. The developer of a rating scale must take pains to ensure that the qualities identified on the rating scale are consistent with those noted in the instructional objective. Further, clear descriptions of the kind of performance implied by each point on the scale are essential. Otherwise, the rater will have difficulty in deciding exactly where along the scale a mark should be made that references the quality of an individual student's performance.

Suppose that a music teacher was interested in determining how well a student could sight-read a given piece of music. He or she could develop a rating scale that might include the following directions and sample item:

DIRECTIONS: Circle the appropriate number for each item. The numbers represent the following values.

> 5 = outstanding
>
> 4 = above average
>
> 3 = average
>
> 2 = below average
>
> 1 = unsatisfactory

1. To what extent does the person play the appropriate note?

> 5   4   3   2   1

The rating scale shown does not give the rater very specific information regarding what is implied by each rating. For example, what, specifically, separates "outstanding" from "above average," "above average" from "average," and so forth? The item might be improved somewhat by changing the descriptors for each step on the scale in the following way:

> 5 = always
>
> 4 = frequently
>
> 3 = occasionally
>
> 2 = seldom
>
> 1 = never

While there still may be some confusion about which rating a given performance ought to be given, in general these descriptors are more informative than the initial set. (For example, few would have difficulty with "always" or "never." There may be some problems with "frequently," "occasionally," and "seldom," but they probably would occasion less difficulty than "above average," "average," and "below average.")

Sometimes it is useful to add descriptive phrases at various points along the scale to indicate behaviors that students should demonstrate to earn a given point rating. Suppose, for example, that a teacher was evaluating performances of students who were giving individual speeches. He or she might wish to use a rating scale something like this:

5	4	3	2	1
Demonstrates a continuous unity of thought. Points are clear and related to the topic.		Demonstrates a generally logical flow. There are occasional "drifts" from main topic.		Rambles consistently. Presentation lacks coherence. Topic never comes into focus.

Inclusion of these descriptors contributes to the accuracy of the rating process. Also, if this scale is shared with students in advance of their speeches, it provides them with useful cues as they prepare for their presentations.

In summary, then, rating scales are useful for making judgments about physical kinds of student performances where proficiency cannot be assessed properly through the use of pencil-and-paper tests. Probably the most difficult part of constructing good rating scales involves providing clear descriptions of the specific kind of performance that would merit a rating at each point on the scale.

Evaluative Checklists

Checklists share certain characteristics with rating scales. Both are used to gather information about physical kinds of student behavior that do not lend themselves well to assessment techniques of a pencil-and-paper test variety. Both depend upon the student behaviors that are the focus of interest as being clearly observable. (The teacher has to be able to see or hear what the student is doing to make a judgment and note this information on the rating scale or checklist.)

A major difference between rating scales and checklists is that rating scales generally provide teachers with more flexibility in determining the degree of adequacy of a given learner's performance. While nearly all rating scales allow teachers to make judgments at any one of a number of points along a scale (for example, on a five-point scale, a teacher might choose to mark any one of the following: 5, always; 4, frequently; 3, occasionally; 2, seldom; 1, never), large numbers of checklists allow only for a "yes/no" decision. That is, a checklist usually is employed when there is an interest only in the presence or absence of a given behavior. When the behavior is indeed present, the checklist format does not lend itself well to making judgments about the relative quality of the behavior.

Suppose, for example, that a teacher was interested in monitoring the progress of individual students on a term-paper project. The teacher might prepare a checklist such as the following to note how far along each learner was on the term-paper assignment.

STUDENT'S NAME: _____

	Yes	No
Topic selected and approved		
Rough outline turned in		
Final outline turned in		
Note cards turned in		
First draft turned in		

Essay Items

Essays are very powerful test items in that they have the technical capability of assessing students' thinking at virtually any level of the cognitive taxonomy (knowledge, comprehension, application, analysis, synthesis, and evaluation). Although essays are capable of testing students' thinking skills at a variety of levels, as a practical matter, they are used best to assess thinking at the higher levels (application, analysis, synthesis, and evaluation) than at the lower levels (knowledge and comprehension).

In general, essays are not preferred for testing students' abilities to think at the levels of knowledge and comprehension because they require so much time to correct. Alternative testing techniques, such as multiple choice, matching, and true/false, are available. These require much less correction time, and they are perfectly capable of assessing knowledge-level and comprehension-level thinking.

A significant "plus" for the essay format is that questions can be generated relatively quickly. In fact, essay questions are so easy to write that sometimes it is a temptation for us to prepare them too hastily. Carelessly written essay items are likely to produce frustration for students taking the test as well as for the teacher who, when working through a stack of student papers, may wonder "how could so many of them have missed the point?"

In thinking about preparing an essay item, one problem we face is that of content coverage. Because of the time required for students to write responses to essays, typically only very few essay items can be included on a given exam. This can result in a very limited sampling of content unless the few essay questions (typically one or two, rarely four or more) are written carefully. One of the authors, for example, remembers vividly his own frustration when a final examination in a course in Western civilization (a course characterized by an incredible diversity of content) included only a single essay question focusing on an obscure event in Greek history (*very* obscure in the mind of the author of your text!). It was doubtful that responses even of those who did brilliantly on the question gave the instructor an adequate picture of students' understanding of the range of content covered in the course.

Maintaining a consistent pattern of scoring when correcting essays prepared by different students presents the teacher with a real challenge. Correction takes a long time, particularly when large numbers of students are involved, and fatigue can interfere with even our best intentions to apply the same standards to the last paper as to the first.

One interesting dimension of the consistent-grading issue is sometimes referred to as the "halo effect." A halo effect may be initiated when a teacher notes that an essay he or she is about to read has been written by one of his or her "good" students. Because of a predisposition to believe that such an individual would be unlikely to do anything but good work, there is a tendency for the teacher to be less critical of what the student has written in response to the essay question. Thus, the halo the teacher sees surrounding the student in terms of his or her general performance is transferred to his or her work on the essay. The halo effect can result in a student receiving a higher grade on an essay than he or she would have received had the teacher been unaware of the name of the individual who prepared the essay response in question.

Although problems of content selection and correction consistency are very real, they can be overcome. We can begin by clearly structuring the essay task for the student. This means that we need to be as precise as possible regarding what the student should include in the essay and the approximate quantity of prose that should be provided. Note the differences between the two following sets of instructions for completing an essay item that were provided to students in a high school biology class:

A. Write an essay in which you discuss the chromosome hypothesis and the gene theory.

B. Write an essay, about five pages in length, in which you compare and contrast the chromosome hypothesis and the gene theory. In your response, include specific references to (1) essentials of each position, (2) modifications that have been made to each position since it was initially developed, and (3) strengths and weaknesses that have been attributed to each view by critics.

A student receiving instructions similar to those in A may be inclined to ramble. The language used to describe the task is imprecise. (The word "discuss," for example, is a very vague guide to what the student should write about.) Further, there are no references to how long the response should be. A student might write a paragraph, or he or she might write eight pages. In light of these vague instructions, the teacher would likely receive a set of papers that would be difficult to assess because each student was forced to determine more or less for himself of herself what the task was.

The set of directions in B is much better. Students have a clear focus regarding the topics to be covered in their response. Further, an approximate length condition is imposed ("about five pages"). Because of these guidelines, the teacher is likely to have a much better set of papers. Further, correction will be easier than in the case of the set of papers coming from students given the A directions, because, at a minimum, the teacher can look to see whether each essay (1) compares and contrasts the chromosome hypothesis and the gene theory, (2) outlines essentials of each, (3) notes changes in each position since it was first postulated, and (4) describes strengths and weaknesses of each position as viewed by critics. These common "must-be-included" features help the teacher to look at each essay in the same way. They help to maintain consistency of grading from paper to paper. Box 13.3 is an exercise in writing essay test questions.

In preparing and grading essay items, a number of procedures can be used to professionalize our practices. Among these are the following:

1. Complete a sample response to each essay item administered to students.
2. Take steps to keep from learning the name of the writer of a given response until after grading it.
3. Read all answers provided by all students related to one essay item before going on to consider answers to other items on the test.
4. Read responses to each item more than once.
5. Adjust scoring criteria in light of a content analysis.

Let us look at each of these procedures in some detail.

Completing a Sample Response. Once we have written an essay question, it makes sense to sit down and write out an answer ourselves. Although this procedure takes time, it can help us spot potential weak-

Box 13.3

Improving the Quality of Essay Test Questions

Below are a number of poorly written essay questions. Try your hand at rewriting each question to turn it into a better item. Be prepared to tell the instructor why your rewritten version is superior to the original.

1. Compare and contrast the underhanded versus the overhanded method of shooting a free throw.

2. Analyze the president's policy on Iran.

3. Suggest possible changes in the nature of plane geometry theorems that might result in a new geometry based on the assumption that parallel lines meet at some point this side of infinity.

4. Contrast alternative explanations for the growing of suburbs.

5. Contrast the two poets' use of alliteration.

6. Analyze critically the theory of plate tectonics.

What Do You Think?

Write an essay item that you might give to students focusing on a subject you might be teaching. Be sure that your essay requires thinking beyond the levels of knowledge or comprehension. Ask your instructor to comment on the adequacy of your item.

---

nesses in the language of our question. Further, the contents of our own answer can suggest some criteria that can be used for grading student responses. If we wish to do so, we can assign a certain number of points to each piece of specific evidence we provided in our own responses. When the same kinds of evidence surface in the student papers, those points can be awarded to the students. (Of course there will be evidence in the student papers we may not have thought of which we will want to credit. But, in general, this system does begin to give us some idea of the kind of content we are expecting to see in our student responses.)

Maintaining Anonymity of the Essay Writer. Because of the halo effect and other problems that might interfere with the fairness of our judgment when we know the identity of the individual who has written an essay, it is desirable to establish some scheme to obscure the identity of the writer until after we have completed the grading process. Some teachers cover over student names with a card paper clipped to student answers and then shuffle the stack. Others assign students a code or a number at the beginning of the term. Students write their codes rather than their names on their papers. The teacher does not determine the identity of the student until after the correction process has been completed and grades are entered into a grade book where numbers or codes assigned to each student are identified. Certainly other schemes might be devised to achieve the same objective of maintaining name anonymity until after grading has been completed.

Grading All Student Answers on One Item Before Going on to the Next. When faced with a stack of examination papers, there is a natural tendency to start with one student's answers and grade his or her answers to all questions that have been asked before going on to another student's paper. Because criteria for grading one item may differ markedly from criteria for grading another, it makes better sense to grade all student responses to one item before grading responses to others. That is, we should grade all answers to question 1, then we should grade all answers to question 2, and so forth. This procedure will make for greater consistency in scoring than will the alternative of reading through responses one student has made to all questions before going on to responses of another student.

Repeated Readings of Responses to Essay Items. If time permits, it is a sound practice to read responses that students have made to an individual essay item several times. Although we try to keep our general mood from influencing our judgment, there are times when we are likely to be more generous than others when reviewing students' responses. If possible, read papers once, then wait at least 24 hours before shuffling and reading them again. This will reduce the likelihood of making serious judgment errors because of our particular mental frame of mind at the time we were correcting the student responses.

Adjusting Scoring Criteria in the Light of Content Analysis. The first step in a content-analysis process is for the teacher correcting students' work to note on a sheet of paper each different piece of significant pertinent information that students have provided in response to the question. The "significant pertinent information" might be in the form of key words, of concepts, or of short phrases. The first time that an individual item of information is encountered in a student paper, the teacher writes it on his or her sheet. Subsequent references to similar information on papers written by other students are noted as tally marks following the original key word, concept, or short phrase.

When this process has been completed, the teacher has a profile of the information provided by the class in response to the essay item. The frequency of mention of certain information can suggest how well the students understood pertinent points. It may be that this content analysis would prompt the teacher to rethink his or her weighting of the importance of certain of the points that might have been included. In this event, the teacher might wish to adjust his or her scoring of individual student responses.

Some teachers we know have found it useful to post all responses and tallies from the content analysis on the board. This information can serve as a good basis for a debriefing session. Further, with this material before them, the class might even be involved in a discussion centering on how much credit or weight ought to be given to each element of information in a completed essay. Such a discussion can help to sharpen students' understandings of the components of a high-quality essay response.

In summary, essays are especially useful for making judgments about students' abilities to engage in higher-level thinking skills. Among difficulties with essays are (1) the time required for correction, (2) the inability to sample a broad range of content by asking large numbers of essay questions on a given test, and (3) maintaining consistency of grading practices. There are, however, procedures we can follow to deal with these problems. Properly constructed and evaluated, essay tests represent a powerful tool in our assessment repertory.

Completion Items

Completion items share with essays the feature of requiring students to write responses in their own handwriting. However, they are much less powerful in terms of the kinds of thinking they can assess. Generally, completion items are most useful for assessing student thinking at the lower cognitive levels of knowledge and comprehension. It is very difficult to prepare completion items capable of testing higher-level thinking abilities of students.

Completion items are easy to construct. They are capable of sampling a broad range of content. Individual items do not ordinarily require a great deal of time to correct. Consequently, a teacher can include a large number of completion items on a given test or examination.

A problem with completion items relates to their scoring. It is very difficult to construct items for which only one answer is logically correct. It is especially difficult to decide what to do about student answers that are partially correct. To get some perspective on this correction issue, look at the following completion-type item:

The individual re-elected president of the United States in 1984 was ———— .

Now probably most students would write in Ronald Reagan. But there are other plausible answers as well. For example, how would a teacher deal with such alternatives as "a man," "an actor," "a Republican," "a conservative," "a Californian"?

To avoid correction problems, it is essential that completion items be written so that the type of response is very clear. For example, the item about the president could have narrowed the range of acceptable (or potentially acceptable) answers considerably had it been phrased like this:

The name of the president of the United States who was re-elected in 1984 is _____ .

The inclusion of the word "name" would eliminate many of the logical alternative responses that would have been acceptable given the original phrasing of the item.

In addition to providing for clarity of expected response, it is important that each completion item have only one blank space in which students can write. Further, this blank ought to come toward the end of the item. This arrangement gives the student time to pick up relevant cues regarding the nature of the expected response. An item with many blanks that are placed at random is almost sure to result in little other than confusion. Consider this horrible example:

_____ affects _____ independently of _____ except on those occasions when _____ and _____ stand inversely related.

To eliminate some scoring problems, teachers often provide students with a selection of answers, some correct and some incorrect, from which they are to draw their responses. Students must use only answers provided on the list. Thus, students can be held accountable both for correct word choice and for spelling (the word is there; the student has only to copy the word correctly to spell it right).

But this kind of revision alters the format of the completion item into a modified matching item. Further, it introduces the possibility of being able to guess the right item. However, some teachers are willing to make this exchange to simplify their correction chores. An example of this kind of modification is provided here:

STUDENT'S NAME: _____

Completion Item

Directions: A number of blanks appear in the following short paragraph. Below the pargraph you will find a list of terms. Select appropriate terms from this list and print them carefully in the proper blanks. Include only terms included in the list at the bottom of the page. You will be expected to spell these terms correctly. In recent years, there has been a trend for people to move away from the core of a city toward the surrounding suburbs. Sociologists call this movement_____. Another urban phenomenon involves movement of people from one social class to a part of the city occupied by people in another social class. This is termed _____ . When a new group in a city succeeds in taking over a neighborhood, a situation termed _____ results. When minority members of a community are removed by majority members, we have a situation called _____ . When this causes married couples to move to a locale where neither set of parents is resident, their new family residence is said to be _____ . The group an individual interacts with over time on a more or les continuous basis is called a (an) _____ group.

recurrent	suburbanization	succession
allotropic	invasion	concession
neolocal	separation	expulsion
patrilocal	segregation	deviance

In general, completion items do not represent a particularly good technique for assessing students' proficiencies. In most cases, multiple-choice, true/false, and matching items are to be preferred. These items have the capacity to assess knowledge- and comprehension-level thinking, as do completion items; but, unlike completion items, they are much easier to correct.

Matching Items

Matching items are used to measure students' thinking at the levels of knowledge and comprehension. (Although it may be possible to construct matching tests to assess higher-level thinking, this is not usually done.) Matching items enjoy a number of "pluses" in the eyes of classroom teachers. They are relatively easy to construct. They can be corrected quickly. And there is little danger that one student's test will be graded according to a standard different from that used for another student's test.

Difficulties that do arise with the use of matching items are usually associated with poor item construction. These problems can be overcome if we pay attention to a limited number of basic principles of sound matching item construction.

First, all terms in a given matching item should focus on a single topic or theme. Students become confused when they are confronted with a matching item containing an array of unrelated terms and definitions. To avoid this possibility, we want to restrict our focus and to cue students to what that focus is by mentioning it by name at the beginning of the matching item. For example, a test including the names of a number of Confederate generals on one side and a number of exploits associated with them listed on the other ought to be labeled "Matching Quiz: Confederate Generals."

As a rule of thumb, the list on the right-hand side (the one providing alternative answers from which students are to select answers should contain about 25 percent more items than the list on the left-hand side. For example, if there were 10 definitions with blanks on the left, then there might be 12 or 13 terms from which students might choose on the right.

The practice of placing more options on the right makes it possible for a student to miss one question without being forced, as a consequence, to miss another. When there is an identical number of items in both left- and right-hand lists, the double penalty for a missed question comes into play. (In such a situation, for example, a student who incorrectly identifies term "d" as his or her response to definition 1 rather than to definition 3, which is correct, will end up having wrong responses both for definition 1 and definition 3.)

Another principle of matching test construction is to have the entire test printed on one page. It is absolutely unacceptable for any portion of either the left-hand list or the right-hand list to be carried over to a second page. When this formatting error is committed, many students fail to realize that part of the test is on another page, which results in additional errors.

Always provide clear directions for matching tests. Students must be given instructions that direct them specifically to place the letter identifying a particular term in the right-hand column in the blank provided before the appropriate definition in the left-hand column. When explicit directions are not provided, students tend to draw lines connecting definitions to terms. This results in a confusing spider web of lines that can tax a teacher's weary eyeballs beyond endurance when there are many tests to correct. Further, directions should make clear to students that only one correct term is provided for each definition listed in the left-hand column. See Box 13.4 for an example of a properly formatted matching test.

When these principles of construction are followed, students should have few difficulties with matching tests that can be attributed to formatting problems. The principles are learned easily, and teachers who are comfortable with them find matching tests to be very useful vehicles for gathering data about learners' control of definitional kinds of information.

Box 13.4

Sample Matching Test

MATCHING TEST: YOUR NAME: _____
TENNIS TERMINOLOGY

DIRECTIONS: Find the term in the right-hand column that is defined by the definition in the left-hand column. Place the letter identifying this term in the blank space provided before its definition. Only one term is correct for each definition. Please do *not* draw lines connecting definitions to terms.

_____ 1. The point that, if won, wins the match for a player.

_____ 2. The area between the net and the service line.

_____ 3. Hitting the ball before it bounces.

_____ 4. Stroke made after the ball has bounced, either forehand or backhand.

_____ 5. The line that is perpendicular to the net and divides the two service courts.

_____ 6. The initial part of any swing. The act of bringing the racket back to prepare for the forward swing.

_____ 7. A ball hit high enough in the air to pass over the head of the net player.

_____ 8. A ball that is served so well that the opponent fails to touch it with his or her racket.

_____ 9. A shot that bounces near the baseline.

_____ 10. Start of play for a given point.

a. ace
b. backswing
c. center service line
d. deep shot
e. forecourt
f. set point
g. lob
h. match point
i. serve
j. volley
k. dink
l. ground stroke

Multiple-Choice Items

Experts in measurement hold multiple-choice items in especially high regard. Multiple-choice items can be adapted to a tremendous variety of subject matter content. They can be scored easily. And they have the capacity to test not only for knowledge and comprehension but for some higher-level thinking abilities as well.

In terms of basic format, a multiple-choice item consists of two basic parts: (1) a stem and (2) some alternative choices only a few of which (usually only one) logically relate to the stem. Among the alternative choices there is (are) a (some) correct answer(s) and some others that are called distractors. The difficulty of the item depends in large measure on the level of sophistication needed by a student if he or she is to identify the correct answer(s) from the distractor alternatives.

It is no easy task to prepare multiple-choice items where distractors appear as really plausible answers. It requires a great deal of time to prepare these items. But the effort is necessary if we really want to check on students' understanding. If we are too hasty and prepare items where distractors are not plausible, we are likely to reveal the correct answer even to students with only marginal knowledge of the material on which they are being tested. A number of basic principles need to be kept in mind as we prepare multiple-choice items.

First, we need to be sure that the stem of the item is clear and grammatically correct. The alternative answers should be grammatically consistent with the stem. Consider this example:

Nils Johannsen, in his novel of the Canadian prairies, *West From Winnipeg*, called trapping an
   a. science.
   b. art.
   c. duty.
   d. nuisance.

A student totally unfamiliar with the novel who read the question carefully would identify "b" as the correct answer simply because it is the only choice logically consistent with the article "an" at the conclusion of the stem. To correct this problem, the writer of the stem might have concluded it in this way: ". . . called trapping a (an)". This version makes any of the four alternatives grammatically plausible.

A stem that is too brief fails to cue the student regarding what kind of information he should be looking for in the list of alternatives. Consider this example:

Roger Williams
   a. sailed on the Mayflower.
   b. established the Thanksgiving tradition.
   c. founded the Rhode Island colony.
   d. developed the first rum distillery in the New World.

Because the stem is so incomplete, the students really are faced with four true/false items to ponder than with one good multiple-choice item.

The task for the student, in other words, is not well defined. A far better way of formatting this question would be this example:

The founder of the Rhode Island colony was
   a. Sir Walter Raleigh.
   b. John Winthrop.
   c. Roger Williams.
   d. William Bradford.

As noted earlier in this discussion, multiple-choice items can be designed to test students' ability to think at a number of cognitive levels. Let us examine some examples of multiple-choice items designed to assess thinking at different levels of sophistication.

Knowledge Level. Recall that at the level of knowledge we are interested only in determining the extent to which youngsters can recall specific information. Multiple-choice items are easy to construct for this purpose. Indeed, it is likely that most teacher-prepared multiple-choice items are designed to test thinking at this level. The following is an example of a knowledge-level multiple-choice item:

A belief that an individual has the right not only to succeed but also has the duty or obligation to succeed is referred to by sociologists as the
   a. multiplier theory.
   b. mobility ethic.
   c. transference syndrome.
   d. neolocal tendency.

Comprehension Level. Multiple-choice tests designed to test students' thinking at the level of comprehension require them to demonstrate an understanding of a number of elements in a given situation that are related to one another in some kind of a systematic fashion. Comprehension requires students to demonstrate an ability to perceive the proper interrelationship of these elements. Figure 13.1 is an example of a comprehension-level multiple-choice item.

Application Level. Application-level multiple-choice items require students to take information learned in one setting and use it correctly in another. Suppose, for example, that students had been exposed to the concept of "horizon of worker expectation" in a previous lesson focusing on the economy of Yugoslavia. We might develop an application-level test item related to this concept that would look like this:

In a social system where workers were allowed to vote on how profits of their employing firms were to be spent, we logically would expect a worker near retirement to

Directions: Look at the chart. The chart indicates
that between 1960 and 1986 there was a trend for
the percentage of classroom teachers to do what
as compared to the percentage of other public
school staff? (Circle the letter before the best
choice. There is only one correct response.)

a. decrease
b. increase
c. stay about the same
d. cannot tell, given the information on the chart.

Classroom Teachers as a Percentage of Total
Public School Staff in school Years Ending in
1960, 1970, 1986.

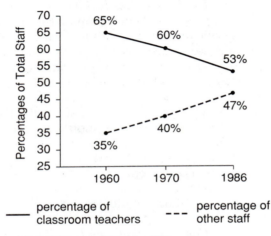

SOURCE: Stern and Chandler 1987. p. 42.

Figure 13.1

a. support expenditures for plant improvement projects rather than
   expenditures for workers' benefits.
b. support expenditures for workers' benefits rather than for plant
   improvement projects.
c. support nearly all efforts of younger workers to improve plant efficiency.
d. support nearly all efforts of younger workers to gain agreements
   to improve working conditions at a time to begin ten years after a
   contract settlement had been reached.

   Analysis Level. Analysis requires students to make inferences.
That is, they are asked to go beyond what is given. To accomplish this,
they examine information that may provide some relevant clues and that

will provide a data base for their analytical thinking activities. Analysis-level multiple-choice questions are difficult to construct. They require considerable teacher time to prepare. For this reason, some teachers prefer to use essay examinations when testing for analysis-level thinking. We do not mean to suggest, however, that it is not worth committing the time to develop analysis-level multiple-choice questions. Despite the preparation time required, there is some compensation in that they take little time to correct.

Often multiple-choice items at the level of analysis present a good deal of information to students along with the stem and the alternative answer options. This information becomes the data base to which the student refers in responding to the multiple-choice item. Often a number of multiple-choice items at the level of analysis will require the student to work with a single set of information items. An example of an analysis-level multiple-choice item is presented here:

Ellison had the flair of genius. But he was not a genius. Though pedestrian in his approaches, he was yet a phenomenon. His was a talent of concentration, not of innovation. No other man of his time rivaled his ability to shunt aside irrelevancies to focus on a problem's essentials. For him, non-critical considerations were trifling bits of detritus to be swept away in a moment. His resolute attack on the nuggety essence of an unresolved issue obviated even the serious probability of egregious error. Contemporaries described his reason as "glistening." Only an audacious few ventured public challenges to his positions. It is not too much to say that he lived out his days surrounded by a nervously-approving silence. Later generations have seen his conclusions as less than revolutionary. But, in his own time, Ellison's ability to "will" an impeccable solution to a complex issue made others seem small figures who were destined ever to walk lightly in the dark shadows of a giant.

One assumption revealed in the preceding paragraph is
a. Ellison was truly competent, but he had a flair for impressing people with the logical structure he built to support his solutions.
b. Ellison really was a genius whose "glistening" logic resulted in novel solutions to problems.
c. Today, people tend to be more impressed with Ellison than they were in his own day.
d. Ellison's form probably was a more significant contributor to his reputation than was the substance of his thought.

Synthesis Level and Evaluation Level. It is possible to prepare multiple-choice questions at levels higher than that of analysis. However, they are very difficult to write. Many teachers prefer essay items for assessing synthesis-level and evaluation-level thinking.

True/False Items

True/false items, though generally used by teachers to assess knowledge-level thinking, do have some limited applications at a few higher cognitive levels. True/false items can be prepared relatively quickly. They provide a format whereby each student is likely to have his or her work graded in the same manner as every other student. They can be graded quickly.

But a number of disadvantages of true/false items should be noted. For one thing, they tend to encourage guessing. Since there are only two choices, a student has a 50:50 chance of getting an item correct even when he or she has no grasp whatsoever of the material.

Another difficulty with true/false items has to do with having to prepare statements that are absolutely "true" or absolutely "false." Much of the content we treat in our courses tends more toward gray than toward black or white. For this reason, some teachers feel constrained by the true/false format, which, they feel, forces them to steer away from the main focus of the instruction to find the odd example that indeed is absolutely true or absolutely false.

When a decision has been made to prepare a true/false test, several basic principles need to be followed. Items selected must be clearly "true" or "false." Further, very specific instructions need to be provided to students regarding how answers should be recorded.

Often, true/false tests are prepared with blank spaces in front of each item. Students are directed to place their responses in the blanks. If this format is followed, students should be directed to write out the entire word "true" or "false" or to place a symbol such as a "+" for true items and a "−" for false items. It is *not* a good idea to direct students to write the letter "t" in the blank before "true" items and the letter "f" in the blank before "false" items. Some students may produce hybrid letters that, when looked at in one way, appears to be a "t" and, when looked at in another way, appears to be an "f."

Grading problems associated with how students fill in blanks in front of true/false items can be eliminated by doing away with the blanks themselves. In their place, it often is convenient simply to print the words "true" and "false" in front of each item. When this is done, students are directed to circle the appropriate word. This format has been followed in the sample true-false test provided in Box 13.5.

As noted at the beginning of this discussion, most true/false tests are designed to test students' ability at the level of knowledge. With some work, they can also be used to test other levels of thinking. Box 13.5 features an example of a true/false test designed to test comprehension-level thinking.

Box 13.5

Sample Comprehension-Level True/False Test

Data to Be Used in True/False Test

Projected Demand for New Elementary and New Secondary Teachers*

Number of New Teachers Needed (in thousands)

Year	Elementary	Secondary
1990	165	75
1991	163	92
1992	163	103
1993	161	112
1994	157	123
1995	157	120

DIRECTIONS: Use the data above as you respond to the following true/false items. If the statement is true, circle the word "true." If the statement is false, circle the word "false."

true   false   1. In none of the years listed is there expected to be a demand for more secondary school teachers than for elementary teachers.

true   false   2. The decline in demand for new elementary teachers is predicted to begin before the decline in the demand for new secondary teachers.

true   false   3. There will be a greater growth in demand for elementary teachers than secondary teachers in the years between 1990 and 1994.

true   false   4. The greatest year-to-year growth in demand for new secondary school teachers will occur between 1993 and 1994.

true   false   5. There will be a demand for more new elementary teachers in 1995 than in 1990.

*Data are from Joyce D. Stern (ed.) and Marjorie O. Chandler (assoc. ed.). The Condition of Education. 1987 edition. Washington, D.C.: U.S. Department of Education, Center for Education Statistics, 1987. p. 46.

Using Test Results to Make Judgments About the Instructional Program

One use of test results that inexperienced teachers sometimes overlook is their value in determining strengths and weaknesses of the instruction that preceded the test. This is quite easy to do when test items are identified clearly with individual instructional objectives. In such cases, it is relatively easy to look at test results and make some general conclusions about content students learned relatively well and about content they may have learned less well. When this kind of analysis is not possible (a situation likely to occur when test items are not tied clearly to individual instructional objectives), there is a tendency, especially for inexperienced teachers, to feel that their whole program has been a failure when students miss more than a few questions. In fact, there is a possibility that students have mastered most of the material presented very well and that the missed items related only to certain parts of the content that was presented. But, when individual questions are not identified clearly with specific objectives, it is not possible for a teacher to locate with confidence a potentially minor component of his or her instructional program that students may not have understood well.

In addition to preventing unnecessary self-criticism by allowing for ready identification of isolated weak spots in the instructional program, tying test items to specific instructional objectives saves time. Obviously it is much more efficient to spend a little time revising an occasional weak spot in a unit than in scrapping the entire unit out of a faulty conviction that the entire instructional plan was a failure.

Using Test Results to Grade Students

Of all the tasks they must perform, awarding grades ranks close to the bottom of the preferred activities list of many teachers (perhaps even of a majority). Grading requires us to look at test scores and other evidence for the purpose of making judgments about individual students. Typically, these judgments are converted to letter grades ranging from "A" for the most outstanding work through "F" for failing work.

In grading, we need to consider two basic concepts: fairness and specificity of communication. Fairness requires that grades not be awarded capriciously. Grades must reflect some levels of performance that are known to individual students. Should youngsters ever infer that this is not the case and that grades are being awarded on the basis of some arbitrary whim of the teacher, their performance levels are sure to fall off.

Grades should communicate something specific to parents and administrators. This means that a grade of "A" in a given class should communicate something clearly different from what is communicated by a grade of "B." Levels of competence implied by grades of "A," "B," "C," "D", and "F" should be clear to students, parents, and administrators who see these grades. Regrettably, these differences, in many schools, have been and continue to be poorly defined.

Three basic schemes have been used in secondary schools as bases for awarding letter grades. There are differences among them in terms of their individual capacities to communicate differences in the levels of competence of youngsters receiving different grades. These basic schemes are designed to award grades, respectively, on the bases of (1) individual improvement, (2) individual performance as compared with group performance, and (3) individual performance as compared with a predetermined standard. Let us look at each of these arrangements in some detail.

Individual Improvement

Grades awarded on the basis of individual improvement require the teacher to administer an initial test of a student's understanding and then a second test (or tests) after he or she has been exposed to the instructional program (typically an instructional unit). When this has been accomplished, students receive grades based on the amount of improvement shown between scores on the initial test and scores on the test(s) given at the end of the instructional program. Students showing the high improvement scores receive the better grades.

There is a certain humanistic appeal to the idea that learners should be awarded grades based on their individual improvement scores. Clearly the scheme does place the teacher's focus on the individual student. Too, the approach suggests a grading practice consistent with many educators' enthusiasm for individualized instruction. But there are dangers associated with the procedure that may be overlooked by its proponents.

When individual improvement becomes the basis for grading, students showing the greatest individual gains will be awarded the highest letter grades. Suppose that we had a youngster who, on an initial test, received a score of 9. On the test given at the conclusion of the instruction unit, this same student received a score of 50. Subtracting the initial score of 9 from the final score of 50, we would find that this youngster had achieved a very large gain, namely, 41 points.

Now let us suppose in this same class that there was another student who had an initial test score of 80 and a final test score of 93. The difference between this individual's initial and final test was only 13 points. Following the principle that the highest grades should go to students with the largest point differences between initial and final test scores, the first student would be awarded a higher letter grade than the second student. Yet, the final test score clearly implies that the second student mastered more of the course content than did the first.

Of the problems associated with this grading approach, the first relates to something that statisticians call "regression toward the mean." Regression toward the mean tells us to be very suspicious of scores on an initial test that are either extremely low or extremely high. Very low scores are thought to be due in part to some chance factors or "bad luck" that caused students to miss more items than they really ought to have missed. Very high scores are thought to be due to chance factors or "good luck" that caused students to answer a few items correctly even though they really didn't know the correct answers.

Regression toward the mean tells us that, on any subsequent test (as, for example, the test given at the end of a unit of instruction), extremely low scorers may well score higher than they did on the initial test (that is, their scores might be higher or closer to the average or "mean") and extremely high scorers may well score lower than they did on the initial test (that is, their scores may be lower or closer to the average or "mean"). What all this means for a grading scheme based on individual improvement is that those students who score very poorly on an initial test enjoy a considerable advantage over students who score very well in an initial test in terms of their ability to "improve" their performances as measured by tests given at the end of an instructional unit. This scheme makes it easier for a student who does poorly on the initial test to receive a high letter grade than for a student who does well on the initial test.

Another problem for students who score high on the initial test is something called the "topping-out effect." Let us see how this might work. A student who scores 9 out of a possible 100 on an initial test enjoys a logical possibility of improving his or her score by 91 points, assuming that the second test also has 100 points possible ($100 - 9 = 91$). On the other hand, a student who scores 83 on the initial test has his or her improvement limited by the topping-out effect. Since only 100 points can be awarded on the second test, this individual has the possibility of improving his or her score only by 17 points ($100 - 83 = 17$). In a system that awards letter grades on the basis of improvement scores, the latter student has a severe competitive disadvantage relative to the student who does poorly on the initial test.

A final difficulty with this arrangement is that a given letter grade does not necessarily imply something specific about the level of competence of each student who receives this grade. For example, suppose that we decided to award grades of "A" to students who "improved" at least 50 points between an initial test of 100 total points and a final test of 100 total points. Note the initial test and final test scores for each of the following students who received a grade of "A":

	Initial Test Score	Final Test Score
Noel Baker	9	60
Sam Johannsen	44	95
Sydney Lofflin	4	55
Wendy Pharr	48	99

Clearly students Johannsen and Pharr, as measured by their final test scores, seem to have mastered the content more adequately than have students Baker and Lofflin. Yet all four students qualify for a grade of "A" under this "improvement" system. Although all receive "A's," it seems clear that these "A's" do not refer to a common level of competence.

In summary, the defects of the individual improvement approach are so severe that it should not receive serious consideration for use. Other alternatives are much more attractive from the standpoint of being fair to youngsters at all ability-levels and from the standpoint of assuring that a given grade refers to a specific level of competence.

Individual Performance as Compared with Group Performance

More commonly used than individual improvement grading is a scheme that awards letter grades to students in a class based on how their performance compares with that of other learners in the class. Sometimes this kind of grading is referred to as norm-referenced grading. The idea here is that an individual student is graded in reference to the "norm" for the group of which he or she is a part. Norm-referenced grading awards higher grades to students scoring above class averages and lower grades to students scoring below class averages (see Box 13.6).

In implementing a norm-referenced system, we ordinarily make some sort of a determination of the percentages of students in our class who will receive each letter grade. Because of differences in courses, students, school settings and other variables, there is no established set of "correct" percentages of "A's," "B's," "C's," "D's," and "F's" for every classroom situation. For example, one teacher might have a class of very bright and hard-working students. Another might have a group charac-

Box 13.6

Basing All Grades on the Normal Curve

Mr. Jones, a new teacher, read that human ability tends to be distributed in a fashion that can be depicted graphically by a bell-shaped curve. That is, there are smaller numbers of higher- and lower-ability people than average-ability people.

Mr. Jones decided that this information could be used as a rational basis for awarding grades to the 32 students in his class. After some further reading, he decided that the top 3.6% would receive "A's," the next 23.8% "B's," the next 45.2% "C's," the next 23.8% "D's," and the lowest 3.6% "F's."

What Do You Think?

Think about this scheme. Then, respond to these questions.

1. In general, how do you think students would respond to this scheme? Why?

2. Would students tend to work harder or to do less work given this arrangement? Why?

3. Would this be a fair grading arrangement? Why, or why not?

4. What would grades awarded under this system tell us about the individual competence of youngsters' receiving each grade?

5. Suppose that you decided to write a letter to Mr. Jones commenting critically on this system. What would you say?

terized by large numbers of indifferent students of modest intellectual gifts. It would hardly be fair to allow the grading system to require that the same percentage of "A" grades be given by each of these two teachers.

One approach to the fairness issue has been to provide teachers with a general range of percentages to which teachers can refer in deciding how many "A's," "B's," "C's," "D's," and "F's" to award. A scheme might be developed that provided teachers with these general ideas for distributing their grades:

A = 5 to 20 percent of students   D = 5 to 20 percent of students

B = 20 to 30 percent of students   F = 0 to 5 percent of students

C = 30 to 50 percent of students

Note that in this scheme the teacher is not required to give any failing grades. It is important in using a norm-referenced system that youngsters recognize that the adopted system does not require some students to fail. This is important for several reasons. First, students approach courses in a more positive frame of mind when they realize that everyone in the class has the potential, at least, to pass. Second, mandating a certain percentage who must fail makes little educational sense. In a single class of learners, perhaps one with students who are academically talented, even those who score at the bottom of the class on tests may have mastered enough material to go on to more advanced work with little difficulty. In such a situation, clearly they have not failed. Rather, they simply have not mastered course work at as high a level of sophistication as have many of their classmates.

Individual Performance as Compared with a Predetermined Standard

"Criterion-referenced grading" is the term generally used to describe practices according to which letter grades are awarded on the basis of a comparison made between a student's performance and some pre-established standard. Typically, different levels of performance are required of youngsters who will receive different letter grades.

Criterion-referenced grading allows for clear communication of the level of competence implied by each letter grade. The standards for individual letter grades can be disseminated easily to students, parents, administrators, and others who may have an interest in this matter. When this is done, little doubt remains regarding what is meant by an "A," a "B," a "C," and so forth.

In a criterion-referenced grading system, each student is potentially capable of achieving any grade. No arbitrary percentages of "A's," "B's," "C's," "D's," and "F's" are established in advance that must be awarded. In this system, there is no particular advantage given to very low-achieving students (as in individual improvement) and no particular disadvantage is given to very high-achieving students (again, as in individual improvement grading). It is logically possible for all students to get "A's." Similarly, it is logically possible (though unlikely) for all students to receive any other available grade. The determinant of the grades that are awarded is simply student achievement in terms of the pre-established performance standard for each letter grade.

As might be imagined, the real challenge for the teacher in using a criterion-referenced grading system is establishing the appropriate standards of achievement for each grade level. Beginning teachers and experienced hands who are new to this grading approach often find that they must teach units several times before they are satisfied with the criteria they have established for each grade. In general, we want to keep grading standards rigorous enough to prevent students from doing hasty and sloppy work but not so rigorous as to make it impossible for them to earn "A's" and "B's."

Some teachers find it useful to specify criteria in the form of grading contracts. Each contract specifies what must be done to earn a given grade. There are different contracts for students interested in seeking each grade. (Usually there are no contracts for "D's." "D's" tend to be awarded to students who fail to complete part of the work on "A," "B," or "C" contracts. "F's" are awarded to those who fall hopelessly short of their contractual obligations.)

Another possibility for awarding grades using a criterion-referenced scheme involves the use of instructional objectives. Recall that each complete instructional objective includes a reference to a "condition" or kind of testing and a "degree" statement about how well a student must do to achieve the objective. The test mentioned in each instructional objective is not, itself, tied directly to letter grading. These tests are used only to determine whether or not the teacher should consider a given student to have achieved the objective. In a criterion-referenced grading scheme, letter grades are determined by considering the total number of instructional objectives a particular student has mastered.

Let us see how such a plan might work. Suppose that during a given grading term students had had an opportunity to achieve a maximum of 40 instructional objectives. Under these conditions, we might develop a grading system based on instructional objectives' attainment that would look like the following:

Total Number of Instructional Objectives = 40

Grade	Number of Instructional Objectives Achieved
"A"	36–40
"B"	32–35
"C"	28–31
"D"	24–27
"F"	23 or fewer

Whether framed by learning contracts or around instructional objectives' attainment, criterion-referenced grading systems have much to commend them. They can communicate clearly the levels of competence implied by each letter grade. Further, no particular groups of students are placed in positions of either special advantage or special disadvantage. Finally, they serve well the need to let students know that grades are being awarded according to practices that are consistent and equitable.

Key Ideas In Summary

1. "Measurement" and "evaluation" are related, but not synonymous, terms. Measurement refers to the process of using specific tools to gather information. Evaluation uses the results of measurement to make judgments. In education, these judgments often refer to students' academic progress.

2. "Summative evaluation" occurs at the end of an instructional sequence. It provides a measure of what a student has learned after he or she has already been exposed to teaching related to a given topic. "Formative evaluation" occurs as the instruction on a new topic is occurring. Its purpose is to provide feedback to students regarding how well they are mastering the material. Results also cue teachers to problems that are being experienced by individual students. These results sometimes lead teachers to make changes in their instructional programs so that students will be better able to master the content.

3. Teachers use a number of informal evaluation techniques to gather information about their learners. The choice of a specific informal technique depends on the specific kind of information the teacher needs. Teacher observation, student-produced headlines and articles, one-on-one teacher-student discussions, and student-produced tests are a few examples of informal evaluation techniques that teachers use.

4. Standardized tests are tests that are prepared by professional evaluation specialists. They are given to students in many classrooms. Their purpose is to provide some indication of how individual students and classrooms compare with national or regional averages. Results of standardized tests are rarely used by teachers for the purpose of awarding grades.

5. Teacher-made tests are what most teachers use to gather information and make judgments about the progress of the students in their classes. There are many widely-used formats for teacher-made tests. Among examples found in many secondary classrooms are multiple-choice tests, matching tests, true-false tests, completion tests, essay tests, rating scales, and checklists. Each of these test types has individual strengths and weaknesses in terms of the kinds of learning it adequately assesses.

"Yes, Albert, your class average is 'grody to the max'."

6. There are several approaches to awarding letter grades. The least desirable is grading students on test score differences between the beginning and the end of a unit of instruction. This scheme may be very unfair to bright students. Norm-referenced schemes tend to award grades to an individual student based on how well he or she did in comparison to others in the class. This arrangement needs to be implemented in a way that students understand the teacher is under no obligation to fail some students in the class. Criterion-referenced grading assigns grades to students on the basis of their performance as compared to a pre-established performance level. One problem teachers face in implementing criterion-referenced grading is deciding just how high a standard should be set for each letter grade.

POSTTEST

DIRECTIONS: Using your own paper, answer these true/false questions. For each correct statement, write the word "true." For each incorrect statement, write the word "false."

_____ 1. "Formative evaluation" takes place as new content is being taught to assure that students are mastering information needed for subsequent learning.

_____ 2. Informal evaluation procedures are rarely used by secondary school teachers.

_____ 3. The term "standardized test" is used to describe a test prepared by an individual teacher for use in his or her own classroom.

_____ 4. In criterion-referenced grading, a student's grade is determined by his or her performance as it compares with scores of other students in the group.

_____ 5. Grading students on the basis of how much progress each person in the class makes as compared to his or her standing at the beginning of the term may work to the disadvantage of very bright students.

Bibliography

BLOOM, BENJAMIN S. (ED.). *Taxonomy of Educational Objectives: Handbook I: The Cognitive Domain*. New York: David McKay Co., Inc., 1956.

BLOOM, BENJAMIN S.; MADAUS, GEORGE F.; AND HASTINGS, J. THOMAS. *Evaluation to Improve Learning*. New York: McGraw-Hill, Inc., 1981.

GOOD, THOMAS L. AND BROPHY, JERE. E. *Looking in Classrooms*. 4th Edition. New York: Harper and Row, Publishers, 1987.

NOWAKOWSKI, JERI R. "On Educational Evaluation: A Conversation with Ralph Tyler." *Educational Leadership, 40*, (May 1983): 24–29.

POPHAM, W. JAMES (ED.). *Criterion-Referenced Measurement: An Introduction*. Englewood Cliffs, NJ: Educational Technology Publications, 1971.

SAX, GILBERT. *Principles of Educational Measurement and Evaluation*. Belmont, CA: Wadsworth Publishing Company, Inc., 1974.

SCRIVEN, MICHAEL. "The Methodology of Evaluation." In Rubert W. Stake, et al., *Perspectives on Curriculum Evaluation*. AERA Monograph Series on Curriculum Evaluation, No. 1. Chicago: Rand McNally, 1967. pp. 39–83.

STERN, JOYCE D. (ED.), AND CHANDLER, MARJORIE O. (ASSOC. ED.) *The Condition of Education* 1987 edition. Washington, DC: U.S. Department of Education, Center for Education Statistics, 1987.

STUFFLEBEAM, DANIEL L. AND SHINKFIELD, ANTHONY J. *Systematic Evaluation*. Boston: Kluwer-Nijhoff Publishing, 1985.

TUCKMAN, BRUCE WAYNE. *Evaluation of Instructional Programs*. 2nd ed. Boston: Allyn and Bacon, Inc., 1985.

TYLER, RALPH W. *Basic Principles of Curriculum and Instruction*. Chicago: The University of Chicago Press, 1949.

PART III

Formal Planning

CHAPTER 14

Planning Instructional Units

AIMS

This chapter provides information to help the reader to:

1. Describe the purpose of an instructional unit.
2. Point out some advantages of long-term instructional planning.
3. Identify common elements found in many instructional units.
4. Explain steps that are followed in planning an instructional unit.
5. Prepare an instructional unit for use in a secondary school classroom.

PRETEST

DIRECTIONS: Using your own paper, answer these true/false questions. For each correct statement, write the word "true." For each incorrect statement, write the word "false."

_____ 1. The kind of planning that goes into selecting content for a book is identical to the kind of planning involved in planning an instructional unit.

_____ 2. One purpose of task analysis is to determine what students will need to be able to know and do to master an instructional objective.

_____ 3. There is a single format for instructional units that is used by nearly all teachers in all schools.

_____ 4. Unit generalizations are succinct summaries of understandings that, it is hoped, students will have as a result of their exposure to unit content.

_____ 5. Unit planners should avoid giving any thought to providing suggestions regarding unit evaluation procedures.

Introduction

Instructional unit plans include information relating to a part of a larger topic or course. They vary greatly in length. Many of them are designed for between one and three weeks' instructional time. However, sometimes they are shorter, and sometimes they are longer. The specific length of a given unit will depend on such things as the kind of content treated, the nature of students for whom the program has been planned, the types of instructional techniques employed, and the priorities of the people who designed it.

The unit preparation process helps teachers to think carefully about a number of program dimensions. For example, since most units will require generalizations, instructional objectives, suggested teaching techniques, recommended evaluation procedures, and lists of learning materials, developers must take time to make decisions about these issues. Further, since units are planned before the content they describe is taught, teachers have time to think carefully about their procedures before lessons are introduced to students. This often allows for potential problems to be identified and remedied before programs are introduced to students.

Students have difficulty managing extremely large doses of content. Preparing instructional units allows teachers to think about this problem and to create units that, individually, focus on relatively small amounts of content.

Not all units are developed by teachers or groups of teachers. Some are available from commercial sources. In many cases, teacher-prepared units are more functional than commercially-prepared units. Units developed by individuals other than the people who will teach the content may not be well suited to the specialized needs of students in a particular classroom or school. Additionally, the priorities of these developers may be at odds with those of the teachers who will teach the program described in the unit. Finally, instructional units developed by others do not command much emotional commitment from teachers. The act of creating a unit often motivates people to give their best effort when they teach the program they have designed.

Completion of an instructional unit requires the developers to make decisions about planning processes and formatting. Issues that must be faced are more complex than those that must be considered when content is being selected for inclusion in a textbook. This is true

"According to the unit plan you sent me, you're supposed to be lecturing on the halogens. There seems to be a bit of a 'truth in advertising' problem here."

because instructional units must provide information that goes beyond a simple breakdown of content. Units must also include suggestions for transmitting content to learners and for evaluating their progress.

Once basic decisions about unit content have been made, unit developers must make decisions about formatting. Formatting decisions relate to the issue of displaying unit content. A number of formats have been developed for doing this. In the sections that follow, some approaches to both unit-planning processes and unit formatting are introduced. In addition, an example of a completed instructional unit is provided.

Instructional Units: The Planning Process

There is no standard set of steps associated with the unit-planning process. However, though individuals may vary somewhat in their approach to instructional unit planning, many teachers follow somewhat similar procedures. The steps outlined here would be familiar to large numbers of instructional unit developers. These steps are:

1. Selecting a unit title.
2. Identifying a major goal.
3. Checking mandated-content regulations.
4. Identifying major generalizations and concepts.
5. Developing instructional objectives and allocating teaching time.
6. Performing a task analysis.
7. Determining appropriate beginning points for instruction.
8. Selecting an instructional strategy for each objective.
9. Developing evaluation procedures.
10. Identifying learning resources.

Selecting a Unit Title

Instructional units organize instructional programs for a portion of a course. The specific title chosen should capture the essence of the content to be covered during the one-to-three week period when the unit will be taught. Unit titles ordinarily are short. Sometimes even one-word titles are used. Some examples of unit titles are "The Halogen Family" (chemistry), "The Lake Poets" (English), "Perimeters and Areas of Triangles" (mathematics), and "The Progressive Era" (history). Some districts provide teachers with curriculum guides that include suggested unit titles. In other places, teachers are free to select their own titles. (See Box 14.1).

Identifying a Major Goal

Goal statements in instructional units try to explain benefits that will come to students as a result of their exposure to the content to be treated. These are often expressed in rather general terms. They are intended to provide a student or a parent with some basic information about the kinds of learning experiences students may encounter as the unit is taught.

Box 14.1

Selecting Titles of Units

To someone who has never confronted the process, selecting unit titles may appear easy. It isn't. Each unit represents a segment of a course. There must be some general unity to the content. Individual units cannot contain too much information. If they do, students experience difficulty in mastering the content. On the other hand, if units include too restricted a body of content, it becomes necessary to develop a large number of them. This can result in confusing fragmentation.

Suppose you were interested in teaching a one-semester course in a middle school, junior high school, or senior high school. (You choose the course.) There are about 16 instructional weeks. Try to identify titles of five or six units you would teach. Indicate how much time would be devoted to each.

1. _____   (time required _____)
2. _____   (time required _____)
3. _____   (time required _____)
4. _____   (time required _____)
5. _____   (time required _____)
6. _____   (time required _____)

Share your titles with your instructor. Be prepared to answer these questions:

1. How did you decide on your titles? On time requirements?

2. Did you consider some alternative titles? If so what were they, and why did you reject them?

Suppose an English teacher were preparing an instructional unit entitled "The Epic Hero Theme in American Novels." The teacher might prepare a general goal statement something like this:

> This unit is designed to foster students' appreciation of the form, extent of use, and purposes of the "epic hero theme" in American novels.

Checking Mandated-Content Regulations

Once a title has been selected and a unit goal has been written, some instructional unit developers face another task. They must consider whether their state, district, or school has any regulations concerning specific information that must be taught that relates to the unit topic. In some parts of the country (Texas is an example), state regulations require teachers to document their coverage of certain information that is mandated by law.

In instances where some content to be covered in an instructional unit may satisfy certain legal requirements, teachers take care when they are preparing units to note the specific requirements that are being met. This enables them to document coverage when administrative authorities ask for evidence that mandated content is being taught.

Identifying Major Generalizations and Concepts

The function of generalizations (often there are several, but sometimes only one) in a unit is to provide a succinct distillation of content to be covered. They tend to represent a summary of "truth" insofar as "truth" can be determined given the present state of knowledge. (See Chapter 5 for more information about generalizations).

Generalizations take the form of relationships among concepts. Concepts are labels that are used to categorize information that shares certain common characteristics. Concepts can be loosely thought of as "terms." To understand a generalization, a student must grasp the concepts embedded within it. Suppose a high school sociology teacher decided to use the following generalization as one that would provide a focus for an instructional unit entitled "Urban Growth and Cultural Change":

> When urbanization occurs rapidly in a country, differences in status among people in various social classes become more pronounced.

In planning this unit, there would be a need to consider which of the concepts in this generalization might pose problems for students. The teacher might conclude that most students were reasonably familiar with concepts such as "country" and "people." However, terms such as "urbanization," "status," and "social class" logically could be identified as concepts that would be less well known. These concepts might be targeted for special emphasis in the unit.

In selecting which concepts to emphasize, unit planners must consider that certain kinds of concepts are more difficult for learners to grasp than others. The characteristics that define a given concept are referred to as its "attributes." For example, the attributes of the concept "triangle" are (a) a two-dimensional closed plane figure that has (b) three sides and (c) three interior angles. Some concepts, such as "triangle," have only a few defining attributes. Other concepts are complex and have numerous defining attributes. Two examples of complex concepts are "democracy" and "socialization."

Topics covered in many instructional units contain complex concepts. More-complex concepts require more time to teach than less-complex concepts. This means that unit developers must adjust the anticipated time required to teach the unit in light of the sophistication of the concepts to be taught.

Developing Instructional Objectives and Allocating Teaching Time

Instructional objectives describe the specific behaviors students should be able to demonstrate as a consequence of their exposure to material taught during the unit. Objectives are tied closely to major concepts that have been selected for emphasis. The development of objectives related to these concepts helps focus learners' attention on their importance.

A good deal of artistry is required of unit developers as they determine how many instructional objectives to include. The number should not be so large that each objective embraces an extremely limited amount of content. On the other hand, the number should not be so small that each must stretch across vast quantities of information. For a one-to-three week instructional unit, many teachers find that five to eight objectives will suffice. Some good units have fewer; others have more.

Some objectives require more sophisticated thinking of students than do others. For example, an algebra teacher might have one objective related to developing students' abilities to recognize meanings of terms including "variable" and "factoring." Recognition is not a particularly sophisticated thinking skill. The time required to transmit the necessary information to students and for them to master the material probably will not be great.

This same teacher might have another objective calling on students to apply skills to which they have been introduced to solve a number of factoring problems. This task involves more sophisticated mental operations than does the objective related to recall of terms. It is logical that more instructional time will be required to prepare students to succeed at the factoring task than will be required to prepare them to succeed at the term-recognition task.

In recognition of differences in time required for students to master behaviors in individual objectives, many instructional unit developers make some suggestions regarding how much teaching time might be devoted to each. First, a judgment must be made regarding how much time is required to teach the total unit. This decision will be based on such considerations as the nature of the students, the unit developer's past experience in teaching similar content, and the complexity of the material. The time required may have to be adjusted when the unit is being taught for the first time.

Once an estimate of the time required to teach the entire unit is made, the unit developer makes recommendations regarding teaching time for content related to each objective. In making these time decisions, the number of objectives and the complexity of each are considered. For example, suppose a unit developer decided that a unit would require 15 instructional days, with one additional day provided at the end for a unit test. If there were six instructional objectives, suggested teaching times might be listed as follows:

Objective 1 (knowledge level) 1 day

Objective 2 (knowledge level) 2 days

Objective 3 (application level) 2 days

Objective 4 (application level) 3 days

Objective 5 (application level) 3 days

Objective 6 (analysis level) 4 days

This arrangement does not necessarily imply that all instruction related to objective 1 would precede instruction related to objective 2, all related to objective 2 would precede instruction related to objective 3, and so forth. It is possible that instruction related to an individual objective may occur at different times during the period the unit is taught. The times indicated merely suggest the **total** instructional time recommended for teaching content related to a given objective.

For additional information regarding types of objectives and formatting of objectives, see Chapter 5, "Selecting Content and Establishing Objectives." Box 14.2 contains an exercise in planning an instructional unit.

Task Analysis

Task analysis is a planning activity that begins once instructional objectives have been prepared. During task analysis, unit developers identify major tasks that students will need to accomplish if they are to grasp content associated with each objective. Each objective that has been prepared for a unit needs to be task analyzed.

Task analysis involves identification of specific information students will need. It begins with this question: "What will students need to know or be able to do to master this objective?" Suppose this objective were under review:

Box 14.2

Preparing a Unit Title, a Unit Goal Statement, Focusing Generalizations, and Instructional Objectives

Identify a title for an instructional unit you would develop for a secondary school subject you would like to teach. Then, prepare a goal statement, one or more focusing generalizations, and about five instructional objectives. Share this material with your course instructor for comments:

Unit Title: _____

Goal Statement: _____
_____
_____

Generalization(s): _____
_____
_____
_____
_____

Instructional
Objectives: 1. _____
_____
_____

2. _____
_____
_____

3. _____
_____
_____

4. _____
_____
_____

5. _____
_____
_____

Share these completed unit components with your instructor.

On an essay examination, each student will compare and contrast relative strengths and weaknesses of the North and South at the beginning of the Civil War. Special reference must be made to each section's (a) industrial capacity, (b) military strength, and (c) transportation networks.

The unit developer might conclude that students would need to know some of these things:

- boundaries of the North and South
- industrial characteristics of the North and South
- military strengths of the North and South
- railway lines in the North and the South
- roads in the North and the South
- navigable waterways of the North and the South
- how to make comparisons in written form
- how to make contrasts in written form

Other items might be added to the list. The idea is not necessarily for the unit developer to prepare a long list. The purpose is to include those items that represent what students must be able to do to master the objective. This kind of explicit information provides some guidelines that can help users of the unit to develop appropriate lessons.

Determining Appropriate Beginning Points for Instruction

Once needed information has been identified, unit developers move on to consider how content should be sequenced. Usually an easy-to-difficult sequence is selected. However, this does not always mean that the most basic item of information identified through task analysis will be taught first. Selection of a beginning point must first consider what students already know and are able to do.

For example, it might be that most students in the classroom are already familiar with the least complex information on the list. If this is the case, another "entry point" for instruction is selected. The idea is to select a beginning point that takes advantage of past learning and begins new instruction at a place where the content begins to move beyond what students already know.

Determining appropriate entry points requires unit developers to know a great deal about the students for whom the unit is intended. If the individual preparing the unit has taught these students, then students' past performances can provide some general guidelines regarding what students already know. If this is not the case, it sometimes is feasible to administer simple diagnostic tests.

Diagnostic tests, often formatted in true-false or multiple-choice test form, are designed to provide the unit developer with some indication about how much information on the task-analysis list students already know. Results may suggest logical beginning points for instruction. Since students differ in what they know, there may be different entry points for different students.

Selecting an Instructional Strategy for Each Objective

Instructional strategies are systematically arranged teacher activities. One is developed for each objective. Each selected strategy is designed to promote mastery of the objective to which it refers. Many different strategies may work well. For this reason, unit developers usually are careful to avoid the implication that strategies they propose are the only ones that might be appropriate. Often language such as "suggested instructional strategies" is found in instructional units.

Though several strategies may be equally capable of promoting mastery of a given objective, successful strategies follow this important rule:

> Instructional objectives requiring more sophisticated student behavior require more sophisticated and time-consuming instructional strategies.

This simply means that it takes longer to teach complex thinking and skills than to teach simple thinking and skills. An art teacher needs less time and a smaller variety of teaching activities to help learners describe features of a famous statue than to teach them to design and sculpt a small statue of their own.

Developing Evaluation Procedures

Teachers use both informal and formal evaluation procedures. Specific guidelines for preparing and using a number of these were introduced in Chapter 13, "Measuring and Evaluating Learning." Results of these assessments are often used as a basis for awarding grades. Because of the importance that grades assume for students and parents, fairness suggests the need for the assessments on which grades are based to be clearly tied to the instructional program.

Unit developers who are concerned about this issue often include as part of the unit examples of assessment procedures that are tied to each instructional objective. Development of assessment procedures at the same time the other components of the unit are developed greatly increases the chance that students will be evaluated on content related to what has been taught in the unit. When formal and informal evaluation procedures are hastily developed by teachers at some later date, there is always a possibility that some items may bear little relationship to what students have been taught. This can result in grading practices that give spurious impressions of students' mastery of unit content.

Identifying Learning Resources

Information sources are needed by teachers and by students as they begin work on a new unit. Lacking such sources, frustration is certain to result. As a guard against this possibility, unit developers often provide a list of relevant resources in the unit.

In preparing the unit, developers frequently identify both resources that are of interest to teachers and resources that students will use. Resources may include references to specific books, films, maps, filmstrips, cassettes, software, newspapers, and other media containing information relevant to the unit topic.

Available resources change over time. Further, some excellent materials may have been overlooked by those who developed the unit. Consequently, it is a common practice in many units to refer to "suggested resources." This leaves the door open to the possibility that teachers who use the unit may identify and use other relevant sources of information. (See Box 14.3.)

Instructional Units: Formatting

Instructional units can be formatted in many ways. Some school districts provide standard formats and request that all units follow a standard layout. Others permit unit developers to make their own formatting decisions.

Major headings used in unit documents may vary. Headings focusing on such components as "unit title," "suggested instructional strategies," and "suggested learning resources" are found in many documents. Places where states, districts, or individual schools require certain elements of content to be taught may feature a "mandated-content" section. Where there are not such requirements, this section will be absent.

Typically, many major unit headings will parallel names of steps in the unit-planning phase. For example, the "unit title" provided on the formatted document acknowledges, in written form, the decision made during the "selecting-unit-title" phase of the planning process. Often an "evaluation" section will be provided to display testing suggestions identified during the "developing-evaluation-procedures" phase of planning. There may be other parallels as well.

On the other hand, some planning activities will not lead to the development of special sections on the completed unit document. For example, "performing a task analysis" and "determining appropriate beginning points for instruction" are important planning activities. Results of these activities will not be reflected in unit-document headings called

Box 14.3

Identifying Learning Resources

Teachers use many learning resources to support their instruction. Beginning teachers sometimes fail to recognize how many information sources are available to supplement what might be provided in the course text.

Select a unit title you might like to teach. Prepare a list of teacher resources (items that might help enrich your knowledge of the focus topic) and student resources (items that students could use to learn more about the topic). Ask your course instructor for ideas about where to locate this kind of information. Consider organizing your material under the headings provided below. (Feel free to modify them, as appropriate.) Present your list to your instructor for review:

1.0 Teacher Resources
   1.1 Books
   1.2 Journal and Newspaper Articles
   1.3 Films and Filmstrips
   1.4 Audio and Videotapes
   1.5 Computer Software
   1.6 Manipulatives and Other Tangible Objects
   1.7 Maps, Charts, Photographs, Drawings, Paintings
   1.8 Other Resources

2.0 Student
   2.1 Books
   2.2 Journal and Newspaper Articles
   2.3 Films and Filmstrips
   2.4 Audio and Videotapes
   2.5 Computer Software
   2.6 Manipulatives and Other Tangible Objects
   2.7 Maps, Charts, Photographs, Drawings, Paintings
   2.8 Other Resources

"task analysis" and "entry points." Rather, information gathered during these phases of planning will be incorporated in decisions related to instructional strategies. The "instructional strategies" section of the unit document, then, will result from a combination of planning decisions related, respectively, to (1) task analysis, (b) determination of appropriate beginning points, and (c) selection of a strategy.

One format for an instructional unit might have these eight components:

1. Unit title.
2. Goal statement.

These teachers are participating in a workshop. They are learning procedures they will incorporate into new unit plans they are developing. *Photo courtesy of National Science Teachers Association.*

3. Mandated content to be covered.
4. Focus generalization(s) and related concepts.
5. Instructional objectives and suggested time allocations.
6. Suggested teaching strategies.
7. Examples of evaluation procedures.
8. Suggested learning resources.

This is not intended to suggest that these eight major headings represent the best approach to organizing content in an instructional unit. They are, however, representative of the organizational schemes found in many units. They represent a beginning point for prospective unit developers to consider as they think about how they would like units of their own design to be formatted. The section that follows introduces an example of an instructional unit that has been formatted using these eight headings.

Instructional Unit: An Example

Title

The American Revolution

Unit Goal

This unit introduces students to the American Revolution and places particular emphasis on the Revolution's role in joining citizens of the former colonies in a common military cause that, in the end, led them also to recognize that they shared certain cultural, political, and economic interests.

Mandated Content Related to this Unit

State-Content Mandates:

• Major Events Leading to the Revolutionary War
• Key Military Events of the Revolutionary War and their Consequences
• Lasting Influences of the Revolutionary War

Local Mandates: none
School Mandates: none

Focus Generalizations

1. The American War for Independence was a true revolution in that its upheavals began because of a challenge to legitimate authority and its consequences presented the world with a set of novel assumptions about the proper relationship between governments and citizens.

Important Concepts:

- revolution
- independence
- authority
- legitimate authority

2. The pressures of war led the colonists to downplay the many differences that divided colony from colony and to emphasize points of common political and military interest.

Important Concepts:

- colony
- colonist
- political interest
- military interest

3. In part, the ultimate success of the Americans in the War for Independence resulted because of British manpower shortages and transportation difficulties.

Important Concepts:

- manpower
- transport
- logistics

Instructional Objectives and Suggested Teaching Time for Each

1. Each student will recognize events leading to the American Revolution by responding correctly to at least 6 of 8 items on a matching quiz that requires them to match actions taken by the British Government to actions taken in response by the American colonists. (cognitive: knowledge)

Suggested time allocation: 1 day

2. In an essay, each student will compare and contrast British and American advantages at the time the Revolutionary War began. Each essay will make specific references to at least two British advantages, two British disadvantages, two American advantages, and two American disadvantages. (cognitive: analysis)

Suggested time allocation: 2 days

3. Each student will identify American approaches to financing the war by responding correctly to at least 8 of 10 true-false questions. (cognitive: knowledge)

Suggested time allocation: 1 day

4. Students will identify key military developments of the Revolutionary War and their importance by responding correctly to 6 of 8 multiple-choice items. (cognitive: comprehension)

Suggested time allocation: 2 days

5. Each student will analyze results of the Revolutionary War on an essay in which specific references are made to (a) political results, (b) social results, (c) economic results. (cognitive: analysis)

Suggested time allocation: 2 days

6. Each student will indicate more interest in the American Revolution at the conclusion of the unit than at the beginning as indicated by a comparison of scores on a pre-unit and a post-unit attitude inventory. (affective)

Suggested time allocation: No separate allocation. The instruction in the entire unit is related to this objective.

Suggested Teaching Strategies

INTRODUCING THE UNIT.   Point out locations of Britain and the United States on a large world map. Explain to students that over 3,000 miles of ocean separate the two places. Take time, too, to point out location of important terrain features of eastern North America, particularly the Appalachian Mountains. Explain to students that very few of the American colonists lived west of the Appalachians at the time of the Revolutionary War. Point out that, at the time the war started, about 9 million people lived in Britain and about 2 million people in the North American colonies.

Ask students to think about this information. Use a brainstorming activity to generate responses to these questions: (Write answers on the chalkboard.)

What advantages might the British have had?

What disadvantages?

What advantages might the American colonists have had?

What disadvantages?

Discuss student responses. Prepare a list of student ideas, duplicate it, and share it with members of the class. As the unit is taught, ask students to take notes about the accuracy or inaccuracy of some of the ideas that were developed during the brainstorming activity.

INSTRUCTIONAL OBJECTIVE. 1. Divide class into five groups. Assign each group to one of these events:

- Proclamation of 1763
- Sugar Act of 1764
- Stamp Act of 1765
- Declaratory Act of 1766
- Townshend Acts of 1767

Ask members of each group to become familiar with (a) the British motive behind the action and (b) the reaction of the American colonists to it. Students may use any available learning resources. Ask two students from each group to explain responses to (a) and (b). Ask another two students to briefly debate this statement: "Resolved that the action of the British was more justified than the reaction of the Americans." Conclude with a general class discussion. List individual events on the chalkboard. Help students to summarize what happened and to think critically about the relative merits of British and colonial actions.

Prepare a large chart. Begin by writing the following headings across the top of the chalkboard or across the top of a large sheet of butcher paper:

British Station Troops in Boston (1768)

Parliament Repeals Townshend Acts but Leaves Tax on Tea (1770)

Parliament Passes Tea Act (1773)

Parliament Passes "Intolerable Acts" (1774)

Parliament Sends Troops to Lexington and Concord

Along the side of the chalkboard or butcher paper, write these labels:

Why British Took this Action

Colonists' Feelings about this Action

Ask students to volunteer information to fill in the chart. They are free to consult any available information sources. Write information in appropriate places. Conduct a discussion focusing on (a) any points of agreement between the British and the colonists, (b) differences in British views and colonists' views, and (c) possible explanations for these differences. Ask students to predict some possible actions the colonists might have taken as a result of their disagreements with these British actions. Ask students to check their predictions against what really happened by referring to any available information sources.

INSTRUCTIONAL OBJECTIVE 2.   Divide students into four groups. Assign each group to prepare one of the following lists:

List of British advantages at the beginning of the Revolutionary War

List of British disadvantages at the beginning of the Revolutionary War

List of American advantages at the beginning of the Revolutionary War

List of American disadvantages at the beginning of the Revolutionary War

Provide time for students to work with information sources in class as they seek to complete their lists. Ask a member of each group to list items on his or her group's list on the chalkboard. Discuss as a group.

Assign each student to write two "newspaper editorials" based on the information about British and American advantages and disadvantages at the beginning of the Revolutionary War. Editorials should be restricted to no more than four paragraphs each. The students should assume they are writing these editorials in the very earliest stages of the Revolutionary War. The title of one editorial should be "Why the British Will Win." The title of the other should be "Why the Americans Will Win." Encourage students to put in specific details to support positions taken in each editorial. Post editorials. Read several editorials to the class, and discuss issues that are raised.

Prepare a short lecture focusing on relative merits of the British army and the colonial forces at the beginning of the Revolutionary War. Point out British dependence on the musket and on traditional tactics of marching massed troops in columns toward the enemy. Point out the colonials' familiarity with the rifle, and cite its advantage over the musket (stress accuracy of shooting over long distances). Point out professionalism of British army and the lack of a history of taking orders on the part of the Americans. Point out that many Americans had grown up with firearms and required little familiarization with them when they became involved in military units.

Use maps of colonial North America as a focus of a discussion centering on transportation. Point out sparse network of roads. Ask such focus questions as these:

> What might these roads suggest about the time needed to move people and goods from place to place?

What does the existence of good transportation have to do with what people living in one place might know and feel about people living somewhere else? Do you think people living in Virginia felt they had much in common with people in Massachusetts? What might roads have had to do with these feelings? What problems might have resulted as the colonists prepared for war as a result of these feelings?

Do you think a person could have traveled from Virginia to Massachusetts faster by land or by sea in the 1770s? Why do you think control of the sea lanes was so important during the Revolutionary War? If the colonists had had a navy more powerful than that of the British, would there have been a Revolutionary War? What do you think would have happened?

INSTRUCTIONAL OBJECTIVE 3. Write this question on the chalkboard:

When a country is involved in a war, its government is often short of money. Why?

Discuss this issue as a class. Then ask students to suggest kinds of things governments do to raise money to pay for wars and to support fighting forces. Make a list of student ideas. Ask students to copy ideas on their lists and to add new information as they learn it.

Invite someone who lived in this country during World War II (or, perhaps, someone from Great Britain) to speak to the class. Ask the person to speak specifically about kinds of things the government did that resulted from special strains caused by the war. For example, rationing of food, gasoline, and other commodities might be mentioned. Tax rates went up. There were restrictions on air and train travel, with military personnel getting priority. Automobile production stopped. Construction on schools and other projects slowed. Consumers faced many kinds of shortages. If the speaker doesn't do so, point out to students that wars are very expensive. They destroy property and they require vast amounts of money to support military activities. (Remind students to add any new ideas about how governments pay for wars to their lists.)

Ask students to work with learning resources to determine what problems the American colonists faced as they sought to pay costs associated with the American Revolution. Ask them to compare and contrast what was done at the time of the Revolutionary War with some of the things done during World War II.

INSTRUCTIONAL OBJECTIVE 4. On the chalkboard, lay out a time line covering the years 1775 through 1781. Ask students to identify major events in the war that occurred during this period. Write them on the time line at the appropriate places. Ask students to make copies of the time line.

Divide students into several groups. Assign members of each group a one-or-two year period on the time line. Each group should gather information to explain each major event that occurred during its assigned time span and its consequences. Conclude by asking students to refer to their time lines as volunteers from each group explain their findings. Students should take notes as the information is reported.

Consider organizing a debate on this topic: "Was there a single, 'most important' event that resulted in the defeat of the British in the Revolutionary War?"

INSTRUCTIONAL OBJECTIVE 5.   Ask students to research the Treaty of Paris of 1783. Assign teams of students to gather information about each of the following questions. Assign one question to each team:

1. What issues was France interested in, and how did the Treaty's results affect France?

2. What issues was Spain interested in, and how did the Treaty's results affect Spain?

3. What issues were the Americans interested in, and how did the Treaty's results affect the former American colonists?

4. What issues were the British interested in, and how did the Treaty's results affect Britain?

Ask a representative of each group to write information regarding each country on the chalkboard. Refer to this information. Discuss, focusing on the general question: "Who were the major winners and losers of the Treaty of Paris?"

Organize students into pairs. Provide each pair with background information focusing on the American Declaration of Independence of 1776 and the French Declaration of the Rights of Man of 1789. Ask each pair to compare the two documents in terms of what each has to say about human rights. How are they similar? How are they different? Is it accurate to say that the American Declaration of Independence may have influenced the French Revolution's Declaration of the Rights of Man?

Prepare a large chart on the chalkboard. Across the top, write these labels: "political conditions," "social conditions," "economic conditions." Down the left side write: "Before the Revolution" and "After the Revolution." Assign several students to use resource materials to find information for each "cell" of the chart. The individual cells are:

political conditions - before the Revolution

political conditions - after the Revolution

social conditions - before the Revolution

social conditions - after the Revolution

economic conditions - before the Revolution

economic conditions - after the Revolution

After information has been gathered, ask students to share what they have found with the class. Enter information into the chart on the chalkboard. Conclude with a discussion. Consider these focus questions:

What differences in each area do you observe before the Revolution and after the Revolution?

How do you account for these changes?

Were lives of people in the former colonies better or worse as a result of the Revolution? Why do you think so?

INSTRUCTIONAL OBJECTIVE 6.   There are no suggested teaching activities that are uniquely tied to objective 6. All instruction in the unit has some relationship to this affective objective.

Concluding the Unit

Tell students to imagine that the British had won the Revolutionary War. Ask them to suppose they are travel writers for an Australian newspaper. They have been assigned to write a feature article for their paper. The title of the article is "Life in British North America Today." Ask students (or teams of students) to write this article. Read several articles aloud. Discuss as a class what our lives might be like today as British subjects.

Organize class members into a number of discussion groups. Give each group about 10 minutes to generate as many responses as possible to this question:

What features of our lives today can be traced to the outcome of the Revolutionary War?

At the end of the 10-minute period, reorganize the class into a large group. Ask representatives from each group to share findings. Write ideas on the chalkboard. Discuss findings. Consider making copies of this information and distributing it to students.

Suggested Evaluation Procedures

INSTRUCTIONAL OBJECTIVE 1: MATCHING

Events Leading to the Revolution

DIRECTIONS: The information on the left describes an action taken by the British. The information on the right describes what the colonists did in response to the British action. You are to find the colonial response on the right that matches the British action on the left. Put the letter of the colonial response in the blank before the British action that led to this response. There is only one correct answer for each item.

_____ 1. Parliament passes Proclamation of 1763.

_____ 2. Parliament passes Stamp Act in 1765.

_____ 3. Parliament passes Townshend Acts in 1767.

_____ 4. Parliament acts to station more soldiers in Boston, 1768.

_____ 5. Parliament repeals Townshend Acts except for a tax on tea, 1770.

_____ 6. Parliament passes Tea Act, which gives the East India Company a monopoly on the tea trade, 1773.

_____ 7. Parliament passes the so-called "Intolerable Acts," 1774.

_____ 8. Parliament, declaring Massachusetts to be in a state of rebellion, sends British troops to Lexington and Concord, 1775.

a. Colonists convene a Second Continental Congress and establish an army.

b. Colonists convene the First Continental Congress and establish the Continental Association to boycott British goods.

c. Colonists ignore Parliament and continue settling lands west of the Appalachians.

d. A cargo of tea on a British ship destroyed by Boston Tea Party.

e. Colonists invite Louis XVI, king of France, to Boston for an emergency meeting.

f. Colonists organize new boycotts of British goods after violent protests by residents of Massachusetts.

g. Colonists clash with British soldiers. The so-called Boston Massacre results.

h. Benjamin Franklin leads an angry, anti-British mob down the streets of Philadelphia.

i. Colonists in 12 of the 13 colonies refuse to import British goods.

j. Colonists boycott British goods and organize the Sons of Liberty.

[Key: 1C, 2J, 3F, 4I, 5G, 6D, 7B, 8A]

INSTRUCTIONAL OBJECTIVE 2:   Essay

Relative Advantages of the British and Americans

DIRECTIONS: Write an essay, not to exceed three pages in length, in which you compare and contrast advantages and disadvantages of the British and the Americans at the beginning of the Revolutionary War. Cite at least two advantages and two disadvantages for each side.

Possible responses:

Examples of British Advantages:

- larger total population
- well-trained professional army
- powerful navy
- money for military supplies
- help from Loyalists and from some Indian tribes
- government that was used to dealing with military affairs

Examples of British Disadvantages:

- long, 3,000-mile supply lines
- manpower shortage; had to hire mercenaries
- dependence on muskets rather than rifles
- also faced military troubles with nations in Europe
- not fighting for homeland

Examples of American Advantages:

- fighting at home
- familiarity with rifles
- willingness to use new tactics
- familiarity with terrain

Examples of American Disadvantages:

- relatively small, weak naval forces
- lack of well-established formal military organizations
- suspicions among different colonies

- no strong central government with authority to assure adequate funding for troops and supplies
- limited manufacturing capability

INSTRUCTIONAL OBJECTIVE 3: TRUE/FALSE

American Financing of the Revolutionary War

DIRECTIONS: Some of the following statements are true. Others are false. Circle the word "true" before true statements, and circle the word "false" before false statements.

true   false   1. In general, the Americans experienced less difficulty in paying for troops and equipment than did the British.

true   false   2. Though the Continental Congress experienced problems in other areas, members had little difficulty in raising money to pay for the Revolutionary War.

true   false   3. Part of the money to pay for the American war effort came from loans from wealthy Americans.

true   false   4. Many American merchants refused to accept currency issued by the Continental Congress.

true   false   5. Americans during the war took pride in the fact that no money to support the Revolutionary War effort was borrowed from any European country.

true   false   6. Legislatures of the individual colonies were eager to send money to support the American war effort.

true   false   7. During the Revolutionary War, because authorities had difficulty raising money, large numbers of individuals who fought on the American side were not paid.

true   false   8. France provided financial help to the Americans during the Revolutionary War.

true   false   9. Part of the difficulty the former colonists faced in raising money for the war was the inability of the Continental Congress to exert strong authority over the individual colonies.

true   false   10. Financial problems sometimes made it difficult for the Americans to keep large numbers of troops in the field at the same time.

[Key: 1 false, 2 false, 3 true, 4 true, 5 false, 6 false, 7 true, 8 true, 9 true, 10 true]

INSTRUCTIONAL OBJECTIVE 4: MULTIPLE-CHOICE

Military Developments during the Revolutionary War

DIRECTIONS: This is a multiple-choice test. There is only one correct response for each item. Circle the letter that precedes the answer you have selected.

1. The early fighting of the war took place in

    a. New England
    b. Pennsylvania and New York
    c. Virginia
    d. The southernmost colonies

2. The Americans won each of these battles EXCEPT:

    a. Vincennes
    b. Cowpens
    c. Yorktown
    d. Bunker Hill

3. The American victory at Saratoga prompted

    a. France to enter the war on the side of the colonists.
    b. the British to seek terms of surrender from the Americans
    c. Italy to join the war on the side of the British.
    d. the British to abandon their use of the musket.

4. One important result of the raids on the British coast by the American John Paul Jones was that they

    a. forced the British to keep part of their fleet in home waters.
    b. demonstrated that the American navy had grown to be larger and more powerful than that of the British.
    c. led to sympathy on the part of British citizens for the cause of the American colonists.
    d. discouraged the French from entering the war on the side of the British.

5. The colonists received a great deal of help in the war at sea when ships of which one of the following countries joined the colonists in their war against the British?

    a. Italy
    b. Spain
    c. Portugal
    d. France

6. The major British defeat that led to the end of the war involved troops led by George Washington and foreign troops led by

    a. The Marquis de Lafayette
    b. Casimir Pulaski
    c. Friedrich von Steuben
    d. Thaddeus Kosciusko

7. At various times during the Revolutionary War, the British occupied each of these two cities:

    a. Richmond and Philadelphia
    b. Pittsburgh and Richmond
    c. Boston and New York
    d. New Orleans and Pittsburgh

8. The main significance of the American victory at Vincennes was that it

    a. drew Spain into the war on the side of the Americans.
    b. established American control over the area between the Appalachian Mountains and the Mississippi River.
    c. represented the first important victory of American troops under the personal leadership of George Washington.
    d. effectively ended the war and led directly to the peace conference at Paris in 1783.

[Key: 1 a, 2 d, 3 a, 4 a, 5 d, 6 a, 7 c, 8 b]

INSTRUCTIONAL OBJECTIVE 5: ESSAY

DIRECTIONS: Write an essay, not to exceed four pages in length, in which you analyze the impact of the American Revolution on American life. In your essay, make specific references to (a) political results, (b) social results, and (c) economic results of the war.

    Possible Responses:

Examples of Political Results:

• The British left; a new nation was created.

- Many people who had remained loyal to the British left the new country to settle in Canada or the West Indies.
- New state governments that were created tended to favor weak governors and strong legislatures.

Examples of Social Results:

- Several states passed laws abolishing slavery.
- Laws were passed in most states that either outlawed or severely restricted the importation of new slaves into the country.
- Human rights concerns raised in the Declaration of Independence led to such reforms as upgrading of conditions in prisons.

Examples of Economic Results:

- Vast new lands between the Appalachian Mountains and the Mississippi River became available for settlement.
- New world trade opportunities became available to American merchants.
- The new country was left with enormous debts that were owed to other countries such as France that had supported the American cause.

INSTRUCTIONAL OBJECTIVE 5: ATTITUDE INVENTORY

Relative Interest in the American Revolution as a Topic

DIRECTIONS: Look at the list of topics from early American history that are provided on page 385. Notice that a blank is provided before each topic. You are to place a rating from 1 to 3 in the blank provided for each topic. An explanation of the meaning of each rating point is provided below:

1. I have little or no interest in this topic. I would not like to spend more time learning about it.
2. I have a moderate amount of interest in this topic. Under certain conditions, I might like to learn more about it.
3. I have a great deal of interest in this topic. I definitely would like to learn more about it.

Box 14.4

Unit-Development Checklist

Prepare a complete instructional unit on a topic of your choice or as directed by your instructor. Use the checklist to assure that all key parts have been included. Some instructors may also wish to review and approve individual components as they are developed.

Date Completed	*Date Approved*	
_____	_____	1. Unit title selected
_____	_____	2. Goal statement completed
_____	_____	3. Mandated content (if any) identified
_____	_____	4. Focus generalizations and major concepts identified
_____	_____	5. Instructional objectives prepared and an estimated teaching time identified
_____	_____	6. Suggested teaching strategies described for each objective
_____	_____	7. Examples of evaluation procedures completed
_____	_____	8. Suggested learning resources identified

_____ The Age of Discovery
_____ The Early Colonial Period
_____ The Late Colonial Period
_____ The Revolutionary War Period
_____ Articles of Confederation to Constitution

[Note: This is an example of an attitude inventory that can be given twice, once at the beginning of the unit and once at the end. The hope is that students, on average, will rate their interest in the American Revolution higher at the end than at the beginning. Students need to be told that their responses will have no bearing whatever on their grades.] Box 14.4 contains a unit-development checklist.

Suggested Learning Resources

BOOKS: GENERAL REFERENCE

Bliss, George A. *The American Revolution: How Revolutionary Was It?* New York: Harper and Row, 1980.

Carrington, Henry B. *Battle Maps and Charts of the American Revolution.* Salem, N.H. Ayer Company, Publishers, 1974.

*Fast, Howard. *Citizen Tom Paine.* 2nd edition. New York: Grove Press, 1983.

Gephart, Ronald E. (ed.). *Revolutionary America.* Washington, DC: United States Government Printing Office, 1984.

Lancaster, Bruce. *The American Revolution.* Boston: Houghton-Mifflin Company, 1986.

*Meltzer, Milton. *The American Revolutionaries: A History in Their Own Words.* New York: Harper and Row Junior Books, 1987.

Miller, John E. *Triumph of Freedom.* Westport, CT: Greenwood Press, 1979.

Smith, Barbara. *After the Revolution: The Smithsonian History of Everyday Life in the 18th Century.* New York: Pantheon Books, 1987.

York, Neil L. *Mechanical Metamorphosis: Technological Change in Revolutionary America.* Westport, CT: Greenwood Press, 1985.

[*Books marked with an asterisk are of primary interest to students. Others may be of interest both to teachers and students.]

BOOKS: SCHOOL TEXTS

Boorstin, Daniel J. and Brooks M. Kelley. *History of the United States.* Lexington, Massachusetts: Ginn and Company, 1986.

Green, Robert P. and Laura L. Becker. *American Tradition.* Columbus, OH: Merrill Publishing Company, 1986.

May, Ernest and others. *American People.* Evanston, IL: McDougal-Littell, 1986.

Patrick, John and Carole Berkin. *History of the American Nation.* New York: Macmillan Publishing Company, 1987.

Todd, Lewis Paul and Merle Curti. *Triumph of the American Nation.* Orlando, FL: Harcourt, Brace, Jovanovich, 1986.

OVERHEAD TRANSPARENCIES

"The Revolutionary War." Set of 12 color transparencies. Available from: Social Studies School Service, P.O. Box 802, Culver City, CA 90232-0802.

REPRODUCIBLE SPIRIT MASTERS

"Activities for Students—the Colonial and Revolutionary Periods: 1492–1789." 50 spirit masters or 50 photocopy masters. Available from: J. Weston Walch, Box 658, Portland, ME 04104-0658.

16MM FILM

"Prelude to Revolution." 13-minute-long film. Available from: Encyclopedia Britannica Educational Corporation, 425 N. Michigan Avenue, Chicago, IL 60611.

VIDEOCASSETTE

"The American Revolution." Available from: Guidance Associates, Communications Park Box 3,000, Mt. Kisco, NY 10549.

SOUND FILMSTRIPS

"America Rises: From Colonies to Nation." 5 color filmstrips and 5 accompanying cassette tapes. Available from Encyclopedia Britannica Educational Corporation, 425 N. Michigan Avenue, Chicago, IL 60611.

"The American Revolution: Two Views." 4 color filmstrips and 4 accompanying cassette tapes. Available from Social Studies School Service, P.O. Box 802, Culver City, CA 90232-0802.

COMPUTER SOFTWARE

"The American Revolution." Tutorial and quiz on highlights of the American Revolution. 3 diskettes. Available for Apple computers only. Available from Social Studies School Service, P.O. Box 802, Culver City, CA 90232-0802.

"Revolutionary War: Choosing Sides." Computer-based role- playing exercise. 1 diskette. Available in either Apple or IBM- PC formats. Available from Social Studies School Service, P.O. Box 802, Culver City, CA 90232-0802.

SIMULATION

"Independence: A Simulation." Involves students in a simulation of events surrounding the Revolutionary War. Available from Social Studies School Service, P.O. Box 802, Culver City, CA 90232-0802.

POSTERS

"American Patriot Posters." Set of 10 color posters of such Revolutionary War-era patriots as Franklin, Revere, and Washington. Available from Social Studies School Service, P.O. Box 802, Culver City, CA 90232-0802.

Key Ideas in Summary

1. Instructional units are an important planning vehicle. They contain information about instruction related to a given topic within a course. They vary greatly in length; however, many secondary units consume

from two to three weeks' instructional time. They provide a general framework for instruction to which teachers can refer as they prepare individual lessons.

2. Instructional units vary in terms of the information they contain. Information can be formatted in a variety of ways. Many units include a goal statement, some focus generalizations, a list of instructional objectives, suggested teaching strategies, suggested assessment procedures, and a list of learning resources.

3. A number of decisions must be made during the instructional unit-planning process. Unit development often requires that decisions be made regarding (a) selecting a title; (b) identifying a major goal; (c) checking mandated-content regulations; (d) identifying major generalizations and concepts; (e) developing instructional objectives and allocating teaching time; (f) performing a task analysis; (g) selecting instructional strategies for each objective; (h) identifying evaluation procedures; and (i) identifying learning resources.

4. There are two general sources of instructional units. Some are available from commercial firms. Others are developed by individual teachers or groups of teachers. In general, those that are teacher-developed describe programs that are better fitted to the students who will be taught unit content. This is true because teachers are better positioned to understand characteristics of their own students than are commercial firms who may have little grasp of local conditions.

5. Generally, unit developers try to avoid highly prescriptive language in their units. Often units will contain qualifiers such as "suggested strategies" or "suggested assessment procedures." The idea is to provide some general guidelines for individuals who will teach the content, but not to insist that a specific set of approaches is the only one that will work. The frequent use of the term "suggested" invites users to modify their approaches in light of their own judgments about what is best for their students.

POSTTEST

DIRECTIONS: Using your own paper, answer these true/false questions. For each correct statement, write the word "true." For each incorrect statement, write the word "false."

_____ 1. Unit instructional objectives tend to describe what students should be able to do as a result of instruction with more precision than do unit goals.

_____ 2. Instructional units developed by teachers who will use them tend to describe programs that are better suited to the needs of students in those teachers' classrooms than do commercially-prepared units.

_____ 3. It is not unusual to find a list of suggested instructional strategies in an instructional unit plan.

_____ 4. Scholars have found that concepts included in instructional units vary little in their complexity.

_____ 5. Generally teachers prefer to teach units developed by others rather than units developed by themselves.

Bibliography

ARMSTRONG, DAVID G. *Developing and Documenting the Curriculum.* Boston: Allyn and Bacon, 1989.

DENTON, JON J.; ARMSTRONG, DAVID G.; AND SAVAGE, TOM V. "Matching Events of Instruction to Objectives." *Theory Into Practice* (Winter 1980): pp. 10–14.

DICK, WALTER AND CAREY, LOU. *The Systematic Design of Instruction.* New York: Nichols Publications, 1984.

GAGNE, ROBERT M. AND BRIGGS, LESLIE J. *Principles of Instructional Design.* New York: Holt, Rinehart, and Winston, Inc., 1974.

KEMP, JERROLD E. *The Instructional Design Process.* New York: Harper and Row Publishers, Inc., 1985.

POSNER, GEORGE S. "Pacing and Sequencing." In Michael J. Dunkin (ed.). *The International Encyclopedia of Teaching and Teacher Education.* Oxford, England: Pergamon Press, 1987. pp. 266–272.

ROMIZOWSKI, A. J. *Producing Instructional Systems.* New York: Nichols Publications, 1984.

CHAPTER 15

Sequencing Instruction: Lesson Planning

AIMS

This chapter provides information to help the reader to:

1. Recognize that some sequences of instruction have more potential for promoting learning than others.
2. Describe features of several schemes for sequencing instruction.
3. Point out how principles of instructional sequencing are followed in preparing a lesson plan.
4. Recognize common features of lesson plans.
5. Develop a lesson plan format.
6. Prepare a complete lesson plan that follows a prescribed format.

PRETEST

DIRECTIONS: Using your own paper, answer these true/false questions. For each correct statement, write the word "true." For each incorrect statement, write the word "false."

_____ 1. Concern for sequencing instruction is an issue that has begun to interest educators only in the last 30 years.

_____ 2. A chronological approach to sequencing is often followed in history lessons.

_____ 3. Lesson plans always involve plans for instruction that last no longer than a single class period.

_____ 4. Many lesson plans include information relating both to what the teacher will be doing and what the students will be doing as the lesson is taught.

_____ 5. Lesson plans sometimes include ideas for enrichment activities that are to be made available to able students.

Introduction

Instructional units provide general guidelines for teaching a course topic that may last several weeks. Lesson plans focus on shorter time periods. They provide quite specific information about how content introduced in one or more class sessions will be organized, sequenced, and delivered.

Some school districts have policies requiring teachers to prepare and maintain files of lesson plans. Administrators may use lesson plans to verify that teachers are covering content mandated by state law or local policy.

Even where there are no stringent requirements placed on teachers to develop and keep formal lesson plans, many experienced teachers prepare them. They do this because the process of lesson planning helps them organize instruction. The thought that goes into lesson planning tends to result in purposeful and effective teaching. Additionally, completed lesson plans can help teachers keep on task. For example, if during a spirited discussion the teacher temporarily forgets his or her place, the situation can be quickly remedied by a glance at the lesson plan.

Though lesson plans are often provided by textbook publishers and other commercial sources, most teachers develop their own. While individual teachers may borrow ideas from lesson plans developed commercially or by other teachers, they usually find lesson plans they develop themselves to be more responsive to the special needs of their own students. The ability to prepare lesson plans is one of the professional skills teachers are expected to have when they assume their first positions.

Preparation of good lesson plans requires familiarity with some important sequencing approaches. Several of these are introduced in

Instructional planning is an important teacher responsibility. *Photo courtesy of Mimi Forsyth/Monkmeyer Press Photo Service.*

the next section. This section is followed by a discussion of several more sophisticated sequencing schemes that have evolved from these basic approaches. Another major chapter section focuses on the issue of lesson plan formatting. An example is provided of a complete lesson plan that has been developed according to a format that includes elements common to many lesson plans.

Basic Approaches to Sequencing Lesson Content

Lesson planners base sequencing decisions on a limited number of basic sequencing approaches. Among them are (1) the chronological approach, (2) the part-to-whole approach, (3) the whole-to-part approach, (4) the topical approach, and (5) the mixed approach.

The Chronological Approach

As the name suggests, time is the key to sequencing lesson content when a chronological approach is selected. Chronological sequencing makes sense only when the lesson deals with content that can logically be tied to different time periods. The sequence most frequently features introduction of "older" content before "newer" content. On some occasions, teachers find it appropriate to reverse the sequence.

Chronological sequencing often is selected as an approach to sequencing content to be introduced in a history lesson. (However, the chronological approach certainly is not the only sequencing approach history teachers use in planning lessons.) Chronological sequencing may also be appropriate for teaching lessons in other subjects. For example, an English lesson focusing on the development of different rhyme schemes over time might be chronologically sequenced.

The Part-to-Whole Approach

Part-to-whole sequencing of lesson content features introduction of simple, less complex content before more difficult and more complex content. The idea is to build students' confidence by introducing them first to lesson material that can be easily understood. Mastery of this material leads logically to more complex understandings that require a solid grounding in the more basic information.

For example, in a chemistry lesson focusing on teaching students how to balance equations, it is common for teachers to begin with quite simple equations. The teacher takes time to explain to students exactly how the process works and to respond to questions. Only after this basic information is in hand does the teacher proceed to introduce students to more complex balancing problems. The ability to solve these problems depends on students' understanding principles introduced earlier in the lesson when less complex examples were presented.

"We will now consider pre-articulated, written, behavioral objective, clarified, instructional equipment selected, process orientation planned, teaching/learning strategy codifications. Or, as some people call them, lesson plan books."

Part-to-whole sequencing is featured in lessons prepared for many secondary school subjects. The approach is suitable for any lesson having content that can be easily broken down into relatively simple parts. Once this task is accomplished, the teacher simply sequences the lesson in such a way that relatively simple and easy information is taught before students are challenged with more sophisticated and complex content.

The Whole-to-Part Approach

The whole-to-part approach reverses the general pattern featured in the part-to-whole approach. A whole-to-part lesson may begin with a broad overview of what is to be covered. The idea is to provide students with a good context for learning. By providing them with the "big picture" first, teachers hope that the more detailed information to follow will make better sense. This general overview is followed by introduction of more specific information. The specific information allows students to better understand components that go together to make up the "whole" to which they have been introduced during the first part of the lesson.

Whole-to-part sequencing may be used in planning lessons for many secondary school subjects. For example, in geography, this sequence may be appropriate for an introductory lesson on "Political Divisions of North America." The lesson might begin with an overview of the continent with special attention to political boundaries. With this information as a background, the teacher might then involve students in activities that would focus their attention on a number of specific political divisions existing at various places within the continental "whole." The purpose of such a sequence would be to highlight the individual political divisions in terms of how they relate to the continent-wide pattern.

The Topical Approach

Sometimes, content of a lesson consists of a number of topics that are relatively independent of one another. When this is the case, the decision about which to teach first is left purely to the discretion of the teacher. When a topical approach to sequencing is taken, there is an assumption that the order in which topics are introduced will have little influence on student learning.

For example, secondary science teachers often teach a lesson early in the semester that is designed to orient students to the science laboratory. Such a lesson will frequently feature a number of topics such as (1)

Box 15.1

Sequencing Content: Basic Approaches

Select a topic from a subject you might like to teach. Suppose you were going to develop a lesson focusing on a certain aspect of this topic. Lay out at least two alternative content sequences based on two or more of the following approaches.

1. The Chronological Approach.
2. The Part-to-Whole Approach.
3. The Whole-to-Part Approach.
4. The Topical Approach.
5. The Mixed Approach.

Ask your instructor to review and critique your response to this exercise.

---

equipment storage, (2) safety procedures, and (3) responsibilities of lab partners. None of these topics must necessarily precede or follow any of the others. Teachers could logically sequence them in any order.

The Mixed Approach

Often, sequencing in lessons reflects a combination of basic approaches. For example, a lesson in English might provide students with a brief introduction to both American poetry and drama during the 1890s. Content could be sequenced in several ways. One option might be to follow this order: (a) 1890–1894: American poetry; (b) 1890–1894: American drama; (c) 1895–1899: American poetry; (d) 1895–1899: American drama. This sequence reflects a combination of a chronological approach and a topical approach. Box 15.1 is an exercise in sequencing content.

Formal Sequencing Approaches

The basic sequencing approaches provide a general intellectual backdrop for more formal sequencing approaches. These more formal approaches describe in considerable detail what should be done first, second, third, fourth, and so forth as a lesson develops. The idea behind these formal approaches is that some sequences will result in better student learning than others. This position has long historic standing.

Centuries ago, the ancient Spartans recognized that it was critical for students to grasp certain highly important information. Teachers in Sparta developed a four-part learning sequence that worked well with many of their learners. Teachers were advised to (1) introduce material to be learned, (2) ask students to think about the information, (3) repeat the material again and work individually with students until they believed they had it memorized, and (4) listen to students as they recited the material (Posner 1987).

In Ancient Sparta there was a limited quantity of information students were expected to know. There was widespread agreement on what this information was. There was little change in the nature of this information over time. Students were expected to know material well enough to repeat it flawlessly from memory. Given these assumptions and expectations, this suggested sequence worked well.

Centuries later, Roman Catholic schools run by the Jesuits developed quite another set of guidelines for teachers in their schools. The Jesuits called on teachers to (1) begin instruction by presenting information slowly enough for students to take notes; (2) pause periodically to explain difficult parts of new content; (3) relate new material to other subjects; (4) ask students to memorize the new material; (5) assign monitors to work with individual students and check on their recitations of memorized material; (6) conclude with a discussion and an interpretation of the meaning of the new content; and (7) reward the best-performing students to provide an incentive for further learning (Posner 1987).

Still another set of guidelines was introduced in the 19th century by the famous learning theorist Johann Friederich Herbart. Herbart's theory of "apperception" suggested that learning takes place when ideas that are already in the mind contact other ideas. If there is a logical relationship between existing ideas and new information, then this new information more easily becomes part of a person's store of knowledge. This view provided an important rationale for diagnosing learners to determine what they already knew. The purpose was to determine whether there was some relationship between existing knowledge and content that was about to be introduced.

Herbart developed a five-part sequence of instruction. Its purpose was to ensure that teachers presented lessons in a way consistent with his views of how learning occurs. The steps in Herbart's recommended sequence are: (1) preparation, (2) presentation, (3) association (tying new information to old information), (4) generalization (stating broad applications of knowledge), and (5) application (Meyer 1975).

Herbart's theory of apperception has been displaced by more contemporary learning theories. However, his five-step plan for sequencing lesson content still is widely used because the steps are consistent with many modern views of learning as well as with the apperceptionist position from which they originally evolved.

Suggested guidelines for sequencing lesson content continue to be developed. One that has attracted a wide following was introduced in 1977 by Madeline Hunter and Douglas Russell. They suggested that a sequence of instruction should follow these basic steps: (1) anticipatory set (taking action to help students focus their attention on the instruction to follow); (2) objective and purpose (taking action to help students understand what they will be able to do as a consequence of their exposure to the lesson); (3) instructional input (conveying relevant content to students); (4) modeling (providing students with examples of what they should be able to do as a result of the lesson); (5) checking for understanding (taking action to ensure students have information they will need to master the objective); (6) guided practice (monitoring students as they begin work on tasks asking them to apply new content); and (7) independent practice (assigning students to use new content under conditions where they will not have the benefit of direct teacher assistance) (Hunter and Russell 1977, pp. 86–88).

Another sequencing scheme, based on the work of Gagne and Briggs (1974), was introduced by Denton, Armstrong, and Savage (1980). This sequence features these steps: (1) emphasizing objectives (advising students about what they will be expected to be able to do as a result of exposure to the lesson); (2) motivating learning (working to establish students' interest in the lesson's content); (3) recalling previous learning (helping students recognize the connection between what they have learned previously and the new material); (4) presenting new information (introducing students to the new content); (5) recognizing key points (helping students to differentiate between highly important information and less-important information); (6) applying new information (providing students with opportunities to use new information); and (7) assessing new learning (taking action to evaluate what students have learned and to provide feedback to them in light of this evaluation) (Denton, Armstrong, and Savage 1980, pp. 10–14). Box 15.2 is a formal sequencing exercise.

Though there are differences among the sequencing schemes that have been introduced here, certain common features are shared by several of them. For example, an emphasis on having students "do something" with new content is a recurring theme. Similarly, the idea that teachers should monitor students' performances to check for understanding is common to several of these sequencing models. The similarity of "steps" in more recent sequencing schemes such as those introduced by Hunter and Russell (1977) and Denton, Armstrong, and Savage (1980), reflects their research base. Teacher-effectiveness researchers have consistently found improved student learning to be associated with lessons that allow students to apply what they have learned and with lessons featuring careful teacher monitoring of their progress (Good and Brophy 1987).

Box 15.2

Formal Sequencing Exercise

A number of formal sequencing approaches have been developed. Formats suggested by Hunter and Russell (1977) and by Denton, Armstrong, and Savage (1980) are widely used. These two formats (and many other formal sequencing approaches, too) share many common features.

Select a topic you might wish to teach. Sequence a lesson focusing on this topic using the Hunter and Russell format. Next, sequence a lesson with the same content using the Denton, Armstrong, and Savage format. Then, respond to these questions:

1. In what ways did you find the two sequencing approaches different?
2. In what ways did you find the two sequencing approaches similar?
3. Which of the two approaches did you find easier to use?
4. Do you think you would have any problem using another sequencing scheme should your school district have adopted one different from either the Hunter and Russell format or the Denton, Armstrong, and Savage format?

Formatting Lesson Plans

Lesson plans specify what is to be accomplished during a given lesson that is presented as part of a unit. Lessons often last for only a single instructional period. Some lessons, however, may last longer. Only rarely will a single lesson cover a time longer than two successive class periods.

Lesson plans contain quite detailed information about what will be happening in the classroom during the time period covered. A number of formats have been developed for organizing this information. Though there are many place-to-place variations, a number of elements are common to many lesson plans. Lesson plans frequently include major headings such as the following:

1. Lesson topic.
2. Lesson purpose.
3. Long-term objective.
4. Lesson objective.
5. Relevant mandated content.
6. Suggested sequence of instruction.

7. Suggestions for meeting special needs.

8. Suggested lesson evaluation procedures.

9. Needed learning resources.

Lesson Topic

This component of the lesson plan is self-explanatory. It is simply a statement that succinctly labels the content to be taught. The need to identify a specific lesson topic helps teachers to think carefully about the central focus of their lesson. The topic places important "boundaries" around what is to be covered and helps teachers "stay on track" as subsequent elements of the lesson are planned.

Lesson Purpose

The lesson purpose consists of a brief statement about the aims of the lesson. This section of the lesson plan is designed to communicate the general intent of the lesson to a principal, another teacher, a parent, or some other interested party. Lesson-purpose statements are short; often one or two sentences will suffice.

Long-term Objective

Often, individual lessons are part of an instructional unit. When this is the case, the lesson plan makes reference to the unit instructional objective that provides the focus for the lesson. Sometimes the relevant unit objective may be referenced only by number (e.g., Long-term Objective: 3). Some lesson developers prefer to write out the relevant objective in its entirety. It is not always the case that an individual lesson will relate to only one unit objective. When a lesson provides learning experiences related to several objectives, each is referenced in the lesson plan.

Lesson Objective

Lesson content often ties to a specific unit instructional objective. Additionally, each lesson includes a narrower objective that relates specifically to the material it introduces. This is the lesson objective.

The lesson objective helps the writer of the lesson plan to maintain a focus on activities that will help students to maintain a focus on activities that will help students learn the material. When a lesson is part of an instructional unit, mastery of the lesson objective represents a check on students' progress toward mastery of the broader objective(s) in the instructional unit.

Box 15.3

Dealing with Mandated Content in Lessons

Some states, districts, and even individual schools have regulations regarding what kind of information must be taught to students in different courses. Ask your instructor whether your state has any requirements mandating that certain content be taught. Then, respond to these questions:

1. If there are state content requirements, do any of these requirements refer to content commonly taught in a course you might teach? If yes, cite some examples.

2. If there are no state mandates in your state or if mandates do not affect your subject area, would you favor that the local school district or your own school develop some "required" elements of content for each course? If your answer is "yes," cite some examples of kinds of things you would like to see required in your own subject area.

3. What are your personal reactions to the idea of mandating content? What are strengths and weaknesses of mandated content regulations? Why do you think so?

Relevant Mandated Content

Some states, districts, and schools have policies that require certain elements of content in certain courses. For example, there might be a requirement that all beginning algebra classes provide students with opportunities "to work with linear equations to graph equations and inequalities." If part of the lesson were designed to provide students with this kind of experience, then this relevant mandated content would be noted on the lesson plan. This information provides documentation to verify that mandated content is being taught. (See Box 15.3.)

Suggested Sequence of Instruction

Often the suggested-sequence-of-instruction section is the most lengthy part of a lesson plan. Some lesson plans take a rather informal approach to this lesson plan feature. They simply list some of the things the teacher will be doing as the lesson is introduced. Others follow one of the formal sequencing approaches, for example the scheme developed by Hunter and Russell (1977) or the scheme introduced by Denton, Armstrong, and Savage (1980). The purpose of this part of the lesson plan is to describe in a quite explicit fashion what will be done at different points during the time the lesson is being taught.

Some teachers prefer to describe only what the teacher will be doing. Others find it useful also to describe what students will be doing at each step of the lesson's development. Inclusion of this information in the lesson plan serves as a prompt to them to remind students to do specific things at appropriate times during the lesson.

Suggestions for Meeting Special Needs

There are many differences among students in secondary school classrooms. This section of the lesson plan, when it is included, provides suggestions for dealing with some important individual differences. For example, there may be some ideas for providing additional learning experiences for very bright students. Similarly, there may be suggestions for transmitting content to learners who are poor readers. There may be mention of possible "reteaching" techniques to be used with students who fail to grasp the content as it is initially presented in the lesson.

Often, the content of this section of the lesson plan reflects the priorities of the lesson plan developer. In some places, school districts may have specific requirements regarding kinds of information that must be included.

Suggested Lesson Evaluation Procedures

The suggested lesson evaluation procedures describe what the teacher intends to do to check on students' grasp of the material that has been introduced in the lesson. Ordinarily this is not a formal test. It may involve asking students questions about new content, asking them to prepare something using new information, or requiring them to solve problems using techniques that have been presented. Suggestions in this part of the lesson plan prompt the teacher to take deliberate action to determine how well students have grasped what has been taught.

Needed Learning Resources

One of the most frustrating experiences teachers face is finding themselves well-launched into a new lesson only to discover that they lack some needed equipment or materials. The needed-learning-resources section of the lesson plan is designed to eliminate this unpleasant experience. This part of the degree plan lists information sources for students and needed support equipment. Careful thought about these issues at the lesson-planning stage can greatly diminish problems when the lesson is taught.

A Sample Lesson Plan

The lesson plan sample introduced here includes each of the elements described in the previous section. This format is not the only one teachers use, but it is a reasonably representative example.

There is no intent to suggest that the content presented and organized in this lesson represents the only way this information could have been presented. The purpose of this example is simply to suggest an organizational scheme. Another teacher might have employed the same format to transmit the basic information using different instructional procedures.

Note that the developers of this lesson plan chose to lay out an instructional sequence that follows the Hunter and Russell (1977) approach. Material in this section could just as easily have been organized to be consistent with the Denton, Armstrong, and Savage (1980) scheme or with some other approach.

Topic: American Advantages and Disadvantages at the Beginning of the Revolutionary War.

Purpose: To develop students' critical thinking skills by having them compare and contrast American advantages and disadvantages at the beginning of the Revolutionary War.

Long-term Objective(s): [See "Critical Thinking Skills," State Competency 36].

Lesson Objective: At the conclusion of this lesson, each student, defending his or her choice with supporting evidence, will identify at least two advantages and two disadvantages faced by the Americans at the beginning of the Revolutionary War.

Relevant Mandated Content(s): State Key Concepts 28.1; 32.4; 32.6 [under "Concepts Related to Conflict"].

Sequence of Activities

1. To capture students' attention and to help them begin to think about the issue of comparative advantage, contrast strengths and weaknesses of "smooth bore" and "rifled" weapons (anticipatory set).

2. To help students as they begin thinking about conditions faced by opposing sides at the beginning of wars, point out that opposing sides often start with different advantages and disadvantages. Explain that this lesson will look at these advantages/disadvantages (objective and purpose).

3. Begin with a short lecture focusing on two or three American military strengths and weaknesses at the beginning of the Revolutionary War. Explain how these influenced the behavior of the American forces during the early fighting (instructional input). Next, conduct a brainstorming activity. Ask students to develop a list of some other possible American advantages and disadvantages at the beginning of the Revolutionary War. Ask students to make a copy of this list.

4. Have students check the accuracy of information on their lists by referring to library resources gathered in the room. Take one item on the list the students developed during the brainstorming activity. Talk the class through the procedure of using the library resources to check on its accuracy (modeling). Ask one or two students to repeat in their own words the procedures to be followed (checking for understanding). Divide the class into several groups. Ask each group to work with the library resources to determine the accuracy of one or two items from the list developed during the brainstorming activity. Additionally, ask each group to suggest one implication for American strategy that might have resulted from one of the documented advantages or disadvantages. Monitor students as they do this activity (guided practice). Assign one member from each group to share findings with the class.

5. Ask each student to write an editorial titled "American Prospects for Victory: How Good?" (independent practice).

Meeting Special Needs

A. *More able students:* Organize a debate to be presented to the class: "Resolved that the Americans had more advantages than disadvantages at the beginning of the Revolutionary War."

B. *Slow learners; poor readers:* Provide a short typed summary, no more than two to three pages in length, of American advantages and disadvantages at the beginning of the Revolutionary War.

C. *Reteaching:* Work with students to fill in ideas on a blank retrieval chart with "American Advantages" and "American Disadvantages" as the major headings.

Box 15.4

An Example of Sequencing Using the Denton, Armstrong, and Savage (1980) Format

The sample lesson provided in this chapter illustrates how content might be sequenced using the Hunter Russell (1977) format. There are other sequencing schemes that would have worked equally well. One of these was introduced by Denton, Armstrong, and Savage (1980). The material introduced here demonstrates how the "suggested sequence of instruction" section of the sample lesson plan might have looked had it been formatted according to the Denton, Armstrong, and Savage approach.

1. *Emphasizing Objectives.* Point out to students that in nearly all wars each side starts with certain advantages and disadvantages. Explain that this lesson is designed to help them understand American advantages and disadvantages at the beginning of the Revolutionary War.

2. *Motivating Learners.* Explain to students that weaponry played an important part in the American victory in the Revolutionary War. Display diagrams showing the interior of a shotgun and a rifle. Point out the smooth bore of the shotgun and the "rifling" of the rifle. Ask questions such as these:

   a. Why is there a difference in the interior of the shotgun barrel and the rifle barrel?

   b. Which would be the better weapon if the objective was to hit distant targets?

Explain that many fighting on the American side used rifles, a weapon usefule for engaging the enemy at a distance. The British, on the other hand, tended to favor muskets. As do present-day shotguns, muskets used by the British have smooth bores. Ask students to think about the British use of the musket.

   a. What did the musket suggest about the nature of fighting that the British expected? (Point out the expectation of close engagement of forces where great accuracy was not necessary.)

   b. How might the American rifle have been an American advantage in the war? (Solicit student ideas.)

3. *Recalling Previous Learning.* Remind students of difficulties faced by the British troops in the French and Indian War. Point out that the Indian allies of the French knew the terrain better than the British. Explain that this was an "advantage" for the Indians and a "disadvantage" for the British. Ask students to recall what problems this disadvantage produced for the British during the early years of the French and Indian War. Conclude with a discussion of this general question: "Does each side always begin a war with some advantages and some disadvantages?"

4. *Presenting New Information.* Provide a short lecture focusing on strengths and weaknesses of the American mili-

Box 15.4 *cont.*

tary forces at the beginning of the war. Emphasize such points as these:

Strengths

- not constrained by tradition to use only a few predictable tactics
- good knowledge of the terrain
- willingness to use rifles, not muskets
- large population familiar with use of firearms

    Weaknesses

- no formal standing army at the beginning of the war
- troops not willing to take orders
- little assurance that soldiers would receive their wages regularly
- few trained as professional soldiers

    Follow this lecture with a brainstorming exercise. Write "advantages" and "disadvantages" on the chalkboard. Write down student ideas under each column during the brainstorming activity. Leave this information on the board for use later in the lesson.

5. *Recognizing Key Points.*   Randomly select one or two students. Ask each to explain what is meant by a "disadvantages" and an "advantage." Have each student provide an example of one American disadvantage and one American advantage at the beginning of the Revolutionary War. Clarify any misunderstandings.

6. *Applying New Information.* Explain to students that they will be working in groups to identify American disadvantages and advantages at the beginning of the Revolutionary War. Write the words "advantages" and "disad-

vantages" on a blank page sheet of overhead projector acetate.

Explain to students that their task will be to use the text and other available resources (handouts, reprints of articles, library books on the revolution, filmstrips set up with a projector in a back-of-the room carrel, and so forth) to identify American advantages and disadvantages. Point out locations of these resources, describe one American "advantage" and one American "disadvantage." Explain why you have categorized each item under its respective heading. Tell students that you will be asking them to seek out and explin information about advantages and disadvantages using resources available in the classroom.

Randomly select one or two students. Ask them to repeat back the general instructions they are to follow. Be sure that all class members understand that their task will be to (a) use available learning resources in the classroom as they (b) identify and list both "advantages" and "disadvantage" of the Americans at the beginning of the Revolutionary War and (c) understand why each listed item was either a "disadvantages" or an "advantage."

Divide class members into groups having approximately five students each. Assign each group to work with their texts and other information resources with information about the American Revolution. Ask each group to develop lists of American "disadvantages" and "advantages" at the beginning of the Revolutionary War.

Box 15.4 *cont.*

Ask students to use the lists of ideas on the chalkboard that were generated during the brainstorming exercise at the beginning of the lesson. Ask them to find information that either supports the accuracy of these ideas or that suggests they are inaccurate. Each group should prepare a revised list of "disadvantages" and "advantages." The revised lists will consist of (a) ideas from the original brainstorming list for which supporting evidence was found in the resources and (b) new ideas not included on the brainstorming list but that were suggested from working with the learning resources.

Conclude by asking a member of each group to share the group's list with the class. As representatives for each group report, prepare a master list of "disadvantages" and "ad-

vantages" on the chalkboard. Lead a discussion focusing on the relative importance of each item on the final list.

7. *Assessing New Learning.* Ask students to write a short simulated newspaper editorial on this topic: "American Prospects for Victory: How Good?" Students are to presume that are writing this editorial at the very beginning of the Revolutionary War. Their task is to weigh American "disadvantages" and "advantages" to support their conclusion. Point out to students that they are to prepare their editorials as if they had no knowledge of the final outcome of the war. Review editorials, correct errors, and provide suggestions to students.

Lesson Evaluation

Provide students with a mixed list of items, some of them representing advantages and some of them representing disadvantages for the Americans at the beginning of the Revolutionary War. Ask students to identify the advantage and the disadvantage. Ask them to cite reasons for their choices.

Needed Resources

Course text, supplementary texts, and library resources including books, periodicals, filmstrips, and other materials with information about American advantages and disadvantages at the beginning of the Revolutionary War. Among specific items to be included will be texts by Boorstin and Brooks, Garraty, and Patrick and Berkin; the filmstrip "America Rises from Colony to Nation"; and selected articles from *American Heritage, American History Illustrated, Military History*.

Key Ideas in Summary

1. Lesson plans focus on shorter periods of time than do instructional unit plans. They provide information about how content will be introduced over one or two class periods. Only rarely are lesson plans designed to cover a longer period of instructional time.

2. Most lesson plans are developed by the teachers who use them. Though lesson plans are available from commercial sources, these commercial plans do not generally respond as well to unique conditions characterizing individual classrooms as do those created by the individuals who will implement them.

3. A number of basic approaches to sequencing content have evolved. Among these sequences are the following: (a) the chronological approach; (b) the part-to-whole approach; (c) the whole-to-part approach; (d) the topical approach; and (e) the mixed approach.

4. Formal sequencing approaches build on several basic approaches. They provide quite specific guidelines as to the kinds of things teachers should do first, second, third, and so forth in introducing content to learners. The issue of formal sequencing has a centuries-old history. Modern examples, including formats suggested by Hunter and Russell (1977) and Denton, Armstrong, and Savage (1980), are rooted in the results of teacher-effectiveness research.

5. A number of formats have been developed for organizing the content of lesson plans. Though individual formats vary, many of them share some common features. One example of a lesson plan format includes these components: (a) lesson topic; (b) lesson purpose; (c) relevant mandated content; (f) suggested sequence of instruction; (g) suggestions for meeting special needs; (h) suggested lesson evaluation procedures; and (i) needed learning resources.

POSTTEST

DIRECTIONS: Using your own paper, answer these true/false questions. For each correct statement, write the word "true". For each incorrect statement, write the word "false".

_____ 1. Today, the belief that some instructional sequences are better than others has been generally discredited.

_____ 2. It is possible to combine a thematic approach and a chronological approach to sequencing in a single lesson.

_____ 3. An individual lesson plan typically will include a listing of all instructional objectives related to the instructional unit that is being taught.

_____ 4. Lesson plans ordinarily do not make reference to needed learning materials.

_____ 5. Teachers usually buy their lesson plans from commercial sources.

Bibliography

DENTON, JON J.; ARMSTRONG, DAVID G.; AND SAVAGE, TOM V. "Matching Events of Instruction to Objectives." *Theory Into Practice* (Winter 1980); pp. 10–14.

GOOD, T. L. AND BROPHY, J. E. *Looking in Classrooms.* 4th edition. New York: Harper and Row, Publishers, 1987.

HUNTER, MADELINE AND RUSSELL, DOUGLAS. "How Can I Plan More Effective Lessons?" *Instructor* (September 1977), pp. 74–75; 88.

LOGGINS, DENNIS; COWAN, RAY; DALIS, GUS; AND STRASSER, BEN. "Elephants Are Easier to Recognize than Good Lessons." *Thrust for Educational Leadership* (October 1986), pp. 40–43.

MEYER, ADOLPHE E. *Grandmasters of Educational Thought.* New York: McGraw-Hill Book Company, 1975.

POSNER, GEORGE S. "Pacing and Sequencing." In Michael J. Dunkin (ed.). *The International Encyclopedia of Teaching and Teacher Education.* Oxford, England: Pergamon Press, 1987. pp. 266–272.

PART IV

Instructional Concerns

CHAPTER 16

Dealing with Exceptional Learners

AIMS

This chapter provides information to help the reader to:

1. List events that have contributed to the increased diversity of learners found in secondary classrooms.
2. Define the problems that might cause a student to be classified as a slow learner.
3. Identify concrete actions that can be taken to help accommodate the needs of slow learners.
4. List the measures that can be taken to help students with limited English proficiency.
5. State how the treatment of handicapped students has changed.
6. Define the basic provisions of Public Law 94-142.
7. Identify specific actions that can be taken to accommodate different handicapping conditions.
8. Describe some concerns of individuals who have not supported special programs for gifted and talented students.
9. Define two basic approaches that have been used to meet the needs of gifted and talented students.

PRETEST

DIRECTIONS: Using your own paper, answer these true/false questions. For each correct statement, write the word "true." For each incorrect statement, write the word "false."

_____ 1. Secondary schools in the United States have always placed a priority on developing programs to provide educational experiences for students with special needs.

_____ 2. Development of gifted and talented programs has sometimes been hindered because of a perception that they are elitist and discriminatory.

_____ 3. Slow learners in the classroom are easily accommodated by simply slowing down the pace of instruction.

_____ 4. Public Law 94-142 mandated the creation of special classrooms for all handicapped learners.

_____ 5. The "acceleration approach" to gifted and talented education is the most popular approach.

Introduction

The last students were filing out of the building at the end of the day. First-year teacher Jorge Maldonado slumped in the chair behind his desk. He fought exhaustion as he tried to prepare himself mentally to plan tomorrow's classes. He did not look forward to the process. To date, he had been less than satisfied with his own performance. No matter what he tried, some students simply didn't seem interested.

Feelings such as Jorge Maldonado's are common among beginning teachers. A major contributor to their frustration is the unexpected student diversity they find in their classrooms. Though many beginning teachers come from fine preparation programs that have provided excellent information about the range of students in today's schools, learning about this diversity in the congenial atmosphere of a college classroom is quite different from confronting it every day as a teacher.

Differences among students in secondary students today are more profound than they have ever been. Middle schools, junior high schools, and senior high schools enroll students from many cultural and linguistic backgrounds. Intelligence levels vary enormously. Every socio-economic stratum in the nation is represented. In recent years, organized groups have recognized that some kinds of students within this diverse mix have not been well served by the "traditional" secondary school program. Their efforts have resulted in attempts to provide special kinds of educational services directed at students with special needs. Among these are needs of slow learners, students with various handicapping conditions, gifted and talented students, and students speaking a language other than English as their first language.

Special Programs: A Historical Perspective

For many years, the nation's secondary schools did not provide instructional experiences designed to meet needs of special populations of students. Early secondary education in the United States was directed primarily at preparing sons of an aristocratic leadership to assume positions of responsibility in business and government.

With few exceptions, early secondary schools were unapologetically elitist. Talent was assumed to reside almost exclusively in the minds of the sons of the upper classes. A few people, Thomas Jefferson, for example, suggested that there might be such a thing as a "natural aristocracy" and that the sons of quite ordinary people might be a part of this group. Jefferson recommended the establishment of procedures to identify these students so that they could be provided with special training (Schnur 1980). Jefferson seemed to build a case for a school system that would identify gifted and talented students and educate them in a way to take maximum advantage of their talents. However, Jefferson's was an isolated voice. Further, he believed that the number of "natural aristocrats" to be found among the common people was likely to be very small.

The view that the major audience for secondary schools consisted of children of a narrow elite began to break down during the second and third decades of the 19th century. Horace Mann was especially influential in changing attitudes about the purposes of education. Mann was an advocate of the "common school," an institution that would bring learners from all social classes together in the school. This kind of social mixing was, in Mann's view, an essential ingredient of a democracy that depended for its existence on mutual understanding among diverse groups.

While Mann's views, in time, greatly expanded the proportion of the population of young people who enrolled in both elementary and secondary schools, they tended to run counter to any effort to provide special programs for gifted and talented students. Such programs, when proposed, were often attacked on the grounds that they sought to impose an intellectual caste system on public schools—something that many viewed as incompatible with democratic values.

Reluctance of secondary schools to offer special programming for gifted and talented students was paralleled by a disinclination to provide special instruction for other groups as well. The idea that schools should be "democratic" suggested that no special programs should be implemented that might result in some students receiving more teacher attention than others.

For example, in 1919 the parents of a student with cerebral palsy attempted to enroll their child as a regular student in a Wisconsin school. The school denied the student admission, and the parents took their case to court. In its ruling, the Wisconsin Supreme Court upheld the decision of the school district pointing out that the presence of a child with a handicapping condition in a regular classroom would have a "depressing and nauseating" effect on teachers and students and would require too much teacher time (Colachico 1985).

The view that secondary schools should not provide special instruction for learners with unique needs began to be challenged during the first three decades of the twentieth century. One force influencing this change was a dramatic expansion in the numbers of young people who continued their education into the secondary school years. Throughout the 19th century, most students received only an elementary education. Secondary students, by and large, were academically talented young people who were preparing to go on to colleges and universities. Young people with handicapping conditions, language differences, and economic problems at home simply were not enrolled as students. When a much broader range of students began to appear in the secondary schools, a real need was generated to respond to some special needs that had rarely been seen at this level of education in the past.

The trend toward paying more attention to special student groups within the total secondary school population began to accelerate in the late 1950s. A key event during this period was the launch of the first Soviet earth satellite, Sputnik I, in 1957. This event stirred many concerned citizens to look seriously at American educational practices. Some of them concluded that the schools were not doing a good job of preparing the nation's brightest students. A number of new programs specifically directed at gifted and talented students began appearing in the 1960s. Much less was heard about the old argument that special programs for bright students were "undemocratic."

The Vietnam War and its accompanying social upheavals had a great influence on school programs throughout the 1960s and on into the 1970s. Violence in the nation's inner cities drew attention to the plight of economically deprived learners and learners from minority groups. Increasingly schools attempted to mount programs designed to serve special needs of these groups.

A very important result of the unrest of this period was a growing realization that organized pressure groups could achieve significant change. Increasingly, parents of students with special needs gathered together and lobbied politicians at the local, state, and federal level to win support for programs designed to meet the unique needs of various groups of learners. Many of these lobbying efforts were successful.

Large numbers of new programs began to be installed to meet needs of slow learners, language-minority students, handicapped students, economically deprived students, and gifted and talented students.

Slow Learners

Defining the term "slow learner" is difficult. Slow learners have been thought of as including those individuals who are not learning at a rate designated as average for a given grade level (Bloom 1982). If the term "average" is used to indicate the mean of the population, by definition, one-half of the students in school will be below average and, therefore, "slow." For many teachers, a slow learner is one who has difficulty keeping up with the pace of instruction provided to the class. An individual who might be labeled as slow in comparison to an exceptionally able group of learners might be perfectly normal if compared to a group of less talented students. In addition, a learner who might be slow in grasping one concept or one subject might be very quick to grasp another concept or body of knowledge. Therefore the teacher should keep in mind that slow is a relative term. It is important not to label students as slow and to treat them as if they are unable to achieve at a satisfactory pace. (See Box 16.1.)

As many as 25 to 50 percent of students in typical secondary school classrooms may be classified as slow learners. These students have special needs that tax the creativity of even experienced teachers. Part of the difficulty stems from slow learners' self-image problems. Many of them see themselves as predestined for failure.

There is a sequence of frustration that characterizes many slow learners. First, they have difficulty learning new content. This, in turn, leads to feelings of failure. These feelings result in a poor self-concept. The poor self-concept is accompanied by low levels of motivation and interest in school tasks. Discipline problems with teachers often result. These conflicts erode relationships between these students and their teachers and further reinforce the notion that "failure is inevitable." For many students, dropping out of school is the final step in this sad sequence.

There are several things that teachers can do to meet the needs of slow learners. An important first step is for them to realize that these students do not want to be slow learners. They want to do well in school and to be successful. However, many of these students have had so many failure experiences that they have stopped trying. Some slow learners work hard to convince their teachers that they do not care and that school

Box 16.1

Remove Slow Learners from the Classroom

The presence of slow learners in secondary classrooms is resulting in a waste of academic talent. Teachers have to gear instruction to the lowest common denominator. This slows down the progress of the brighter youngsters and leads to boredom. If we want significant reform in education we need to remove this handicap and encourage our brighter students. One way we can do this is to follow the pattern of some other countries.

Students could be tested as they enter high school and assigned either to an academic or a vocational track. This would benefit everyone. Slower learners would be in a vocational track and would not be asked to compete in situations where they have little opportunity for success. The brighter students could be challenged and allowed to progress much faster. Teachers would have their job simplified because they would not have to plan for such a diversity of learning abilities. Taxpayers would benefit because funds would be spent more efficiently.

What Do You Think?

1. Do you agree that everyone would benefit from this plan? Why or why not?

2. Can you think of any possible negative effects of this plan?

3. What track would you be in if you had been tracked as you entered junior high?

4. Can you think of any major flaws in this proposal?

---

achievement is unimportant to them. Although this might be what these students express, it often is not an expression of their true feelings.

Lack of success in the secondary classroom is often related to students' lack of prerequisite knowledge, experience, or skills. Since this is the case, teachers at this level need to work closely with slow learners to determine what they know before instruction begins on a new topic. When students are found to be weak in some areas, additional instruction on previously introduced material may need to be provided.

Another common problem of slow learners is an absence of good work habits and study skills. Many of these young people have not received the help they need at home and may even have a home life that facilitates a careless and undisciplined approach to life. Some individuals simply do not know how to study or how to complete assignments. To remedy this situation, many teachers have found it useful to model appropriate learning and study techniques for these young people. Showing these students concrete examples of properly completed assignments, giving them clear step-by-step instructions, and pairing them with successful students are among other approaches that can help improve inadequate work and study habits.

Many slow learners have not developed good thinking skills. They do not know how to approach a problem or how to think about an issue. "Thinking aloud" is one way teachers provide help to students with this problem. To implement this procedure, the teacher identifies a problem similar to one that might be assigned to students. The teacher talks to students about the thinking processes he or she uses to identify key aspects of a problem and to work through to a reasonable conclusion. Thinking aloud procedures are sometimes also used by teachers in working with students to improve their abilities to take notes and to organize information.

Some slow learners may appear to be slow because they seem unable to grasp the ideas and concepts presented to the class. One of the sources of difficulty may be that the material is not presented in a manner that is compatible with their personal learning styles. Some students can listen to verbal explanations and quickly grasp the material. Others need to see or visualize how it is organized. Still others require concrete illustrations and examples. To accommodate possible differences in student learning styles, teachers need to use a variety of presentation modes.

The pace of instruction is another variable that may have to be considered in working with slow learners. The pace might be too fast for some individuals. As they become lost and frustrated, problems begin to mount. One way of altering the pace is to emphasize key ideas to be learned fairly early in an instructional sequence. Once this has been done, questions can be asked of individual students to ascertain who has and who has not grasped the information. Students who have the new content in hand can be assigned enrichment activities calling on them to apply basic information that has been learned. Slower students can be grouped together and retaught the material. When this is done, ordinarily some attempts are made to vary teaching techniques somewhat from those used when the content was initially introduced to the whole class.

Slow learners often have negative self-concepts. To the extent possible, teachers of these students strive to provide opportunities for these individuals to succeed. Where possible, lessons are designed to take advantage of whatever academic strengths these students might have. Developing some instruction around areas that are of great personal interest to these students often will increase their levels of motivation. As students experience more success, their levels of self-confidence go up. They feel better about themselves. This, in turn, makes it more likely that they will approach new learning tasks optimistically.

One way some teachers attempt to assure that slow learners experience some success is to reduce levels of competition among students in the classroom. Where competition is keen, slower learners often sense little possibility of achieving success. A few negative experiences may reinforce self-images that, even at the beginning of the school year, may not be positive. Cooperative learning activities often work well with these students. (For more information about cooperative learning, see Chapter 9, "Learning in Groups.")

Limited-English-Proficient Students

In the last several decades the United States has experienced an enormous wave of immigration. These immigrants have arrived from around the globe and have brought with them a wide diversity of primary languages other than English. It is estimated that approximately 5 million students, or about 10 percent of the school-age population, speak languages other than English as their primary language (Borich 1988, p. 280). The addition of these newly arrived immigrants to the pool of students already residing in the United States who speak a language other than English at home has made English proficiency an important educational policy issue.

The failure to provide an adequate education for many of these students is an educational failure of great magnitude. Individuals need to become proficient in English in order to achieve success both in school and out. Those who fail to achieve a minimum level of proficiency experience frustration in school and tend to drop out. This results in a tremendous social and economic loss for these students as individuals and for the nation as a whole.

In recognition of this problem, the Bilingual Education Act was passed in 1968. It calls for initial school instruction to be provided in a learner's native language. This pattern is to continue until the student's English proficiency reaches a level sufficient for him or her to compete effectively in classrooms where English is the exclusive medium of instruction.

The importance of providing educational services for students with a home language other than English was further highlighted in a 1974 U.S. Supreme Court decision, *Lau v. Nichols*. The effect of this decision was to require school districts to develop methods to ensure that students with limited proficiency in English would not be deprived of a meaningful education. The Court emphasized that merely providing the same textbooks and curriculum for those who did not understand English was not meeting the standard of equal treatment (Lopez 1978, p. 4).

In response to concerns about non-native speakers of English, schools have become increasingly sensitive to these students' needs. Many special programs have been established to work with these students and to provide conditions that will allow them to succeed academically. Even where special programs to serve needs of non-native speakers of English are highly developed, these students continue to spend a good part of the school day in regular classrooms. Hence, most secondary school teachers may expect to work with such students from time to time. (In some places, teachers have many such students in all of their classes.)

A good deal of sensitivity is required of teachers who wish to work successfully with students who do not have good control of the English language. These students' self-concepts are closely tied to their own cultures. Teachers must take care not to imply that something is "wrong" with a non-English-speaking group. Students need to be motivated to learn English, but they also need to retain a pride in their own heritage. (See Box 16.2.)

This suggests a need for teachers to become sensitive to the cultural contexts from which non-native speakers of English come. When teachers understand the values of these cultures in areas such as relationships to adults, relationships with others, the importance of the family, the role of cooperation and competition, and common child-rearing practices, the likelihood increases that the teacher will communicate with these students in ways that convey sensitivity and respect. These kinds of teacher attitudes can make these students much more open to the school's instructional program.

The heavily verbal nature of much secondary school instruction poses particular problems for students with limited English proficiency. When possible, teachers working with these students need to supplement verbal instruction with concrete examples including models, graphs, paintings, photographs, and other representations of content that can be appreciated by individuals with limited reading and speaking abilities in English. Some teachers have found it useful to tape parts of their lessons. Tapes are given to students who can play the tapes under the teacher's supervision (often in a learning carrel situation that allows the student to use headphones to listen to the tapes) and ask questions about any parts that are not well understood.

For some non-native speakers of English, proficiency in the written language comes more quickly than proficiency in the spoken language. Many of these students find it much easier to follow written instructions

Box 16.2

Much Ado About Nothing?

The following statement was made by a radio talk-show caller.

> All of this attention to the problems of limited English speaking youngsters is absurd. For years immigrants came to the United States, learned how to communicate in English, and went on to attain success without these costly programs. Bilingual programs only serve to delay the learning of English and the transition of the youngster into mainstream America. If they are going to succeed in this country they will need to learn English, and they need to do so as soon as possible. They should be immersed in English and not allowed the crutch of continuing in their native language. I'm all for making English the official language of the United States and eliminating all of these special programs for the non-English speaking.

What Do You Think?

1. Do you agree or disagree with this statement? Why or why not?
2. Do you agree that special programs slow down the transition of individuals to English?
3. Is the statement about past generations making the transition to English a valid one?
4. What might be other consequences of eliminating programs for limited-English-proficient students?

---

than spoken instructions. Teachers who work with these students have often found it useful to write down assignments rather than give them orally.

When instruction is provided orally, teachers need to avoid using slang expressions or obscure vocabulary. Such terminology stands as an important obstacle for students with limited proficiency in English. It is an unnecessary barrier. Generally, teachers can convey the same information using more standard terminology.

Often it is necessary for teachers to modify their instructional pace when they work with limited-English-proficiency students. Though many of these students are intellectually capable, they often have insufficient control of English to profit from instruction that moves quickly from point to point. It is particularly useful to slow the instructional pace at the beginning of a new unit of learning. This allows students to master basic material, and this kind of learning acts as a good motivator when additional information is introduced.

Sometimes a lack of English gets in the way of students' levels of performance on tests. For example, such a student may do poorly on an algebra test. He or she might be perfectly capable of doing the required mathematics, but be puzzled by some of the written directions. Confusion about this information could result in errors having little to do with his or her understanding of the relevant mathematical content.

Handicapped Students

Educators have a long history of concern for working with individuals with special needs. For years, handicapped students received some training in public schools in so-called "special classrooms." Teachers interested in working with this population received special training and were assigned as special education teachers. In general, there was an assumption that these learners would not be present in regular classrooms or instructed by regular classroom teachers. This long-standing tradition began to be questioned seriously in the middle 1950s.

The beginnings of change trace to a court decision that had nothing to do with handicapped learners. This was the famous *Brown v. Board of Education* case that was decided in 1954. This decision involved the issue of racial segregation and declared that separate schools for white and black students were inherently unequal. The decision of the Supreme Court included language that suggested the opportunity for an education was a right which was to be made available to all individuals on equal terms (Colachico 1985).

Subsequent investigations revealed that many handicapped students were not being served by the public schools. Many were simply staying at home. There were concerns about the adequacy of the education being provided to those handicapped students who were attending school. Critics pointed out that they were being unfairly isolated from contact with non-handicapped students and that this was discriminatory. Recommendations were made to include both handicapped and non-handicapped learners in regular classrooms. Handicapped students' self-esteem would improve, and non-handicapped students would overcome fear and prejudice toward individuals with handicapping conditions.

Public Law 94-142

As a result of a continuing interest in the needs of handicapped citizens, the U.S. Senate in the early 1970s held a number of hearings on the status of education for handicapped individuals. Senators learned that over one million handicapped young people in the country were receiving no educational services whatever from the schools. These findings and continued pressure from constituencies representing the interests of handicapped individuals led to the enactment in 1975 of the Education for All Handicapped Children Act, Public Law 94-142. This piece of legislation has been called the "Bill of Rights for Handicapped Children."

Public Law 94-142 was a very different kind of federal legislation for educators. Traditionally, most federal laws established certain goals or objectives. Means of achieving these goals or objectives had been left largely to state and local school authorities. Public Law 94-142, on the other hand, not only specified goals and objectives but went on to describe in very specific terms about how schools should achieve these goals and objectives. Some of the required processes have resulted in dramatic changes in schools' responses to the needs of handicapped learners. To understand these changes and their implications for the regular classroom teacher, let us review some of the major provisions of the law.

1. *Each identified handicapped child will receive a free, appropriate education.* This means that the schools will assume the cost of educating the handicapped student. An "appropriate education" was defined as one that is designed to meet the particular needs of individual students with handicapping conditions.

2. *Handicapped learners will be educated in the least restrictive environment and with nonhandicapped peers when that placement is appropriate.* The response to this provision of the law is often referred to as "mainstreaming." This means that, whenever possible, these students are to be educated in regular classrooms. The regular classroom teacher is expected to provide much of the instruction to handicapped learners.

3. *The instruction for handicapped learners is to be based on an Individualized Education Program (I.E.P.).* The Individualized Education Program (I.E.P.) is a management tool. It requires school professionals and parents of handicapped students to identify (a) short- and long-term goals for the students, (b) the resources to be committed to the program, (c) the dates when the services are to be rendered, (d) who is to deliver the instruction, (e) the extent to which the student is to be involved in regular education programs, and (f) how the student's progress is to be evaluated. The I.E.P. requirement imposes several responsibilities on classroom teachers. First of all it requires participation in meetings to develop and monitor the I.E.P. In addition, teachers are expected to be capable of diagnosing entry-level achievement of the learners, identifying long and short term goals, delivering instruction to the students, and evaluating their progress. Some teachers have been

To the extent possible, students with special characteristics are "mainstreamed" in regular school classrooms. *Photo courtesy of David Strickler/Monkmeyer Press Photo Service.*

frustrated by the time demands imposed by this portion of the law. Box 16.3 is a sample individualized educational plan form.

4. *Procedural safeguards were established to cover the identification, placement, evaluation, and due process rights of handicapped learners.* Once a handicapped student is identified, both educators and parents must be involved in determining what constitutes an "appropriate" educational program. Often a committee known as an admissions, review, and dismissal (A.R.D.) committee is formed. This committee involves a representative of the district qualified to supervise or provide services to the handicapped learner, the teachers of the student, the parents, and, sometimes, the student. Parents have a right to demand a hearing if they disagree with what is written in the I.E.P. Parents who are dissatisfied with a diagnosis and prescription provided by the school district are usually allowed to demand an independent

Box 16.3

SAMPLE INDIVIDUALIZED EDUCATIONAL PLAN FORM
STUDENT: _____   SUBJECT AREA: _____
TEACHER: _____   ENTRY DATE: _____
SUMMARY OF ENTRY-LEVEL PERFORMANCE: _____
_____
_____

PRIORITIZED LONG-TERM GOALS: _____

Behavioral Objectives	Materials or Resources Needed	Person Responsible to	Date Started	Date Ended	Date of Evaluation

Continuum of Services Hrs. Per Week Committee Members:

Regular Classroom   _____   _____
Resource Teacher in
    Regular Class   _____   _____
Resource Room   _____   _____
Specialists (specify)   _____   _____
Counselor   _____   _____
Special Class   _____   Date I.E.P. Approved_____
Others   _____   Meeting Dates_____

evaluation. This provision means that communication between the parents and the school must be kept open and that the school personnel must be very professional in their diagnosis and treatment of the student.

5. *Each school district must specify the procedures to be used to prepare personnel to work with handicapped learners.* In addition, the law requires teacher-education programs to better prepare future teachers to deal with the specific needs of handicapped students.

Kinds of Handicapping Conditions

Teachers who work with mainstreamed students need some basic understanding of the kinds of handicapping conditions they may encounter among learners in their classrooms. Any attempt to categorize handicapping conditions is risky. First, broad categories often mask differences among individuals within each category. Further, a good many students are likely to have multiple handicaps. For example, someone who is visually impaired may also be emotionally disturbed.

In general, a handicapped student can be defined as "an individual who has a mental or physical condition that prevents him or her from succeeding in a program designed for individuals who are not characterized by this condition or these conditions." Various authorities use different schemes to organize handicapping conditions into categories for purposes of description and analysis. For our purposes, we will consider the major kinds of handicapping conditions to be (1) mental retardation, (2) hearing impairment, (3) speech impairment, (4) visual impairment, (5) learning disability, (6) physical and health impairment, and (7) emotional disturbance. In the following sections, we will outline major characteristics of each condition and provide suggestions for adapting classroom instruction to meet special needs of learners having conditions cited.

MENTAL RETARDATION. Mental retardation is a term that is difficult to define with any degree of precision. In general, a person is thought to be mentally retarded when his or her intellectual development is (1) significantly below that of age mates and where (2) potential for academic achievement has been determined to be markedly less than for so-called "normal" individuals who are otherwise similar to the individual in question.

Historically, IQ scores were often used to determine whether a person properly could be categorized as mentally retarded. A problem with using IQ scores for this purpose is that people who may appear to be mentally retarded on the basis of an IQ test may be perfectly capable of functioning in a normal fashion under other conditions. For example, people with very low IQ scores may do very well in certain kinds of job roles after leaving school. Because of this, the American Association of Mental Deficiency (AAMD) advocates a broader measure of mental retardation than the IQ test. The AAMD suggests that a person who is mentally retarded is characterized by "deficits in adaptive behavior." This means that an individual who is mentally retarded cannot function as a normal person might function within the typical range of life situations. The individual who can function within this typical range is not classified as mentally retarded regardless of how he or she might fare on an IQ test (Payne et al. 1979).

We need also to remember that mental retardation is not in every case a permanent condition. There are people who, because of early home and family environments, may appear to be mentally retarded at some fairly early point in their lives. Such individuals may appear to be perfectly normal at later periods of their lives if they have been placed in enriched environments where special help is provided (Payne et al. 1979).

Traditionally, it has been a practice to describe several categories or levels of mental retardation. Generally the terms "educable," "trainable," and "severely" or "profoundly retarded" are used. The type of mentally retarded individual most likely to be assigned to spend part of the school day (perhaps a full day) in the regular classroom is the individual classified as "educable." Educables represent by far the largest percentage of individuals who are mentally retarded.

We cannot speak with great authority regarding what kinds of achievement might be expected from educable youngsters. Some experts suggest that they cannot be expected to succeed at work much more demanding than that offered in a typical sixth-grade classroom. But there are so many differences among individuals in the educable category that generalizations of this kind are hazardous. It is fair to say that these learners can profit to some extent from the school program. To the individual teacher falls the task of diagnosing each educable youngster with whom he or she works and of devising learning experiences (in concert with parents and other school officials) that are reasonable.

Working with Educable Students. Educable students tend to have rather short attention spans. Further, they tend to become frustrated rather easily. Many educable students, by the time they reach secondary school, have experienced a long history of failure in school. Consequently, they tend to see themselves as failures even before they start on a new task. Some may not even be willing to try. In general, these youngsters have difficulty in grasping abstract ideas or complex sequences of ideas (see Box 16.4).

In teaching educable learners, lessons should be short, direct, and to the point. Material should be presented in short sequential steps. There ought to be large numbers of very concrete examples to illustrate new ideas. Material that is introduced in prose form should be reinforced with additional visual and oral presentations. Some teachers have found it useful to assign one of the nonhandicapped students in the class to work with an educable student as a tutor. Frequently a peer tutor will be able to explain material in simpler, more direct language than the teacher. Certainly, peer tutoring programs can offer a good supplement to what the teacher does.

Teachers must monitor their vocabularies very carefully when directing comments to educable students. This is particularly true when providing directions. Often, educable students' failures can be attributed as much to their lack of understanding regarding what they are to do as to their difficulty with accomplishing an assigned task.

Box 16.4

Sensitive Treatment of Educable Learners in the Regular Classroom

When you were in school, there may not have been any students in your classes who would be formerly categorized as "mentally retarded-educable" (though perhaps there were). But you very likely had some classes that included individuals who simply appeared to be much less bright than most others in the class.

What Do You Think?

Spend a few moments trying to recall any students similar to those mentioned in the paragraph above. Then, respond to these questions.

1. In general, how did your teachers treat these youngsters? Can you recall some specific examples?

2. How did these youngsters react to school? Were they active in the extracurricular program? Were they generally popular? How would you assess their general social standing in the school?

3. Have you kept track of what has happened to any of these people in the years since you graduated from high school? What are they doing? Are some of them doing things that you never would have predicted?

4. How would you prepare other students in your class if you learned that you would have some "educables" on your roster? Would you say anything at all? Would you choose to remain silent? Or would you follow some other course of action?

5. Knowing what you know about "educables," how might you make assignments in such a fashion that they would enjoy some potential for success? Would everybody in the class be doing the same thing at the same time? If not, how would you manage several different kinds of activities at the same time?

Educable learners frequently require more time to accomplish a given task than do nonhandicapped learners. Teachers need to be cautious about establishing tight, overly restrictive deadlines for these students. Often it is better to have them accomplish fewer tasks, even though each task takes some time to complete, than to push them to work on more tasks than they can get done. Self-esteem is enhanced when a learner has an opportunity to get the job done. Consequently, allowing educable students sufficient time to complete their work can enhance their self-images.

Finally, teachers need to be very careful about exposing educable students to situations that are highly competitive. It is particularly important to avoid placing them in situations where they have to compete against nonhandicapped students. An educable learner can be absolutely devastated when he or she is forced to compete in a situation where he or she has almost no prospect of doing anything but losing. Such an experience can be a great humiliation, and it can lead to a greatly diminished interest in the school program.

HEARING IMPAIRMENT.   Students who are hearing impaired tend to fall into two broad categories. On the one hand, there are students whose hearing loss is so profound as to preclude their ability to acquire normal use of the oral language. These individuals are classified as "deaf." On the other hand, there are students with a hearing loss that is serious but not so serious as to have prevented them from acquiring normal speech patterns. These individuals are classified as "hard of hearing."

There are great differences among hearing-impaired students. For example, some are unable to hear certain pitches. Others require different levels of amplified sound. Some will have had a hearing loss since birth. Others may have suffered a hearing loss after some oral language proficiency has developed. A characteristic shared by large numbers of hearing-impaired learners is a difficulty in developing proficient oral language skills. A great deal of emphasis in school programs for these students is placed on improving their performance capabilities with the spoken language.

About 5 percent of the school-aged population is estimated to suffer from some degree of hearing loss. Of this 5 percent, only about 1.5 percent are thought to require special educational services. Even students with quite severe hearing losses are capable of functioning satisfactorily in regular classrooms. Teachers do need to exercise care to assure that these youngsters understand what is going on. School hearing specialists can provide practical guidelines.

Working with Hearing-Impaired Students. Many students who suffer severe hearing losses have been taught to attend very carefully to visual cues. Many know how to read lips. Because of their dependence on visual signals, students with hearing losses must be introduced to learning material in such a fashion that they can take advantage of their visual learning skills. For teachers, this suggests a need to face hearing-impaired students when introducing new information and providing directions. Teachers with hearing-impaired learners might also consider using overhead projectors rather than blackboards. (Overheads permit teachers to face the class while writing information on the acetate sheets. On the other hand, when writing on the blackboard, a teacher may be talking with his or her back turned to the class.) It is a good idea, as well, for teachers of hearing-impaired students to remain relatively stationary while they are speaking. Trained lip readers find it difficult to follow comments being made by a person who is in motion.

Assignments and other directions ought to be provided in written form. (They can be oral as well, but the written material can go a long way toward eliminating potential confusion.) When a lecture format is used, it is helpful to provide class members with a general printed outline (including at least major headings) of the material to be presented. This helps students to keep up as the lecture is presented. It is a good idea to provide students with lists of important and potentially confusing words in advance of the lecture. This is particularly critical when words to be used may have multiple meanings. (Consider, for example, the differences in meaning attached to the term "market" as it is used in everyday conversation and the term "market" as it is used in the discipline of economics.) Specialized usages need to be explained on the lists themselves. A discussion in advance of the lecture will also prove helpful.

In general, hearing-impaired students do best when instruction is well organized and systematic. The easier it is for such students to recognize the organizational scheme of the lesson, the better they are likely to do. All students tend to become confused when they do not understand what a teacher is attempting to accomplish at a given point during a lesson. For hearing-impaired students who lack the communication channels open to nonhandicapped learners the task of keeping on track with the teacher presents a real challenge. For these students, well-organized instructions (which, indeed, can benefit *all* students) is essential.

Some hearing-impaired students may wear hearing aids or other mechanical devices designed to enhance their ability to compensate for their hearing loss. Teachers need to understand how these devices work. For example, they should know how batteries are replaced in a hearing aid. It may be a good idea for them to have a supply of batteries (and perhaps certain other critical components) on hand so that minor repairs can be made in the classroom. Certainly some advice from school hearing specialists ought to be solicited regarding what properly can and cannot be done in this connection.

SPEECH IMPAIRMENT. Identification of students with clearly defined speech impairments is difficult. Even the most clear-cut definitions of speech impairment still require the individual making a decision about a given student to use a good deal of personal judgment. In general, an individual is thought to suffer from impaired speech when his or her speech differs significantly from the speech of others of the same age. Speech problems encompass a wide range of difficulties. These relate to such things as voice quality, problems of articulating certain sounds, and stuttering.

Because speech impairments do not present so clear-cut and obvious obstacles to learning as do such handicaps as hearing impairment and visual impairment, there is a tendency for some teachers not to take them as seriously as they should. A very important side effect of speech impairment, and one that occurs in a distressingly high number of students suffering from this problem, is a low self-image. Out of their frustration at their inability to speak normally, there is a tendency for many learners with speech impairments to conclude that they are inferior or even incompetent. The dropout rate among students with speech impairments is quite high.

Working with Students with Speech Impairments. Many students with speech impairments can profit from work with a trained speech therapist. A good many districts have such individuals on their professional staffs. But classroom teachers, too, can do a great deal to help these students. In general, these students need a good deal of emotional support. As noted, they tend to suffer from negative self-image problems. Thus teachers must take care to avoid placing learners with speech impairments in situations that call unnecessary attention to their handicap.

For example, in classroom discussions, it may be wise to call on students with speech handicaps only when they raise a hand and indicate a willingness to volunteer a response. When such a student begins to speak, he or she should be allowed to complete what he or she has to say without interruption or correction. Praise and other kinds of positive reinforcements should be provided when these individuals volunteer a remark in class.

Some teachers have found it prudent to talk to other members of the class, at a time when speech-impaired students are absent, about the desirability of not criticizing or making fun of their speech handicap. Support from other students in the class can make it much more comfortable for a learner with a speech impairment to speak up.

Finally, it is a good idea for the teacher to provide opportunities for speech-impaired students to speak with the teacher on a one-to-one basis. This kind of a setting provides an opportunity for the teacher to boost the morales of such students by making sensitive supportive comments to them individually. Further, it affords the student an opportunity to talk to the teacher about course work (or other matters) without fear that he or she will experience a communication difficulty that might prompt ridicule from other class members.

VISUAL IMPAIRMENT.   The term "visual impairment" implies a variety of deficiencies related to the sense of sight. Some visually impaired individuals have no sight whatever. However, most in this category have some sight. Some see a world that is blurred, dim, or out of focus; others may see only parts of objects. Federal education officials have estimated that about one tenth of 1 percent of the school-aged population is blind or partially sighted.

Whenever assignments are written on the chalkboard or written information is passed out, the teacher must make special arrangements to communicate with visually handicapped students in the class. In some cases it may be sufficient to explain this information orally. In other situations, it is useful to provide a recorded version of the material that visually handicapped learners can take with them to play on personally owned cassette recorders.

A problem shared by all individuals with severe visual handicaps has to do with personal mobility. In time, people with visual handicaps develop good mental pictures of areas they visit frequently. But they require some experience in a new environment before a mental picture develops. Thus it is useful for teachers to arrange for students with severe visual handicaps to visit classrooms at times when class is not in session to allow them to learn configurations of furniture and other features of the room. When changes in these arrangements are made, teachers must make a special effort to familiarize visually handicapped students with the new classroom configuration.

LEARNING DISABILITY.   The term "learning disability" is a very broad one. Some students who are not learning disabled at all have been so labeled simply because certain teachers have experienced difficulty in communicating with them. Properly, a student classified as learning disabled is one who exhibits a disorder in one or more of the basic psychological processes involved in understanding or using spoken or written language. These disorders may be revealed in such areas as listening, writing, reading, spelling, or computing. Sometimes learning disabilities are referred to by such terms as "perceptual handicaps," "minimal brain disfunctions," and "dyslexia." Fundamentally, then, the student who is characterized as having a learning disability experiences difficulty processing sensory stimuli.

Individuals with learning disabilities often experience difficulty in following directions. They may appear disorganized. Teachers often find that they are unable to get started on assigned tasks. Many learning disabled students have a low tolerance for frustration. Some become tense and appear to be incapable of doing anything when they sense that they are being pressured by the teacher. Handwriting of these learners often appears disorganized. Letters within words may be inconsistent in size. There may be letter reversals. In terms of their oral communication, some learning disabled students have unusual speech patterns in which, for example, words may be out of sequence.

Working with Learning Disabled Students. Most students who suffer from learning disabilities need special help in the area of organization. Such learners, for example, frequently experience great difficulty in differentiating between critical material in an assignment and other information that is much less important. In working with learning disabled students, it is desirable for teachers to take time to highlight key ideas and to provide students with ways of organizing these ideas into a meaningful pattern.

Because of a typically low toleration for frustration, learning disabled students often have a hard time dealing with alternatives. Teachers can reduce unnecessary anxieties of such learners by limiting the number of alternatives confronting them.

In general, by the time they reach the secondary school level, learning disabled students have experienced a good deal of frustration and failure. Consequently, many of them suffer from low self-concepts. Anything the teacher can do to help them grow in terms of their own self-confidence should be encouraged. In a supportive classroom environment, many of these students *can* learn.

PHYSICAL AND HEALTH IMPAIRMENT.   Physical and health impairment is a broad category that includes many different kinds of specific conditions. In general, students in this category include those who have limitations that may interfere with school performance or attendance that are related to physical abilities or medical conditions. About half of them have suffered from a crippling disease.

Working with Students with Physical and Health Impairments. The range of conditions in this general category makes it impossible to provide recommendations that would be appropriate for every handicapped student who is either physically or health impaired. For teachers, the appropriate initial step is to gather complete information regarding the specific physical and health handicaps of learners in their classes. Meetings or conversations with parents, counselors, and others with relevant information are certainly appropriate. Once specific information is in hand, teachers can consider what modifications might have to be made in the instructional program to make it appropriate for each physically or health handicapped student.

Information about specific handicaps may result in any one of a number of actions being taken by the teachers. For example, a physical or health limitation may make it impossible for a given student to complete certain tasks at as fast a rate as nonhandicapped students. In such a case, special time allowances may need to be made. For another learner, perhaps one who must use a cumbersome walker, it might be necessary to rearrange furniture in the room to make it possible for this individual to move into the area and slip into a seat. Space for special equipment needed by some physically or health handicapped students will need to be found.

In general, physically and health handicapped students are fully capable of meeting the intellectual challenges of instruction in regular school classrooms. The challenge comes not so much in devising unique methods of presentation as it does in accommodating limitations pertaining to learners' physical and health characteristics. When arrangements can be made, many students in this category do very well as students in regular classrooms.

EMOTIONAL DISTURBANCE.   Emotionally disturbed students have been defined as those who display "a marked deviation from age-appropriate behavior expectations which interferes with positive personal and interpersonal development" (Turnbull and Schulz 1979, p. 41). Many classroom teachers find emotionally disturbed students difficult to work with. In part this results from a tendency of some emotionally disturbed learners to engage in behaviors that are disruptive to classroom instruction.

A number of schemes have been developed to categorize types of behavior of emotionally disturbed learners. One scheme identifies five separate kinds of behaviors thought to be characteristic of these students. According to Payne et al. (1979, p. 35), these individuals are thought to

1. Have problems achieving in school that cannot be explained by sensory or health factors.

2. Have problems establishing and maintaining satisfactory interpersonal relationships with others.

3. Have a tendency to demonstrate inappropriate feelings and actions under normal circumstances.

4. Be characterized, in many instances, by a pervasive mood of unhappiness or depression.

5. Have a tendency to develop physical symptoms such as pain or emotional symptoms such as fear as a consequence of their problems.

Some emotionally disturbed students may be defiant, rude, destructive, and attention seeking. Others may be fearful and withdrawn. One of the authors once taught a group of emotionally disturbed students, one of whom, at a moment's notice, would explode and begin to throw books, desks, and any other available objects. In the same class, there was a boy who would begin to cry and start running to a corner of the room when he was greeted with a friendly "good morning" from the teacher.

Most emotionally disturbed students have difficulty coping with their environments. Their difficulty in making needed adjustments frequently distracts them from tasks associated with completing school-related work. Consequently, a lack of academic success often ensues. Problems in the academic area often lead to self-concept problems. Self-concept problems lead to anxieties, and these anxieties often result in behaviors that are unacceptable in the context of the school. In essence, many of these become caught up in a cycle of failure. Teacher efforts in working with students of this type are directed at breaking this destructive pattern of behavior.

Working with Emotionally Disturbed Students. Teachers need to attend to four basic concerns in planning instructional programs for emotionally disturbed students. First, activities need to be success oriented. That is, there must be a reasonable chance for the student to accomplish what he or she is asked to do. Second, teachers must be specific in terms of communicating their behavioral expectations to these students and consistent in enforcing these expectations. (We cannot be "hard nosed" one day and a "soft touch" another day.)

Third, teachers must minimize distractions. These learners tend to be diverted very easily from assigned tasks. Efforts must be undertaken to reduce the potential for shifting their attentions away from required work.

Fourth, the teacher needs to help emotionally disturbed students realize that there is a clear and definite relationship between their behaviors and consequences flowing from these behaviors. Many such students do not make an immediate connection between something that happens to them (receiving a low grade, for example) and what it was that they did that resulted in the occurrence of that "something." Large numbers of these individuals believe the world to be a totally capricious place where anything that happens to them occurs because of random chance or bad luck. Teachers need to make the effort to help them appreciate that there is a connection between what a student does and what happens to him or her.

A general concern related to some extent to all four of these major areas is the issue of motivation. By the time many emotionally disturbed learners reach even the junior high school level, they have experienced so much failure that they begin to doubt that anything taught in school can be mastered. Further, many suspect that school learning simply isn't useful. Many emotionally disturbed students go to great lengths to avoid becoming involved in academic tasks. In considering the issue of motivating emotionally disturbed learners, the teacher needs to devise ways to convince them that the subject, if mastered, will provide a personal benefit. Identified benefits need to have immediacy. It does little good, for example, to tell an emotionally disturbed student, "You should do this because ten years from now it will help you get a better job."

Beyond motivation, there is a need to develop instruction in such a way that potentials for success are maximized. One approach to this problem is to cut large tasks into small pieces. Emotionally disturbed students are much less likely to be intimidated when a small piece of a larger task is assigned than when they are asked to complete the entire larger task before being credited with satisfactory performance. When material is introduced in small steps and positive feedback is provided at the successful conclusion of each step, the emotionally disturbed student is encouraged to keep on task.

Behavior patterns of emotionally disturbed children are variable. We must recognize that not all emotionally disturbed learners are likely to engage in disruptive behavior in class and hence, immediately catch the teacher's attention. Some emotionally disturbed students may be withdrawn and passive. Sometimes these students are experiencing more severe problems than those whose outward symptoms may appear to be more obvious. With such students, the teacher needs to build trust and to eliminate a potentially debilitating fear of failure.

Finally, teachers with emotionally disturbed students in their classes must understand that such problems are not likely to go away overnight. In many cases, emotional disturbance has developed over a period of years. Consequently, even teachers who approach such young people with compassion and understanding do not achieve quick results. Teachers who work with emotionally disturbed students often have to be satisfied with small, incremental changes. Box 16.5 deals with your feelings about working with handicapped students.

Gifted and Talented Students

In 1971 the U.S. Commissioner of Education prepared a status report for Congress on education for the gifted and talented. This report pointed out that specific programs for the gifted and talented were extremely few in number. The report stimulated considerable interest in such programs. In 1972, Congress established the Office of Gifted and Talented within the U.S. Office of Education. Gifted and talented learners were defined by Public Law 91-230 as "children who have outstanding intellectual ability or creative talent, the development of which requires special activities or services not ordinarily provided by local education agencies" (United States Statutes at Large 1971,

Box 16.5

Feelings About Working with Handicapped Students

What Do You Think?

Please respond to each of the following questions.

1. As you review the different handicapping conditions, which students do you think would be most difficult for you to reach? Why?

2. What could be done to alter your instruction to accommodate students with that particular handicap?

3. The attitude of the teacher is very important in working with handicapped learners. What is your attitude regarding teaching these learners? Is it positive or negative? What can be done to improve your attitude?

4. As you review this chapter, what particular skills and knowledge do you still need to acquire to be successful in teaching handicapped learners? How will you acquire these skills and knowledge?

p. 153). In 1974, responding to additional public interest, Congress, in Public Law 93-380, provided federal funds to local and state agencies for the specific purpose of improving programs for the gifted and talented.

Since the middle 1970s, there has been a steady expansion of programs to serve gifted and talented students in the schools. At least some schools in all areas of the country have such programs. Increasing numbers of colleges and universities are offering courses on education for the gifted and talented. At this time, only a few states require teachers who work with gifted and talented students to hold a special teaching certificate. However, requirements in this area are tightening, and we may expect more states to have such requirements in the future.

In summary, political factions supporting expansion of programs for gifted and talented learners have enjoyed a large measure of success over the past 10 to 15 years. There is reason to expect a continued expansion of special programs for gifted and talented students in the years ahead. This by no means suggests that controversies regarding these programs do not continue to rage (see Box 16.6). We will be exploring some of these in subsequent sections.

Who Are the Gifted and Talented?

Much of the controversy surrounding programs for the gifted and talented centers on difficulties in deciding exactly which students are gifted and talented. Some have argued that gifted and talented students should be identified by standard intelligence tests. Various cutoff points have been suggested. A number of programs have used minimum measured IQs between 120 and 135 as evidence of "giftedness" (Daurio 1979).

Others have challenged the reliance on standardized IQ scores to identify gifted and talented children. Some have argued that measured IQ, by itself, is too narrow a criterion to use for identifying students of exceptional ability. Others, particularly those concerned with education of students from minority groups, point out that standardized IQ tests are culturally biased. That is, they fail to account for the special values, abilities, and specific cultural-based knowledge of young people from racial and ethnic minorities (Bruch and Curry 1978). Consequently, large numbers of minority group students who are truly gifted and talented will not score well on standardized IQ tests. Note that the arguments of minority critics are not against the important of intelligence as one characteristic of gifted and talented students. Rather, they charge that standardized test scores are an inappropriate measure of this intelligence.

In addition to intelligence, it has been suggested that gifted and talented students are characterized by an ability to pursue a given objective tenaciously over a long period of time until it is achieved. The high level of personal involvement in their work of gifted and talented individuals has been well documented through the years (Roe 1953; Terman 1959; MacKinnon 1965). Task commitment then is thought to complement intelligence as one of the characteristics of gifted and talented students.

The elements of intelligence and task commitment suggest that gifted and talented students not only have above-average intellectual abilities but that they characteristically bring these abilities to bear on some task in a purposeful way. It is not just the intelligence itself but what is done with the intelligence that is important. Some specialists in gifted and talented education contend that the simple willingness of a student with high intelligence to keep at a task is not sufficient evidence of the existence of giftedness. There must also be some measure of the

Box 16.6

Are Programs for Gifted and Talented Students Racist?

Recently, a caller on a radio talk show made these comments about a proposed new program for gifted and talented students in the school district.

Look, let's think about this thing as it really is. Whose kids are really going to benefit from this program? In my mind these classes are going to be filled with the kids who live in the fancy houses on the hill. This whole program is simply a political ploy to get the enthusiastic support of these upper-income people. Lots of these folks have all but had it with public education. I mean they are hacked off about busing, about special programs for minorities, and a bunch of other programs that primarily have benefited blacks and Hispanics. They can't oppose these programs directly. To do so would be to leave themselves wide open to the charge of racism. Instead, they have adopted the code words "gifted and talented" programs to hide behind. These programs will result in setting up a situation in the school where their youngsters, disproportionate numbers of whom will be identified as gifted and talented, will not have to rub shoulders in their classes with blacks and Hispanics. The gifted and talented program is a godsend for racists who have long sought a legal mechanism for resegregating the schools.

What Do You Think?

Read the comments carefully. Then, respond to these questions.

1. Are gifted and talented programs promoters of racism? Why, or why not?

2. How do you assess the general logic of this caller's arguments?

3. Suppose that you were interested in establishing a gifted and talented program that would not be open to charges that it was promoting racism. How would such a program be organized?

4. Suppose that you were the superintendent of the school district that had established the gifted and talented program to which this caller was referring. Suppose that the radio station gave you time to respond to the caller's concerns. What would you say?

nature of what is achieved as a result of the commitment to the task. People such as E. Paul Torrance (1970) have advocated expanding the definition of gifted and talented students to include the dimension of creativity. That is, students who are gifted and talented not only have above-average intellectual abilities and a commitment to task completion but they also tend to complete tasks in unusual, nontraditional ways.

A leading authority in gifted and talented education, Joseph S. Renzulli, has pointed out that a long history of research supports the conclusion that giftedness involves an interaction among the factors of intelligence, task commitment, and creativity (Renzulli 1978). Logically, then, selection procedures used to identify students for inclusion in gifted and talented programs ought to include evidence related to all three areas. As Renzulli (1978) points out, too frequently measures of general intellectual ability alone have been used to identify gifted and talented students. Selection procedures of this type tend to include some students who properly ought not to be included. And they tend to exclude some students who properly ought to be included.

Perhaps the overreliance on measures of intelligence noted by Renzulli results from the abundance of tests to measure general intellectual ability and the relative scarcity of reliable measures of "task commitment" and "creativity." It may well be that the availability of the tools of measurement has prompted undue attention on the factor of intelligence. Box 16.7 is an exercise in identifying criteria for selecting students for a gifted and talented program.

An increasing appreciation of the point that giftedness is a composite of several variables has led administrators of many programs for the gifted and talented to use a variety of information sources as bases for making decisions about which youngsters will participate. The program for Mentally Gifted Minors in California, for example, selects youngsters based on (1) tests of intellectual ability, (2) records of school achievement, and (3) judgments of teachers, psychologists, and administrators. Further, because of concerns about culturally biased intelligence tests, "scores from IQ tests are inadmissable as the main criterion for excluding or including the child in the program" (Olstad 1978 p. 187). Although there are differences in specific procedures, the California pattern of looking at several kinds of information is one supported today by many administrators of programs for the gifted and talented.

Kinds of Programs for Gifted and Talented Students

In general, programs for gifted and talented students sort into two broad categories: enrichment and acceleration. Enrichment programs try to meet needs of these students by providing them with additional or different kinds of learning experiences from those provided for other learners. In programs of this kind, gifted and talented students progress through the school program at the same rate as other students.

Acceleration programs, on the other hand, are designed to increase the pace at which gifted and talented students complete their schooling.

Box 16.7

Criteria for Selecting Students for a Gifted and Talented Program

What Do You Think?

Suppose that you had been asked by your principal to provide a set of guidelines for identifying students for a pilot gifted and talented program to be started in your school. How would your guidelines address these questions?

1. How much emphasis would you attach to information you might have about a student regarding (a) his or her IQ, (b) his or her task commitment, and (c) his or her creativity?

2. How would you propose to measure the quality of task commitment?

3. How would you propose to measure the quality of creativity?

4. What provisions, if any, would you suggest to (a) enable students selected initially to drop out of the program and to (b) enable students not selected initially to qualify for the program at a later date?

5. To what extent would your selection guidelines make provisions for selecting minority group students who might not score well on ordinary IQ tests because of culture bias?

For example, a given gifted or talented student might complete the high school program in only two years. As in enrichment programs, students in acceleration programs generally are provided with more challenging content than that provided to other students.

Profound philosophical differences tend to divide proponents of enrichment programs and acceleration programs. In the sections that follow, we shall look at some practices recommended by partisans of each view. We shall also examine some arguments that have been made to support and to criticize each of these positions. A status report on the enrichment versus acceleration debate will conclude this discussion.

ENRICHMENT.   Enrichment consists of learning experiences and activities that are above and beyond those of the regular curriculum (Renzulli 1977). Enrichment programs attempt to stretch gifted and talented students by exposing them to experiences that challenge them to make maximum use of their considerable capabilities. Enrichment is thought to be democratic in that it provides opportunities for gifted and talented learners to be exposed to learning experiences appropriate to their needs without removing them from contact in regular classes with more typical students.

A number of authorities have developed guidelines for enrichment programs. One of the best known of these is the "enrichment triad model" developed by Joseph S. Renzulli (1977). Renzulli suggests that an enrichment program ought to provide three categories of experiences for learners: (1) general exploratory experiences, (2) group training activities, and (3) individual and small group investigations of real problems.

General exploratory experiences. Learning experiences in this category are designed to introduce students to contents not ordinarily treated in the regular school curriculum.

Group training activities. Learning experiences in this category seek to familiarize students with rational thinking processes and with feeling and valuing processes.

Individual and small-group investigations of real problems. Learning experiences in this category involve students in activities where they apply what they have learned to solve real problems. There is an emphasis on students' developing learning products for which there is a demonstrated need in the real world.

Programs for the gifted and talented that are built around the enrichment triad model attempt to accommodate two key concerns. On the one hand, there is an effort to provide learning experiences that are different from what students otherwise would encounter in the school program. Provision of different experiences assures that these students are not simply being introduced earlier to material that they might encounter at a later date in the regular school program. Where this principle has not been observed, gifted and talented students in the ninth grade, for example, have simply been exposed to eleventh- or twelfth-grade content early. This then creates a problem for teachers when these students reach the eleventh or twelfth grade in that they have already been exposed to the learning experiences typically provided during those years. Because of these difficulties, it has become fairly common for enrichment programs to avoid duplication of content offered in the regular curriculum.

A second concern addressed by the enrichment triad model has to do with a conviction that giftedness implies not simply a set of descriptive characteristics about a given student but, rather, a capability to utilize innate talents in a productive way (Delisle 1980). According to this understanding, many enrichment programs require gifted and talented students to engage in activities that result in some kind of "observable end product" (p. 11). In the enrichment triad model, the category of experiences labeled "individual and small group investigations of real problems" attempts to accommodate this need.

The "enrichment" approach is the most popular approach for dealing with the needs of gifted and talented students. It enjoys considerable support from parents, counselors, and administrators. It is consistent with the view of the school as a place where students of all kinds come together. Further, it poses few serious administrative problems.

Some groups oppose enrichment programs on the grounds that they do not sufficiently challenge the abilities of bright students. They feel that enrichment approaches unnecessarily slow the progress of talented learners through the school program and that they are a response more to the school's managerial needs than to gifted-and-talented students' academic needs.

ACCELERATION.   Acceleration involves gifted and talented students in "progress through an educational program at rates faster or ages younger than conventional" (Pressey 1949, p. 2). Advocates of acceleration reject the premise that students in schools must proceed through the program one grade and one year at a time. Rather, they take the position that, when capable, students should be provided opportunities to complete the program more quickly. Partisans of acceleration suggest that any potential benefits of keeping bright students in classes with their age mates are outweighed by the potential for boredom and failure to make maximal use of their capabilities. Gifted and talented students, so say advocates of acceleration, should be provided with opportunities to progress through school at rates consistent with their abilities.

There are two basic types of acceleration: subject matter acceleration and grade acceleration. Subject matter acceleration permits a student to take a given course earlier than would normally be the case. For example, a student in grade 8 might be allowed to take an introductory calculus course, usually a grade 12 elective. Grade acceleration occurs when a student is allowed to skip an entire grade to take a complete program of courses that is more advanced than that ordinarily taken by a student of his or her age.

One of the best known acceleration programs that has evolved over a number of years has been part of Julian C. Stanley's Study of Mathematically Precocious Youth (SMPY) (Stanley 1978). In the SMPY program, mathematically talented youths are permitted to take advanced mathematics classes. They are assigned to work with a mentor who is another mathematically talented young person who has mastered the content of at least the first year of university-level calculus. Further, provision has been made for students in the program to earn college credit for advanced work in mathematics when they are able to complete advanced college-level courses successfully. Stanley's program has been in operation for over ten years. It has proved to be highly successful.

"Your semester project proposals are always interesting, Schuyler. Last fall's light-hearted musical rendering of *The Scarlet Letter* certainly cut new ground. But, I ask you, is the world ready for *Silas Marner Meets Godzilla*?"

A number of students in the program have entered college with a substantial number of hours completed at entrance. Many have gone on to complete advanced degrees at an unusually early age. Despite the success of SMPY and other acceleration programs, the principle of acceleration continues to inspire a good deal of debate. Let us look at some arguments that have been put forward both by proponents and opponents.

Students who are involved in accelerated programs are generally supportive of their experiences. These students are eager to move ahead faster than they could were they locked into the traditional grade-by-grade and course-by-course approach. They graduate from high schools and universities while still quite young. As a result, these students can enjoy the personal satisfaction of making meaningful contributions to society for many years. Proponents of acceleration contend that this is good both for the gifted and talented young people and for our society as a whole.

Critics, however, point out that involvement in accelerated programs can cause difficulties. They believe that they can place too much pressure on some students. For example, since selection procedures are not absolutely reliable, some individuals may be placed in such programs who should not be there. When this happens and students fail, there can be severe damage to their self-image.

In addition, some people argue that the social adjustment of students in accelerated programs may suffer. For example, how is a bright 12 year-old who is accelerated to the twelfth-grade going to handle the male-female relationships that are common at that grade level, or how is a gifted 15 year-old who has already completed college going to function in a world that has many restrictions on hiring individuals under 18 years of age?

Despite a considerable body of research that supports the acceleration approach, the percentage of gifted and talented students in accelerated programs remains small when compared to the percentage enrolled in enrichment programs. Arguments of those opposing acceleration still are widely accepted by many educational policy makers. For this reason, it is probable that enrichment programs will continue to outnumber acceleration programs for quite some time.

Key Ideas in Summary

1. The diversity of students in secondary classrooms is greater today than it has ever been. The range of students to be served makes it difficult for teachers to discharge their ethical obligation to assist all learners to achieve their fullest potential.

2. The mission of the contemporary high school has expanded from that of the early high school. No longer is the high school the special preserve of the wealthy or the college bound. It is an institution for "all of the young people, from all of the families."

3. Early attempts to provide special programs for the gifted and talented often suffered because they were viewed as elitist programs that catered mainly to the children of the privileged classes.

4. Teaching slow learners is one of the most frustrating experiences for secondary teachers. Nearly every secondary level class will include students who might be classified as "slow." The sequence of failure

and frustration experienced by slow learners can lead to serious class-room and school problems. Diagnosing the problems, teaching study skills and study strategies, delivering clear and concrete instruction, changing the pace of classroom activities, providing for alternative learning styles, and modeling thinking are strategies that can be useful in teaching learners who may be falling behind age level norms in achievement.

5. In recent decades the number of limited-English-proficient students has expanded greatly as large numbers of immigrants have entered the United States from all over the world. The standard textbooks and standard procedures used to teach those who are proficient in English are ineffective in reaching many students who are not native speakers of English. The drop out rate among these students is high. A beginning step for a teacher dealing with limited English proficient learners is to become aware of these students' cultural norms and values. It is important to help them preserve their cultural identity and pride as they make the transition to English. Using different forms of communication, limiting the amount of verbal interaction, eliminating slang expressions, allowing learners to proceed at their own pace, and altering testing procedures are useful techniques for helping them attain success in the classroom.

6. Public Law 94-142 declared that handicapped students will be educated in the "least restrictive environment." That means that the teacher may have learners with a variety of handicapping conditions in the regular classroom. The regular classroom teacher needs to understand the nature of various handicapping conditions and how to meet those special needs in the classroom. In addition, teachers need to know how to diagnose problems and how to plan individualized and sequential instruction for these students.

7. The federal government has been increasingly interested in programs for the gifted and talented since the early 1970s. Among other things, the federal government provides some support money for gifted and talented programs that is paid to states and to local school districts.

8. The types of programs provided to gifted and talented students tend to be of two basic types. One type attempts to provide enrichment experiences for gifted and talented students who continue to be enrolled in regular classrooms. The other type attempts to accelerate the progress of gifted and talented learners through school by allowing them either to skip grades or to enroll in more advanced course work. The most popular choice of programs by most educators is the enrichment alternative.

POSTTEST

DIRECTIONS: Using your own paper, answer these true/false questions. For each correct statement, write the word "true." For each incorrect statement, write the word "false."

_____ 1. Horace Mann advocated a public school system that would accommodate the needs of students from all levels of society.

_____ 2. Slow learners in the secondary classroom are generally not much of a problem because, by this time, slow learners have dropped out of school.

_____ 3. A basic step for teachers in meeting needs of limited-English-proficient students is to develop an understanding of these students' cultures.

_____ 4. To meet Public Law 94-142's requirement that all students be provided with an "appropriate education," schools need do nothing more than place each handicapped student in a regular classroom for some portion of the school day.

_____ 5. The "enrichment approach" is the one that is generally favored by administrators and teachers.

Bibliography

BLOOM, BENJAMIN S. *Human Interaction and School Learning*. New York: McGraw-Hill, 1982.

BORICH, GARY. *Effective Teaching*. Columbus: Merrill Publishing Company, 1988.

BRUCH, C., AND CURRY, J. "Personal Learnings: A Curent Synthesis on the Culturally Different Gifted," *The Gifted Child Quarterly*. (Fall 1978): 313–321.

COLACHICO, DAVID. *The Education For All Handicapped Children Act: Legislation for Academic Equality (A Historical Study of Public Law 94-142)*. Unpublished record of study, Texas A&M University, 1985.

DAURIO, S. "Educational Enrichment Versus Acceleration: A Review of the Literature," in George W.; Cohn, S.; and Stanley, J. (eds.), *Educating the Gifted: Acceleration and Enrichment*. Baltimore: John Hopkins University Press, 1979.

DELISLE, J. "Education of the Gifted: Coming and Going," *Roeper Review*. (May–June 1980): 11–14.

LOPEZ, M. "Bilingual Education and the Latino Student," in Valverde, L. (Ed.) *Bilingual Education for Latinos*. Washington, DC, Association for Supervision and Curriculum Development, 1978.

MacKinnon, D. "Personality and the Realization of Creative Potential," *American Psychologist* (April 1965): 273–281.

Mitchell, B. "What's Happening to Gifted Education in the U.S. Today?" *Roeper Review* (May–June 1980): 7–10.

Mitchell, P., and Erickson, D. "The Education of Gifted and Talented Children: A Status Report," *Exceptional Children*. (September 1978): 12–16.

Olstad, D. "The Pursuit of Excellence Is Not Elitism," *Phi Delta Kappan* (November, 1978): 187–188, 229.

Payne, J. S.; Kaufman, J. M; Patton, J. R.; Brown, G.; and De Mott, R. M. *Exceptional Children in Focus: Incidents, Concepts, and Issues in Special Education*. Columbus, OH: Charles E. Merrill Publishing Co., 1979.

Pressey, S. *Educational Acceleration: Appraisal and Basic Problems*. Bureau of Educational Research Monographs, No. 31. Columbus: Ohio State University Press, 1949.

Renzulli, Joseph. *The Enrichment Triad Model: A Guide for Developing Defensible Programs for the Gifted and Talented*. Wethersfield, Conn.: Creative Learning Press, 1977.

Renzulli, Joseph. "What Makes Giftedness: Re-examining a Definition," *Phi Delta Kappan* (November 1978): 180–184, 261.

Roe, A. *The Making of a Scientist*. New York: Dodd, Mead & Company, 1953.

Schnur, J. "Teachers for the Gifted—Past, Present and Future," *Roeper Review*. (May–June 1980): 5–7.

Stanley, J. "SMPY's DT-PI Mentor Model: Diagnostic Testing Followed by Prescriptive Instruction," *Intellectually Talented Youth Bulletin* Vol. 4, no. 10 (1978): 7.

Terman, L. and Others. *Genetic Studies of Genius: The Gifted Group at Mid-Life*. Stanford, Ca.: Stanford University Press, 1959.

Torrance, E. Paul. "Broadening Concepts of Giftedness in the 70's," *Gifted Child Quarterly* (Winter 1970): 199–208.

Turnbull, A. P., and Schulz, J. B. *Mainstreaming Handicapped Students: A Guide for the Classroom Teacher*. Boston: Allyn and Bacon, 1979.

United States Statutes at Large. 91st Congress, 1970–1971, Vol. 84, Part 1. Washington, DC: U.S. Government Printing Office, 1971.

CHAPTER 17

Responding to Reading Problems

This chapter provides information to help the reader to:

1. State some things teachers can do to create conditions that encourage students to read.
2. Identify several different reading levels that might be found among students in a given classroom.
3. Describe an informal reading inventory.
4. State some processes that can be used in analyzing reading material.
5. List approaches that can be used during the prereading phase in order to improve students' reading comprehension.
6. Define some types of vocabulary words likely to give secondary students problems.
7. Define "three-level guides," "pattern guides," and "study-skills" guides.
8. Describe the importance of the postreading phase.

PRETEST

DIRECTIONS: Using your own paper, answer these true/false questions. For each correct statement, write the word "true." For each incorrect statement, write the word "false."

_____ 1. The level of students' interest in the content influences the relative degree of difficulty they will experience in reading a given prose selection.

_____ 2. Since diagnosis of students is so complete at the elementary level, there is little merit in secondary-school teachers' taking time to diagnose students in terms of their reading abilities.

_____ 3. The Fry Readability Graph can be used to determine the approximate grade-level reading difficulty of a given piece of prose material.

_____ 4. The cloze procedure and the Fry readability graph are alternative procedures that provide exactly the same information.

_____ 5. The basic goal of strategies used during the reading phase is to help students understand how to extract meaning and make connections between and among the ideas and concepts they are reading.

Introduction

Most secondary school teachers view themselves as experts in the subjects they teach. Their enthusiasm for their subjects may lead them to overlook one of the essentials for success in the classroom—students' ability to read and understand the material. If teachers expect students to develop desired levels of competence, they must consider how they learn through reading. Postman (1979, p. 165) pointed out the important linkage between reading and competence in school content areas in his statement, "Biology is not plants and animals. It is language about plants and animals. History is not events. It is language describing and interpreting events."

Secondary teachers often take the reading abilities of their students for granted. They assume that the students have learned the requisite reading skills in the elementary grades. However, this often is not the case. Even the most talented students occasionally have difficulty with some of the material presented. Some students find reading so difficult that they do not succeed on many of their school tasks.

Creating Conditions to Stimulate Reading

Secondary teachers in the content areas have an obligation to help students learn to read and comprehend the material presented in class. Part of this obligation requires them to create conditions that support

"Dyslexia? But she's had all her shots!"

learning from reading. A beginning point in creating these conditions is the modeling of reading by the teacher. Teachers may tell students that reading is important; however, the evidence of a person's values is seen in the actions that are taken. Teachers need to be observed reading books, newspapers, and magazines and deriving personal enjoyment from this activity.

A second step in creating conditions that support reading is to help students realize that reading is an important part of all aspects of life. Throughout their lives, individuals read material ranging from comics to job applications to legal contracts. Teachers can help students reach this understanding by providing for a variety of reading materials in the classroom. These can range from newspapers to technical journals. A corner of the classroom or a special table can be set aside where high-interest reading material can be kept.

One teacher, for example, had success in motivating students to work on reading comprehension by keeping the state Department of Motor Vehicles booklet containing the information needed to obtain drivers

These students are working in a reading laboratory that features special instructional-support equipment. *Photo courtesy of Hugh Rogers/Monkmeyer Press Photo Service.*

licenses. Often copies of rules and regulations for football, basketball, and other sports are popular with students. Other possibilities include high-interest materials such as popular magazines and books. When students have completed assignments or otherwise have some available time (perhaps before or after school) they can be invited to use these items. One football coach, for example, stimulated an interest in reading by making copies of the sports section of several major newspapers available on a daily basis. Students, both athletes and nonathletes, were invited to stop by his office in the morning to read the newspapers. This provided a lively forum for discussion for many students who did not normally spend much time reading.

In many communities, newspaper publishers will make newspapers available for a class of students. They may also have materials that the teacher can use to build content lessons around in the newspapers. Many teachers have found these "Newspaper in the Classroom" materials beneficial in developing students' interest in reading.

Finally, when teachers tell students that it is important for them to read the assigned material, they must be required to *do* something with what they have read. In particular, when it is time to test students on a segment of instruction, some test items should relate to information presented in the required reading. In a survey reported in 1977, one researcher found that a large number of teachers devised tests that students could pass with high scores without doing any of the assigned reading (Rieck 1977).

In addition to establishing basic conditions that emphasize reading, there are a number of more specific approaches that a secondary teacher can use to increase the probability of students' learning through reading. The following sections will introduce some of the approaches that secondary teachers have found useful.

Diagnostic Strategies

The beginning point for solving most instructional problems is diagnosis. Without diagnosis the teacher makes instructional decisions based primarily on conjecture. When this happens, the instructional program often fails. Teachers may become frustrated and blame their students when the primary responsibility for the failure rests with the teachers' own inadequate diagnoses. The probability of success in all aspects of instruction increases dramatically when teachers discover what the students can do and, in response to this information, select appropriate instructional activities.

A distinction should be made between diagnosis as a series of technical steps and the development of a diagnostic sensitivity. There are numerous tests, both formal and informal, that have been developed to help teachers diagnose student difficulties. However, the effective teacher is one who does not merely rely on the results of these tests, but who remains constantly responsive to the clues that students provide regarding their ability to complete reading assignments successfully.

One of the major problems faced by teachers in all subjects is the match between the material and the skill level of the students. Even when teachers have a variety of resources available, they usually have one major text that plays a dominant role. The inability of some class members to read the text may create serious difficulties for the teacher. Teachers need to diagnose the reading-proficiency levels of their students as they compare to the difficulty levels of available course reading materials.

Identifying Reading Levels

Specialists in reading have identified three levels of understanding that can be used in determining whether a student is able to read the material and profit by instruction. These levels are the "independent reading level," the "instructional reading level," and the "frustration reading level". An understanding of a given student's level can help the teacher plan reading assignments that are appropriate.

The reading-proficiency level of a given student may vary depending on reading content. Comprehension, in part, depends on students' prior experiences and prior knowledge. For example, students who are interested in space exploration might be familiar with a high number of specialized terms associated with this topic. As a result, when the subject is space exploration, they may be able to read and understand quite sophisticated material. These same students may find it very difficult to learn from much less sophisticated prose materials that deal with topics with which they are unfamiliar and in which they are uninterested.

Independent Reading Level

Individuals are functioning at the independent reading level when there is a good match between their reading skill and the difficulty of the material being read. The reader can understand what the author is trying to communicate without outside assistance. The reader is familiar with the vocabulary and easily understands the concepts presented. The independent reading level is the level that is best suited for independent study or homework assignments. If students are unable to read the material at the independent level, the time they spend reading the material will be unproductive. Students with a history of academic difficulty may give up if presented with an assignment that is beyond the independent reading level.

Instructional Reading Level

Individuals functioning at the instructional reading level are those who do not have the necessary prior knowledge or reading skill to completely understand the material and concepts contained in the material. However, these individuals are able to comprehend the material when provided with some assistance. Material at this level is appropriate for classroom use when some assistance is available. For example, in-class reading assignments may feature instructional-level materials.

Frustration Reading Level

Individuals functioning at the frustration reading level are unable to handle the material unless given considerable assistance. The gap between the reading ability and the prior knowledge of the student is simply too great and cannot be spanned without considerable individual attention. Because the difficulty of the material clearly exceeds the skill of the student, his or her attempts to read this material may well lead to frustration and anger. These negative emotions are destructive to the development of a positive attitude about both the subject being studied and reading in general. Therefore, teachers should avoid asking individual students to read materials which, for them, are at the frustration level.

Informal Reading Inventories

One way to identify the reading levels of students is through the use of an "informal reading inventory." The informal reading inventory is composed of selections of reading passages that are representative of the types of material students will be expected to read in the class. For example, if the class will be reading predominantly factual or scientific material, the material in the informal reading inventory should be of this type. If the class will be reading different types and styles of literature, the selections should be drawn from these types of literature.

The selections should be drawn from material of varying levels of difficulty. They should be relatively short, approximately 200 to 250 words in length, and should include a logical beginning, clearly develop an idea, and contain a conclusion (Estes and Vaughan 1985).

Selections should be arranged in order of ascending difficulty so that the easiest selections are presented first and the most difficult last. Students are asked to read the material. The teacher watches them as they read. Students' nonverbal actions often will cue the teacher to the levels of frustration they are experiencing in dealing with the reading task. These should be noted. An individual who becomes stressed when reading a selection should not be required to continue.

When students finish each passage, the teacher asks several questions about the reading. These questions require students to recall facts as well as make inferences from the material. Care needs to be taken in asking the questions so that they are clearly related to the information provided in the passage. Poorly framed questions may interfere with student responses and, therefore, lead the teacher to develop faulty conclusions about students' abilities to read and comprehend the assigned material. Since the informal reading inventory presents passages in terms of their difficulty, as the process of reading and questioning continues, the teacher can identify types of material that students can handle at the independent, instructional, and frustration levels.

Informal reading inventories can be used with individual students or with the whole class. Implementing the procedure with the whole class can be a time-consuming approach. In recognition of this difficulty, some teachers prefer to choose a sample of class members. Administering an informal inventory to five or six students will provide a general idea about how difficult students in the class as a whole will find the proposed reading assignment.

Analyzing Reading Material

The general reading difficulty of a specific piece of prose material can be determined by applying one or more readability formulas. "Readability" refers to the relative difficulty of a given prose selection. The readability of a selection varies with the complexity and the length of the sentences, the number of many-syllabled as compare to one- or two-syllabled words, and the number of words that, for some reason or another, the students simply do not know.

Readability formulas are used to identify approximate grade-level readabilities. That is, a given selection might be found to have a grade-level reading difficulty of grade 8, grade 9, grade 10, or some other grade level depending on the results of the application of the readability formula. In using readability formulas, it is important to recognize that grade levels are described in terms of averages. That is, simply because we find a given book to have a readability level of grade 11 does *not* mean that every student in grade 11 can read the material without difficulty. It means that the average eleventh-grader should be able to read the material. The term "average" suggests that, nationally, about half the grade 11 students will be able to read material at this level and about half will experience difficulty.

One of the most commonly used readability formulas is the Fry readability graph developed by Edward Fry. This is a relatively easy procedure to use. It involves selecting a number of 100-word passages from the material to be read and then performing several simple calculations. Plotting the data on the graph provides an estimate of the reading difficulty of the material. The graph and directions for use are presented in Box 17.1.

A readability formula that is very easy to use is the SMOG (Some Measure of Gobbledegook) formula developed by McLaughlin (1969). It is widely favored by busy secondary teachers. The formula requires the teacher to select three 10-sentence passages from near the beginning, the middle, and the end of the material. The number of words with three or more syllables in the 30 sentences is then counted. Words that are repeated are included in the count. If for example, the first ten sentences in the selection contained 10 words with three syllables or more, the second 10 sentences selected contained 15 words with three or more syllables, and the third selection contained 20 words with three or more syllables, the total would be 45.

Box 17.1

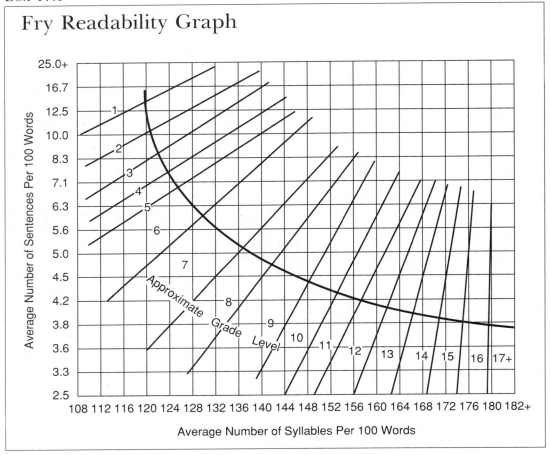

Fry Readability Graph

Average Number of Sentences Per 100 Words

Average Number of Syllables Per 100 Words

The next step in the process is to compare the total with the product of a perfect square (i.e., $5 \times 5, 6 \times 6, 7 \times 7$). The number in our example is 45. The nearest product of a perfect square is 49. We calculate the difference between our number (45) and the closest perfect square to that number (49). In this case, the difference is four ($49 - 45 = 4$). Next, we identify the square root of the perfect square (49). In this case, the square root is seven ($7 \times 7 = 49$). To determine the approximate grade reading-level of this material, we add our difference (4) to the square root (7). In this case we get an estimated grade level of 11 ($4 + 7 = 11$).

Many criticisms of readability formulas have been made. They fail to take into account student interests and motivation, the relationship between prior knowledge of the student and the material, the quality and appropriateness of the visuals that accompany the text, the organiza-

Box 17.1 *cont.*

Expanded Directions for Working Readability Graph*

1. Randomly select three sample passages and count out exactly 100 words each, beginning with the beginning of a sentence. Count proper nouns, initializations, and numerals.

2. Count the number of sentences in 100 words, estimating length of the fraction of the last sentence to the nearest one tenth.

3. Count the total number of syllables in the 100-word passage. If you do not have a hand counter available, simply plut a mark above every syllable over one in each word; then when you get to the end of the passage, count the number of marks and add 100. Small calculators can also be used as counters by pushing numeral 1, then push the + sign for each word or syllable when counting.

4. Enter graph with *average* number of sentences per 100 words and *average* number of syllables; plot dot where the two lines intersect. Area where dot is plotted will give you the approximate grade level.

5. If a great deal of variability is found in syllable count or sentence count, putting more samples into the average is desirable.

6. A word is defined as a group of symbols with a space on either side; thus, *Joe, IRA, 1945,* and *&* are each one word.

7. A syllable is defined as a phonetic syllable. Generally, there are as many syllables as vowel sounds. For example, *stopped* is one syllable and *wanted* is two syllables. When counting syllables for numerals and initializations, count one syllable for each symbol. For example, *1945* is four syllables, *IRA* is three syllables, and *&* is one syllable.

* This extended graph does not outmode or render the earlier (1968) version inoperative or inaccurate; it is an extension.

SOURCE: Edward Fry, "Fry's Readability Graph: Clarification, Validity, and Extension to Level 17," *Journal of Reading* (December 1977): 249.

tion of the material, and the writing style of the author. All of these factors can influence the suitability of a text for a given group of learners.

To make a more accurate determination of the suitability of the material for a given group of students, the teacher can combine readability formulas with the use of the cloze procedure, first introduced by Wilson Taylor (1953). The cloze procedure is a method of systematically deleting words from a prose selection and evaluating the success of the learner in filling in the missing words (Robinson 1971).

The recommended procedure for using the cloze procedure is to select a passage of approximately 300 words from the material to be used in class. Type the first sentence intact and then, starting with the second sentence, begin deleting every fifth word until there are

50 deletions. Each deleted word is replaced with a blank fifteen spaces long. Finish the sentence where the 50th deletion occurs and type one more complete sentence (Estes and Vaughan 1985).

This passage is then presented to the students. They are informed that only one word has been deleted from each blank. Their task is to supply the missing words. The cloze test is then scored by counting the number of exact replacements that are correct. Misspellings can be counted as correct if it is clear that the student's intent was to supply the exact word that was missing from the text. After students have finished working with the test, the teacher grades each student's test. The number of correct replacement words is divided by the total number of words deleted—50—to yield a percent-correct score.

Once percentages have been calculated for individual students, a class average can be determined. The class average is then compared to the following criteria. If the mean of the class is 60 percent or higher, the material is on the independent reading level for the class. If the class mean is between 40 percent and 60 percent, it is on the instructional level. If the mean for the class falls below 40 percent, the material is on the frustration level for the class and should not be used (Estes and Vaughan 1985, p. 40).

In summary, it is important for the teacher to attempt to match student skill levels with the difficulty of the material. The mismatch that often occurs between student skill and material difficulty is one of the most common problems in secondary schools. Making an appropriate match can be facilitated by administering an informal reading inventory to students, determining the readability level of the material that is to be used, and administering a cloze test. Data gathered from these various steps can assist teachers as they work to select reading material that students in their classrooms can understand.

Sometimes teachers are in situations that require them to use reading materials that they know many of their students will find difficult. There are some specific strategies that teachers can use to help their students learn from difficult material. The following section introduces some approaches that have been found to be useful in secondary classrooms.

Instructional Responses to Reading Problems

In planning instructional programs that facilitate reading comprehension it is useful to consider three different instructional phases. The "prereading phase" focuses on actions teachers take before students begin to read. There are numerous useful prereading strategies. The second phase features "during-reading strategies." These are designed to help students derive information as they read assigned materials. The third phase involves implementation of "postreading strategies." These help students to apply what they have learned and to transfer knowledge to new situations.

Prereading Strategies

The previous experience of learners plays a critical role in their comprehension. Prior experience provides students with a frame of reference that helps them fit what is read into a meaningful pattern. To test this principle, find a technical manual in an area you know little about, and try to read it. Even an excellent reader who lacks the necessary background may not be able to derive much meaning from specialized material dealing with sophisticated electrical circuits. The organization, vocabulary and lack of a useful "mental picture" of what is being described make the reading very difficult.

This illustrates what many secondary students experience when asked to read in different subject areas. Students with little previous knowledge or background in the topic being read sometimes feel they are being required to make sense out of a random collection of words. The task they face is extremely difficult. Some of these students simply give up.

There are two major problems that the teacher needs to address in the prereading phase. The first is that secondary students may not have sufficient previous experience in the area being studied. Second, even when they have had appropriate prior experiences, they may not recognize the relevance of these experiences for the assigned reading task. Teachers must help them to identify the connection between prior learning and present academic work. Students need a frame of reference as they attempt to derive meaning from their reading.

The importance of this phase was highlighted by the famous learning theorist, D. W. Ausabel (1963), a quarter of a century ago. He suggested that the use of "advance organizers," broad or general ideas that were provided to the student before beginning the study of material, enhanced learning and retention. These general ideas or organizing frames of reference should be drawn from the previous experience of the student. Several approaches can be used by the teacher to address the problem of providing students with a frame of reference prior to the time they begin reading.

Structured Overview

The structured overview is a graphic display that helps the reader understand the relationship between the concepts or main ideas that are

Box 17.2

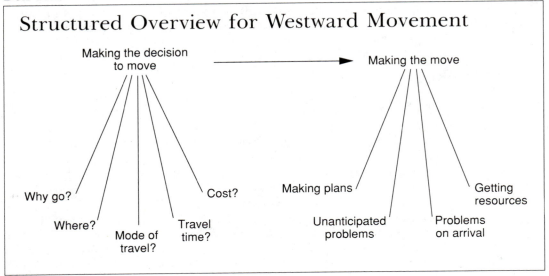

Structured Overview for Westward Movement

going to be read. It typically includes one or more major topics to be covered and questions which, if answered, promote understanding of the topic or topics. (See Box 17.2 for an example of a structured overview). In order for a structured overview to achieve the maximum benefit, students should be involved in its preparation. One way of accomplishing this is to have the students brainstorm what they already know or think they know about some aspects of a topic to be studied. Write responses on the chalkboard or on a blank overhead transparency. Then work together with the class to organize information into a graphic.

For example, students studying the westward movement in American history obviously could not have had direct personal experience in this historic settlement pattern. But many of them will have been involved in a permanent family move. Some of them, too, will have taken an extended trip. These student experiences may be used in the attempt to put together a relevant structured overview.

ReQuest

Another way of providing students with a frame of reference before reading is to identify questions that might be answered during a reading assignment. These questions establish a focus for reading. The ReQuest procedure makes extensive use of questions.

ReQuest is an acronym for "reciprocal questioning." This means that both the students and the teacher are involved in asking and answering questions (Manzo 1969). Student participation in the framing of the questions helps them relate their previous knowledge and their interests to the topic to be studied. A unique and important feature of the ReQuest procedure is that it provides modeling for the students in how to ask and respond to questions. These are the steps that are typically followed when a ReQuest procedure is used:

1. The teacher and the students read the first sentence of a selection together. (If one sentence fails to provide sufficient information for meaningful questions to be asked, the teacher is free to extend the reading to include several sentences.)

2. The teacher closes his or her book while the students keep theirs open. Students may ask the teacher any question they wish that relates to the first sentence (or to whatever length of material they were asked to read). The teacher answers the questions as accurately as possible. The teacher may choose to make some comments to students about the quality of their questions, including some suggestions for improvement.

3. The students then close their books and the teacher asks questions. The teacher should try to ask questions that will help the students recall any previous information they have about the topic or a similar topic and questions that will provide a model for student questioning during their next turn.

4. This procedure may be repeated for several paragraphs until the students can answer a predictive question such as, "What do you think you will find out in the rest of this selection?" Their answers to this question helps them develop a framework for the rest of the reading as well as learning how to ask questions to guide their own reading.

Vocabulary Overview Guide

One of the significant problems for secondary students is understanding the vocabulary words that they encounter in the text. A well-known reading specialist, Robert C. Aukerman, has identified a number of categories of words that frustrate many secondary school readers (1972). Those categories include obsolete words or phrases, colloquial vocabulary, unfamiliar vocabulary and technical vocabulary.

Obsolete terms or phrases are those terms that have either undergone alterations in meaning or have passed out of usage over time. The English language is dynamic and is continually changing. Terms that many of us take for granted are unfamiliar to younger generations. Outdated terms are particularly difficult for many students. Aukerman cites as examples such terms as the following (1972, p. 23). (For those who do not recognize these terms, an explanation has been provided following each.)

arctic
(a rubber overshoe reaching to the ankle or above.)

hooch
(liquor, particularly illicitly distilled liquor.)

lizzie
(Model T Ford)

nosegay
(a small bouquet of flowers)

Colloquial vocabulary occurs frequently in prose selections that attempt to provide the reader with the flavor of regional speech. To accomplish this objective, words may be deliberately misspelled in order to capture the sound of the regional speech. Many students find such writing incomprehensible. For example, Mark Twain's attempts to present to the reader the speech of the Mississippi borderlands in Missouri have charmed many sophisticated readers. However, Twain's language baffles some high school students. The "Irish" English of Mr. Dooley presents even more serious challenges to the typical secondary school reader. The Cornwall dialect in Winston Graham's *Poldark* novels makes no sense at all to many high school students.

Unfamiliar vocabulary includes two kinds of words. One type includes words that students know and may even use but that they have never seen in print. For example, some secondary students may have heard such phrases of foreign origin as "comme ci, comme ca," and be reasonably certain of their meaning, yet they may fail to recognize these phrases when they first encounter them in print.

A second type of unfamiliar vocabulary includes those non-technical words that are simply not known to students. As Aukerman (1972) points out, words of this kind are especially prevalent in the writings of college and university professors who fail to appreciate the limited range of vocabulary of many high school students.

To help teachers who are interested in looking over their texts in order to determine the extent to which unfamiliar vocabulary words are used, Aukerman has developed several lists of what he calls "impedilexae." Impedilexae are words that create reading problems. He has identified lists of impedilexae for the social studies, English, science, mathematics, business, industrial arts, vocational education, and, home economics. Teachers can use the appropriate subject impedilexae to determine which reading material might be likely to cause students difficulty.

"Technical vocabulary" includes the specialized words associated with a particular subject or area of interest. Of all vocabulary problems, teachers are probably most prepared to deal with difficulties associated with technical vocabulary. This is true because teachers do not expect the students to be familiar with these words. Consequently, they typically take time to introduce technical terms to students before they are asked to read materials that contain them.

The kind of technical vocabulary that presents the fewest problems consists of words that are rarely used except in dealing with a specialized subject area. For example, the specialized term "external validity" used by historians in describing procedures followed to establish the authenticity of source material is used in almost no other context.

Another kind of technical vocabulary causes teachers more difficulty. Technical vocabulary of this type has two "lives." On the one hand, these terms are used in a very precise and specialized way by experts in various academic subjects. On the other hand these very same terms are used by the general public to connote things that may be far different from what the terms mean to the academic specialist. For example, the statistician in his or her own specialized use of the term "significant" means to imply that something occurred with a frequency that is demonstrably greater than one would expect from chance or luck. On the other hand, the public uses the term "significant" almost synonymously with the term "important."

Terms that are used one way by specialists and another by members of the general public present students with problems. For example, economists use the term "market" in a very special way. Unwary students may skim over this term when they encouter it for the first time in their text because they believe they already know what it means (a place to buy groceries). To deal with this kind of a situation, teachers need to preview assigned reading carefully and to explain specialized uses of words that students, erroneously, think they already understand.

A Vocabulary Overview Guide can be used to help students overcome vocabulary problems. It outlines steps students are to follow as they work to master unfamiliar vocabulary. The teacher provides the students with a blank form and a set of directions. The directions to the students are as follows.

1. Survey the material to identify the topic.
2. Skim the material and identify unknown vocabulary words. Underline them in pencil or mark them in some way.

Box 17.3

Vocabulary Overview Guide

Chapter Title: The Basics of Economics

Category: Production

Word: Resources

Definition: Anything used to make a product

Clue: people, factories, natural resources

Word: Specialization

Definition: Each person doing one thing well

Clue: plumbers, electricians

Word: _____

Definition: _____

_____

Clue: _____

Category: Consumption

Word: Market

Definition: A meeting together of people to freely buy and sell

Clue: Wants and Demands of people

Word: Income

Definition: What a person makes that can be spent on goods and services

Clue: salary, wages, interest

Word: _____

Definition: _____

_____

_____

Clue: _____

---

3. Try to figure out the meaning of the word from the sentences around it. Then ask someone or use a dictionary to check the meaning.

4. Write the definitions in the text or on paper so that they will be available when you read the text.

5. Read the text.

6. Complete the Vocabulary Overview guide by including the following:

   a. the title of the passage.

   b. categories for grouping the vocabulary words according to topics the words discuss or describe (Give each category a title.)

   c. the vocabulary word.

   d. the definition underneath the vocabulary word.

   e. a clue to help you connect the word to something you already know.

An example of a Vocabulary Overview Guide is provided in Box 17.3. A collection of vocabulary words learned during the semester can help students see how their vocabularies are growing. In addition, teacher review of Vocabulary Overview Guides can help them identify vocabulary words that should be addressed the next time the material is used with a class.

During-Reading Strategies

"During-Reading Strategies" are designed to help students while they are reading a selection of material. The purpose of providing assistance at this stage is to help students gather information in a productive and efficient manner. Many of them do not know how to approach a given selection of material for the purpose of extracting meaning and making connections among "pieces" of information that are presented.

One way to accomplish this purpose is through the use of study guides. Useful guides help students identify their purpose for reading, think about the strategy they will use, and assist them in identifying relationships in the passage they are reading. Secondary teachers commonly use several types of study guides. Among them are three-level guides, pattern guides, and study-skills guides.

Three-Level Guides

Three-Level Guides are designed to develop students' higher-level thinking skills. They help to move beyond the literal meaning of the words they are reading to make inferences and apply new knowledge. Three-Level Guides are organized around three basic questions. Each question establishes a focus on a given level of understanding. The three questions are:

1. What did the material say? (This question is designed to elicit information about students' grasp of the literal meaning of what they have read.)
2. What does the material mean? (This question encourages students to make inferences.)
3. How can I apply this meaning to something else? (This question prompts thought about applications of what has been learned.)

These questions provide guidelines for teachers as they prepare Three-Level Guides related to a specific reading assignment. Using question one as a point of departure, the teacher begins by identifying some literal information contained in the assigned reading. Next, using question two as a beginning point, inferences that might be drawn from the passage are noted. Finally, information that might suggest applications of what has been read is identified. This information is organized and presented for students to use as they read the material. Students are asked to complete the guide as they read. Note the example of a three-level guide provided in Box 17.4.

Box 17.4

Three Level Guide for Math Story Problem

Problem: Tom has 145 boxes of cereal that must be placed on shelves in the supermarket. He is able to place 68 of the boxes on the biggest shelf. He must now place the same number of boxes on two remaining shelves. How many will he need to put on each shelf?

LEVEL 1: Read the problem above. Check those statements that contain important information to help you solve the problem.

_____ Tom works in a supermarket.

_____ There are 145 total boxes.

_____ The boxes contain cereal.

_____ He placed 68 boxes on one shelf.

_____ The remaining boxes are to be placed on two additional shelves with an equal number on each shelf.

_____ There are three shelves total.

LEVEL 2: Check the following statements that contain math ideas related to this problem.

_____ Division is putting an amount into equal groups.

_____ When we take an amount away we subtract to find the amount left.

_____ Adding groups with the same amount is multiplying.

_____ When we put an amount into groups of the same size we divide the amount by the number of groups.

LEVEL 3: Below are possible ways of getting an answer to the problem. Check those that apply to this problem.

_____ $145 - 68$

_____ $145 + 68$

_____ $(145 - 2) + 68$

_____ $(145 - 68) - 2$

Pattern Guides

As they write, authors usually follow a specific organizational pattern. Patterns used by individual authors vary in terms of their purposes. For example, historical material is often written following a chronological sequence pattern. Scientific material often is organized into large categories. Other common patterns found in secondary school reading material are the comparison-and-contrast pattern, the cause-and-effect pattern, or the general-statement-followed-by-supportive-data pattern. The comprehension of material read can be greatly enhanced if the reader is aware of the pattern of organization used in presenting the material. "Pattern Guides" are useful tools for helping students understand and identify these patterns when they are reading.

Pattern Guides can follow several formats depending on the pattern that is followed. Some of them are simply skeleton outlines that list some main ideas with a few missing parts provided for students to fill in as they read. Somewhat more sophisticated Pattern Guides may list some "effects" and call on students to fill in information about their "causes." Some Pattern Guides appear as complex "webs" that display relationships among ideas. Students may be asked to fill in these missing links using information they have derived from their reading.

When constructing a Pattern Guide, the teacher needs first to read the material and identify the pattern of organization. One way of doing this is to look for key words. Words such as "first," "second," "third," "before," and "after" usually indicate a sequential or chronological pattern. Use of the conjunctions "but" and "and" often indicate comparisons or contrasts (Estes and Vaughan 1985, p. 162).

After the pattern has been identified, the teacher decides on a format that will be most appropriate for the organization of the material. When they first introduce Pattern Guides, teachers find it useful to provide students with a considerable amount of information. This information provides useful cues to students as they seek out additional information they will need to find in order to complete the guide. As students become more familiar with the procedure, more and more detail can be omitted. This makes completing the guide more difficult. A final challenge is to have the students learn how to construct their own guides as they approach new material. This process reinforces the idea that authors' patterns vary and that, in part, a successful reading strategy involves the ability to recognize the scheme used by the writer(s) of the assigned material.

Study-Skills Guide

A third type of a guide that can be used for students during reading is a Study-Skills Guide. This guide is designed to help the students monitor their own reading skills and think about the material they are reading. Often, students read their assignments very superficially. They may read the words, but fail to think about what they have learned or about what is important. The Study-Skills Guide prompts students to stop at critical points as they read and respond to questions or engage in an activity. The purpose is to increase their levels of motivation and to help them monitor what they have read. When they find they cannot answer the questions or perform the required activity, they can either re-read the material or seek assistance from the teacher. In time, students begin to incorporate key questions of their own as they read. When this happens, their levels of comprehension increase.

Study-Skills Guides are not difficult to construct. As a first step, the teacher reads through the material and identifies places for students to stop reading. Questions are developed for students when they stop. Sometimes, required activities are described. If questions are used, they should prompt students to monitor their own comprehension and reading strategy. The following are examples of questions that might appear on a Study-Skills Guide.

- Summarize the section you read in one sentence.
- What do you think will happen next?
- What information from this section do you think might be on a test your teacher might prepare?

An example of a Study-Skills Guide is provided in Box 17.5.

Postreading Strategies

Many teachers do not realize that one of the most important steps in helping students learn how to process and comprehend material occurs after students have completed reading. In order for individuals to understand and comprehend new material, they need to relate it to what they already know and understand. This can be done in the postreading phase when students reflect and react to the material they have just read.

Organizing students into small groups often is useful during the postreading phase of instruction. When students are in small groups, there is a possibility for many more individuals to participate than when the class sits as one large group. In particular, there are opportunities for students who have succeeded with the reading assignment to share their understanding with others. The models these students provide can be useful for students who have found the assigned reading difficult and who have failed to gain the hoped-for insights from the reading activity.

A number of postreading strategies have been developed. Among them are Graphic Post-Organizers and Interaction Frames.

Graphic Post-Organizers

The Graphic Post-Organizers' technique is an extension of the Structured-Overview approach discussed earlier (Estes and Vaughan 1985,

Box 17.5

Study Skills Guide

DIRECTIONS: As you read the assigned pages follow the steps listed below. You will be asked to stop your reading at specific places and review what you have read. It is important for you to be aware of how you are thinking about and organizing the material as you read.

STEP 1: Start on page 20 and read to the bottom of page 21. What do you think is important for you to know about this section? _____
_____

STEP 2: After reading to the third paragraph on page 23, write 2 or 3 sentences about what you have learned. If you cannot do this or do not understand what you are reading, what can you do to get help? _____
_____

STEP 3: Before reading the next section, what do you predict will happen?
_____
_____

STEP 4: Read to the end of page 25. Was your prediction correct? What information in this section is likely to be on a test?
_____
_____
_____

STEP 5: Read to the second paragraph on page 27. List in sequence the events that happened. Do you feel you are understanding the material? Would rereading help?
_____
_____
_____

STEP 6: The last sentence of paragraph 3 on page 28 states the main point of this chapter. Rewrite this statement into a question. _____
_____

STEP 7: After finishing the chapter what pictures or images of the events come to mind? _____
_____

How is this like something you know about? _____
_____

What was most difficult to understand?
_____
_____

Would it help to discuss these difficult parts with someone? Write a short summary of what you have read. _____
_____
_____

p. 182). In the Structured-Overview approach, teachers prepare a framework for students to use while they are reading. Graphic Post-Organizers are developed by the students themselves. Students reflect on what they have read and construct their own structure. The process of construction helps them relate what they have read to prior levels of understanding. The technique is designed to help students refine and modify previous information by reflecting on new information and insights they have gained from their reading.

Constructing the post organizer can be done rather simply using 3 × 5 cards of two different colors. Each group of four to six individuals is given a packet of cards. It becomes each group's goal to identify the basic concepts or main ideas that were covered in the passage read. Each group member records on the cards of one color what he or she believes were the major concepts or ideas. Each member then presents these to the rest of the group and defends his or her choice. The group then reaches a consensus on the major concepts or ideas.

Individuals then take the card of another color and identify key information or supporting ideas that fit under each of the major concepts or ideas identified by the cards completed during the first part of the exercise. Individual group members once again defend their choices of supporting information. Finally, each group arranges this information under the appropriate concept or idea.

When members of a group have arranged their cards in a manner that is satisfying to them, they proceed to make a graph or chart. This is simply a visual depiction of the major ideas that have been identified and the important subordinate information associated with each. The graph can be prepared on large sheets of paper or on a blank overhead transparency. Once all groups have completed this phase, the graphs are displayed. They become a focus for a class discussion. The teacher can react to the various organizational schemes. Students often learn that there are several ways to organize what they have read. A discussion of these issues helps students to think about ways of organizing and thinking about what they read.

Interaction Frames

Interaction Frames are especially useful in helping students to organize information from reading selections that refer to interactions between or among two or more individuals or groups. The content students read in their English and social studies classes is often of this type. Interaction Frames are organized around these four basic questions:

1. What were the goals of the various individuals or groups?
2. What actions did they take to try to accomplish these goals?
3. How did the individuals or groups interact?
4. What were the outcomes of the interactions?

Students are asked to repond to these questions. Then, they provide a brief summary of their responses. Often teachers assign students

Box 17.6

Interaction Frames

Faction A   Faction B

Goals of Faction A   Goals of Faction B

1.   1.
2.   2.

Actions: Actions:

1.   1.
2.   2.

How these two factions interacted

Conflicts:

1.
2.

Compromises:

1.
2.

Cooperations:

1.
2.

Results for Faction A   Results for Faction B

1.   1.
2.   2.

Summary

---

to groups for the purpose of responding to questions and preparing summaries. This provides them opportunities to consider thinking processes of others and to reflect more carefully on what they have read. An example of an interaction frame is provided in Box 17.6.

In summary, the postreading phase is one of the most important phases of the comprehension process. It helps students reflect on their own thinking. Activities are designed to help them develop more systematic and sophisticated ways of interpreting information they have read.

Key Ideas in Summary

1. All teachers share in the responsibility to help students learn how to comprehend reading material. Part of this responsibility involves the creation of conditions that emphasize the importance of reading. Teachers establish these conditions by modeling good reading habits, providing a variety of reading material, and testing students over material they have been assigned to read.

2. It is important for teachers to identify the reading levels of students in the classroom. The match between the reading level of students and the difficulty of the material is a critical variable in creating a successful classroom environment. Material that is so difficult that it places students at the frustration level should not be used.

3. Teachers often construct and use informal reading inventories to help them identify the reading level of the students in the classroom. Informal inventories can be used with the whole class or only with those who seem to be having difficulty reading the assigned material.

4. Several formulas for identifying the readability of material are available. Two of the more popular are the Fry Readability Formula and SMOG. Using these formulas in combination with a cloze test can help teachers select material that is appropriate for the reading levels of students in their classrooms.

5. Students' abilities to learn from a given reading assignment, in part, is related to their prior knowledge and experience. Several approaches can be used to help students relate this prior knowledge to the material that is to be read. Among useful approaches are Structured Overviews and ReQuest.

6. Vocabulary difficulties are a prime souce of confusion for students. There are several types of vocabulary that tend to cause problems for secondary students. These include obsolete words or phrases, technical vocabulary, colloquial vocabulary, and unfamiliar vocabulary. Vocabulary Overview Guides are useful in helping students become familiar with potentially-confusing words.

7. Providing guidance during the reading phase prompts students to consider whether or not they are understanding what they are reading. Classroom activities at this time seek to help students develop effective techniques for organizing and understanding the material they are reading. Three-Level Guides, Pattern Guides, and Study-Skills Guides are useful for accomplishing this purpose.

8. Effective postreading strategies help students clarify and modify their conceptual frameworks. A good approach to the postreading phase is to have students work in small groups to reflect on and react to what they have read. In addition, working in small groups provides unsuccessful students an opportunity to observe students who are successful.

POSTTEST

DIRECTIONS: Using your own paper, answer these true/false questions. For each correct statement, write the word "true." For each incorrect statement, write the word "false."

_____ 1. An important part of creating conditions to stimulate reading is the modeling of good reading by the teacher.

_____ 2. A major task of the teacher is to provide for a match between student reading abilities and material difficulty.

_____ 3. Informal reading inventories are readily available from textbook publishers.

_____ 4. A major goal of the prereading phase is to help a reader develop a framework for organizing the material to be read.

_____ 5. Postreading strategies generally can be omitted with little loss of learning.

Bibliography

AUKERMAN, R. C.   *Reading in the Secondary School Classroom.*   New York: McGraw Hill, 1972.

AUSABEL, D. W.   *The Psychology of Meaningful Verbal Learning.*   New York: Grune and Stratton, 1963.

ESTES, T. H. AND VAUGHAN, J. L.   *Reading and Learning in the Content Classroom: Diagnostic and Instructional Strategies,* Second Edition. Boston, Allyn and Bacon, 1985.

FRY, E.   "Fry's Readability Graph: Clarifications, Validity, and Extensions to Level 17," *Journal of Reading* (December 1977): 242–252.

MCLAUGHLIN, G. H.   "SMOG Grading: A New Readability Formula." *Journal of Reading* (May 1969): 639–649.

MANZO, A. V.   "ReQuest Procedure," *Journal of Reading* (November 1969): 123–126.

MOORE, D. W.; MOORE, S. A.; CUNNINGHAM, P. M.; AND CUNNINGHAM, J. W. *Developing Readers and Writers in the Content Areas: K-12.* New York: Longman, 1986.

POSTMAN, N. *Teaching as a Conserving Activity.* New York: Delacorte, 1979.

RIECK, B. "How Content Teachers Telegraph Messages Against Reading," *Journal of Reading* (May 1977): 646–648.

ROBINSON, R. D. *An Introduction to the Cloze Procedure.* Newark, Del.: International Reading Assciation, 1971.

TAYLOR, W. L. "Cloze Procedure: A New Tool for Measuring Readability," *Journalism Quarterly* (Fall 1953): 415–433.

PART V

Professional Concerns

CHAPTER 18

Technology and the Secondary Schools

AIMS

This chapter provides information to help the reader to:

1. Recognize the general impact technology is having on society and schools.
2. Explain some basic differences between modern electronics-based technologies and older mechanical-based technologies.
3. Cite examples of earlier technological innovations and describe their impact on educational programs.
4. Describe some general barriers to the adoption of technological innovations in the schools that began to appear in the early and middle 1980s.
5. Cite examples of a number of emerging technological innovations that have already influenced or are beginning to influence secondary schools' instructional programs.

PRETEST

DIRECTIONS: Using your own paper, answer these true/false questions. For each correct statement, write the word "true." For each incorrect statement, write the word "false."

_____ 1. Microcomputers have more moving parts than typewriters.

_____ 2. Discoveries in microelectronics have made possible many of the newer innovations found in today's secondary schools.

_____ 3. Historically, new technologies have achieved even wider use in the schools than proponents of the technologies had dared to hope for.

_____ 4. One feature that has attracted secondary school teachers to videocassettes is that it is possible to record new information and to replace old information.

_____ 5. CD-ROM is a technology that has become outdated because of its inability to store large amounts of information.

Introduction

Technological change is accelerating. Increasingly, nations' standings in the world are being measured by the level of sophistication of their technology-based industries. Many of the educational reform proposals of the 1980s suggested that American schools were doing too little to prepare students for a world which would demand high levels of technological expertise. An underlying theme of many of these reports is that American students are falling behind their counterparts in other nations in terms of their technological expertise. (For more discussion of this general issue, review material in Chapter 1.)

Secondary schools today are under pressure to increase their use of technology to support instruction *and* to make students more personally familiar with emerging technologies. The second part of this statement reflects an important change from previous efforts to introduce technological innovations into the schools. These earlier innovations included such things as educational films, first introduced in large numbers in the 1930s, and educational television, which attracted a tremendous amount of enthusiasm in the 1960s. In each case, these technologies were proposed as vehicles for supporting instruction. There was little pressure for teachers to familiarize students with film-making technology or with television technology.

Many of the newer technological innovations center around electronics. Computers are a prime example. While one aim of advocates of increased school-use of technology is to use computers to support the general instructional program, this is not the only purpose they have in mind. Additionally, schools are being encouraged to familiarize students with the technology itself. Increasingly students are being taught to become computer-literate or technology-literate. This means that they should leave schools (1) unafraid of new technologies, (2) with abilities to use some of the technologies, and (3) unafraid of a world in which they will be required to master new technologies as they become available.

Why has there been an interest in familiarizing secondary students with these new technologies? One reason this has happened is that new, electronics-based technology has become pervasive in the work place. Education of employees in many industries increasingly depends on sophisticated technology. For example, by the end of 1988, IBM estimated that about 60 percent of all of its internal employee education programs were delivered through communication satellites and educational television (Charp 1988, p. 8). Supporters of new technologies have pointed to successful educational applications in industry as evidence that these applications make sense for public schools as well. Further, computers and other technologies have become pervasive features of the world of work. Increasingly employers expect new workers to be familiar with their use.

Sophisticated production techniques have resulted in dramatic price reductions. For example, word-processing equipment that would have cost $15,000 or more in 1980 can be had today for several hundred dollars. The old equipment was about as large as an upright piano; today's versions fit easily on a portion of a desk top. The low price and convenient size of this equipment has greatly expanded its use. Increasingly, employers expect employees to be familiar with its use. This expectation has encouraged schools to develop instructional experiences designed to produce technology-literate graduates.

Pressures on schools to adopt these newer technologies have been very heavy. Influential school patrons have worked hard to get these technologies into the schools. In some instances, school districts seem to compete with one another in this regard. Public relations brochures from some districts have pointed with pride to the number of computers available per student. Occasionally, the enthusiasm for purchasing new equipment has raced ahead of the efforts to plan carefully for its effective use in school programs. Box 18.1 discusses the high cost of microcomputers in the classroom.

The Nature of the New Technologies

Computers represent only one of the many new technologies that are increasingly being used in today's middle schools, junior high schools, and senior high schools. Others include videocassettes, optical discs, teletex, and videotex. Each of these innovations has its unique characteristics. However, they all share a common characteristic that suggests they are quite different from earlier technological innovations. Specifically, each of them depends on electronic as opposed to mechanical technologies. This has important implications for equipment costs and maintenance.

Box 18.1

Does Student Use of Microcomputers Justify Their Cost?

In secondary school programs, microcomputers are used most frequently by students for the purposes of (a) writing letters and reports, (b) making graphs, (c) making data bases, and (d) writing computer programs. A recent survey reported that 53.5 percent of 11th graders never use computers for writing letters and reports, 78.9 percent never use computers for making graphs, 82.7 percent never use computers for making data bases, and 67.8 percent never use computers for writing computer programs.

What Do You Think?

Read the information on the left, then respond to these questions.

1. Individual microcomputers cost hundreds of dollars. Given the levels of student use indicated in the material noted above, does their purchase represent a wise expenditure of school funds?

2. Some people would suggest that these figures are the result of too few computers in the schools. Others argue that the computers that are there are underutilized. What is your view?

3. Would you expect these figures to be different if a similar student-use survey were conducted 10 years from now? Why, or why not?

By way of contrast, many older technologies made very heavy use of mechanical technologies. Consider, for example, the motion picture projector and the typewriter. Each has dozens of moving parts. These moving parts produce vibration. Mechanical wearing of part on part results in relatively frequent break-downs. Maintenance costs have been high in settings where this equipment has been heavily used.

Innovations depending on electronic innovations have many fewer moving parts (Hawkridge 1983). As a result, there are fewer limits on their speed of operation. Electronic technology depends on an ability to control the flow of electrons through elaborate circuits. Discoveries in microelectronics have led to the production of extremely small electronic devices, especially switches and circuits. Today, thousands of circuits and switches can be embedded on tiny chips, less than one-fourth of a square inch in size. Sophisticated production lines have been set up that allow the relatively inexpensive manufacture of these microchips by the millions. This production system and the high degree of competition in the business have acted to produce electronic devices that are small in size and relatively cheap. Since electronic equipment has few moving parts, maintenance costs often are low. For example, the keyboard on a microcomputer is one of its few moving parts. Maintenance on moving parts of microcomputers often is a fraction of that required for a busy office typewriter.

Forces Supporting Expanded Emphases on New Technologies

National security fears are an important force behind the drive to expand use of new technologies in the schools. One measure of a nation's political power is its economic strength. Economic strength depends, in part, on an educated citizenry that is highly familiar with the latest technologies. Many of the reform reports of the 1980s suggested that students in the United States were being less well prepared for the technical demands of the world of work than they should be. Without this kind of expertise, economic growth could falter. A consequence of such a development might well be a general weakening of the nation's economic health. A weaker economy would be less able to sustain a strong national defense. Hence, the nation's security could be put at risk.

In addition to arguments related to national security, other proponents of technology in the schools point out the personal benefits such programs bring to learners. As far back as the early 1980s the Education Commission of the States pointed out that in the future most American workers would not be engaged in the production of goods. Rather, the future will witness a time when "an increasing percentage of workers will be retrieving, processing, and transmitting information" (Education Commission of the States 1983, p. l). Modern work with information is highly dependent on electronic technologies. Hence, students who become familiar with these technologies in school will have a great advantage in the job market over students who lack such training.

In some respects, American schools enjoy advantages over their counterparts in other parts of the world as they seek to emphasize emerging technologies. This is particularly true with respect to computer technology. In the United States, there are personal computers in millions of homes. As a result, many American students have learned something about computers at home. Indeed, some of them are quite advanced users by the time they enter their secondary school years.

This situation is quite different in many other parts of the world. For example, in Europe, personal computers are very expensive and fewer of them are found in students' homes. Europe lacks the thousands of young people who, on their own, have worked directly with computers before they encounter them in their school programs (Duff 1986). This means that European school programs have to assume that nearly all learners know nothing about computers. In this country, because of their prior experience with computers, some students are able to begin computer work at school at quite advanced levels.

Expansion of computer-related school programs in the United States enjoys one other important advantage over similar efforts in Europe. In this country, educators who are interested in spreading this technology can draw support from large and prestigious university departments of computer science. Strong university computer science departments are not widespread in Europe. Indeed, there is a tendency in some places for computer specialists to be regarded as sophisticated mechanics (Duff 1986). They do not enjoy the high prestige of their American counterparts. As a result, they have less influence on school programs.

Further, the tendencies to downsize electronic equipment and to offer it at lower prices have also interested school leaders in microcomputers and other technologically oriented equipment. The great increase in the volume of school purchases of equipment based on new electronic technologies that began in the early 1980s continues unabated today.

What all of this means is that American schools exist in an environment that is highly receptive to an increased emphasis on new electronic technology. There is political support for this emphasis among the public at large. This support is buttressed by a highly respected technical community that generally is eager to work with school personnel to infuse new technologies into school programs.

Forces Opposing the Spread of New Technologies in the Schools

Barriers facing introduction of new electronic technologies are generally similar to those that have often confronted new innovations through the years. Larry Cuban (1986) has made an extensive study of innovations in the schools. He found that innovations proposed for use in the schools often go through four distinct phases. First is the "exhilaration phase." This phase features announcements by school authorities of marvelous positive changes that will accompany or result from the innovation's introduction. Cuban found that these announcements often have been made by individuals who themselves would not be required to work with the innovation on a day-to-day basis in the classroom.

The next phase is the "scientific-credibility phase." At this point in the process, school officials work hard to discover a research base that supports the innovation's effectiveness. Often there are reports that installation of the change resulted in improvement of student scores as compared to outdated "traditional" methods. If no score improvement can be documented, sometimes there is a reported finding that equivalent scores resulted from use of the innovation at less cost than those achieved when "traditional" approaches were used.

The studies surveyed during the scientific-credibility phase frequently are used to convince authorities to adopt an innovation. Once this decision has been made and the innovation has been introduced, often the innovation is used less extensively than had been hoped. Often, too, its overall effectiveness falls short of initial hopes. This leads to what Cuban has aptly described as the "disappointment phase."

Disappointment frequently is felt most acutely by people who were the strongest supporters of the change. This is particularly likely to be true of administrators who have taken a public stand to back the innovation. This disappointment often leads to a search for explanations about why the innovation failed to live up to expectations. Sometimes teachers are blamed. When this happens, Cuban (1986) suggests that the innovation-introduction cycle has entered the "teacher-bashing phase." When this happens, teachers are sometimes depicted as unbending conservatives who have deliberately stood in the way of an innovation that is "basically sound." Had teachers embraced the innovation enthusiastically, so the argument goes, wonderful results would have been achieved.

Cuban (1986) argues that it is unfair for teachers to be blamed for the failure of many technological innovations to take root. Failure more logically can be attributed to (a) methods used to introduce the change, (b) the nature of the individual innovation, and (c) the character of teachers' working conditions. (See Box 18.2.)

Historically, introduction of innovations has often been a "top-down" process. This means that supporters of innovations such as instructional films, educational television, and programmed instruction did not initially consult with teachers. Rather, they attempted to influence school boards to adopt these technologies. Once convinced, school boards ordered administrators to implement the change, and administrators passed along these instructions to teachers. This pattern left teachers out of the picture until policy decisions mandating innovation adoption were made.

As a result of this process, most teachers had little background knowledge about the innovations. Further, they had little emotional commitment to them. Frequently, with very little (if any) training, teachers were expected to include these new technologies in their day-to-day instructional planning. There was an assumption that teachers would be able to adapt easily to these changes. But, as Cuban has written, "little in the

Box 18.2

Teacher Survey on Low-Tech and High-Tech Innovations

Larry Cuban (1986) argues that many high-tech innovations are not well matched to conditions teachers face in their classrooms. To test this view, interview one or more teachers about four instructional technologies: textbooks, overhead projectors, videocassette players, and microcomputers. Take notes about their responses to each question. Share information with your instructor.

1. As a teacher, how easy do you and your students find each of the following to use?

   - textbooks
   - overhead projectors
   - videocassette players
   - microcomputers

2. As a teacher, how would you rate the flexibility of each of the following? That is, how free are you to schedule the occasions and times of their use?

   - textbooks
   - overhead projectors
   - videocassette players
   - microcomputers

3. How dependable do you find each of the following to be?

   - textbooks
   - overhead projectors
   - videocassette players
   - microcomputers

formal training and early years of a teacher's career . . . nurtures the use of the newer forms of technology" (Cuban 1986, p. 60).

Many environmental variables have interfered with secondary teachers' successful use of innovations. For example, instructional programs requiring the use of educational films and educational television depend on the availability of special equipment. Further, this equipment must be in good working order. Teachers who have planned lessons only to find needed equipment is missing or out of order often have become frustrated with technological innovations. Such stand-bys as chalkboards and textbooks may not be flashy, but they are a highly dependable instructional resource. The perceived reliability of traditional instructional technologies as compared to their suggested replacements has contributed to a reluctance of some teachers to commit strongly to some of the newer technologies.

Some of the early attempts to introduce computers into school programs featured large computers that forced teachers to take students to special classrooms for instruction. Today, microcomputers are available in individual classrooms. While this represents an improvement, teachers often are still concerned about the inability to involve larger numbers of students on this equipment at the same time. This difficulty needs to be compared with the situation teachers face when using one of the most time-tested technologies, the textbook. In most cases, a textbook is made available to every student in the class.

The issue of flexibility-of-use is very important to teachers. Some recommended innovations have placed great constraints on teachers. This has been particularly true in terms of their flexibility to vary scheduling of different learning experiences. Educational television, especially when first introduced on a large scale in the 1950s and 1960s, was an example of a particularly restrictive technology. Broadcast schedules generally required all interested teachers to have their classes prepared to view programs at prearranged times. This took away planning flexibility. Consequently, many teachers found it difficult to integrate educational television into their instructional programs.

More recent innovations have not been so constraining. For example, videotapes of television programs can be used by individual teachers whenever they deem them appropriate (provided, of course, the needed playback equipment and television receivers are available and in working order). In general, it is fair to say that the newer technologies seem to be responding to teachers' desires to exercise more personal discretion over times and occasions of their use.

As noted, early educational television featured centralized broadcasting of programs. From this inflexible beginning, educational television has evolved into a highly flexible instructional technology. This has been especially true since the invention of affordable videotaping equipment. This equipment has placed programming control directly into the hands of individual teachers. Teachers can record and replay programs as they see fit.

Additionally, videocameras have allowed teachers to prepare videotapes of programs of their own making. Many physical education teachers use this equipment. The technology has been enormously beneficial to them in teaching and critiquing complicated skills, for example in tumbling classes. It provides teachers with a means of providing students with immediate visual feedback about their performances.

The newer electronic technologies lend themselves well to decentralized use. More than ever before, teachers are able to use them for purposes they identify and at times of their own choosing. This flexibility of use has the potential to prompt much wider use of some of the newer technologies than of the less flexible innovations introduced before the age of the microchip.

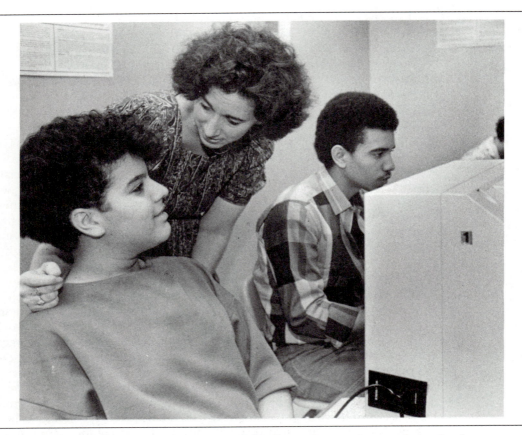

Ever-increasing numbers of computers are available for student use in secondary schools. *Photo courtesy of Maria R. Bastone.*

Some Examples of Technologies Found in the Schools

The technological innovations introduced in this section represent a cross-section of those being introduced into the secondary schools today. Some of them already exist in the schools in very large numbers. Others are just beginning to be incorporated into school programs. Some will not be widely used until the middle and late 1990s. Indeed, some that show promise today may not work out as expected and may never play a large role in secondary school instructional programs.

Microcomputers

The decade of the 1980s witnessed a tremendous growth in the number of microcomputers in the schools. From a modest number at the beginning of the decade, numbers of schools with microcomputers soared to over 90 percent by the middle 1980s (Cuban 1986). Today, it is rare to find a secondary school anywhere that lacks microcomputers.

The great growth in microcomputer numbers does not necessarily suggest that they are "taking over" or even always "very common" in secondary school courses. One reason for this situation has been noted previously. Often there are not sufficient numbers of machines for each student in a class. This has tended to restrict their uses for instructional purposes. In the last several years, a number of firms have begun marketing devices that project images from microcomputer screens on to large wall screens. This equipment has made it possible for teachers to use some programs to good effect with the entire class. However, it still has not resolved the problem of providing all students with frequent access to individual computers for the purpose of improving their personal levels of proficiency.

Without sufficient machines for each student, teachers have often found it difficult to integrate microcomputer use into their regular instructional program. Frequently, the computers have been used to provide enrichment experiences for limited numbers of students. Sometimes teachers have given microcomputer time to students as a reward for successfully completed assignments.

In response to the lack of machines problem, some middle schools, junior high schools, and senior high schools have established special microcomputer laboratories. These are rooms equipped with enough computers to accommodate an entire class. Teachers take class members to the laboratory for lessons involving use of relevant educational software. While these laboratories do provide students with opportunities to work individually on the machines, the need to move out of the regular classroom and the need to work out use schedules with other teachers impose some constraints on their use. (See Box 18.3.)

When budgets allow and when there is sufficient space, many secondary school teachers prefer to have a number of microcomputers located in their regular classrooms. Teachers generally find it easier to integrate the equipment into their programs when it is immediately at hand and when they can use the equipment whenever they deem it appropriate. There has been a tendency for school officials to place more microcomputers into rooms of science and mathematics teachers than of English and social studies teachers (Cuban 1986). In large measure, this has resulted because more and better instructional software

Box 18.3

Have Schools Moved Too Quickly to Buy Computers?

One study revealed that, when junior high school students used microcomputers, they used them fully 60 percent of the time for simple drill-and-practice activities. In other words, the kinds of exercises that have been available for years in workbooks have simply been converted to software. Rather than using the inexpensive workbooks, large numbers of junior high school students now sit at computers and do the same exercises by responding to information on a screen. This represents an unconscionable educational decision. Very low level skill work, that can be very successfully accommodated by workbooks, now is being delivered at an incredibly high cost via computers. In their eagerness to appear "up-to-date," schools have frittered away scarce resources on an expensive and, to judge from how it is being used, an unnecessary technology.

What Do You Think?

Read the comments above. Then answer these questions.

1. Have schools been too quick to purchase microcomputers? Why, or why not?
2. If you were a school official, how would you respond to these comments?
3. Would you expect a survey taken 10 years from now to reveal as much drill-and-practice work on computers?

---

was initially available in science and mathematics than in English and social studies.

Today, large amounts of quality software are available in many areas of the secondary curriculum. Though poor software continues to exist, excellent programs are available. The higher quality software is gradually driving out some of the poorer programs that were made available to teachers in the early 1980s when substantial numbers of computers began to be used in the schools. One result has been a great expansion in the numbers of microcomputers into classrooms of secondary school teachers in nearly all subject areas.

The availability of better software has led to a shift in emphases of school programs that incorporate computer use. The first computer classes in high schools were established to serve needs of students who had an aptitude for mathematics and who were interested in learning programming languages. Some of the more advanced courses of this type featured emphases on sophisticated programming languages that were used commonly in business and research applications of computer technology. In general, the courses provided opportunities for students who, after graduating from high school, might work with large mainframe computers.

The invention of the microcomputer and the expansion of good instructional software have resulted in changes in the ways computers are used in the schools. Some of the traditional computer courses remain. However, the vast majority of students today are likely to encounter computers not in these highly specialized courses but rather in their regular English, mathematics, social studies, and mathematics classes (among others). Improved off-the-shelf software makes it possible for teachers to teach subject-matter content to students, through the medium of the computer, even if the students have no knowledge of computer programming. Students are using computers to master subject-matter content.

Improvements in computer software and increasing teacher expertise in using microcomputers have begun to influence how some content is taught. English teachers have always been interested in improving students' writing skills. Traditionally students have found the process of revising and rewriting to be a tedious, difficult chore. Today's word-processing programs make revision and rewriting relatively easy. As a result, some teachers find that students are willing to do more revising and rewriting than they used to be willing to do.

An important side effect of more instructional applications of microcomputers is an increased student familiarity with computer hardware. Supporters of computer-based instructional programs believe that students who use computers in school will make a relatively smooth transition to using with them in the work place.

Videotape

Audiotaping equipment has been available for many years. The kind of tape used in videotaping is similar in many respects to that used in audiotaping. In videotaping, an electronic record is made simultaneously of both audio and visual information. Tape can be saved for a more or less indefinite period of time. It can be erased, or it can be recorded over as new information is electronically encoded.

There are two general approaches to packaging videotape. Sometimes it is wound on free-standing reels. Today, most tapes are enclosed in cassettes or cartridges, plastic containers that enclose two reels. When the cassette is inserted into a unit that will either record new information or play back previously encoded information, tape moves from one reel to another. Because of their ease of handling, videocassettes have become very popular.

Today, many stores rent videocassettes of popular films for home use. Large numbers of educational programs are also available on cassettes. There has been an enormous growth in numbers of households and of schools with videocassette recording and playback equipment. This has created a huge market for pre-recorded videocassettes and a general decline in their prices, greatly adding to their attractiveness for use in school programs.

Videocassettes are very well adapted to school settings. They can provide instruction that formerly required use of educational films. Further, they can do so at a much reduced cost. A typical half-hour color instructional film may cost as much as $500. Often a videocassette of the same film can be purchased for one-tenth of this amount. With reasonable care, a videocassette will last for many years. Videocassettes are not nearly so vulnerable to the kinds of breaks and tears that often afflict 16 mm films.

Many teachers have found videocassettes to be easy to use and easy to integrate into their instructional programs. A single playback unit in a classroom can serve the needs of an entire class of students provided that television monitor screens are reasonably large and that care is taken to properly arrange student chairs. The videocassettes themselves are not bulky, and lend themselves easily to storage in classroom cabinets. Videocassette technology is very flexible. Teachers are generally free to use programs at times and places of their choosing. Playback equipment is very "user friendly." A newcomer to the technology can become confident and proficient in a very short period of time.

In addition to playing back pre-recorded videocassettes, many teachers are now using combination video-camera/video-recorder equipment to make videorecordings of their own. This equipment is becoming increasingly light, portable, and affordable. Teachers use it to do such things as make video-recordings of student activities of field trips, of art students' first attempts to raise a pot using a potter's wheel, of high school wrestlers' performances during matches, and so forth. They are particularly useful when instruction focuses on a specific skill. Video-recordings can be replayed immediately after they are made and can provide very useful feedback to students. (See Box 18.4.)

Optical Discs

Optical discs are of two basic types, audiodiscs (often simply called "compact discs") and videodiscs. There are several ways information is stored and retrieved, including the increasing use of laser beams. As the discs rotate, laser beams "read" information that has been stored. This information is converted to audio signals, in the case of audiodiscs, and to both audio and visual signals in the case of videodiscs. Since only the

Box 18.4

Planning for Use of Videotaping Technology

Today many schools have videotaping equipment. Teachers use it to make videorecordings of students. It is particularly useful in situations where students are demonstrating a skill. Students can be videotaped and the tape played back so that students can view their performances as they are critiqued by the teacher.

Think about two or three lessons in your own teaching area in which you might use videotaping. Identify the topic and the specific skills you would be looking for.

Topic 1. _____
    Relevant Skill(s) _____
                  _____
                  _____

Topic 2. _____
    Relevant Skill(s) _____
                  _____
                  _____

Topic 3. _____
    Relevant Skill(s) _____
                  _____
                  _____

---

laser beam strikes the disc, there is no physical abrasion. Optical discs will not wear out as a conventional record will after repeated playing because of friction from the tone-arm needle.

Quality of sound reproduction on audiodiscs is superb when they are played through a sophisticated system. In some schools, they are used in the music department by instructors who wish to expose students to the best possible reproduction of the sounds of professional musicians. Generally speaking, however, audiodiscs have not been widely used in other secondary school subject areas.

Videodiscs store both sight and sound signals. They are an attractive medium in that tremendous quantities of information can be recorded on a single disk. Disks are easily stored.

Though still not widespread, videodiscs may have potential to support instruction in many secondary school subjects. This is especially true of "interactive" videodisc systems. These are distinguished from other, "non-interactive" systems. Non-interactive videodisc units operate much like traditional record players. A videodisc is inserted, and it is simply played back in a predetermined sequence from beginning to end. Interactive units, on the other hand, allow users to vary the order, the speed, and the composition of the information that is played back.

Interactive videodiscs involve a combination of video-disc and computer technology. They provide users with a great deal of flexibility. For example, specific portions of recorded programs can be identified quickly. Action can be slowed down to allow students to see how specific parts of complex processes are accomplished. Action can be stopped to permit time for student questions. Sequencing of information that is presented can be varied to meet needs of a specific lesson.

The flexibility of interactive videodisc technology suggests that it may play a larger role in secondary school programs in the years ahead. Present costs for the equipment are quite high, slowing the adoption process. However, as the size of the market and the volume of production increase, prices may well go down. This is likely to be accompanied by increased purchases by middle schools, junior high schools, and senior high schools.

Present price levels are not the only thing that has acted to depress school demand for videodisc equipment. The number of videodiscs available is minuscule compared, for example, with the number of videocassettes. They are also quite expensive. This situation somewhat parallels the circumstances faced by early school purchasers of microcomputers. Initially, little good software was available. That situation has changed tremendously for the better. It may well be the case that, as more schools purchase videodisc equipment, the numbers and quality of videodiscs will increase as well.

A technological feature of present optical discs (both audio and visual) that somewhat diminishes their appeal for teachers is their lack of an erase-and-record-over feature. Optical discs feature microscopic depressions or pits that are scanned by laser beams. The irregularity of the pitted surface reflects light back. Differences in the nature of the reflection (caused by variations on the disc surface) are interpreted by special circuitry into either sound signals (in the case of audiodiscs) or sound and visual signals (in the case of videodiscs). Once a disc has been manufactured, the nature of the pitted surface has become a permanent feature of the disc. Hence, users have been unable to record over encoded material with new audio information or new visual information.

The inability of the optical disc technology to accommodate wishes of some teachers to replace old information on the discs with new information has made the technology somewhat less attractive to many teachers than videocassette technology. Individual videocassettes allow users to keep information for indefinite periods and to erase it and replace it whenever they wish. This provides a great deal of flexibility to instructors. Producers of optical disc equipment have been very sensitive to the limitations imposed by the no-erase-no-new-recording situation. New optical discs and equipment are coming to market that allow users to write, erase, and rewrite optical discs (Tyre 1988). One new technology coats discs with a special heat-sensitive material. The pits in the recorded disc surface are cut into this material. When a user wants to replace existing information with new information, a heat process dissolves the old pits and makes a clean surface. Once the disc has cooled, a recording process cuts new pits in the surface to record the new information.

A very sophisticated optical technology, CD ROM (compact disc, read only memory), has enormous educational potential. CD-ROM technology allows users to intermingle at will existing computer, audio and visual technologies. Present systems are extremely expensive, and widespread school use is some years' distant.

One particularly attractive feature of CD ROM discs is their potential to store vast quantities of information. Alan Kay, one of the leaders in the development of microcomputers, has estimated that the number of CD ROM discs stored in a unit measuring less than one cubic foot in volume would be capable of holding all the information in 200,000 books. This technology may dramatically change how print media are stored. Some libraries may choose to have supplies of CD ROM discs rather than individual books. Users may be provided with book copies printed on the spot by high speed laser printers. The technology may have important implications for secondary school instruction in the years ahead. (See Box 18.5.)

Teletex and Videotex

Videotex and teletex are technologies that have had relatively few applications in secondary schools. Possibly their use may increase in the future. Both technologies depend on large computers, situated at a central location, that send signals to television sets of subscribers. Special decoders on the television sets unscramble these signals and provide a coherent picture on the screen. Subscribers have a way to control specific information they want to view. For example, they may be able to choose specific topics or to "turn pages" to get to particular items they wish to view.

Teletex systems are one-way. This means that users can receive what the computer sends, but they cannot make an active response to it. Some examples of teletex systems are services that keep subscribers up-to-date

Box 18.5

Is Student Learning Being Held Hostage to Uninterrupted Supplies of Electricity?

Microcomputers, videocassettes, optical discs, teletex, and videotex are the products of the microelectronic revolution. All are beginning to play important roles in secondary schools. All have the potential to enrich instructional programs. Yet, there is a down side to the estimable benefits that, optimally, these innovations can provide. Their universal Achilles heel is electricity. Each of these innovations requires uninterrupted supplies of electrical power.

Even today, power outages sometimes last several days. Schools should not become too dependent on technologies dependent on electricity for providing instruction to students. There should always be a place for the textbook and the chalkboard. Natural light allows for some limited use of these traditional technologies even when the lights go out.

What Do You Think?

1. Have schools raced so quickly to embrace technologies that depend on consistent supplies of electricity that students may be at some risk?

2. Will the textbook ever be totally replaced? On what do you base your opinion?

3. Have you experienced a situation where an electrical problem has interfered with a lesson because it was impossible to operate the needed equipment?

---

about fluctuations of stock prices, restaurant menu and price changes, breaking national and local news, and changes in local weather patterns.

Videotex systems are two-way. Subscribers can communicate directly with the controlling computer. Some systems allow users to do such things as make deposits to their bank accounts, make monthly mortgage or automobile payments, reserve theater tickets, and make reservations at certain restaurants.

Experts anticipate future growth of both teletex and videotex systems. Some new services may offer information of particular interest to secondary school teachers. For example, there may be services geared to the interests of government teachers. They could provide current information about committee hearings, status of action on individual bills, and other items of interest to students in a government course. Teachers' professional organizations might use such systems to communicate with their members in individual school buildings. Central administrative offices might use systems to apprise staff members of inservice education opportunities.

"The English Department, Dr. Barton, has rejected your proposal to teach a course on high-tech poetry."

Key Ideas in Summary

1. Economic growth throughout the world increasingly is a function of a nation's abilities to develop and utilize sophisticated technologies. In recent years, some people have felt that the United States has not been keeping up with the technological progress of other nations. One response to this situation has been increasing pressure on American schools to familiarize students with new electronic technologies as a regular part of their school programs.

2. Many of the newer technologies are based on microelectronics. In the past, many innovations involved mechanical rather than electronic technologies. Because mechanical technologies require physical movement of many independent parts, components suffered wear and breakdowns were relatively frequent. Electronic technologies, on the other hand, have few moving parts. There is less wear, and generally they are quite dependable. More importantly, they allow some things to be accomplished at extremely high speeds because they do not depend on movement of individual components.

3. In general, there has been a tendency for equipment based on new electronic technologies to decrease in price over time. Once large-

scale production lines have been established, the per-unit cost of manufacture has gone down. This has made it possible for firms to lower prices once markets have expanded to the point that original start-up costs have been repaid.

4. One of the new technological innovations that today is widely used in many secondary schools is the microcomputer. Many American families own microcomputers of their own, and many American students already have learned a great deal about computer use before they enter secondary schools. It is possible to provide some students with quite sophisticated computer instruction, particularly at the high school level. The situation in the United States contrasts with that in Europe. Few European families own computers. Consequently, not many students have developed a familiarity with the equipment on their own.

5. There are barriers that stand in the way of adoption of innovations. In part, problems stem from improper introduction of these changes. Successful innovations tend to involve teachers early on so as to win their emotional commitment to the change, to be changes that have characteristics perceived valuable by users, and to respond positively to the unique working conditions of individual teachers.

6. Two basic problems school users of microcomputers have faced are (1) small numbers of available computers and (2) low quality of software. Some schools have established special computer laboratory rooms with sufficient microcomputers for every student in a class. Increasingly, teachers are seeking to have additional machines placed in their own classrooms. Early educational software was not particularly good. In recent years, however, there have been dramatic improvements. Today, some excellent software is available to serve needs of secondary teachers in a variety of subject areas.

7. Videocassette technology has experienced a dramatic growth in teacher use in recent years. In part this results from the "user friendly" character of the equipment. Additionally, it is possible for teachers to schedule its use according to their own needs. The ability to record information themselves has attracted many teachers to the technology. This has been particularly true in situations where videocameras are available that allow teachers to make videotapes of students who are attempting to master specific skills.

8. Optical disc technologies are of several types. Audiodiscs record and play back audio information. The quality of sound reproduction is outstanding. Videodiscs contain both audio and visual information. Interactive videodiscs involve a combination of audio, visual, and computer technology. They allow users to vary order of presentation of information, change speeds of playback, and take other actions

to "tailor" playback to their own instructional needs. CD-ROM is an emerging optical disc technology that may have important educational applications. Among other things, CD-ROM discs can store incredible quantities of information on a single disc.

9. Teletex and videotex technologies connect subscribers' television sets to a master computer situated at a central location. Teletex provides information to users, but it does not allow them to communicate responses to the central computer. Videotex is two-way. That is, individuals can communicate with the central computer to do such things as arrange for payment of bills and reserve theater tickets.

POSTTEST

DIRECTIONS: Using your own paper, answer these true/false questions. For each correct statement, write the word "true." For each incorrect statement, write the word "false."

_____ 1. Increasingly, employers are expecting new workers to have some familiarity with the new electronics-based technologies.

_____ 2. Fears that the United States may fall behind other nations of the world has contributed to expanding use of electronic technologies in the nation's schools.

_____ 3. In considering whether to adopt a new technology, teachers are often concerned about the issue of flexibility of use.

_____ 4. Videodiscs are more widely used in secondary schools than videocassettes.

_____ 5. Subscribers to a teletex service have the capability of "talking back" to the controlling computer.

Bibliography

ABRAMS, ARNIE.   "Twelve Modest Proposals for Tomorrow's Technology." *Tech Trends* (January/February 1987): pp. 18–20.

ANDERSON, JOHN J.   "CD ROM: The Continuing Search for a Standard." *Computer Shopper* (May 1987): pp. 5; 28; 294–296.

CHARP, SYLVIA.   "Editorial." *Technological Horizons in Education Journal* (August 1988): p. 8.

CUBAN, LARRY.   *Teachers and Machines: The Classroom Use of Technology Since 1920.* New York: Teachers College Press, 1986.

DUFF, JON M. "From the Desk of the Editor," *The Engineering Design Graphics Journal* (Autumn 1986): pp. 4; 7.

EDUCATIONAL COMMISSION OF THE STATES. *Issuegram* No. 17. Denver: Education Commission of the States, 1983.

HAWKRIDGE, DAVID. *New Information Technology in Education.* Baltimore, Maryland: The Johns Hopkins University Press, 1983.

HEAFORD, JOHN M. *Myth of the Learning Machine: The Theory and Practice of Computer Based Learning.* Wilmslow, Cheshire, United Kingdom: Sigma Technical Press, 1983.

HEINICH, ROBERT; MOLENDA, MICHAEL; AND RUSSELL, JAMES D. *Instructional Media and the New Technologies of Instruction. 2nd ed.* New York: John Wiley and Sons, 1985.

"How Computers are Used—if Used at All." *The Washington Post* (June 6, 1988), p. 15.

LOCATIS, CRAIG N. AND ATKINSON, FRANCIS D. *Media and Technology for Education and Training.* Columbus, Ohio: Charles E. Merrill Publishing Company, 1984.

TANNER, DENNIS F. AND BANE, ROBERT K. "CD-ROM: A New Technology with Promise for Education." *Technological Horizons in Education Journal* (August 1988): pp. 57–60.

TYRE, TERIAN. "Erasable Optical Media Is Closer to Being Real." *Technological Horizons in Education Journal* (October 1988): pp. 68–72.

CHAPTER 19

Legal Issues Affecting Students and Teachers

AIMS

This chapter provides information to help the reader to:

1. Define *in loco parentis* and explain how application of this doctrine has changed in recent years.
2. Differentiate between "substantive" and "procedural" dimensions of due process.
3. Define some principles that govern search-and-seizure procedures in schools.
4. Identify some legal issues associated with the use of corporal punishment in schools.
5. Point out legal implications for teachers of the Family Rights and Privacy Act.
6. Describe different types of teacher contracts.
7. Define some rights of teachers in the areas of AIDS and drug testing.
8. State teacher responsibilities regarding the reporting of suspected cases of child abuse.
9. Describe different types of professional negligence.
10. Explain some limitations school districts face in placing restrictions on out-of-school teacher behavior.

PRETEST

DIRECTIONS: Using your own paper, answer these true/false questions. For each correct statement, write the word "true." For each incorrect statement, write the word "false."

_____ 1. School officials may establish any rules they deem necessary to control the actions and the dress of students when they are on school property.

_____ 2. In cases regarding alleged misbehaviors of students, many courts have considered the extent to which these behaviors have acted to interfere with the learning of other students.

_____ 3. Provisions of the Family Rights and Privacy Act give parents the right to review their children's school records.

_____ 4. School districts are permitted to require their employees to take periodic AIDS and drug tests as a condition of maintaining their employment.

_____ 5. A basic test of negligence that courts frequently apply to teachers is whether a person with similar experience and training would have acted in the same manner.

Introduction

In times past, legal issues rarely concerned secondary school teachers. Principals and teachers exercised an authority over students that was rarely challenged. They made the rules, and students were expected to obey them. Students enjoyed few legal protections. Individuals who failed to conform to school rules could be summarily dismissed. Expelled students had no standing in the courts to challenge expulsion decisions.

Teachers, too, were regarded differently than they are today. Teachers' in-school behavior was expected to be impeccable. Many communities also placed severe restrictions on teachers out-of-school behavior. Often these restrictions were incompatible with the constitutional guarantees enjoyed by other United States' citizens. It was not uncommon for teachers to be criticized (and, sometimes, even to lose their jobs) because of complaints relating to such issues as church attendance, alcohol and tobacco use, and changes in marital status.

Over the last quarter of a century, many court cases have undermined earlier assumptions about legal status of students and rights of teachers. Court challenges and related legislation have resulted in changed

This officer is teaching a lesson focusing on students' rights and responsibilities. *Photo courtesy of Maria R. Bastone.*

relationships among students, teachers, school administrators, and communities. This chapter introduces a number of these changes. The first major section introduces legal issues affecting students.

Legal Issues Affecting Students

Few issues in secondary education have generated as much controversy as has the issue of student rights. In recent years, the legal relationship between students and school authorities has changed dramatically. These changes began accelerating during the 1960s. They continued through the 1970s. By the 1980s, students had come to enjoy legal rights that are largely comparable to those enjoyed by all adult citizens.

In Loco Parentis

The traditional legal doctrine governing the relationship between student and school was known as **in loco parentis**. **In loco parentis** is a

Latin phrase meaning "in the place of the parent." The designated representatives of the school (administrators and teachers) were expected to treat students as a wise parent might. School employees enjoyed some of the same legal protections that parents have. Common law precedents relating to the child-parent relationship were extended to the school. Common law doctrine typically had meant that courts would rarely agree to hear a case brought by a young person who was complaining about some "unjust" parental directive. As extended to the school, *in loco parentis* meant that school authorities did not have to justify actions taken against young people who were judged to have broken the rules. School officials were presumed to be acting in these students' best interests.

The *in loco parentis* assumption began to break down in the 1960s. The doctrine was first challenged at the university level. Later, it was attacked successfully at the secondary and elementary levels. These challenges went forward at a time when many traditional authorities were being questioned. The basic assumption that school officials always acted in the best interests of students was widely attacked. There were particular concerns about expelling students, thereby denying them access to educational services. The negative long-term personal and social consequences that could result from inappropriate expulsion decisions were increasingly recognized. A number of court cases sought to extend constitutional protections to public school students. A landmark case of this kind was the case of *Tinker v. Des Moines Independent Community School District* (1969).

The Tinker case evolved out of a situation that developed in Iowa. In Des Moines, children of several families who opposed the Vietnam War decided to participate in a protest movement that involved the wearing of black arm bands. When school officials learned the protest was about to take place, they quickly adopted a policy banning wearing of armbands at school. Any student who came to school wearing an armband would be asked to remove it. Failure to comply would result in suspension.

Three students wore armbands to school. Administrators enforced the new policy and suspended them. (They later returned after the end of the official protest period.) Suit was brought on behalf of the students. Eventually, the case worked its way to the United States Supreme Court and the Court ruled in favor of the students. In its decision, the High Court viewed the wearing of armbands as symbolic speech. It was argued that the right to wear armbands was protected under the free speech provision of the First Amendment to the United States Constitution.

Court decisions that have helped to define the appropriate legal relationship between school authorities and students have generally focused on two areas. First, there have been a number of cases examining the

Box 19.1

Freedom of Expression in Student Publications

Suppose a group of students in a high school where you were teaching decided to publish a journal to "expose" what was "really going on" in the school. The first issue featured a bitter attack on the principal. She was attacked as someone who "has been dead from the neck up for years." Other articles painted counselors and teachers in a very negative light.

What Do You Think?

1. Do you think these students have a legal right to publish such a journal?

2. Do you think these students' legal position would be different had they published their "exposé" in the regular school newspaper instead of a journal they started themselves?

3. If it were determined that students had a basic right to publish such a journal, are there any kinds of legal restrictions school administrators could place on these students?

4. As a teacher, what do you think your best response to this situation might be?

---

limits of school officials' power to interfere with actions of students. Second, there have been cases centering on the appropriateness or the fairness of the procedures school officials have used in making decisions affecting students' rights.

Subsections that follow introduce some issues that have been addressed in court cases involving students' rights. Box 19.1 discusses freedom of expression in student publications. In reviewing this material, keep in mind that legal guidelines in our system are constantly changing. Principles that seem to have been considered by courts in the past may not be the same ones that will guide courts in the future.

Freedom of Speech and Expression

The Tinker case dealt with this important area. This case was one of many that sought to define the limits of power of school authorities over students' freedom and expression rights. One area that has been of particular concern has been the power of school authorities to limit the publication of "underground" or unauthorized student newspapers. In general, the courts have held that school authorities may abridge students' freedom of speech rights only in cases where it can be conclusively demonstrated that an exercise of these rights will interfere with the educational process. This has meant, for example, that students cannot be prohibited from speaking out or from publishing an unauthorized newspaper, but the time and place where these rights can be exercised can be controlled by school authorities to prevent a disruption of classes.

There have also been court cases focusing on the right of school officials to deal with students' use of profane language. In one case, a student's name was removed from the school's graduation list after he had used language filled with sexual innuendoes during a campaign for a school office. Attorneys for the student challenged this action. The United States District Court and the Ninth Circuit Court supported the student's argument that freedom-of-speech rights had been abridged. However, on appeal, these lower court rulings were overturned by the United States Supreme Court (Baker 1987). In supporting the decision of the school administrators, the High Court suggested that students may be subjected to punishment when the language in school and in school-related activities goes "beyond the boundaries of socially appropriate behavior" (Baker 1987, p. 124).

In another case, school regulations banning the wearing of protest messages were challenged. In this instance, administrators were able to cite several specific incidences of violent disruptions between different ideological factions in the school. In some cases, there were fist fights. The courts viewed this situation as indicative of an interference with the educational process. The school regulations were upheld.

Generally, it is fair to say that students today enjoy constitutionally guaranteed rights to freedom of speech and expression. These rights cannot be arbitrarily abrogated by school officials. When authorities do attempt to regulate student behavior in these areas, they are obligated to establish a convincing link between the behavior and an interruption of the school program.

Student Dress and Appearance

School dress and appearance regulations are a frequent source of irritation between students and school officials. Though there have been many court cases dealing with this issue, judicial decisions have revealed no consistent pattern. In some cases the courts have upheld school dress codes and hair style regulations. When this has been done, the courts have accepted the argument that these kinds of rules are needed to maintain an orderly educational environment. Some decisions have sustained school authorities on the ground that certain regulations regarding dress and hair styles are needed to protect the safety or health of students. For example, schools generally have been found to have the authority to require students with long hair to wear hair nets when working as food servers in cafeterias.

Not all cases in this area have been decided in favor of school authorities. Some decisions have supported challenges brought by students. Often, these decisions have been supported by a court finding that the regulation in question bore no direct relationship to the educational process. For example, school officials may find a certain student dress fad objectionable. Rules preventing students from wearing "objectionable" clothing generally cannot be defended simply because school authorities have labeled a certain style as "unacceptable." Generally, authorities have had to defend such rules in terms of evidence showing that such clothing was interfering with the educational process or posing a health or safety danger.

Due Process

The fairness of school decisions affecting students has been a subject of many court cases. The issue of "due process' has been at the heart of many of these disputes. Due process involves two basic components. The first, the "substantive component," consists of the basic set of principles on which due process is based. The second, the "procedural component," consists of procedures that must be followed to assure that due process rights have not been violated.

The following principles are included in the substantive component of due process:

1. Individuals are not to be disciplined on the basis of unwritten rules.
2. Rules must not be unduly vague.
3. Individuals charged with rules violations are entitled to a hearing before an impartial body.
4. Identities of witnesses are to be revealed.
5. Decisions are to be supported by substantial evidence.
6. A public or private hearing can be requested by the individual accused of a rule violation.

The procedural component of due process involves a specific set of procedures to be followed. With respect to school practice, the following steps are consistent with due-process guidelines:

1. Rules governing students' behavior are to be distributed in writing to students and their parents at the beginning of the school year.

2. Whenever a student has been accused of breaking rules that might result in a due-process procedure, the charges must be provided in writing to the student and his or her parents.

3. Written notice of the hearing must be given, with sufficient time provided for the student and his or her representatives to prepare a defense. However, the hearing is to be held in a timely manner (usually within two weeks).

4. A fair hearing must include the following:

   a. right of the accused to be represented by legal counsel.

   b. right of the accused to present a defense and to introduce evidence.

   c. right of the accused to face his or her accusers.

   d. right of the accused to cross-examine witnesses.

5. The decision of the hearing board is to be based on the evidence presented and is to be rendered within a reasonable time.

6. The accused is to be informed of his or her right to appeal the decision.

Court decisions in recent years have affirmed students' rights to due process. This means that schools are under an obligation to follow the admonition laid down in the Fourteenth Amendment to the United States Constitution that no citizen can be deprived of "life, liberty, or property without due process of law."

Complying with due-process requirements requires a heavy investment of time on the part of school officials. The very complexity of due-process guidelines reduces the likelihood that capricious charges will be made against students. Due-process procedures are required whenever a fundamental right of a student is potentially at risk. In recent years, courts have tended to affirm access to schooling as a right. This has meant that disciplinary actions that could result in either suspension or expulsion must follow due-process guidelines. Let's consider how due-process procedures apply to these two situations. (Box 19.2 looks at the question: Does due process keep "bad" students in school?)

"Suspension" is defined as a temporary separation from school. A suspension of less than 10 days is considered to be a short-term suspension. When a student is faced with a short-term suspension, only minimal due-process procedures are required. In such cases, the student to be suspended must receive (1) at least an oral (preferably a written) notice of the specific charges, (2) an explanation of evidence supporting these charges, and (3) an opportunity to present his or her version of the issue at question. In short-term suspension situations, it is not necessary for legal counsel to be present.

Box 19.2

Does Due Process Keep "Bad" Students in School?

A parent recently made these comments at a local school board meeting:

> My son is in an algebra class with a student who just disrupts the class almost every day. This student interrupts the teacher's explanations, asks irrelevant questions, and works as hard as he can to keep any real teaching from going on. My son is not learning anything.
>
> I have called the principal to complain. She explained that legally it is very difficult to remove a misbehaving student. If this is true, I want you board members to know that I am very unhappy. I would urge your attorneys to get to work on a policy that will get these troublemakers out of the school so that serious students can learn.

What Do You Think?

1. Does this parent have a legitimate concern?

2. How do you think members of the school board might respond to this parent's complaint?

3. Do you think the principal really is in a legal bind, or is the principal simply failing to take appropriate action?

A suspension exceeding 10 days is considered to be a long-term suspension. Long-term suspension is considered to severely challenge a student's right to an education. Hence, there must be implementation of all due-process procedures. This means, for example, that school authorities must be careful to observe all guidelines noted under the procedural component of due process.

"Expulsion" is a very serious action. It permanently separates a student from the school. Consequently, where expulsion is likely to be the end result, very strict and careful due-process procedures must be followed. In most cases, teachers and administrators at an individual school cannot make an expulsion decision. Expulsion tends to be the prerogative of the highest governing officials of a school district. This is true because a failure to follow due-process procedures carefully could result in expensive legal action against the entire school district.

Due-process requirements have important implications for teachers. First, they must understand that students have been legally recognized as citizens whose rights are fully protected by the United States constitution. This status does not necessarily undermine teachers' abilities to control students in their classrooms. The courts generally have affirmed educators' rights to enforce rules that are needed to maintain an orderly and safe educational environment. Educators, however, are obligated to proceed in a fair and appropriate manner in making and enforcing school rules. When this is done, they have little to fear from the courts.

In reflecting on whether rules they have developed are fair and appropriate, teachers find it useful to consider these questions:

1. Is the purpose behind the rule clear?

2. Is the rule consistent with local, state, and federal laws?

3. Is the rule described in clear and precise language?

4. Does the rule have clear relationship to maintaining an orderly educational process and preventing disruptions?

5. Do all students know that the rule has been established?

Search and Seizure

Interest in search and seizure has heightened in recent years as school authorities have become concerned about the use of illegal substances on school campuses. In some places, outbreaks of violence have prompted officials to take action to eliminate weapons from schools. In responding to these situations, school authorities have felt a need to search school lockers, automobiles in school parking lots, and even individuals and their personal possessions. These searches have the potential of violating guarantees against unreasonable search and seizure as outlined in the Fourth Amendment to the United States Constitution.

In considering school cases involving search and seizure, the courts have attempted to strike a delicate balance. On the one hand, they have been interested in preventing unreasonable search-and-seizure activities. On the other hand, they have been interested in preserving school authorities' need to maintain a safe and orderly educational environment.

When considering whether a search is appropriate, school officials must apply four basic tests. The first test concerns the thing or object to be found. The greater the potential of danger of this object to the health or safety of students in school, the greater the justification for the search. A gun or bomb poses an immediate danger. On the other hand, a stolen book generates little threat to students. Hence, school authorities might be on shaky legal ground were they to conduct highly intrusive searches for the purpose of locating a missing book.

A second test relates to the quality of information that has led to the decision to conduct the search. Reliability of individuals who have reported information is a consideration. When several people who are known to be reliable have provided evidence supporting the decision to conduct a search, it rests on stronger legal grounds than, for example, when the decision is made on the basis of a single tip from an anonymous caller.

The third test concerns the nature of the place to be searched. If this is an area where there is a high expectation of privacy, school officials need very good information to justify the search. This would be the case when there was an intent to conduct a search of a student's person. On the other hand, in areas, such as student lockers, where there is less expectation of privacy, less compelling evidence is required to justify the search.

The fourth test involves the nature of the proposed search. Searches of individuals are highly intrusive. Hence, considerable evidence is required to justify them. Additionally, the age and sex of the individuals to be searched is a consideration in such cases.

The case of *Doe v. Renfrow* (1979) illustrates several of these principles. This case involved the use of dogs to search for drugs in a high school. When one of the dogs acted in a manner suggesting that "Diane Doe" had drugs on her person, school authorities required her to empty her pockets and purse. When no illegal substances were found a strip search was conducted. No illegal substances were found. Diane Doe, infuriated at what had happened, filed suit on the grounds that the sniffing of dogs, the search of her pockets and purse, and the strip search had violated her rights.

In its decision, the court held that the sniffing of the dogs was not search and was, therefore, permissible. Too, the court held the emptying of pockets was justifiable because the action of the dogs provided reasonable suspicion that an illegal substance was present. But the court held for Ms. Doe on the issue of the strip search. This was declared to be an invasion of privacy that could not be justified given the evidence school authorities had available to them. Much more convincing evidence would have been needed as a justification for such a highly intrusive search.

Teachers have a duty to protect the safety of their students. If they find objects or substances in the classroom that have the potential to harm students, they have an obligation to remove them. On the other hand, they must recognize that case law in the area of search and seizure does not provide clear-cut guidelines for educators. Given this reality, generally it is not wise for teachers to conduct searches on their own initiative. They should gather evidence and consult with administrative staffs. Administrators, in cooperation with school legal staffs, make a final determination about whether a proposed search is legal and should go forward. Box 19.3 discusses the issue of search and seizure.

Box 19.3

The Issue of Search and Seizure

The Vice-Principal for Discipline was escorting a student to his office. While he was doing so, he noticed a bulge in the student's pants pocket. As they neared the office, the student broke away and bolted for an outside door. Spotting a policeman who was standing outside his office, the Vice-Principal shouted, "Get that student. He's got junk, and he's escaping."

Together, the Vice-Principal and the policeman chased the student. They caught him three blocks from the school. They pulled the student's hand from his pocket. It came out holding a set of drug "works." The policeman wrote up charges. During the trial, the prosecution asserted that the student's possession of "works" was an indication of possession of illegal drugs.

What Do You Think?

1. Do you think the Vice-Principal acted correctly or incorrectly? Why do you think so?

2. Suppose this student argued in court that the evidence used against him had been gathered illegally. Do you think the court would have been receptive to this argument? Why, or why not?

3. How do you think the court ultimately would have ruled in this case? Why do you think so?

Grading Procedures

Not long ago, a high school teacher was called to the administrative office of her school where she was confronted by a student, the student's parents, and an attorney. The teacher was informed that they had come to challenge a grade the student had received in her class. In this instance, the teacher was able to provide documentary evidence to support the award of the grade. This evidence resulted in the challenge to the grade being dropped.

Courts generally have been reluctant to substitute their judgment for that of a teacher in cases involving grades. They have held that teachers have the right to use grades as a measure of academic performance. However, courts have been willing to hear cases where there has been a suspicion that a grade has been awarded capriciously or arbitrarily or where some nonacademic factors have influenced the grades. This suggests that teachers might not be on sound legal ground when they lower grades for disciplinary reasons or for poor attendance (Fisher and Schimmel 1982, p. 338). Attendance can be defended as an appropriate consideration for grading provided that the teacher documents classroom participation as an important part of the learning process.

The importance of documentation cannot be overstated. Because grades are supposed to indicate the academic performance and achievement of students, teachers need to develop record-keeping schemes that provide evidence about students' academic performance. Where this kind of evidence has been maintained, teachers have ordinarily had little difficulty in winning court cases that have challenged grades they have awarded to their students.

Family Rights and Privacy

Concern about potential misuses of school records has been evolving for the last 30 years. There have been fears that comments in school records may permanently stigmatize students and hurt their subsequent educational and employment opportunities. In 1974, the Family Educational Rights and Privacy Act was passed to address this problem.

This act requires schools to protect students' privacy rights by closing the files of students to all individuals except those immediately concerned with their education. Files can be opened only with the consent of the students' parents or, in the cases of students over age 18, of the students themselves. Further, parents of students are permitted free access to all school files and records of their own children. Students over the age of 18 have a similar right to see their own files. After parents have viewed files and records of their children (or after a student over age 18 has viewed his or her own files and records), they may request to amend any record that they believe to be (a) inaccurate, (b) misleading, or (c) in violation of privacy rights.

Parental access to school files has important implications for teachers. They can be sued for defamatory comments written in school records. Comments should include references to specific student behaviors. General judgments about students should be avoided. Comments should relate to students' academic performance and should not be stated in a way clearly designed to cause harm to the student. If comments are not pertinent to the academic performance and if they can be construed as designed to harm the student, legal actions may result (Connors 1981, p. 130).

Legal Issues Affecting Teachers

Teachers' legal concerns do not stop with an understanding of student rights. Teachers themselves also have certain rights and obligations. Their legal rights relate to such issues as conditions of employment, drug-and-alcohol-abuse testing, freedom of expression, private lives, academic freedom, and negligence.

Conditions of Employment

A basic requirement for employment as a teacher in most states is a valid teaching certificate. In some states, school districts are prohibited from paying the salary of a person who does not possess a valid certificate. A number of court cases have declared that those individuals who sign a teaching contract and who lack a proper certificate are "volunteers" who have donated their services to the district. Such voluntarism can be an expensive proposition. It points up the importance of meeting all certification requirements before contracting for employment as a teacher.

Certification is a state responsibility. Each state has a somewhat different set of certification requirements. An individual may meet certification requirements in one state and, upon moving to another state, find that additional requirements must be met. Individuals preparing to be teachers should contact the state department of education in the state in which they hope to work. This office will be able to provide information about the state's certification requirements. (This information may be available from officials in your own teacher preparation program or from your campus placement office.)

Most certification plans require prospective teachers to complete an organized program of study at a college or university. Programs normally are approved by state officials in the state where the college or university is located. Completion of the approved program of study automatically results in the award of an initial teaching certificate.

Teaching certificates are not life-time licenses. They may be terminated for a variety of reasons. Some states require teachers to take additional professional development courses to maintain their certificates. Frequently, too, there are other conditions that can lead to termination of a certificate. For example, many states revoke teaching certificates if holders are convicted of a felony charge. Teachers who have engaged in public displays of immorality or in other extreme examples of socially unacceptable behavior have also lost their certificates. The courts have held that teachers, because of their contact with impressionable young people, can be held to higher standards of personal conduct than the population as a whole.

Teachers' Contracts

Teachers' contracts spell out salary terms and conditions of employment. There are several types of contracts. Typically, new teachers are offered a *term contract*. A term contract provides for employment for a specific time period, usually for one school year. At the conclusion of the term, the teacher is reviewed, and school administrators make either a positive or negative re-employment decision.

A given term contract conveys the right to both contracting parties (the teacher and the school board) to negotiate new terms in any subsequent term contracts. In some states, term contracts are used for all teachers. In other places, regulations require that term contracts be issued only to teachers who are new to the system. Often, after a stipulated number of probationary years, teachers must be offered a different type of contract.

One of the other contract types is the *continuing contract*. Unlike a term contract, provisions of a continuing contract do not have to be renewed after a specified period of time or "term." Continuing contracts are renewed automatically on a year-to-year basis unless they are deliberately terminated by one of the parties. This means that teachers enjoy security of continuous employment. Most continuing contracts provide for salary adjustments to be made at the beginning of each academic year. Often, they contain provisions requiring districts to follow rather strict sets of procedures if they wish to terminate services of continuing-contract teachers.

A third contract type is the *tenure contract*. A tenure contract is similar to a continuing contract in that it stays in force from year to year. A tenure contract usually stipulates that the teacher can be terminated only if certain state statutes governing the behavior of teachers have been violated. (See Box 19.4.)

Tenure contracts have come under fire from some critics on the grounds that they seem to guarantee lifetime employment for teachers. This is a misconception. Tenure does not provide for lifetime employment. What it does do is guarantee the teacher that due process procedures are followed in any proceeding that may lead to dismissal and that dismissal will occur only for specific causes. These causes usually include (a) evidence of gross incompetence, (b) physical or mental incapacity, (c) neglect of duty, and (d) conviction of a crime. In short, a school district must "show cause" and be able to document charges before a tenured teacher can be dismissed.

When a contract is signed by both parties (the teacher and the school board or its designated representative), it becomes a legally binding document. It places certain responsibilities on both parties. School districts that fail to honor a signed contract can be subject to legal action. The same is true for teachers. In some states, a teacher who fails to honor a signed contract can be stripped of his or her teaching certificate.

If a prospective teacher signs a contract and then receives a better offer from a second district, it is unwise for him or her to sign the

Box 19.4

Should Tenure Contracts be Banned?

A representative made these comments in a state-legislature education committee hearing:

> We need to take action now to repeal legislation that requires our districts to issue tenure contracts. Tenure maintains incompetents in our schools. We all know the arguments that principals *do* retain the power to get rid of bad teachers, but these arguments are weak. The reality is that almost no tenured teachers are ever released from their jobs. They are in a position to sit back, use their yellowed old notes, and go through the motions of teaching. Tenure provides for early 'mental retirement.' These people may still be physically in their schools, but their brains have been on 'hold' for years. Let's get rid of this bad legislation and move this dead wood out of our schools.

What Do You Think?

1. *Is* there a danger that laws permitting tenure contracts allow marginally effective teachers to remain in the schools?

2. How would proponents of laws permitting tenure contracts respond to this state representative's arguments?

3. What are your personal feelings about tenure contracts? Why do you feel this way?

---

second contract without first obtaining a release from the first contract. The proper procedure is to contact the first district and ask whether it might be possible to be released from the first contract "without prejudice." In most cases districts will honor this kind of request. They fully understand that they are unlikely to get a first-class effort from an individual who would rather be teaching elsewhere. In those instances where districts refuse to release individuals from the first contract they signed, they are legally obligated to teach in the district for the term specified in the document.

Teacher Dismissal and Due Process

Does a teacher have a right to challenge a non-renewal of a contract or a dismissal from a position? There is no answer that applies to every case. In general, though, the concept of due process is relevant to this situation. Recall that due process requires decisions that affect citizens' rights to be made fairly.

Two basic types of rights are relevant to the discussion of teacher non-renewal or dismissal. "Liberty rights" are rights that free individuals from personal restraints and assure them, among other things, opportunities to engage in the common occupations of life (*Meyer v. Nebraska*, 1923). The liberty-rights concept suggests that school districts cannot use an unconstitutional reason to prevent a teacher from maintaining his or her employment status. For example, teachers cannot be dismissed because of their religious beliefs or because of their race.

"Property rights" are a second category of rights relevant to non-renewal and dismissal disputes. Property rights ensure individuals' rights to the present and future benefits that accrue to them as a consequence of signing a contract. In a number of cases, the courts have wrestled with this question: Is teaching a property right? Generally, the courts have rules that teachers *do* obtain a property right when they enter into a contractual relationship with a school district. Ordinarily this means that a teacher cannot be dismissed during the term of service specified in a contract unless he or she violates some provision of the contract. A small number of contracts contain language within the contract itself that stipulates the contract may be terminated by the school board at any time. In such cases, the teacher has no property right covering the entire term of service. He or she, as the contract stipulates, may be terminated at any time by school board action.

In summary, contracts generally offer teachers some protection from summary dismissal. However, many variables must be considered. These include the type of contract the teacher has signed and the contract's specific provisions. Teachers need to read contracts carefully and to ask for clarification of any unclear language before they sign the documents.

Testing for AIDS and Drug Abuse

Societal concerns about AIDS and drug abuse may affect teachers. Proposals have been made to test all teachers for AIDS and drug abuse. However, these proposals have raised important legal questions. Some authorities believe that requirements calling for universal testing of teachers may violate their constitutionally protected rights. Some court decisions in this area suggest that tests of this type qualify as a form of search. To be legal, these searches must be consistent with protections involving search and seizure as described in the Fourteenth Amendment. Further, schools must be able to demonstrate that they have "a compelling interest" in the results of such tests.

A compelling interest might be demonstrated if school authorities could point to instances where teachers under the influence of a controlled substance or who had the AIDS virus posed a clear threat to students' safety or health. Such evidence has been difficult to gather.

This has been particularly true with respect to AIDS. Most evidence suggests that AIDS cannot be transmitted through the type of teacher-student interactions occurring in most classrooms. Some people who have studied the question believe that school districts will find it difficult to demonstrate a "compelling interest" that will support a policy requiring AIDS testing of all employees.

Recently, one school district decided to require urinalysis as a part of its mandatory physical examinations for teachers seeking tenure. Some teachers challenged this policy in court. The court noted that, before implementing this policy, school officials had found no evidence that any of the district's teachers were using illegal substances. In this instance, the court ruled that the policy constituted an illegal invasion of teachers' privacy (*Patchogue-Medford Congress of Teachers v. Board of Education*, 1986).

Reporting Suspected Child Abuse

Public concerns about child abuse are growing. In 1984 the number of suspected cases of child abuse reached an all-time high of 1,727,000 (Thomas 1987, p. 54). All 50 states and the District of Columbia have laws that require certain categories of individuals to report suspected instances of child abuse.

Because teachers have prolonged contact with young people, they usually are included among groups of people who are required to report suspected child-abuse episodes. Teachers who fail to report such situations may face both criminal and civil charges. A high level of suspicion is not required for reporting suspected cases of abuse. A teacher does not need to know "beyond a reasonable doubt" that a student has been abused. If there is some suspicion that an injury to a student is not the result of some unavoidable action, generally the suspected abuse should be reported.

All states provide individuals who report suspected cases of abuse with some form of immunity from lawsuits. This offers protection to individuals who may be fearful of legal reprisals if they file a child-abuse report. This immunity from lawsuits is not unlimited. It generally requires complainants to file their reports in good faith. If there is evidence that the teacher has filed a suspected-child-abuse report for the purpose of maliciously harming the parents, he or she may be successfully sued by the parents.

Legal Liability

The volume of litigation against teachers has increased in recent years. One of the major categories of liability faced by teachers is **tort liability**.

A "tort" is a civil wrong against another that results either in personal injury or property damage. There are many categories of torts including negligence, invasion of privacy, assault, and defamation of character. The areas that seem to generate the largest number of lawsuits against teachers are (a) excessive use of force and (b) negligence.

Excessive Use of Force in Disciplining Students

Many court cases have focused on the issue of the use of physical punishment for disciplining students. In the case of *Ingraham v. Wright* (1977), the United States Supreme Court ruled that teachers could use reasonable, but not excessive force in disciplining a student. Further, the Court ruled that corporal punishment did not constitute "cruel and unusual punishment" and, therefore, did not violate constitutionally protected rights.

The *Ingraham v. Wright* case hinted at the need to define the phrase "reasonable force." No single court case has done this. However, collectively, court decisions seem to be suggesting that the following factors should be considered when making a decision regarding whether the force used was reasonable: (a) the gravity of the offense; (b) the age of the learner; (c) the sex and size of the learner; (d) the size of the person administering the punishment; (e) the implement used to administer the punishment; and, (f) the attitude of the individual administering the punishment. With regard to this final factor, the courts have looked more favorably on disciplinarians who were not in a state of anger or obviously seeking revenge at the time punishment was administered.

The *Ingraham v. Wright* ruling and others that have been decided have not acted to make corporal punishment legal in all instances. A few states and many local school districts have rules banning the use of corporal punishment in their schools. A teacher who accepts employment in one of these locales is barred from using corporal punishment. A teacher who violates these regulations may lose a job, a teaching credential, or suffer other penalties.

Even in places where corporal punishment is technically permissible, legal action may be taken against teachers who use it. Allegations of too much force by a student or his legal representatives may result in criminal assault and battery charges being filed against the teacher. Local juries in such cases typically have decided them by reference to the *in loco parentis* doctrine. That is, they attempt to decide whether the teacher acted as a prudent parent would have acted under similar circumstances. (See Box 19.5.)

In summary, corporal punishment in schools is a highly controversial issue. Teachers who use it face the possibility of legal action, even if they live in areas where there are no general bans on corporal punishment.

Box 19.5

Corporal Punishment and Control or No Corporal Punishment and Chaos?

A high school teacher recently made these comments:

> Fifty years ago, just the cream of the crop went to high school. They were academically talented kinds who cared about learning. Today we take everybody. Lots of these students would rather be about anywhere than school. They are disruptive. They are disrespectful. There is not one thing the school has to offer that interests them. Though there are not too many of these students, left uncontrolled, they can make it impossible for others to learn. The only language some of them understand is the language of the paddle. A few good licks will often accomplish much more than a thousand "lectures." The choice we have is simple. We retain our right to corporal punishment and retain control. Or, we give it up and accept chaos.

What Do You Think?

1. What major arguments does this teacher make to support the case for corporal punishment?

2. How inevitable is it that "chaos" necessarily follows when teachers are denied the right to use corporal punishment?

3. How would you respond to this teacher's comments?

Many teachers feel that the risks associated with corporal punishment outweigh any benefits.

Negligence

Negligence is defined as a failure to use reasonable care to prevent harm from coming to someone. There are three kinds of negligence: (a) misfeasance; (b) nonfeasance; and, (c) malfeasance. *Misfeasance* occurs when an individual fails to act in a proper manner to prevent harm from coming to someone. Teachers guilty of misfeasance act unwisely or without taking proper precautions. For example, a teacher may not instruct a student in the proper use of equipment or may permit a student to use equipment that is not in good repair.

Nonfeasance occurs when an individual fails to act when he or she has a clear responsibility to do so. This sometimes happens in schools when teachers are away from their places of assigned responsibility. For example, a teacher may be guilty of nonfeasance if he or she slips across the hall for a quick cigarette in a faculty room and, while he or she is gone, a student is injured in the classroom. When they consider nonfeasance cases, the courts typically consider whether a teacher's absence from his or her place of responsibility was justified. For example, if a student was injured in a classroom after the teacher had left the room to extinguish a fire in the hall, the teacher probably would not be found guilty of nonfeasance.

Malfeasance occurs when an individual deliberately acts in an improper manner and, thereby, causes harm to someone. In schools, malfeasance cases ordinarily involve situations where a teacher has acted deliberately and knowingly to harm a student. For example, in attempting to break up a fight, a teacher might lose his composure, get personally involved, and injure a student.

Academic Freedom and Freedom of Expression

Academic freedom issues involve conflicts between teachers' rights to conduct their classes according to their best professional judgments and education authorities' responsibility to see that the authorized program is taught. Court decisions in this area do not reflect a clear and consistent pattern.

One principle that has been generally endorsed is that school officials have rights to impose *some* limitations on teachers' academic freedom. However, where this is done, guidelines regarding what teachers can and cannot do must be clear, defensible, and specific. Courts usually have supported administrators' insistence that teachers teach the content of the course to which they are assigned. For example, in one case the courts ruled against an art teacher who used her instructional time to promote her personal religious beliefs.

On the other hand, the courts have usually decided that school authorities cannot require teachers to avoid controversial issues. In one case, the right of an American history teacher to use a simulation exercise that evoked strong racial feelings was upheld (*Kingsville Independent School District v. Cooper*, 1980). In another case, the court supported a teacher who challenged an administrative ruling banning her use of a particular book. In its decision, the court ruled that the book was appropriate for high school students, that it contained nothing obscene, and that its banning constituted a violation of the teacher's academic freedom rights (*Parducci v. Rutland*, 1979).

"I'm afraid, Mrs. Fullagar, that Christopher had a slight accident in chem lab today."

Freedom of expression relates to the rights of teachers, as individuals, to express their views on a subject freely. Many court cases in this area have involved attempts to punish teachers for out-of-classroom speech. Sometimes districts have attempted to dismiss teachers who criticized administrators or school district policies. A landmark case in this area was *Pickering v. Board of Education of Township School District 205, Will County* (1968).

In this famous case, Pickering, a teacher, had written a letter to the editor of the local newspaper. The letter criticized the way school funds had been allocated. The local school board was angered by the letter. Members of the board claimed that Pickering had made untrue statements and that the letter had damaged the reputations of school administrators and of the school board. Pickering was dismissed. Ultimately, his case worked its way through the court system to the United States Supreme Court.

In making its decision, the High Court considered two key issues. First was the issue of whether a teacher could be dismissed for making critical comments in public. With respect to this question, the Court ruled that teachers have a right to speak out on school issues as part of a general effort to provide for a more informed public. Second, the court considered whether a teacher could be dismissed for making false statements. In its examination of Pickering's letter, the Court found only one false statement. In the absence of any evidence that the statement had been included knowingly or recklessly, the Court decided in favor of Pickering.

It should be noted that in the Pickering case the High Court did *not* approve unlimited freedom of speech for teachers. The decision noted that instances may exist when teachers' freedom of speech may be legally limited. No specific examples of these situations were cited.

Teachers' Private Lives

Traditionally, school boards believed that some restrictions could be placed on teachers' private lives. This position was justified by the argument that teachers are role models for young people. Hence, teachers' out-of-school behavior was a legitimate area of concern of school authorities. This general view has sometimes been supported by courts. In one case, *Board of Trustees v. Stubblefield* (1971), the court supported the view that certain professions, such as teaching, impose limitations on personal actions that are not imposed by other professions.

Courts have considered many cases in which there have been allegations of immoral behavior on the part of teachers. Typically, the courts have dealt quite severely with teachers who have been found to be "immoral." A problem in deriving general principles from these cases is that the terms "moral" and "immoral" tend to take on different meanings from place to place.

One thread that does seem to run through a number of these cases is the concern for the impact of the teacher's behavior on his or her classroom performance and community standing. When an "improper" teacher behavior has been viewed as violating prevailing community standards and when there has been widespread public outrage, the courts have tended to support teacher-dismissal actions taken by school districts. On the other hand, when teacher behaviors have not been shown to have a clear impact on the school and the community, the courts have often held for the teacher and against the school administrative authorities.

Among other teachers'-private-lives issues that have been litigated are situations involving drunk driving, use of illegal substances, church attendance, and personal standards of dress and appearance. In one state, the courts upheld the dismissal of a teacher who had many drunk-driving convictions. But, in another, the courts overturned the dismissal of another teacher with a similar record. A divorced teacher was dismissed from one school district because it was rumored that she was having an affair and was not attending church regularly. The courts, in this instance, not only decided in favor of the teacher but also awarded her substantial financial damages.

Key Ideas in Summary

1. The *in loco parentis* doctrine that formerly governed the nature of the legal relationship between school officials and students has been modified in recent years. In general, court actions have acted to extend to students the full rights of citizenship as protected by the United States Constitution.

2. Rights of school officials to place limits on students' speech, written expression, and dress have been limited by important court decisions. One standard school officials must meet in defending any such limitations is that specific student speech, written expression, or dress clearly interferes with the school's educational program.

3. Students who are accused of rules violations that may result in a suspension of more than 10 days or in expulsion are entitled to due- process protections. There are two major components of due process. The substantive component of due process includes basic principles that are to be followed. The procedural component spells out specific procedures to be followed.

4. School officials have a responsibility to protect students' safety. If teachers or administrators suspect that there are objects in the possession of a student that have the potential to harm others, generally they are justified in making a search. The type of the search that can be legally conducted is governed by such factors as the intrusiveness of the search and expectation-of-privacy level of the place searched.

5. Federal law generally makes it possible for parents and students over age 18 to review school records and to question statements included therein. Regulations also place severe restrictions on school officials regarding individuals who may have access to student records.

6. Teachers' contracts are legally binding documents. It is important for teachers to read contracts carefully before signing them. They need to be particularly aware of the nature of property rights and liberty rights implied by the language of the contract.

7. Public worries about AIDS and drug abuse have led to proposals for general testing of teachers. These proposals have faced a number of legal challenges. Since this form of testing constitutes a search, generally a school district must evidence a compelling need for the tests before the courts will support wholesale testing of the district's teachers.

8. States have laws that require teachers to report suspected instances of child abuse. Failure to report such episodes may result in criminal or civil proceedings against the teacher. Most states have provisions that provide reporting teachers with some immunity from legal actions that might be brought against them by parents of allegedly abused children.

9. Many suits against teachers involve negligence. In general, negligence results when a teacher's actions or inactions have allowed harm to come to a student. Negligence can involve misfeasance, nonfeasance, or malfeasance.

10. A number of cases related to teachers' freedom of speech and teachers' private lives have been considered by the courts. In general, decisions to dismiss teachers in these cases have been upheld when districts have demonstrated a clear erosion of the teacher's class performance or a clear undermining of the teacher's credibility with students, parents, and/or the local community.

POSTTEST

DIRECTIONS: Using your own paper, answer these true/false questions. For each correct statement, write the word "true." For each incorrect statement, write the word "false."

_____ 1. In recent years, most court decisions have tended to strengthen the application of the *in loco parentis* doctrine to teachers.

_____ 2. Because learners have a right to due process, they have a right to be represented by legal counsel at hearings held in response to an alleged violation of school rules that might result in expulsion.

_____ 3. It is permissible for a teacher to sign several teaching contracts and to honor the one offering the best employment terms.

_____ 4. Teachers who report suspected instances of child abuse are at considerable risk of being sued by parents should the charge be found to be untrue.

_____ 5. Academic freedom ensures the right of a teacher to discuss any topic in the classroom.

Bibliography

BAKER, M.   "The Teacher's Need to Know versus the Student's Right to Privacy." *Journal of Law and Education* (Winter 1987): 71–91.

BOARD OF TRUSTEES V. STUBBLEFIELD,   94 Cal. Rptr. 318, 321 (1971).

CONNORS, E.   *Educational Tort Liability and Malpractice*. Bloomington, IN: Phi Delta Kappa, 1981.

DOE V. RENFROW,   (No. *H 70-233* N.D. Ind., 30 August, 1979).

FISHER, L. AND SCHIMMEL, D.   *The Rights of Students and Teachers*. New York: Harper and Row, 1982.

INGRAHAM V. WRIGHT,   430 U.S. 651 (1977).

KINGSVILLE INDEPENDENT SCHOOL DISTRICT V. COOPER,   611 F.2d 1109 [5th Cir. 1980].

MEYER V. NEBRASKA,   262 U.S. 390, 399 (1923).

NEW JERSEY V. T.L.O.,   105 5. CT. 733 (1984).

PARDUCCI V. RUTLAND,   316 F. Supp. 352 [M.D. Ala. 1979].

PATCHOGUE-MEDFORD CONGRESS OF TEACHERS V. BOARD OF EDUCATION, 505 N.Y.S. 2d 888 (N.Y. App. Div., 1986).

PICKERING V. BOARD OF EDUCATION OF TOWNSHIP HIGH SCHOOL DISTRICT 205, WILL COUNTY, 391 U.S. 563 (1968).

ROSSOW, L.   *Search and Seizure in the Public Schools*. Topeka, KS: National Organization on Legal Problems in Education, 1987.

THOMAS, S.   *Health-Related Issues in Education*. Topeka, KS: National Organization on Legal Problems in Education, 1987.

TINKER V. DES MOINES INDEPENDENT COMMUNITY SCHOOL DISTRICT, 343 U.S. 503 (1969).

CHAPTER 20

The Career Secondary Teacher

AIMS

This chapter provides information to help the reader to:

1. Identify the influence of previous experiences on preparation for teaching as a career.
2. State the major components of a preservice preparation program.
3. State a rationale for each component of the preservice program.
4. List advantages and potential limitations of the student teaching component of the preservice program.
5. Point out some common problems experienced by new teachers.
6. List steps that can be taken to reduce stress during the induction phase.
7. List the stages of teacher career development beyond the induction phase.
8. Identify organizational and personal environments that influence transitions to different career stages.

PRETEST

DIRECTIONS: Using your own paper, answer each of the following true/false questions. For each correct statement, write the word "true" on your paper. For each incorrect statement, write the word "false" on your paper.

_____ 1. Because they were once students themselves, most people preparing for careers in education are very well informed.

_____ 2. The quality of instruction provided to prospective teachers during the liberal-arts/general-education component of their preservice programs has been universally praised.

_____ 3. The purpose of student teaching is to train future teachers to teach precisely in the same manner as their supervising teachers do.

_____ 4. One of the major challenges for teachers during the induction phase of their careers is learning how to deal with other adults.

_____ 5. The stages of career development beyond induction do not follow a pattern of linear development.

Introduction

Lettie Jacobs had always wanted to be a teacher. She remembered with fondness her eleventh grade American History teacher. Mr. Yonkers had made history come alive. As a result of his influence, Lettie entered college determined to prepare herself to become an outstanding history teacher. She looked forward to the day when, like Mr. Yonkers, she would excite the minds of eager high school students. She would help them uncover the great lessons for life that could result from studying American history.

The four undergraduate years raced by. Lettie completed her student teaching, walked across the stage to receive her diploma, completed several employment interviews, and accepted a teaching position. Her first year was a disappointment. Teaching was not at all she had supposed it would be. So many students seemed to be unmotivated. Many were even disrespectful. Students certainly seemed to have changed in the years since she had left high school.

The administrative work had been another unpleasant surprise. Some days she spent as much time filling out forms as preparing lessons. How was she supposed to provide a stimulating intellectual atmosphere when so much time was consumed by tasks having little to do with student learning? It was all very frustrating.

Is Lettie's situation unusual? Not at all. Every year new teachers find themselves confronted with a classroom reality that fails to live up to their initial expectations. Some teachers never do adjust to constraints with which they must work. Many of them leave the profession after two or three years in the classroom. On the other hand, others come to terms relatively quickly with classroom realities. They make necessary adjustments and, in many cases, develop into first-rate teachers.

During their professional careers, teachers go through a number of career-development stages. Some attitudes expressed by Lettie Jacobs are typical of individuals during the "induction stage" of teaching. An understanding of the several career stages can help prospective teachers appreciate the kinds of pressures teachers face and some of their typical attitudes at various times during their professional lives.

Pre-Training Phase

Teachers' initial attitudes toward teaching and appropriate teaching behavior are influenced by experiences that they have had prior to beginning a formal teacher preparation program. They have had years of experience as learners in the classroom and have observed a great variety of teachers and teaching approaches. Nemser (1987) notes that the typical person entering a teacher preparation program has had more than 10,000 hours of exposure to teachers. They have taken courses from more than 50 teachers (Ryan 1986). This exposure influences individuals' attitudes and beliefs about teachers' roles. Some of these preconceptions can help an individual move toward success in teaching. Others can be detrimental to their career development.

Prior experiences as students in school tend to give individuals, including prospective teachers, certain ideas about which teacher behaviors are effective and which are not. The intensity and duration of these school experiences sometimes lead people with little or no formal preparation for teaching to assume that they qualify as experts. Casual conversations with individuals from all walks of life reveal that many of them are quick to offer their analyses of the problems of education and to suggest solutions. (See Box 20.1.)

People who enter teacher preparation programs are not representative of the total population of high school students. Their enrollment in a college or university indicates that they generally experienced academic success in high school. This achievement sets them apart from many others who attended high school at the same time they did. Many students who began school with them as early as kindergarten stopped their formal education long before completing a baccalaureate program.

Previous school experiences *do* give prospective teachers some idea of teachers' roles. However, they need to remember that their views of the reality of teaching are selective. What they saw as students in schools may not generalize well to other settings.

Some individuals, at the beginning of their teacher preparation program, place a great deal of faith in their own high school experiences as a guide to their future practices as teachers. Too much reliance on per-

Box 20.1

Individual Students and "Effective" Teachers

"Good" teachers work hard to prepare students for college and university. They give assignments that include challenging reading. They favor essay tests. Typically, they require members of their class to write several short papers each grading term. These papers are carefully reviewed, and students must rewrite them to an acceptable standard.

What Do You Think?

Read the statement above. Then, respond to these questions.

1. In general, do you personally tend to agree or disagree with the statement?

2. In general, what kinds of students might be most likely to profit from instruction of this kind of a "good" teacher?

3. Would there be students in the school for whom this teacher would not be effective? If so, who are these students?

4. Do you think that *any* single set of teacher practices can be devised that would be "good" for every student in a class? Why, or why not?

---

sonal experiences as high school students can leave prospective teachers with an inflexible mind-set as they approach courses and other experiences in the preservice program. People who sincerely believe they already know what it takes to become a "good" teacher may regard requirements in their preparation program simply as hurdles to be overcome in order to qualify for a teaching certificate. They may not commit their intellectual resources to these courses as fully as they commit them to courses in the subject areas they are preparing to teach. As a result, the formal preparation program may have little influence on how they behave in the classroom once they begin teaching.

Many of these who do not appreciate the difficult intellectual work required in preparation for a career in teaching are at what Ryan (1986 p. 11) has termed the "fantasy stage" of career preparation. People at this stage develop mental pictures of themselves functioning in idealized ways as teachers in the classroom. They see themselves acting in the classroom as their favorite teachers behaved. They imagine themselves succeeding with every student. Individuals at the fantasy stage may have an intellectual awareness that some teachers have difficulties with unmotivated learners and with discipline in the classroom. However, they are certain *they* will not experience these difficulties.

People who fantasize about their future success as teachers often fail to take courses in their preservice program seriously. The failure rate among such people both before and during student teaching is high. Few of them develop into competent classroom practitioners.

Pre-Service Phase

The second phase of career development is what is known as the pre-service phase. This means that it occurs before a person obtains certification and enters the "service" of teaching. This phase normally takes place in an institution of higher education. During this phase, prospective teachers follow a course of study that leads to initial teacher certification.

Individuals not familiar with teacher preparation programs sometimes assume that people preparing to be teachers will spend the majority of their time in college taking education courses. This is a misconception. In most programs that prepare individuals for teaching in secondary schools the professional education component, including student teaching, comprises only about 21 percent of the curriculum (Kluender 1984).

There are place-to-place variations in the design of preservice programs. However, there are also many similarities. In part, these similarities result from guidelines and standards imposed by state education agencies and national accrediting agencies such as the National Council for Accreditation of Teacher Education (NCATE). A typical preservice program consists of three general parts: (a) a liberal-arts or general-education requirement; (b) an academic major or teaching specialization; and, (c) a professional education requirement (Kluender 1984).

Liberal Arts-General Education Component

In addition to their special expertise in teaching, teachers are expected to have a well-balanced general education. They need to be sensitive to social and environmental influences, to the historical and cultural context within which they live and work, and to contributions and challenges posed by scientific and technological change (DeLandsheere 1987). The liberal-arts or general-education component comprises about 40 percent of the curriculum for secondary students and is designed to provide future teachers with breadth of knowledge.

Although this area of the preparation program is the one that is most often criticized by those preparing to be secondary teachers, teachers need to realize that liberal arts and other general education courses contribute greatly to teachers' credibility. These courses develop broad understandings and promote the growth of a variety of intellectual interests. Secondary teachers need to realize that they will be teaching students that come from a variety of backgrounds and have a variety of interests. The liberal arts component of the curriculum helps the prospective teacher relate to others who are outside their major area of study.

Regrettably the quality of instruction in this component has not always been good. The uninspired teaching in some of these courses has provided poor models of instruction for future teachers. An organization of major research universities dedicated to improving the quality of teaching in the schools, the Holmes Group, made these comments about this situation: "Few of those teaching university courses know how to teach well, and many seem not to care. The undergraduate education that an intending teacher — and everyone else — receives is full of the same bad teaching that litters American high schools" (*Holmes Group* 1986, p. 16).

The members of the Holmes Group and others who are concerned about the quality of teacher preparation programs are focusing special attention on the quality of these programs' liberal-arts/general-education components. Without improvements, there are fears that the purposes of this part of the preparation program will not be achieved.

The Academic Major or Teaching Specialization

Specific academic majors or areas of teaching specialization are nearly universal features of secondary-level teacher preparation programs. Approximately 39 percent of the preparation program for secondary education is devoted to the academic major. Secondary teachers are expected to have considerable depth of knowledge in the area or areas that they expect to teach.

A concern of many educators is that many academic courses offered by colleges and universities do not match up well with public school curricula. For example, some people with majors in English discover that a large share of the major is devoted to topics in literature rarely covered in high school English programs. Additionally, except for freshman-year courses, relatively few college and university courses provide composition instruction; yet, teaching of writing is considered to be one of the most important professional obligations of high school English teachers.

The argument that courses prospective teachers take in their academic majors should be more closely tied to school curricula has not been universally endorsed. Some people contend that providing future teachers with a knowledge base for teaching is only one function of courses in the academic major. Perhaps more important are the roles these courses play in helping students to develop patterns of serious scholarship, to master the basic methodology of academic disciplines, and to improve their abilities to analyze, synthesize, and evaluate. (See Box 20.2.)

Box 20.2

What Do You Need to Know About What You Teach?

Specific course requirements to qualify individuals to teach individual subjects vary somewhat from state to state and from institution to institution. A number of influences help shape these requirements. National professional organizations for English, science, social studies, mathematics, and other subject-area teachers issue general guidelines. State laws lay out certain minimum requirements. Individual colleges and universities also impose some standards of their own.

Ask your instructor for information to help you respond to these questions:

1. What specific courses are required of individuals preparing to teach in your area of interest? Are teachers required to prepare in a single field? A major field and a minor field? Two equivalent fields?

2. In general, where have requirements related to the teaching fields come from?

3. Does your institution have some requirements of its own that exceed minimum state standards?

4. How do requirements at your institution vary from those at other teacher-preparation institutions in your state?

Professional Education Component

Future teachers take a smaller percentage of courses in the professional education component of their program than in either the liberal-arts/general-education component or the academic-major component. Only about 21 percent of the preparation program for secondary teachers is actually devoted to professional-education-related course work, including student teaching. In recent years there has been a rapidly expanding volume of educational research focusing on classroom instruction. Teacher educators have been increasingly hard-pressed to disseminate this growing volume of information in the small number of required education courses (DeLandsheere 1987). This problem has prompted some colleges and universities to extend the length of the preservice teacher-preparation program to five or more years.

The accelerating rate of development of new knowledge about teaching and learning has important implications for how prospective teachers view their careers. Even teachers who have been trained in extended programs (those lasting longer than four years) cannot become acquainted with more than a fraction of the information that is presently available under the general heading "teaching effectiveness." This reality suggests that preparation for teaching does not end with the conclusion of the preservice program. Rather, preparation is an on-going, career-long obligation. Student teaching, in the past viewed by many prospective teachers as the "beginning of the end" of professional preparation, now more properly is viewed as the "end of the beginning."

Though it is no longer considered the terminal phase in a prospective teacher's preparation, student teaching is still viewed as a highly important component of the preparation program. Historically, student teaching evolved from apprenticeship models of teaching. "Learning to teach" was viewed as a matter of working with a "master" and learning to mimic his or her actions. It was basically a matter of imitation. This view of the student-teaching function has been challenged in recent years (Dunkin 1987).

Mere imitation of an experienced professional's actions can inhibit the development of reflective thinking about what teachers do. Today, many people believe that prospective teachers should not be taught that teaching is a technical activity. There is an increasing realization that the same teacher behaviors or the same lessons will not be effective with all of the students all of the time.

Teacher personalities vary. Students' needs differ. School environments are not the same from place to place. In response to these multiple realities, today's teachers must be prepared to be reflective problem-solvers. They should know how to analyze students' needs, to question themselves about alternative approaches, and to make rational judgments among available options. Today, more sophisticated supervising teachers regard assisting student teachers to develop their analytical skills as one of their important supervisory responsibilities.

Prospective teachers need to realize that even the best student teaching experience does not represent a total preparation for the first teaching position. For one thing, no two school settings are exactly the same. Consequently, it is seldom possible for teaching patterns that work well in one environment to be transferred without modification to another. Inevitably, some adjustment to the different setting will have to be made.

Further, student teaching represents "sheltered reality" (Ryan 1986). The student teaching classroom is shaped to a degree by the procedures and expectations of the supervising teacher. There is an established classroom culture and climate when the student teacher arrives. Further, the supervising teacher and the college or university supervisor are available to help the student teacher over rough spots. Many tasks that teachers perform are not required of student teachers. Beginning teachers find themselves faced with more personal responsibilities than they had as student teachers.

Induction Phase

The "induction phase" is that period following the beginning of the first teaching position. During this time, the teacher gradually learns the full range of responsibilities of a full-time professional. This is a transition time. At the beginning, it is common for new teachers to continue to think of themselves as "prospective" teachers. Most teachers grow increasingly confident during this phase. Toward its end, they tend to view themselves as having the competence of "real" teachers.

Until quite recently little attention was focused on the induction stage. In part, this resulted from several misconceptions about teaching. One of these held that teaching was basically "simple." According to this view, one became professional on the first day of the job as a result of the experience they developed during student teaching. Student teaching was viewed as the end of professional education. No more professional development was thought necessary.

Another perspective held that teaching was basically an "art" or an "innate talent." Some people were born teachers; some were not. Therefore, no assistance during the induction stage was needed. Those who were born teachers would be able to do the job, those who were not could not be helped.

Though there are still proponents of the teaching-is-simple and the teaching-is-art points of view, today most people recognize that teaching is a highly complex activity. Further, there is increasing support for the view that many different kinds of people can learn how to become good teachers, but that development of expertise takes time. This development is an evolutionary process. Teachers continue to learn some new dimensions of their profession throughout their careers (Nemser 1987; Wildman and Niles 1987). The induction stage is a critical component in the development of a highly skilled teacher. Those who are successful in coping with the pressures of this stage develop a foundation for a satisfying and productive career. Those who do not cope well with this stage will usually leave teaching.

Ryan (1986, p. 18) points out that one of the first things that happens to many new teachers is what he calls the "shock of the familiar." Many things new teachers are required to do are familiar to them as a result of their experiences as students and as student teachers. But, for the first time, they alone are responsible for the classroom. Many beginners are surprised at the volume of activity required, the paperwork that must be completed, and the number of meetings that must be attended. Teaching turns out to be far more complex than they had anticipated. Feelings of stress, frustration, and fatigue are common.

During their first year, many teachers find themselves fighting for their professional lives. Large numbers develop serious doubts about their own self-worth and personal dignity (Ryan 1986). Beginning teachers have invested considerable time and money in preparing to enter the profession. The thought that they might not be successful can be devastating. Anxieties are intensified by their recognition that any shortcomings are likely to be very public. Students, administrators, other teachers, and even parents will be aware of their failure.

Patterns of teaching and coping that teachers develop during the induction phase have been found to persist through much of their teaching careers (Moffett, St. John, and Isker 1987). This suggests that new teachers should be provided with special help during this crucial phase. They need to learn productive patterns and coping strategies to minimize the emotional costs of occasional failures.

Some states and a number of individual school districts have adopted formal induction-year programs. These are designed to assist new teachers through this difficult phase of their development. Several of these programs continue to involve college and university education specialists, who provide assistance to the new teacher. Some induction-year programs organize support groups consisting of new teachers in the district. Other programs designate "mentor teachers" to assist the newcomers. Mentor teachers are experienced professionals who are particularly sensitive to the newcomers' problems. They provide guidance and counsel to beginners.

Specific adjustment problems faced by individual teachers vary. However, some difficulties are experienced by large numbers of beginners. Among these are concerns related to (a) instructing and disciplining learners; (b) working with other adults, including administrators, parents, and other teachers; and (c) obtaining resources and materials pertinent to subjects taught (Odell, Loughlin, and Ferraro 1986–1987).

Learners and Discipline

Coping with problems associated with learner misbehavior is one of the most stressful components of the role of the new teacher. Many individuals choose teaching because they sincerely care about young people and have a desire to help them. Beginning teachers find it frustrating to discover that not all youngsters view them positively and that some may not even like them.

In response to initial problems with learners, some beginning teachers go to great lengths to win students' approval. For example, the teacher may try to become a personal friend of a particularly difficult student. This strategy is not usually effective. Although students do want teachers who are warm and friendly, they often are not particularly interested in becoming close personal friends. They may resent obvious overtures of an inexperienced teacher who wants to become "one of the gang."

Additionally, attempts to establish close personal ties with students can undermine a teacher's ability to exercise authority. Learners may use the teacher's apparent need for personal friendship as a kind of "emotional blackmail." Students may hint that any attempt of the teacher to exercise authority may threaten the friendship. If the teacher gives in to this "blackmail," classroom control and respect are likely to erode. A final result may be a more strained relationship between the teacher and the students than existed before the teacher tried to become one of their "friends."

In the long run, relationships with learners become more positive when students recognize that the teacher is a friendly, but firm, professional. Teachers who insist on certain patterns of behavior and who expect learners to perform well academically communicate several important messages. First, students understand that the teacher sincerely believes lessons that are being presented are important. Second, high teacher expectations communicate a statement about the teacher's belief in learners' abilities. These "messages" can have a positive impact on the members of the class. This kind of professional communication between teachers and students, over time, builds mutual respect and diminishes the potential for disruptive student behavior. (Box 20.3 explores characteristics of an "ideal" induction program.)

Working with Adults

Though teachers spend much of their time in schools working with students, many adults — administrators, other teachers, and parents — are also part of their work environment. New teachers need to understand that the school principal and other school administrators have many roles to play in addition to attending to the needs of new faculty. They must evaluate staff members, enforce state and local policies, manage large budgets, work with parents, and look after a variety of special school needs. These responsibilities place heavy time demands on administrators.

In a large high school, new teachers may rarely see the school principal except in large-meeting settings. They may initially feel that the school administration is indifferent to their concerns and needs. This is not true. Most administrators *do* care about new teachers and would like to help ensure their success. After all, a smoothly functioning school staffed with competent teachers makes the work of school leaders much easier. However, the demands placed on principals' time often precludes the close working relationship that many new teachers desire.

Sometimes new teachers experience difficulties in establishing positive relationships with other teachers. Teachers are similar to many other people who work together. Over time, individual friendships and

Box 20.3

Characteristics of an "Ideal" Induction Program

This chapter introduces a great deal of information about problems teachers face during the induction phase of their professional careers. Think about what you have read and about what you know from other sources about adjustment problems of new teachers. Suppose you were in a leadership position in a school district. What five things might you include in a special program to make induction into the profession easier for beginning teachers?

1. _____

_____

2. _____

_____

3. _____

_____

4. _____

_____

5. _____

_____

groups of like-minded individuals develop. The new teacher may experience an initial feeling of being an outsider. In time, most newcomers find people to whom they can relate, and they develop a network of friends within the school.

An additional strain often occurs when the new teacher realizes that the patterns of operation in the school are different from those experienced in student teaching. There is a tendency for beginners to judge the new situation as not quite as professional or "good." This judgment often creates a defensiveness on the part of the experienced teachers. New teachers need to learn to withhold judgments until they are in a position to understand the unique problems of the school where they are working and to have earned some credibility as a successful professional.

Relationships with parents sometimes create stressful situations. Many new high school teachers will discover that they are dealing with parents who are much older than they are. In many cases, parents are as old as new teachers' own parents. They may find it hard to talk confidently with these parents about their children. Though a few parents are difficult, most are extremely interested in the welfare of their children. They view teachers as allies in the personal and intellectual development of their youngsters. New teachers who approach parents in a professional manner and who demonstrate that they are knowledgeable about their subject and teaching have little difficulty in gaining parents' respect.

The Induction Year: Some Suggestions

There are a number of things that new teachers can do to ease their own transition from college or university student to teacher. First, they can begin by developing some realistic self-expectations. Particularly, they need to understand that the development of a professional teacher is a process that continues throughout a career. They are not going to know all they would like to know when the first day of school starts. Beginners need to view themselves both as learners and teachers and to avoid harsh self-judgments when things do not go well.

Second, they should seek out an experienced teacher as a friend and mentor. This should be someone with whom ideas can be shared freely and who will listen and react to frustrations. Every teacher in the schools today went through an induction stage. Many teachers remember the experience well and will be pleased to help newcomers through this challenging adjustment period.

Third, newcomers should recognize that the first year of teaching is unique (Ryan 1986). It is a time when new teachers learn a tremendous amount about their new profession. Often, they are unaware of how much then need to learn. As a result, some new teachers become very discouraged concerning their ability to cope with the demands of teaching. New teachers should recognize the uniqueness of the first year and make a personal commitment, even before the first year begins, to teach at least two years. Often there are amazing differences in the levels of performance and confidence between the first and the second years.

Finally, newcomers must recognize that teaching is a demanding, stressful activity. All teachers, newcomers included, need to develop ways to counterbalance this stress with other activities. Many people find exercise programs or other group activities to be helpful. Reserving time for activities not associated with the professional demands of teaching can diminish stress and contribute to teachers' general effectiveness in the classroom.

Beyond Induction

Generally, all teachers pass in sequence from the preservice stage into the induction stage of their careers. Those that remain in the profession branch off into one of several career stages beyond induction.

Service on committees is a career-long feature of a teacher's professional life.

These include (a) the competency-building stage, (b) the enthusiastic-and-growing stage, (c) the stable-and-stagnant stage, (d) the career-frustration stage, and (e) the career-wind-down stage (Burke, Christensen, and Fessler 1984).

The Competency-Building Stage

Many teachers who have dealt successfully with survival issues of the induction stage move to the competency-building stage. As the name implies, people at this stage focus on developing their overall teaching expertise. Many of them actively seek out professional workshops and graduate-level courses that have promise of helping them become more proficient teachers. This stage may last several years.

The Enthusiastic-and-Growing Stage

Most frequently, this stage is the next one entered by individuals who feel they have developed high levels of teaching proficiency during the competency-building stage of their careers. Teachers tend to be increasingly confident about their ability to do well in the classroom. This confidence then stimulates an excitement about teaching. People at this stage tend to look forward to going to school each day. They derive a great deal of satisfaction from their career.

It is common for people at this stage to develop interests in sharing their enthusiasm and expertise with others. They often volunteer to lead workshops and make inservice presentations. They serve willingly on professional committees. They seek out opportunities to work with new teachers and student teachers. In summary, individuals in this stage of development tend to be confident in their ability to manage and teach learners and are eager to share their expertise.

The Stable-and-Stagnant Stage

Not all teachers go through competency-building or enthusiastic-and-growing stages. Some enter a career stage known as the stable-and-stagnant stage immediately after the induction phase. Other individuals, who for a time may have been in the competency-building stage or the enthusiastic-and-growing stage, may also enter the stable-and-stagnant stage. Individuals in this stage tend to have given up on the ideal that they can play an important role in education. They may well have a low sense of efficacy and self-esteem. They often question their abilities to teach the students assigned to them. They may doubt students' ability to learn.

Teachers at this stage often put relatively little effort in their work. Many of them have concluded that there is little payoff for devoting time and energy to planning and teaching. They may do just enough to be considered competent. Few believe they will ever be considered excellent teachers. Many individuals at this stage devote their energies to activities outside of school. For example, they may spend increasing amounts of time on a hobby, or they may develop a small part-time business. Their personal satisfactions come from activities other than teaching, and teaching is generally viewed only as a means of providing a steady income.

The Career-Frustration Stage

Individuals at this stage have become disillusioned with teaching. They have concluded that they can have no impact on young people. These teachers often have negative expectations of learners in the classroom and are very critical of other educators. They often dread going to school and may be openly hostile to students and other teachers.

A part of the frustration of individuals at this stage stems from their fear that they cannot escape from teaching. They feel trapped because they can identify no other job for which they have the necessary qualifications. Many of these people went into teaching with very high expectations. Their inability to obtain the successes that they anticipated contributed to their frustration and bitterness. Sometimes these teachers blame students, parents, administrators, or society for their inability to achieve success.

In time, some of these people develop enough interests outside the school to provide them the satisfactions they do not find in teaching. In fact, the personality transformation that takes place when these individuals are out of the school environment can be startling. A few of them succeed in switching to careers they like better. Many of them, though, remain in the schools. Their presence is an ongoing challenge to teachers and administrators who look more positively on their career roles.

The Career-Wind-Down Stage

People in the career-wind-down stage are preparing to leave teaching. Some of these individuals are approaching the end of a long career in the classroom. Others have made definite plans to change careers. Still others are assuming other roles within professional education, perhaps as counselors or administrators.

Attitudes of people at this stage vary in terms of their own feelings about teaching. Those who have had productive and satisfying careers may continue to be very positive and successful until their last day in the classroom. Those who have been dissatisfied may put forward only minimal efforts and be very ineffective during the career-wind-down stage. (Box 20.4 is an exercise in identifying career stages.)

Influences on Career-Stage Changes

A number of professional and personal circumstances go together to influence the career stage that a person enters (Burke, Christensen, and Fessler 1984). Individuals may move back and forth between stages at different points of their career.

The stages to which teachers move are greatly influenced by the nature of the school and the community where they work. Among the important professional circumstances that influence their movement into or out of a given stage are (a) the general school climate,

Box 20.4

Teachers and Their Beyond-Induction Career Stages

Teachers may pass through a number of career stages after the induction stage. Among these are the (a) the competency-building stage; (b) the enthusiastic-and-growing stage; (c) the stable-and-stagnant stage; (d) the career-frustration stage; and (e) the career-wind-down stage.

Work with two or three other students to recall teachers you have had. Try to identify at least one individual whose behavior patterns suggested that he or she might have been at each of these five stages. Make some brief notes about kinds of behaviors that led you to your conclusions.

Competency-building stage _____
_____
_____

Enthusiastic-and-growing stage _____
_____
_____

Stable-and-stagnant stage _____
_____
_____

Career-frustration stage _____
_____
_____

Career-wind-down stage _____
_____
_____

(b) rules and regulations of the school and the school district, (c) the management style of the administrators, (d) the nature of support provided by local professional organizations, (e) community expectations of schools and teachers, and (f) the trust and status accorded to teachers within the community. There are great place-to-place differences in these circumstances. It is quite common for teachers who find themselves very unhappy in one setting to blossom and develop into satisfied professionals in another.

Changes in teachers' personal lives can also cause them to move in and out of different career stages. Marriages, divorces, births, deaths, illnesses, family problems, and changes in economic circumstances can affect how teachers feel about themselves and their roles as teachers. The process of growing older tends to be accompanied by changing interests and priorities. These, too, can influence attitudes about teaching.

Most teachers adjust to these changes and continue to be effective in the classroom. Newcomers to the profession need not fear these adjustments; they are simply part of the process of living. They should recognize, however, that their values and personal priorities may vary over time as personal, social, and employment environments change.

"Of course I believe that a teacher should offer a positive role model; however . . ."

Career Stages: Implications for Prospective Teachers

At the United States Mint, giant presses strike sheets of metal to create shiny new coins. Once the sheets are struck, the process is complete. New coins need no more work. They are ready to go into circulation until they wear out.

Teachers are not produced like coins. There is no clear ending to the preparation process. The making of a teacher is an ongoing process. It begins years before they enter the classroom. It continues throughout the duration of their professional careers.

Unique constellations of circumstances act to make individual teachers develop in different ways. Depending on these variables, they may pass through any one of a number of career stages during the years they are in the classroom. Some of these stages tend to be more associated with personal career satisfaction than others. For people contemplating a future as classroom teachers, an understanding of these career stages can be very useful.

Teachers, similar to other human beings, are not hopelessly buffeted by forces they cannot control. They have personalities that have an interactive relationship with their professional environment. By being sensitive to conditions associated with career stages characterized by high degrees of satisfaction with teaching, teachers can determine early on to make choices to work for those kinds of conditions. Those who do this can exercise positive control over their career destinies. People who take charge of their professional lives are likely to develop into well-adjusted, committed, and competent teachers. The profession awaits them.

Key Ideas in Summary

1. Influences on the classroom behavior of someone planning to become a teacher begin even before the formal preservice preparation program. Prospective teachers bring with them memories and impressions about teaching resulting from exposure to over 10,000 hours of instruction and more than 50 different teachers.

2. Impressions about the characteristics of "good" teaching that individuals bring with them to their initial courses in the preservice program need to be examined critically. One difficulty is that there are tremendous differences among schools and learners. Teacher behaviors that were effective in one setting may not work well at all in another.

3. The preservice education program is divided into three major parts. One of these focuses on content in the area of teaching specialization. Another centers on the liberal education courses thought to be essential for all educated people. There are often referred to as the academic foundation or "core" courses. The third part of the program consists of professional education courses. Professional education courses, including student teaching, comprise about 21 percent of the total program for secondary students.

4. Student teaching is one of the most important phases of the preservice preparation program. The best student teaching experiences are those that allow student teachers to design, teach, and critique their own instruction with a view toward developing an ability to respond flexibly to changing conditions. Among the worst are those where students are expected to imitate the behaviors of their supervising teachers. These are particularly inappropriate in that they may lead student teachers to assume that the behaviors that worked in one school context can be successfully transported without modification to another.

5. The induction phase teachers go through after they assume their first teaching position can be a challenging time. They often discover that teachers have more roles and responsibilities than they had learned from their student teaching experience. Whether a teacher has a smooth or shaky induction experience greatly influences whether that teacher will remain in the profession.

6. New teachers face a number of problems. They need to learn how to work smoothly with several important groups. These include students, other teachers, administrators, and parents. They must locate and develop instructional materials especially suited to the content they are teaching and to the needs of learners in their own classrooms.

7. As teachers mature, they may pass through one or more career stages. There is no predictable sequence of stages through which each teacher will pass. The specific career stages experienced by a given teacher will depend on influences of both personal and organizational environments.

8. Among important career stages are (a) the competency-building stage, (b) the enthusiastic-and-growing stage, (c) the stable-and-stagnant stage, (d) the career-frustration stage, and (e) the career-wind-down stage. Some teachers may pass through all of these stages. Others may pass through only a few. Some individuals may move back and forth between the different stages depending on a number of variables.

9. It is important for teachers to be aware of the different stages and of the influences that can move them from one stage to another. This kind of understanding can help them to exercise more personal control over their careers and to derive more personal satisfaction from teaching.

10. Teachers' professional development does not stop with the awarding of the initial teaching certificate and the beginning of the first teaching position. It is a career-long process.

POSTTEST

DIRECTIONS: Using your own paper, answer each of the following true/false questions. For each correct statement, write the word "true" on your paper. For each incorrect statement, write the word "false" on your paper.

——— 1. Individuals enrolled in a teacher-preparation curriculum spend the majority of their time in courses focusing on teaching.

——— 2. One major purpose of an academic major is to provide prospective teachers with information that, ultimately, they will pass along to the students they will teach.

——— 3. Teachers' attitudes towards teaching as a career usually become more positive during their first year of teaching.

——— 4. Typically, a teacher will have passed through the induction phase before he or she enters the enthusiastic-and-growing stage.

——— 5. Movement in and out of the various stages of career development are influenced by the organizational and personal environments of the individual teacher.

Bibliography

BOLAM, R. "Induction of Beginning Teachers," In Dunkin, M. J. (ed.), *The International Encyclopedia of Teaching and Teacher Education.* New York: Pergamon Press, 1987. pp. 745–757.

BURKE, P. J., CHRISTENSEN, J. C. AND FESSLER, R. *Teacher Career Stages: Implications for Staff Development.* Fast back #214, Bloomington, IN: Phi Delta Kappa Educational Foundation, 1984.

DELANDSHEERE, G. "Concepts in Teacher Education," In Dunkin, M. J. (ed.), *The International Encyclopedia of Teaching and Teacher Education.* New York: Pergamon Press, 1987, pp. 77–83.

DUNKIN, M. J. (ED.). *The International Encyclopedia of Teaching and Teacher Education.* New York: Pergamon Press, 1987.

HITZ, R. AND ROPER, S. "The Teacher's First Year: Implications for Teacher Educators," *Action in Teacher Education.* (Fall 1986): pp. 65–71.

HOLMES GROUP. *Tomorrow's Teachers.* East Lansing, Mich.; Holmes Group, 1986.

KLUENDER, M. M. "Teacher Education Programs in the 1980s: Some Selected Characteristics," *Journal of Teacher Education* (July–August 1984): 33–35.

LIGHTFOOT, S. L. "The Lives of Teachers." In Shulman, L. and Sykes, G. (eds.). *Handbook of Teaching and Policy.* New York: Longman, 1983.

MOFFETT, K. L., ST. JOHN, J. AND ISKER, J.   "Training and Coaching Beginning Teachers: An Antidote to Reality Shock," *Educational Leadership* (February 1987): 34–36.

NEMSER, S. F.   "Learning to Teach."   In Shulman, L. S. and Sykes, G. (eds.).   *Handbook of Teaching and Policy*.   New York: Longman, 1983.   pp. 150–170.

ODELL, S. J., LOUGHLIN, C. E. AND FERRARO, D. P.   "Functional Approach to Identification on New Teacher Needs in an Induction Context," *Action in Teacher Education* (Winter 1986–87): 51–57.

RYAN, KEVIN.   *The Induction of New Teachers*.   Fastback #237, Bloomington, IN: 1986.

STONES, E.   "Student (Practice) Teaching."   In Dunkin, M. J. (ed.).   *The International Encyclopedia of Teaching and Teacher Education*.   New York: Pergamon Press, 1987, pp. 681–685.

WILDMAN, T. AND NILES, J.   "Essentials of Professional Growth," *Educational Leadership* (February 1987): 4–10.

Author Index

Subject Index